SECOND EDITION

Strategic Human Resource Management

Charles R. Greer

Texas Christian University

Upper Saddle River, New Jersey 07458

Library of Congress Cataloging-in-Publication Data
Greer, Charles R.
Strategic human resource management / Charles Greer.—2nd ed.
p. cm.
Includes bibliographical references and index.
ISBN 0-13-027950-1
1. Personnel management. I. Title.
HF5549 .G6923 2000
658.3—dc21 00-058863

Editor: Melissa Steffens
Managing Editor (Editorial): John Sisson
Editorial Assistant: Samantha Steel
Assistant Editor: Jessica Sabloff
Media Project Manager: Michele Faranda
Executive Marketing Manager: Michael Campbell
Managing Editor (Production): Judy Leale
Production Editor: Emma Moore
Production Assistant: Keri Jean
Permissions Coordinator: Suzanne Grappi
Associate Director, Manufacturing: Vincent Scelta
Production Manager: Diane Peirano
Design Manager: Patricia Smythe
Cover Design: Bruce Kenselaar
Cover Art/Photo: Bob Commander/Stock Illustration Source, Inc.
Associate Director, Multimedia Production: Karen Goldsmith
Manager, Print Production: Christina Mahon
Composition: Rainbow Graphics
Full-Service Project Manager: Rainbow Graphics

Credits and acknowledgments borrowed from other sources and reproduced, with permission, in this textbook appear on appropriate page within text.

14 15 16 17 18 19
ISBN 0-13-027950-1

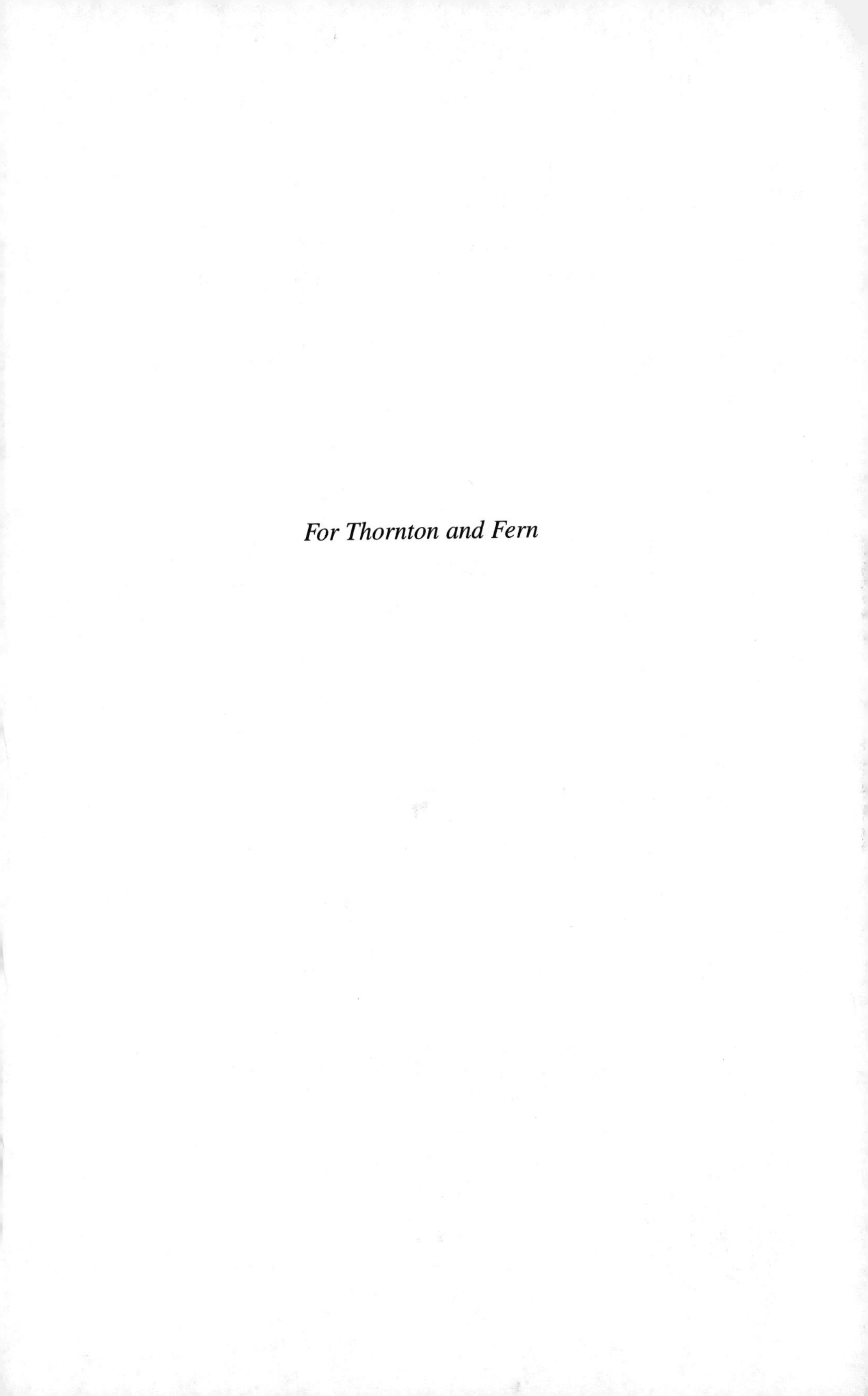

For Thornton and Fern

Contents

Preface

This book deals with the interaction between strategy and human resources, as approached from a general managerial perspective. This approach has been adopted for its relevancy to managers in general, as opposed to only human resource specialists. Major features of the book include an investment orientation toward human resources and comprehensive discussions of the environment of human resources, strategy formulation, human resource planning, strategy implementation, the performance impact of human resource practices, and human resource evaluation. Extensive examples of applications of strategic human resource management in specific companies are provided throughout the book.

This book is designed for use by MBA and Executive MBA students, graduate students in specialized human resource management programs, and other graduate students focusing on administration. The book is also suitable for advanced undergraduate courses focusing on the strategic aspects of human resource management. In keeping with the general managerial perspective, discussions are presented from a practical point of view. The cases at the end of each chapter are designed to stimulate thought and discussion of important strategic issues.

The conceptual framework for this book, presented in Figure P-1, is composed of a mission statement and nine components corresponding to individual chapters that draw from the principles of human–capital theory, strategic management, strategic planning, environmental analysis, human resource planning, strategy implementation, and principles of evaluation. It also incorporates principles of rational and comprehensive strategic planning. The framework begins with an assumption that the company has a *mission* of obtaining an appropriate rate of return for shareholders while complying with the interests of the company's other stakeholders, including employees and governmental agencies. Assuming such a mission, the framework of this book begins with development of an *investment perspective* for guiding managerial decisions regarding strate-

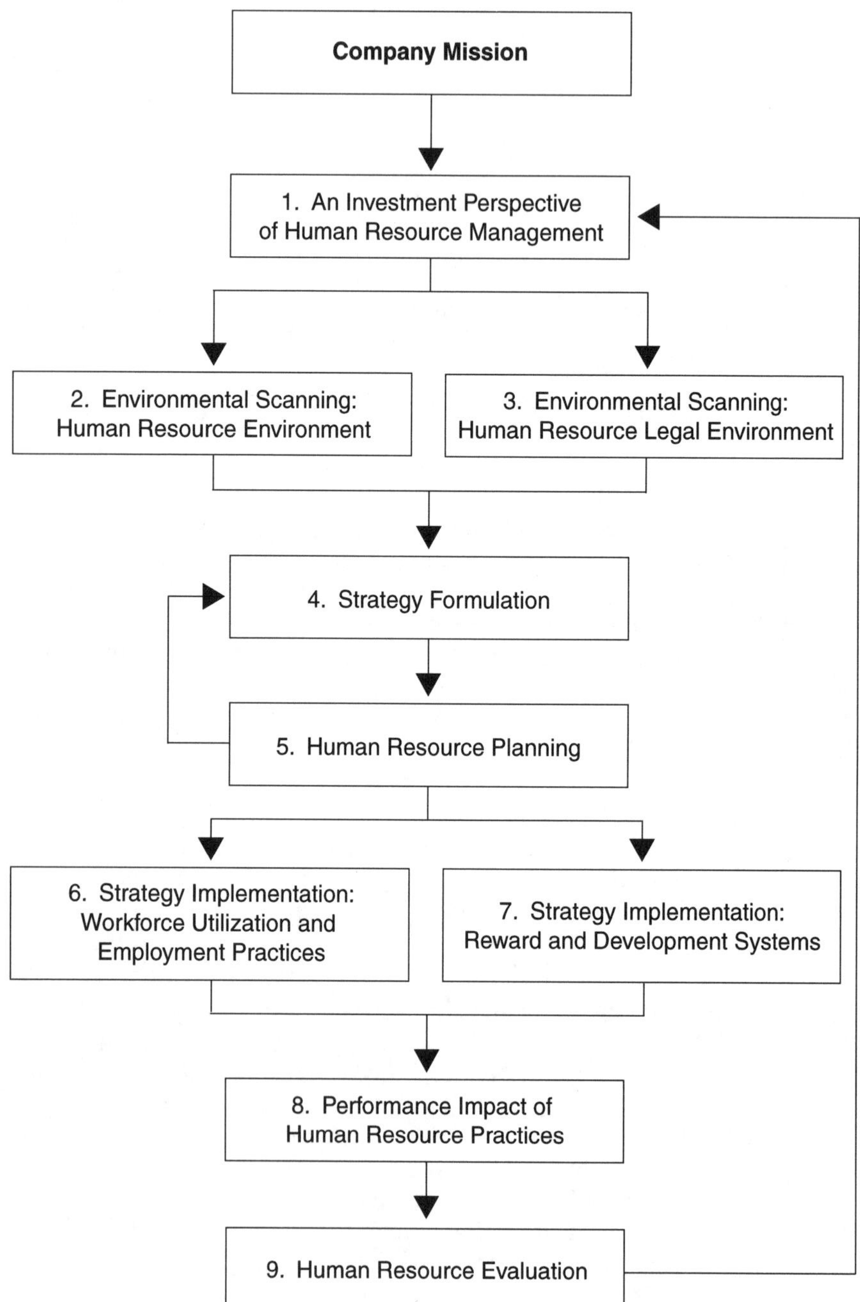

FIGURE P-1 Strategy and Human Resources

gic human resource issues. The investment perspective is consistent with mission statements of economically rational organizations. This perspective provides a rational, financially justifiable basis for analyzing the value of alternative human resource strategies, policies, and practices.

A thorough understanding of the investment perspective is critical for human resource executives and managers who wish to play a strategic role in their organizations. As will be discussed in Chapter 1, senior mangers are accustomed to evaluating returns on investments in various endeavors. Human resource executives are being required to provide better justifications for the resources devoted to human resource programs. Just as financial outlays for plant and equipment are evaluated from an investment perspective, expenditures on human resource activities, such as training and development, also should be evaluated in terms of return on investment. Additionally, the investment perspective provides a valuable general managerial framework for evaluating programs, policies, and activities in terms of their ability to enhance and preserve the organization's investment in its human resources.

The second and third components of the conceptual framework are the *general environment* and *legal environment* of human resource management, respectively. An informed awareness of environmental trends and developments is required before managers can examine intelligently the potential opportunities and threats to which strategies must be directed. Because the environment of human resource management and the broader economic environment have changed so dramatically, a great deal of attention has been devoted to these developments in Chapter 2. In addition to these massive changes, the legal environment of human resources continues to evolve and expand. As will be discussed in Chapter 3, in some respects the legal environment itself has become a source of uncertainty. Although in the past human resource strategists may not have incorporated the legal environment in their conceptual frameworks, further expansions of the law into areas of employer and employee relationships have made it a critical component of strategic analysis. For example, whether an employer chooses to manufacture in the United States or locate production facilities offshore may be highly dependent on trends in the U.S. legal environment.

Strategy formulation is the fourth component in the framework. The framework's investment perspective drives the formulation of strategies for dealing with opportunities and threats in the environment. Human resources and human resource management can play major roles in the organization's overall strategy, particularly when human resources are viewed as providing a major competitive advantage. As will be discussed in Chapter 4, some authors define *strategic human resource management* as the effective application of the organization's human resources to accomplish the organization's overall strategies. Such definitions have only an implementation perspective, while other authors also see strategic human resource management as being integrated with strategy formulation. The latter perspective will be employed in this book. Human resource strategies are narrower in focus than the domain of strategic human resource management. *Human resource strategies* define the manner in which the organization's practices, programs, policies, and activities will be aligned to obtain consistency with the organization's overall strategies. Such strategies play an implementation role and are valuable means of obtaining direction, consistency, and coherence in human resource efforts.

Human resource planning is the fifth component in the conceptual framework. Through such planning, which is discussed in Chapter 5, organizations prepare to match resources with the requirements needed for implementation of strategies. Human resource planning is positioned after strategy formulation although it can occur before or simultaneously with strategy formulation. Such planning can provide strategic input for strategy formulation when it identifies a competitive advantage deriving from the organization's human resources. Nonetheless, in many organizations, strategy formulation occurs first, and then human resource planning is conducted to either determine the feasibility of the strategy or as a prelude to implementation of the strategy. The planning feedback loop to strategy formulation in Figure P-1 indicates the function's formulation roles of feasibility assessment and identification of competitive advantage.

The sixth and seventh components are involved with *strategy implementation.* These components consist of two broad groups of human resource practices through which human resource strategy is implemented. The first deals with the efficient utilization of human resources, employee shortages, employee surpluses, and special challenges. Included in these broad groups of implementation activities are cross-training and other actions that create flexibility in the utilization of the workforce, strategic recruiting, minority and female recruiting, selection, flexible retirement, redeployment, early retirement, downsizing, layoffs, terminations, and special actions for dealing with dual-career couples. These activities are discussed in Chapter 6. The second broad group, which is discussed in Chapter 7, includes reward systems and development activities. The discussion of reward systems includes performance measurement and several strategically oriented compensation approaches such as skill-based pay, broadbanding, compensation systems, and team-based pay. The discussion of development includes training programs, training methods, apprenticeships, and management development programs.

The eighth component, which describes the *impact of human resource practices* on firm performance, is presented in Chapter 8. The discussion reports research results on the question of whether the performance effects of human resource practices and systems are contingent on business strategies and contextual factors.

The ninth and final component is *human resource evaluation.* This component includes general approaches to evaluation and specific applications to various human resource practices and activities. As will be discussed in Chapter 9, in the past organizations did not place much emphasis on evaluating human resource management. However, global competitiveness pressures have created increased needs for justifying the use of resources. As a result, there should be much greater emphasis on evaluation in the human resources area in the future. As noted in Figure P-1, after evaluations are conducted, the results are fed back into the investment component in an iterative manner. The evaluation of human resource programs and activities then becomes an input in the next round of strategic decision making.

As the reader will note, numerous examples of human resource practices are provided throughout this book. These examples often involve companies that are exemplary in some aspect of strategic human resource management. Nonetheless, given the dynamic environment in which these companies currently operate, it is acknowledged that over time some of these companies may encounter difficulties. Hopefully, the reader will not discredit the principles for which the examples are offered because of difficulties in other aspects of a company's performance. In addition, in an attempt to provide a more comprehensive treatment of the issues addressed in this book, numerous endnotes have been used to give credit to the sources of the material and to provide sources where the reader may find more information. All endnotes cite references, and none is for supplemental or explanatory purposes. Thus, the reader need not refer to the endnotes except in those cases in which there is interest in learning more about a particular issue.

Acknowledgments

I would like to express my appreciation to several people who provided assistance to this project in many ways. First of all, a special thank you is owed to my editor, Melissa Steffens, and my production editor, Emma Moore. Their patience and good humor were greatly appreciated. Thanks also to Linda Begley of Rainbow Graphics. I also am indebted to Aparna Casella and Kathy Livingston who provided research assistance with the first edition and Suzanne Lindquist who helped with this revision. Their many hours in the library and on the Internet are greatly appreciated. A special note of gratitude is owed for the human resource insights of Alan Speaker, Senior Vice President of Synhrgy HR Technologies, Alpharetta, Georgia, and former vice president of Human Resources of Burlington Northern. Thanks also to Larry Peters and Stu Youngblood, my colleagues in human resources at Texas Christian University. A note of gratitude is also owed to David Lei, Southern Methodist University, for sharing his insights on strategic management, and to Robert Kolodinsky, Ph.D. student at Florida State University, for his comments on the manuscript and the preparation of accompanying materials.

Several reviewers contributed to this book through their comments on the first or second editions. These reviewers were Rich Arvey, University of Minnesota; Brian Becker, SUNY Buffalo; Elmer H. Burack, University of Illinois at Chicago; Jack L. Howard, Illinois State University; Douglas McCabe, Georgetown University; Kelly A. Mollica, Wake Forest University; Wayne Rockmore, East Tennessee State University; Marcus Sandvor, Ohio State University; Scott Snell, Pennsylvania State University; George Spindler, University of Chicago; and Charles Vance, Loyola Marymount. And thanks also to Dr. Vance's anonymous students who provided very specific and helpful comments. Any remaining weaknesses or faults are, of course, attributable to the author.

Charles R. Greer
Fort Worth, Texas
September 2000

CHAPTER 1

An Investment Perspective of Human Resources

As indicated in the Preface, the conceptual framework for this book begins with an investment perspective for guiding managerial strategic decisions regarding human resources. Human resource management practitioners and management scholars have long advocated that human resources should be viewed from an investment perspective. Current practices in many organizations indicate that employees are viewed as valuable investments. However, some still view their employees as variable costs of production, while physical assets are treated as investments. When employees are viewed as variable costs, there is little recognition of the firm's contribution to their training or the costs of recruiting and training their replacements. Likewise, there is less incentive to provide training or make other investments in them. A respected human resource scholar described the existing state of affairs as follows:

> I am constantly amazed at the contrast between the concern that strategists show for potential capital costs and the casual indifference they tend to display toward potential human resource costs (until, of course, the latter have gotten completely out of hand).[1]

A focus solely on investment in physical resources, as opposed to human resources, is shortsighted. Strategists have found that having superior production facilities or a superior product are usually not enough to sustain an advantage over competitors. Physical facilities can be duplicated, cloned, or reverse-engineered and no longer provide a sustainable advantage.[2] Strategists James Quinn, Thomas Doorley, and Penny Paquette have argued that "maintainable advantage usually derives from outstanding depth in selected human skills, logistics capabilities, knowledge bases, or other service strengths that competitors cannot reproduce . . .".[3] Thus, with their perspective, there is recognition of the importance of having superior human resources. There is little doubt that organizations will need to invest heavily in their human resources in order to be competitive during the twenty-first century. Management scholar Edward Lawler has described these investment requirements as follows:

> To be competitive, organizations in many industries must have highly skilled, knowledgeable workers. They must also have a relatively stable labor force since employee turnover works directly against obtaining the kind of coordination and organizational learning that leads to fast response and high-quality products and services.[4]

According to Lawler, these investments will become increasingly important due to forecasts of shifts in skill needs from manual to cerebral.

Contemporary management practices indicate that many leading companies have recognized the strategic importance of human resources and have adopted an investment perspective toward these resources. Further, there is greater awareness of the costs of treating employees as variable costs, which is beginning to change views of human resource practices.[5] There is also a growing recognition of the relationship between companies' overall strategies and their human resource practices. For example, companies pursuing strategies of innovation have the potential to be severely damaged by turnover because of reliance on individual expertise and unrecorded knowledge that has been quickly acquired. Accordingly, such companies tend to provide greater job security for some employees.[6] A final reason for beginning this book with an investment perspective is to reinforce the idea that for human resource management to play a meaningful role in the strategic management of organizations, it must be viewed as contributing to the bottom line. An investment perspective provides a valuable guide for strategic management.

This chapter begins with consideration of factors relevant to strategy-based human resource investment decisions. Factors to be discussed include the organization's managerial values, risk and return trade-offs, the economic rationale for investments in training, the investment analysis approach of utility theory, and outsourcing as an alternative to investments in human resources. Following the discussion of these factors, specific investments in strategy-related training and development will be considered. This discussion will include investments in the future "employability" of employees, current practices in training investment, on-the-job training, management development, prevention of skill obsolescence, and reductions in career plateauing.

Practices for investing in improved retention and reduced turnover will be discussed, beginning with an examination of organizational cultures that emphasize interpersonal relationship values. This will be followed by discussions of effective selection procedures, compensation and benefits, job enrichment and job satisfaction, practices providing work life balance, organizational direction, and other practices that facilitate retention. Next, there will be a discussion of the costs of downsizing and layoffs. This will be followed by a discussion of how to avoid business cycle–based layoffs, alternatives to layoffs, and employment guarantees. There will also be a discussion of the relationship between job insecurity and work effort. Nontraditional investment approaches will also be examined. These include investments in disabled employees, investments in employee health, and countercyclical hiring.

HUMAN RESOURCE INVESTMENT CONSIDERATIONS

Several factors will be considered in the discussion of strategic human resource investment decisions. As noted earlier, these will include management's values, views of risk, the economic rationale for investment in training, utility theory, and alternatives to human resource investments. Investments in training are covered in this chapter because they are fundamental to the formation of human capital. Firms also invest in many other human resource practices with the expectation that there will be impacts on performance and financial returns. Chapter 8 is devoted entirely to the important topic of the potential returns from investments in various human resource practices.

Management Values

Fundamental values must be addressed in many human resource issues, particularly those involved in major strategic initiatives. When senior managers formulate and implement strategies, their values and philosophies are communicated to members of the organization through human resource policies and practices.[7] For example, senior managers who are committed to the preservation of the organization's human resources can manage the stress associated with major strategic events, through such measures as dealing with rumors and providing accurate information, so that misinformation does not have such a debilitating impact on employees.[8] How employees are treated following significant strategic events, such as a merger or acquisition, is a reflection of these values and communicates whether the organization views employees from an investment perspective. Those adopting an investment perspective seek to enhance the value of their human capital or, at the very least, prevent its depreciation.

Risk and Return on Investment

Although there are a number of important benefits to investments in human resources, such investments contain an element of risk. Investing in human resources is inherently more risky than investing in physical capital because the employer does not own the resource. Employees are free to leave, although contractual arrangements may limit their mobility. In order for investments in human resources to be attractive, the returns must be great enough to overcome the risks. Further, for some investments, such as cash outlays to maintain no-layoff policies, the benefits are not easily quantified and there are meaningful costs. Decision makers have to be prepared to trade off current costs for long-term strategic benefits, such as a more flexible, committed workforce and related positive aspects of the organizational culture to which such policies contribute.[9]

Economic Rationale for Investment in Training

Because human resource investments frequently involve training, it is instructive to consider the difference between specific and general training. Nobel Laureate economist Gary Becker has written extensively on this subject. His distinction between specific and general training in human capital theory provides guidance for understanding when employers will provide training. The decision whether to invest in training and development depends, in part, on whether the education imparts skills that are specific to the employing organization (specific training) or are general and transferable to other employers (general training). Employers generally invest in or pay part of the cost of *specific training* because employees cannot readily transfer such skills to other employers. Employers recoup their investments after employees complete training by paying employees only part of the revenue derived from their increased productivity (marginal product). Conversely, conventional *human capital theory* predicts that employers will pay for none of the cost of *general training* because employees can transfer skills developed at employers' expense to other employers. Accordingly, employers would rather hire an employee who has the requisite general skills. When employees having the requisite general skills cannot be hired, the employer must invest in general training without assurance that the unskilled employee will remain employed long enough after training for the employer to recoup the investment.[10]

In reality, employers probably invest in general training more than the specific and general training rationale would suggest. A recent study has found the following:

> under certain conditions [use of employment contracts and retention of employees based on productivity] the firm may share the costs of and returns on investment in general human capital and pursue no lay-off policy. General human capital will have the same implications as firm-specific capital.[11]

General training can be obtained in on-the-job training as well as in formal programs such as tuition reimbursement. It also can occur unintentionally simply as a by-product of the work situation as employees learn work skills that are applicable to other employers. Employers may make general training investments in employees by paying a wage during training, which has been reduced by the training costs. Employers also can recoup some of their investments in general training because employees incur costs of mobility, such as the costs of finding new jobs and relocating. If the costs of mobility are high enough (moving expenses, realtors' fees, psychological costs of moving children, etc.) the employer can pay a wage lower than the employee's new general skills would warrant at other places of employment.[12]

Labor economists also argue that employers are more reluctant to lay off employees in whom they have invested in specific training. (When employers pay part of the costs of general training, the firm also will be reluctant to lay off workers who have received this training.) Like general training, specific training can be obtained through formal programs. It also can be obtained through on-the-job experience, as much of what employees learn on the job tends to be of a specific nature. Employees who receive specific training from an employer receive a lower wage after training than their productivity would warrant because no other employers have use for these specific skills.[13] Thus, it is likely that the employer will have invested more heavily in these employees and would not want to lose the investment.

To a certain extent, the distinction between general and specific training is misleading. There are probably few skills that have no transferability to other employers. Likewise, probably few skills are completely general. Further, employers do not seem to make clear distinctions between general and specific training.[14] There are many considerations in layoff decisions in addition to the employer's investment, such as equity, contractual obligations, and different business needs. Nonetheless, the concepts of specific and general training can provide insights on the conditions in which investments in human resources are more favorable.

Utility Theory

In considering investments in human resources in terms of hiring or development of current employees in order to pursue given strategies, there must be a method for evaluating the financial attractiveness of such investments. There must also be a method to be used in "selling" the investment to senior management. These tasks may be accomplished by determining the returns for such investments through cost–benefit analytical approaches such as utility analysis. *Utility theory* attempts to determine the economic value of human resource programs, activities, and procedures. As such, utility theory might be used to determine the dollar value of a selection test that enables an employer to identify and hire managers for a specific job whose productivity is higher than those hired without the test. The calculations of utility might involve several variables. For example, validity of the selection test would be a critical variable, in that it provides an indication of the predictive ability of the test. Additionally, the increased production, its contribution to profitability, and the standard deviation of the contribution, would be variables in the calculations. Finally, other variables might be included in the analysis, such as the cost of testing enough applicants to obtain a sufficient number having scores above the cut-off point.[15]

Brian Becker and Mark Huselid's study in a national retailing company provides another example of an application of utility theory. Becker and Huselid's analysis explained return on sales for each store on the basis of the performance appraisals of the store supervisors. Their statistical analysis also controlled for differences in the supervisors' educational levels and their commitment to the company. Their study demonstrated that better estimates of the standard deviation of the performance appraisal variable could be obtained through a model based on the use of accounting data (return on sales) rather than the more commonly used subjective approaches. This study helps to enhance the legitimacy of utility theory for applications in real business environments.[16] An example of the application of utility analysis to a strategic selection problem is provided in Chapter 9.

Outsourcing as an Alternative to Investment in Human Resources

As indicated earlier, investments in human resources should support the organization's strategies. Unless there is the potential to build capabilities that provide an advantage over competition, cost considerations often lead to the rational decision to outsource through specialized service providers rather than invest in human resources. In general, *strategic outsourcing* is advocated where (1) world-class capabilities and a strategic advantage cannot be developed, (2) the resources devoted to services performed internally will be greater than those needed to outsource the service, and (3) excessive dependency on suppliers can be avoided. When an activity is performed internally at a higher cost, the misallocated resources will put the company at a disadvantage to its competitors.[17]

Firms have been outsourcing human resource activities at a phenomenal rate. Furthermore, they have been outsourcing a wide range of activities. For example, firms routinely outsource the administration of 401(k) plans, executive search activities, payroll functions, employee assistance programs, human resource information systems, benefits administration, and outplacement. As a result of the demand for outsourcing, a whole new service industry of personnel service providers has been created, often by human resource executives who were downsized during the 1980s and early 1990s. Although many firms have been willing to outsource a wide range of their human resource activities, virtually all of them have retained the critical and sensitive functions of performance management, employee relations, and labor relations.[18] Because of the importance of outsourcing, Chapters 2 and 6 discuss the topic in greater detail.

INVESTMENTS IN TRAINING AND DEVELOPMENT

Specific investment approaches will be examined in this section, beginning with new approaches, which result in enhanced "employability" of employees.

Investments in Employability

While there have been dramatic declines in the prevalence of employment security policies, some companies are now investing in their human resources by providing developmental experiences that make employees much more employable should the employment relationship end. These developmental investments might include the provision for growth opportunities, a learning environment, training, and retraining. Having a workforce that is characterized by its employability is probably a necessary prerequisite for corporate survival. General Electric's experiences provide an example of the new employability approach. In the aftermath of General Electric's workforce reductions of 25 percent, there was recognition by its chief executive officer (CEO) Jack Welch that the company would have to attract quality employees with desirable achievement opportunities instead of job security policies.[19] Welch, who was widely regarded as one of the most visionary and effective CEOs, was strongly criticized for his actions as indicated in the following passage:

> Welch says that when he took over, the need for change was obvious, and he moved quickly. He was vilified as heartless in his zeal to reshape the corporation by eliminating jobs, earning himself the nickname "Neutron Jack." When Welch left a GE facility, the story went, the building was still standing but the people were gone.[20]

Interestingly, Welch stated that strong managers, like him, produce the only real job security in the current environment. His rationale was that such managers make the major structural changes necessary to increase their companies' competitiveness and ultimate survivability, often through the elimination of unneeded jobs. Conversely, he argued that weak managers, who do not take such actions, endanger the competitiveness of their companies, ultimately causing the loss of jobs.[21]

Because the types of experiences that result in future employability (e.g., valuable learning experiences and progressively more challenging assignments) are typically not the result of chance, and are instead the product of intentional developmental programs, they involve resource allocations or monetary outlays and will be considered as investments in this discussion. Kanter's description of the employability concept is summarized in the following discussion:

> If security no longer comes from being *employed*, then it must come from being *employable*. In a post-entrepreneurial era in which corporations need the flexibility to change and restructuring is a fact of life, the promise of very long-term employment security would be the wrong one to expect employers to make. But *employability security*—the knowledge that today's work will enhance the person's value in terms of future opportunities—that is a promise that can be made and kept. Employability security comes from the chance to accumulate human capital—skills and reputation—that can be invested in new opportunities as they arise.[22]

Bruce Ellig, the former Vice President of Human Resources for Pfizer, has provided another view of the concept of employability and the respective obligations of employers and employees:

> [I]t is hard to argue against a position that says individuals have a responsibility to be the best they can be to improve their employability, and employers have a

responsibility to ensure they are getting the best results from each employee before terminating them. This means that the employer has an obligation to coach and counsel as well as to provide appropriate training programs. Training programs provide the opportunity to improve existing skills and/or acquire new ones. It is the employer's responsibility to make such opportunities available; it is the employee's responsibility to take advantage of them.[23]

Current Practices in Training Investments

As indicated earlier, heavy investments in training will be necessary for future strategies and competitive advantage. Nonetheless, U.S. companies seem to lag behind the practices of companies in several other industrialized countries. For example, a study by the Congressional Office of Technology Assessment reported that "auto workers in Japan receive more than three times as much training each year as workers in American-owned assembly plants in the U.S."[24] U.S. workers not going on to college do not receive the training of their counterparts in other industrialized countries. In contrast, technical workers in other industrialized countries are often trained in well-developed *apprenticeship programs*. Approximately 59 percent of the German workforce has been trained through apprenticeships. In Japan, new employees often receive months of training by their employers.[25] Japanese companies are investing in human resources by training these workers.

There are some notable exceptions to the U.S. tendency to lag behind the Japanese and Germans in employee training. One of the most progressive examples of investment in training technical and production workers is provided by Corning, Inc. Corning's experience demonstrates that a company can earn high returns by investing in human resources. At one point, Corning faced a common dilemma of many U.S. companies in that its foreign competitors had acquired the same technology that had enabled it to be dominant in the past. Given its competitors' lower labor costs, it had to adopt a different approach unless it moved its production facilities overseas. Corning decided that to compete on a global basis it would need a world-class workforce. It reopened a plant in Blacksburg, Virginia, and staffed it with 150 production workers from a pool of 8,000 applicants. Although most of those hired had completed at least one year of college, Corning invested in extensive technical and interpersonal skills training. Training took up 25 percent of total working time during the plant's first year of operation. The plant's empowered workers take on duties previously performed by managers and use their broad range of skills in a team-based approach. An intensive emphasis on skills is maintained as workers must master three skill modules within two years in order to retain their jobs. In contrast to the narrow job definitions in many U.S. plants, the Corning plant has only four job classifications instead of the previous 47. Because of the workers' broad skills, the plant can retool quickly. The result is that during the first 8 months of operation, the plant made \$2 million in profits in contrast to an expected \$2.3

million start-up loss. Because of these successes, Corning is adopting the same approach in 27 other factories.[26]

Some other well-managed U.S. companies also have invested heavily in training employees who work in teams. These companies include A. O. Smith, Boeing, Cummins, Ford, General Electric, IBM, Kodak, Motorola, Polaroid, Procter & Gamble, and Xerox.[27] Another example of a company that invests heavily in training is the Dana Corporation. Like Corning, the Dana Corporation has used training as a means of gaining an advantage vis-à-vis its competitors. In a recent year, Dana invested $10 million in training 8,500 employees with the expressed purpose of enabling them to meet competitive needs.[28] Companies in *Fortune*'s best 100 companies to work for also provide extensive training:

> So the 100 Best are making major investments in employee education at multimillion-dollar facilities and through generous tuition-reimbursement programs. On average, the 100 Best lavished 43 hours of training on each employee . . . Some companies have begun to advertise these learning labs in their recruitment materials. At brokerage firm Edward Jones (No. 11), new brokers are immersed in 17 weeks of classes and study sessions at a cost of $50,000 to $70,000 per head. "We consider training an investment rather than an expense," explains Dan Timm, a principal at the St. Louis company.[29]

On-the-Job Training

On-the-job training is another way in which an employer may invest in human capital needed for strategic advantage. Such investments may be made by structuring a job so that employees learn while they work. For example, employees' skills may be increased by learning how to perform new tasks or operate new equipment. Employers may structure jobs so that these skills may be learned from other employees. They may also give employees time to learn new procedures or how to operate new equipment through self-instruction, such as by reading technical manuals, or by learning new software through self-instruction. Employers may also absorb the costs of lower productivity while workers lacking relevant skills learn through interaction with skilled employees or through trial-and-error processes.

Gary Becker has noted that on-the-job training's impact on workers' productivity levels is frequently underrated.[30] Likewise, economist Lester Thurow argues that on-the-job training provides the bulk of skills used on the job while formal education serves a *signaling function* of communicating to employers the trainability of job applicants.[31] Economists calling attention to the importance of on-the-job training point out that a worker's productivity is determined by the capital intensity of the job; type and extent of on-the-job training provided; the worker's ability to learn from the training, which is signaled by education; and how the jobs are structured, such as their promotion possibilities and responsibility level.[32] The contribution of on-the-job training to productivity has also been hypothesized to vary according to occupation as a result of differences in such factors as the rapidity of skill obsolescence and difficulty of job tasks. The contribution to worker productivity of on-the-job training has been verified in an empirical analysis of governmental employees with on-the-job training being measured by the employees' years of job experience.[33]

Investments in Management Development

The continued development of managerial personnel is a critical strategic issue in most organizations and a particularly difficult challenge given the massive shifts in strategy. Before considering management development, it is useful to quickly review some evolving and forecasted trends in the managerial environment. It is clear that organizations are becoming less hierarchical and that many middle-management positions have been eliminated. Further, larger numbers of workers are better educated and many are professionals. As a result, they expect to participate more in decision making. In the future, more work is expected to be performed in task force or project teams, power will be shared, managerial status will be deemphasized, and leadership responsibilities may be rotated.[34] Because of the participative aspect of these empowerment trends, many professionals and highly educated employees may have more exposure to managerial responsibilities and may develop related skills as a natural part of their work.

An important management development approach has been to rotate managers through successively more challenging assignments. Frequently, these *job rotation programs* seek to provide a broad view of the organization and as a result, may involve interdepartmental or *cross-functional assignments*. Use of job rotational programs is positively correlated with company size and is used most in transportation and communications and least in service industries.[35]

Advantages of job rotation include the development of generalists, avoidance of overdependency on one supervisor, the challenge of new assignments, avoidance of dead-end career paths, cross-fertilization of ideas gained in other settings, increased interdepartmental cooperation as a result of the establishment of personal networking, and evaluation by different superiors in different settings. From a strategic perspective, a major advantage is that such programs develop a pool of managers who have been exposed to an area of the business who can then provide management talent in the event that there is an unexpected or sudden increase in the level of business in that area. Such rotational programs are also widely used for high-potential or fast-track managerial personnel.[36]

Conversely, the disadvantages of such job rotational approaches include the institutionalization of short-term perspectives because of frequent changes in assignments as one is "rotated out," underdeveloped peer relationships, reduced loyalty to the organization if rotations are too frequent, expense when the rotation involves a geographic move, and personal impact on the employee and family.[37] Other disadvantages include productivity losses due to the learning time required after each new job assignment, and the complications of rotations involving geographic transfers of dual career families.

Aside from job rotational approaches, other methods of management development include sending high-level executives and less senior high-potential managers to executive development programs at leading universities. Shorter in-house training programs for less senior managerial personnel and more junior high-potential managers are quite common. Use of residential university programs has been found to be most likely in the financial industry and least likely in services.[38]

More systematic approaches toward in-house and off-site management development programs have been recommended by human resource practitioners and scholars. In some organizations, such approaches are evident. From the author's personal observations of in-house programs for project managers in large banks and insurance companies, several companies are taking an investment perspective in systematic developmental approaches. Such programs involve high-level management in the analysis of the skills needed and in pilot tests of program content. They are also conducted on a continuous basis, as opposed to one-shot training sessions. They also utilize customized cases and materials, involve participants in exercises in which skills are developed and practiced, provide exercises in which participants apply program content to real problems that they currently have, and communicate either implicitly or explicitly that the managers are of critical importance to the organization.

Although these positive trends have been observed, a continuing problem exists. Management training is still an early casualty of budget cuts when companies encounter economic downturns. Unfortunately, in many organizations, management development is given a low priority and is viewed more as an avoidable cost rather than an investment. Where management development has to be "sold," it is important to build in several of the components just noted to include specification of the results expected and how they will be measured.[39] Given the expense of some programs such as executive MBA programs, it will be important to be able to determine the returns on the investment. Unfortunately, most cost-effectiveness studies of development programs have focused only on individuals and not on organizational impact or have used only subjective measures of organizational impact.[40]

Prevention of Skill Obsolescence

Technological change is often a cause of *skill obsolescence* in engineering, science, and the professions. Because of the rapidity of change, the knowledge half-lives in electrical engineering and computer science are five years and two and one-half years, respectively.[41] In addition, other professionals and managers run a risk of having their skills become obsolete because of changes in technology and methods. Technological change appears to affect individuals differently, as some grow and develop along with new technology while others fall behind.[42] Because technological obsolescence can limit an organization's strategic alternatives, obsolescence in this area can be devastating and companies should have a strong incentive to invest in its prevention.

A model using both expectancy theory and human capital theory has been developed to explain such differences in individuals' responses to changing technology. Given the critical strategic impact of technological change, such explanations should be of value to strategists. The model identifies motivation, along with individual, organizational, and external factors as determinants of whether individuals will develop the skills needed for new technology. Employees' expectations of their ability to acquire new skills and the perceived reward instrumentality of such skills help explain employees' motivation for skill acquisition. Such motivation is also related to the expected costs of investing in skill acquisition and the length of time for returns to be accrued. Nonetheless, the payback period can be misleading as there are several individual difference variables, such as breadth of interests, education, aptitude, and personality variables, that also affect individuals' acquisition of new skills.[43]

A number of suggestions have been offered for the prevention of obsolescence. One suggestion is to provide challenge, particularly of a technical nature for technical specialists, in all phases of their careers. Individuals who face such challenges are less likely to become obsolete in later career stages. Likewise, responsibility, authority, participation, and employee interaction also appear to be related to the prevention of obsolescence. Periodic reassignments requiring new learning also help to prevent obsolescence and facilitate development. It is important to prevent employees from becoming overspecialized. Although the organization may benefit in the short term, excessive specialization may be exploitative and not be in either the individual's or the organization's long-range best interests. Organizations can explicitly encourage employees to stay abreast of developments in the field by incorporating knowledge acquisition activities and accomplishments in performance evaluation and reward systems. Organizations also can set goals for updating knowledge and reward such goal accomplishments. In addition to these suggestions, funding attendance at conferences and providing time to read professional literature can help to prevent obsolescence.[44]

An example of one company's intensive efforts to prevent obsolescence is provided by Hewlett-Packard. The company's approach with its engineering workforce has involved the establishment of cooperative programs with universities. In one year alone, 1,000 Hewlett-Packard employees were able to take courses at Stanford University while another 200 took courses at California State University, Chico. Although Hewlett-Packard is a company involved at the leading edge of rapidly changing technology, it also will be important for other companies in lower-technology industries to make investments in their current employees.[45] As the rapid rate of technological change continues, the problem of obsolescence will need continued attention.

Reductions in Career Plateauing

Career plateaus occur when employees have occupied a job in an organization for some period of time, have mastered all aspects of the job, and have low prospects for promotion. Eliminating or reducing the incidence of plateaus is important because they have the potential to create resentment and a sense of futility. As a result, there may be reductions in productivity. Plateaus are a natural consequence of a lack of organizational growth or change. They also occur because of the pyramidal shape of organizations and organizational inflexibility. Other, more employee-specific causes of plateaus are the personal choices of employees, lack of career skills resulting from naive perceptions of organizational realities, and lack of requisite skills for promotion.[46]

Employees also may lack appropriate skills because changes in the external environment and resultant shifts in strategies may not have been anticipated in a company's managerial development programs. In such instances, the company may be forced to hire managerial talent from outside. Aside from the expense of external hiring there may be detrimental effects on morale. Further, those brought in may not have sufficient knowledge of the primary business to be effective.[47] A lesson to be derived from such situations is that investment in developmental programs is not sufficient for the avoidance of plateaus. Instead, alternative future strategic scenarios must be considered in the planning of developmental assignments in order to have promotable managers.

Another cause of plateaus is related to developmental programs. Companies sometimes make inflexible decisions about which employees should continue in management development programs or those who should be placed on a fast track. Sometimes, these decisions are based on performance during the early stages of an employee's career. Further, the decision may be made in the manner of a single elimination tournament in which one failure to be promoted or one unsuccessful performance may cause a manager to be taken out of the developmental program. Those left out of developmental programs or fast-track assignments are often relegated to dead-end career paths and become plateaued. In essence, the early identification of fast trackers may become a self-fulfilling prophecy. Furthermore, perceptions of being plateaued tend to have the greatest detrimental impact on job satisfaction and company identification for employees who have less rather than more tenure on the job.[48]

Plateaus also may be avoided by more deliberate identification of *stars* (outstanding performers with high potential) and *solid citizens* (satisfactory or outstanding performers with less potential). More developmental assignments, challenges, and lateral moves for both categories can produce a pool of qualified managerial talent that should enable the organization to be more flexible and adaptive to strategic needs. Job rotation for plateaued employees also can reduce frustration and increase the chance for improved performance. The stress associated with career plateauing also may be reduced by managerial actions that provide recognition and appreciation in the absence of promotions, job enrichment, mentoring assignments, and lateral transfers that provide growth opportunities also may be helpful in this regard.[49]

INVESTMENT PRACTICES FOR IMPROVED RETENTION

Companies invest in their workforces when they pursue practices and develop programs that increase retention. By failing to make such investments, they incur the high costs of turnover. Coarse-grained estimates place the costs of turnover at 150 percent of exempt employees' compensation and at 175 percent for nonexempt employees.[50] The determinants of turnover are reasonably well understood as there has been a great deal of research on the topic. Accordingly, there are sound practices that employers can follow in order to retain their employees.

Organizational Cultures Emphasizing Interpersonal Relationship Values

One of the most important determinants of employee retention is the organization's culture. By investing in human resource practices that ultimately affect the organization's culture, firms can influence retention. A longitudinal analysis examined the retention of 904 college graduates hired by public accounting firms over a six-year period. The study found a difference in retention related to the culture of the firms. For employees of firms with cultures characterized by interpersonal relationship values (respect for people and a team orientation), the median for retention was 14 months longer than in firms with cultures reflecting task values (detail and stability). Interestingly, the effects of the culture emphasizing interpersonal values appeared to be universal and were not contingent on employee characteristics.[51] Other research has found higher retention in "fearless cultures" in which employees can speak up in order to challenge the status quo without being concerned about retribution. Retention improves with other related aspects of culture such as positive relationships with superiors, absence of conflict-laden relationships, having input into decisions, less emphasis on formal authority, information sharing, and support for employees.[52]

Effective Selection Procedures

When firms hire employees that match well with the organization, the job, and their coworkers, there is an increased likelihood of retention. Recent survey research indicates that careful selection is the most widely used method for retaining front-line employees.[53] In addition to the use of selection procedures, such as valid tests and improved interviewing processes to obtain better job matches between employee job qualifications, the use of realistic job previews (RJPs) also can increase retention. RJPs attempt to show applicants what the actual job is going to be like. As a result, there is less likelihood that applicants will accept jobs that fail to conform to their expectations. The exact means by which RJPs influence retention is the subject of some debate because there are several variables that can have an impact on their ability to affect retention. Nonetheless, RJPs provide a useful means for increasing retention in many circumstances. In addition, the use of biodata, which are data on objective characteristics such as years of experience, bilingualism, and college education, improves retention.[54]

Compensation and Benefits

Equitable compensation is important for employee retention. In turn, greater compensation equity occurs with fair appraisal reviews, equitable ratios of inputs (e.g., effort, skill, education) to outputs (various rewards), exclusion of politics in compensation decisions, fair compensation structures, and communication of compensation procedures. Increased retention also occurs with performance-based compensation, pay incentives, and benefits that are valued by employees. Not surprisingly, the most frequently used approach for retaining senior executives is to improve their compensation and benefits. Companies in *Fortune*'s top 100 list typically offer both high compensation and generous benefits. For example, Merck has extraordinary benefits, and its pay ranks at the top of the scale. Merck employees have received $60,000 in stock options over the past decade while the average stock option gain for nonexecutives at Cisco Systems has been $150,000. At WRQ software, employees pay nothing for their health care. At J. M. Smucker, the jelly maker, voluntary turnover in a recent year was only 5 percent. One of the company's benefits is a savings plan for which the company provides 50 percent matching contributions.[55] Retention bonuses provide a direct example of how compensation is being used to keep the companys's good employees:

> For many companies seeking to hang onto employees, "retention bonuses" have become the tool of choice . . . The [oil] industry is offering bonuses of 15% to 50% of one year's pay, spread over three years, to employees who stick around . . . Employers have to bolt their back doors, i.e., to fend off recruiters and minimize staff turnover because it is so expensive. Experts, such as those at the Hay Group consulting firm, estimate that finding and training a replacement costs 50% to 60% of the departed employee's annual compensation.[56]

Job Enrichment and Job Satisfaction

Job-enrichment practices, such as those building in increased responsibility or autonomy, knowledge of results, meaningful work, knowledge of how assigned tasks contribute to the greater activity of the larger organization, and skill variety, have been found to produce moderate reductions in turnover. Practices that enhance job latitude and job satisfaction also have a positive impact on employee retention. However, when high-performing employees feel undervalued, they tend to have higher turnover rates.[57] Another company from *Fortune* top 100 companies provides a good example of the retention effects of job enrichment and job satisfaction:

> "Being at a good company is like having a good wife," says Floyd Williams, a senior production manager at sports gear maker K2 (No. 52), who gushes about the opportunity to work on as many as 25 projects at a time. "When you get used to a certain level of freedom and excitement, you don't want to leave." In fact, none of Williams' three marriages has lasted as long as his 28-year career with the company. "One wife told me it was either K2 or me. And I said, 'Well, I'm not leaving K2!' "[58]

Practices Providing Work Life Balance

In addition to job-related factors and the work environment, the opportunity to obtain a balance between work and home life also has a positive impact on retention. Alternative work schedules, child care services, and provisions for family leave also facilitate retention. (The Family and Medical Leave Act sets minimum standards for family leave.) Conversely, unreasonable workloads are associated with turnover. It is no surprise that many companies in *Fortune*'s list of the best 100 companies to work for provide such benefits. Flextime is offered at 59 of these companies, while 18 provide opportunities for telecommuting. These top employers include a wide range of practices for balancing work and family life. For example, Deloitte and Touche has adopted flextime and telecommuting practices. Janus Investments has generous time-off practices. Unum provides subsidized child care for employees earning less than $40,000. The accounting firm Plante and Moran provides child care on Saturdays during tax season. The SAS Institute, the statistical software developer, has a 35-hour week and provides employees child care at a rate of $250 per month. It also provides 12 holidays per year and free medical care on site. At First Tennessee Bank, 91 percent of employees are on flextime.[59]

Organizational Direction Creating Confidence in the Future

When employees are confident about their organization's future direction, they are more likely to stay. Thus, setting a clear direction for the future and building confidence in the vision for the future should help improve retention.[60] The following excerpt from *Built to Last: Successful Habits of Visionary Companies* provides an example of such direction:

> Merck, in fact, epitomizes the ideological nature—the pragmatic idealism—of highly visionary companies. Our research showed that a fundamental element in the "ticking clock" of a visionary company is a core *ideology*—core values and sense of purpose beyond just making money—that guides and inspires people throughout the organization and remains relatively fixed for long periods of time. . . . we describe, support, and illustrate this crucial element that exists paradoxi-

cally with the fact that visionary companies are also highly effective profit-making enterprises.[61]

Strategic direction and strategies will be discussed in detail in Chapter 4.

Retention of Technical Employees

Retention of information technology specialists and other technical employees is a particular concern for many employers. The demand for such specialists and other highly skilled employees is so strong that companies have been very innovative in their retention efforts. For example, Burlington Northern Santa Fe has implemented a career development institute in which employees can learn new computer languages and other technical skills. The company also has increased the amount of communication with its technical employees and has helped develop their business knowledge and awareness. Alcon Laboratories also has implemented special measures to help retain information technology employees. The company has a well-deserved reputation for being a very stable employer. It also offers very attractive compensation and benefit packages and gives employees the "red carpet" treatment. In addition, the company has a dual career ladder or track program for its information technology professionals. Like many other companies, Alcon allows casual dress and has implemented innovative work schedules such as allowing employees to work 80 hours in nine days in order to gain an additional day off.[62]

Other Practices in Facilitating Retention

Opportunities for training, new learning, growth, and promotion also have positive impacts on retention. Similarly, liberal transfer policies tend to reduce employee turnover. When employees can transfer, they have the opportunity to leave problem situations and are less likely to leave the organization. In addition, effective management of diversity and prevention of sexual harassment tend to increase retention.[63] Marriott International, another of *Fortune*'s top 100 employers, has a workforce consisting of more then 50 percent minorities. The company has an excellent reputation for training and advancement opportunities and has a voluntary turnover rate of 37 percent even though the company operates in a low-wage industry. Enterprise Rent-A-Car also provides excellent opportunities for advancement as it moves new college graduates quickly into management jobs.[64]

A summary of these positive influences on employee retention is presented in Table 1-1.

INVESTMENTS IN JOB-SECURE WORKFORCES

Companies also invest in their human resources when they keep employees on the payroll through business downturns. Nonetheless, by the 1980s and 1990s, it

TABLE 1-1 Investment Opportunities for Improving Employee Retention

- Organizational Culture Emphasizing Interpersonal Relationship Values
  - Team Orientation
  - Respect for People
- Effective Selection Procedures
  - Use of Realistic Job Previews (RJPs)
  - Use of Biodata
- Compensation and Benefits
  - Equitable Compensation
    - Fair Appraisal Reviews
    - Equitable Input-to-Output Ratios
    - Exclusion of Political Factors
    - Fair Compensation Structures
    - Communication
  - Performance-Based Compensation
  - Pay Incentives
  - Valued Benefits
- Job Enrichment and Job Satisfaction
- Practices Providing Work Life Balance
  - Alternative Work Schedules
  - Family Leave
  - Child Care Services
- Training and Opportunities for Personal Growth
- Opportunities for Promotion
- Organizational Direction Creating Confidence in the Future
- Liberal Internal Transfer Policies
- Effective Management of Diversity
- Prevention of Sexual Harassment

became clear that employment security policies were often untenable, and downsizing became a daily feature of the business press. However, companies differed in the extent to which they resorted to downsizing or layoffs as many of the best ones did little or no downsizing. Although some companies provide employment security to enhance their chances of remaining union free, others provide such security for other workforce advantages. Increasingly, companies find that they must operate in environments characterized by rapidly evolving technological change, compressed product life cycles, and heavy emphasis on quality. In many such environments, greater employment security helps companies obtain the commitment, flexibility, and motivation needed from their workforces.[65] Indeed, three of *Fortune*'s 100 best companies to work for have official no-layoff policies—Southwest Airlines, Harley-Davidson, and FedEx—and another, Hewlett-Packard, has been a leader in workforce security for decades.[66]

Recognition of the Costs of Downsizing and Layoffs

Although there are many associated costs, downsizing is a fact of life in the United States, and layoffs occur with downturns in the business cycle. A strong labor market eliminated most cyclical layoffs in the late 1980s and 1990s, but frequent downsizing has continued into the twenty-first century. Downsizing is commonly linked to competitively driven structural changes in organizations, although it also is triggered solely by attempts to cut costs. Nonetheless, the costs of downsizing and layoffs are becoming better understood.[67] (The costs of downsizing are addressed in greater detail in Chapter 8.) For example, a study of approximately 100 surplus workforce situations revealed that it would have been more cost effective not to have laid off workers in 30 percent of the situations and to have laid off fewer workers in 20 percent.[68] Layoffs have been criticized on the grounds that they are sometimes inefficient, relative to other cost-reduction strategies. A major inefficiency or cost associated with downsizing or layoffs is that a firm's layoff practices may make it less attractive as a potential employer. A typical result of downsizing is that another 10 to 15 percent of an organization's workforce will often quit after layoffs. The uncertainty of future employment often causes some of the better, more mobile employees to leave. These, of course, are the employees that the acquiring organization would like to keep.[69]

Numerous other costs are involved in layoffs. One of the major costs is incurred in bumping practices. Because layoffs are typically conducted by inverse seniority, invariably where there is a union contract, employees with less seniority are "bumped" out of their jobs by more senior employees whose jobs have been targeted for elimination because of a lack of work. A chain reaction then occurs as more senior employees bump those with less seniority until, as in a game of musical chairs, the least senior is left without a job.[70] The width of the seniority unit that will govern bumping rights determines the impact of bumping. Narrower seniority units or definitions prevent a senior employee from displacing a junior employee in a job in which he or she is not qualified. With broader seniority units or definitions, senior employees can bump into new jobs for which they lack skills. As a result, training is needed for them to reach the proficiency levels of the junior employees who were bumped. Unions generally argue for broader seniority units on the basis of fairness while employers seek narrower definitions in order to minimize the dysfunctional aspects of bumping.[71] In addition to bumping costs, there are also severance, administrative, and intangible costs. Intangible costs sometimes involve declines in morale of the remaining workforce and disruption of work group synergy.[72] These costs are presented in Table 1-2.

Avoiding Business Cycle–Based Layoffs

The advisability of laying off workers during economic downturns has been questioned by some companies and management scholars.[73] Although the *no-*

TABLE 1-2 Costs of Layoffs

Costs Related to "Bumping" Less Senior Employees
- Reduced Productivity During Learning Periods
- Costs of Training Employees Assigned to Other Jobs
- Wage Supplements for Reassignments to Jobs Receiving Lower Compensation

Costs Related to the Termination of Employees
- Separation Payments
- Higher Rates for Unemployment Compensation
- Depletion of the Firm's Investments in Training Employees

Administrative Costs
- Human Resource Processing Activities
- Clerical Expenses
- Costs of Conducting Medical Examinations of Laid-Off Employees
- Increased Supervisory Obligations for Managers of Reassigned Employees

Intangible Costs
- Decline in Morale of Remaining Employees
- Disruption of Efficiencies in Work Processes
- Higher Incidence of Accidents
- Depletion of Goodwill
- Irregular Age Distributions
- Voluntary Turnover Prompted by Layoffs

Source: Adapted from Dan L. Ward. "Layoffs: What Does Flexibility Really Cost," in Richard J. Niehaus and Karl F. Price (Eds.), *Creating the Competitive Edge through Human Resource Applications*. New York: Plenum Press, 1988, pp. 169–91.

layoff policies of such companies as Southwest Airlines and Lincoln Electric are well known, there have been other examples from contemporary experience such as in Germany when a financially strapped shipbuilding company loaned 68 skilled workers to Daimler-Benz for one year. Another example is provided by the Sony Corporation. Sony's refusal to lay off employees in its San Diego plant after a decline in sales paid off in increased employee commitment and increased performance in following years.[74] As Akio Morita, the chairman of Sony, has stated:

> American management treats workers as just a tool to make money. You know, when the economy is booming, they hire more workers, and [when] the recession comes, they lay off the workers. But, you know, recession is not caused by the workers.[75]

Other leading U.S. companies that have offered *employment guarantees* in the past have included Johnson Wax, Nucor Corporation, Worthington Industries, Hewlett-Packard, and Hallmark.[76] Hewlett-Packard has stated that a central concept in its culture and human resource philosophy is the sharing of responsibilities in economic upturns and downturns. When orders at some of its manufacturing plants were lower than expected, employees were allowed to voluntarily go on leave without pay but with continued benefits and a guarantee of getting their jobs back after their return. After conditions deteriorated further, almost the entire nonsales workforce was furloughed two days per month without pay. Senior management were not furloughed and continued to work full schedules, but their pay was reduced by 10 percent.[77]

Alternatives to Layoffs

In contrast to periods of permanent structural change when a downturn is expected to be of relatively short duration, alternatives to layoffs are often feasible. When companies avoid layoffs, they preserve their investments in employees' skills and are able to avoid the expense and delay of hiring and training new employees once the recovery begins. When employees change employers, there is some loss of productivity because, if employed for more than a short time, they have acquired specific skills that do not apply to the new employer. Although layoffs are numerous, there is empirical evidence that firms attempt to avoid layoffs, thereby preserving their investments in human resources. A study of manufacturing firms found that they retain approximately 8 percent more labor during downturns than needed for production. Even after some excess labor is used in alternative assignments such as maintenance of equipment and training, approximately 4 percent is hoarded.[78]

There are a number of alternatives having the potential to reduce the number of layoffs in the short term, although layoffs are better avoided through the use of long-term alternatives. Some of these alternatives deal with shutting off the inflow of personnel into the organization. When the inflow is shut down, attrition can then help draw down excess employees. Unfortunately, during general downturns, attrition usually does not have the desired impact. For attrition to have an effect, there must be high turnover. When a downturn is sudden and severe and turnover is low, attrition may not work quickly enough to save labor costs.[79] Another set of these actions involves some form of redeployment of current employees or curtailment of subcontracts and reassignment of work from contractors to the company's own employees. A different set of actions involves sharing the economic loss through work sharing or incentives for early retirement. (The latter course of action can be quite expensive and is not always acknowledged.) Unsurprisingly, the survey of manufacturing companies noted earlier indicated that nonunion firms place greater importance on reductions in hours as an alternative to layoffs (69 percent and 37 percent, respectively).[80]

There are a few other short-term alternatives to layoffs, some of which involve pay cuts. Cuts may be accompanied in some instances by fewer days worked or with commitments from management that it will make it up to employees when conditions improve. Unpaid leaves of absence are also alternatives. Those taking leaves are guaranteed the job at the end of the leave.[81]

Actions or tactics useful for avoiding layoffs in the long term are presented in Table 1-3. One of the initial tactics is to conduct human resource planning with employment stability as a goal. As with the short-term tactics, several are related to the inflow of personnel into the organization. A lean staffing approach, staffing for the long term, and focusing on nonspecialists where possible will help to establish appropriate inflows. Greater flexibility in job assignment may be gained by providing employment guarantees in return for reductions in numbers of job classifications.[82] Another set of actions or tactics is related to maintenance of a productive workforce through training or retraining, judicious termination of unproductive employees, and using human resource buffers to supplement understaffing.

The feasibility of *buffering* appears to be increasing. As will be discussed in Chapter 2, the range of jobs for which temporary or contract employees are used is expanding. For example, the services of accountants, computer technicians, engineers, and financial managers are increasingly being obtained on a temporary or contract basis.[83] Another example of *flexible employment arrangements* comes from the entertainment industry. The Disney Company's Walt Disney World has three classifications of employees: (1) full-time, in which employees work no fewer than four days and 20 hours per week; (2) casual regular, in which weekly minimums of one day and maximums of less than four days apply except during peak periods when more days may be worked; and (3) casual temporary, in which employees work during peak periods or as needed in nonpeak periods.[84]

A tactic oriented more toward the long term involves linking larger proportions of employee compensation to company performance, which has the effect of reducing costs during downturns.[85] Of course, employees would no longer be assured of an even income stream but the likelihood of being laid off would decrease. As discussed in Chapter 7, profit sharing and stock options have

TABLE 1-3 Techniques for Avoiding Layoffs in the Long-Term

Actions to Be Taken

- Direct Human Resource Planning Toward Employment Stability
- Place Emphasis on Training and Retraining
- Maintain Lean Staffing Even During Periods of Prosperity
- Maintain Stability with Buffers (Overtime, Vendors, Part-Time Workers)
- Correct Poor Performance and Terminate When Warranted
- Select New Employees with the Goal of Long-Term Retention
- Use Probationary Periods for New Hires
- Focus Hiring Toward Nonspecialists Where Possible
- Teach Employees Skills Needed for Next Stage of Product Life Cycle

Source: Adapted from James F. Bolt. "Job Security: Its Time Has Come," *Harvard Business Review* 61, no. 6 (1983): 115–23; and Joseph T. McCune, Richard W. Beatty, and Raymond V. Montagno. "Downsizing: Practices in Manufacturing Firms," *Human Resource Management* 27, no. 2 (1988): 145–61.

become common compensation components in many companies. As profit sharing, stock options, and other forms of variable pay account for greater proportions of employee compensation, there could be reduced layoffs when economic conditions deteriorate.

Employment Guarantees

Although the distinction between no-layoff policies and employment guarantees may be artificial, the latter, although a somewhat elastic concept, may take the concept a step further. *Employment guarantees* have been defined in the popular management literature as "oral agreements to move heaven and earth to avoid layoffs."[86] Employment guarantees are made feasible by many of the same actions as no-layoff policies. One of most important tactics is understaffing. Companies such as IBM and Motorola staff some of their operations with 70 to 85 percent of the number of permanent employees needed for production at normal demand levels. The difference in labor needed is usually made up with overtime, temporary employees, subcontracting, or employees contracted on a short-term basis. A second tactic is *flexibility in job assignment*, which is made possible by employees who can perform several tasks and the absence of restrictive work practices such as narrow task definitions. Such flexibility also is supported by retraining for those whose skills have been made obsolete by technological advances and redeployment of excess labor. An innovative tactic is to redeploy extra personnel into sales. A more common redeployment may be assignments to maintenance activities. A third tactic, *work sharing*, involves sharing the available work by reducing the number of hours for each employee. However, work sharing or job sharing may not be legal in some states.[87] (The topic of workforce flexibility is discussed in greater depth in Chapter 6.)

Numerous benefits to employment guarantees have been found, many of which should have a positive impact on strategy implementation. Most of these benefits are simply the obverse of how employees act when they are insecure about their jobs. Several benefits result when a work scarcity mentality is avoided. These include volunteering ideas for labor savings, working at an optimal pace, foregoing restrictive work practices, and performing tasks beyond the job description. Other benefits appear to be related to increased receptivity of employees to changes. These include accepting management-initiated changes, working overtime even when inconvenient, volunteering for job-broadening training, deployment flexibility, and increased loyalty. Additional benefits include increased retention, morale-related productivity gains, elimination of bumping costs, elimination of the need for early-retirement incentives, and reduced hiring and training costs during postrecessionary periods.[88]

The Work Effort and Job Security Relationship

Some companies have learned hard lessons that employees may not be willing to be sufficiently flexible in their work assignments when their employers have employment security policies.[89] Unfortunately, high-standards companies that provided such employment security in the past may have endangered their own adaptability and survival through these enlightened or progressive human resource practices. Not only have some employees failed to reciprocate by making personal adjustments needed for the welfare of the company, employees may become shielded from the realities of the marketplace and too complacent in today's era of intense competition. Interestingly, with an appropriate level of job insecurity, employees may work harder. A recent field study has found an inverted "U"–shaped relationship between job insecurity and work effort. As presented in Figure 1-1, effort increases as insecurity escalates from low to moderate levels, but it declines with high levels of insecurity.[90] The implications for human resource investment policy are that there may be trade-offs between the benefits of employment security policies and the costs—to include the amount of effort that may be expected from employees. However, this relationship is obviously only an average tendency to which there are many exceptions.

ETHICAL IMPLICATIONS OF EMPLOYMENT PRACTICES

Downsizing, layoffs, terminations, and other employment practices often involve ethical issues. When these actions are implemented unfairly or without regard to the dignity and rights of employees, there are ethical problems as well

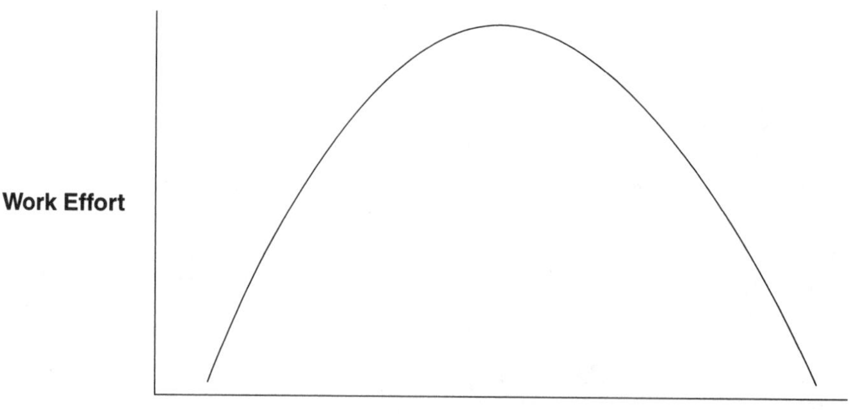

FIGURE 1-1 Relationship Between Job Insecurity and Effort

Source: Approximation of an inverted U relationship based on results reported by Joel Brockner, Steven Grover, Thomas F. Reed, and Rocki Lee Dewitt. "Layoffs, Job Insecurity, and Survivors' Work Effort: Evidence of an Inverted-U Relationship," *Academy of Management Journal* 35, no. 2 (1992): 413–42. Reprinted by permission of *Academy of Management Journal.*

as adverse performance effects. A Japanese company's recent attempt to lay off one of its workers provides an example of the ethical issues of such actions in another culture. Japanese companies have traditionally offered lifetime employment and have set the example for employment security practices throughout the world. However, many Japanese companies have bloated workforces, and lifetime employment has eroded somewhat, even though layoffs are opposed by Japanese culture and restricted by law. As a result, some companies have attempted to get some of their lower-performing employees to quit.

Sega Enterprises, Ltd., the producer of video games, wanted to lay off Toshiyuki Sakai, one of its employees in Tokyo. Sega proceeded to inform Sakai that his performance was substandard and offered him a severance package. He refused to quit and rejected the package.[91] The following account of the company's treatment of Sakai after he turned down the company's severance offer raises some important ethical concerns:

> Three days later, Sega told Mr. Sakai to take home all personal belongings, turn in all company property and report to an office dubbed the "Pasona Room," after the English word personnel. He arrived to find the room empty, except for a desk, three chairs, a bare locker and a telephone that couldn't make outside calls. Mr. Sakai was given no work to perform and allowed no diversions. He was being laid off, Japanese style. "I'm not going to be able to hold out for a day of this," Mr. Sakai recalls thinking. Months later, however, he was still clocking 40 hours a week there . . . Mr. Sakai had written orders to stay in the room every day from precisely 8:30 A.M. to 5:15 P.M . . . In late April, Sega announced a plan to cut its work force by one-quarter . . . By June, 750 employees had accepted severance packages. Mr. Sakai claims that Sega used the Pasona Room to frighten others into taking its buyout offers. "Everyone's afraid they might be the next to be thrown into solitary confinement," he says.[92]

NONTRADITIONAL INVESTMENT APPROACHES

Investments in Disabled Employees

A nontraditional area of human resource investment involves providing support for programs that return disabled employees back to the workforce. Frequently, companies deal with employees who have become disabled by relying on the company's long-term disability insurance policy to provide economic support. Unfortunately, there is little emphasis on facilitating the employee's return to the job. In contrast, companies such as 3M and Eastman Kodak have developed programs that enable disabled workers to return to work.[93] According to 3M's rehabilitation program supervisor, "Returning an employee to work makes good economic sense. With today's electronic aids and devices, we can return almost any worker to most any job."[94]

Aside from the economic motivations for investing in disabled workers, the law provides additional incentives. As will be discussed in Chapter 3, the

Americans with Disabilities Act of 1990 (ADA) requires employers to make reasonable accommodations for such workers. In addition to preserving the company's investment in the employee, there are obvious humanitarian benefits as well. Unfortunately, many companies are not aware of the support services that rehabilitation organizations provide or the devices that enable a disabled employee to perform the job again. Often, relatively inexpensive devices or aids can allow a physically disabled employee to be a productive worker again. Such approaches include raising the height of desks in order to provide wheelchair access, providing curb ramps for wheelchairs, providing appropriate handrails, simple changes in rest room facilities, lowering elevator controls, and removing structural barriers such as revolving doors. Simple changes such as alterations in the job may also be made, such as allowing physically disabled workers to work shorter hours. Other inexpensive approaches include providing battery-powered scooters, computer attachments that enable the deaf to make telephone calls, and computerized speech-recognition aids. In order to facilitate the exchange of knowledge on how to accommodate disabled workers, companies such as AT&T, Du Pont, Hartford Insurance, IBM, and Sears are sharing with other companies the knowledge they have acquired in accommodating disabled workers.[95]

The return from investments in disabled workers can be quite attractive. One large Chicago bank changed the job of a transcriptionist so that only dictated work is typed. The employee, who is blind, types dictated work at up to 96 words per minute without errors.[96] The experiences of Pennsylvania Power and Light Company (PP&L) provide further endorsement of investing in disabled workers. PP&L found the quantity and quality of work performed by 12 part-time disabled workers to be equivalent to that of other employees in its cash receipts department. Further, to the extent that such programs can enable disabled workers to continue work, there may be some ability to limit insurance rates.[97]

Ironically, advances in medical technology may allow even more disabled people to join the workforce. People who would not have survived a disease or injury in the past may now live, but may be disabled. Further, with increasing life spans, there is greater likelihood that people will experience a disabling condition.[98] Disabled workers may become an even more attractive source of labor when there are labor shortages.

Investments in Employee Health

Another nontraditional investment approach involves improvement of employees' health. Such investments can increase the productivity of employees. For example, in underdeveloped countries, increasing the quality of nutrition and providing basic medical care can increase the productivity of employees and would thus constitute investments in human resources. Companies operating maquiladoras in Mexico have learned that they must furnish two meals a day to ensure that their workers are receiving sufficient nutrition. As a result, some of the better employers place a great deal of emphasis on high-quality food service as well as medical services. Companies from the United States and other industrialized countries that have maquiladora plants in Mexico commonly operate medical clinics at the plants, which provide treatment for employees and their dependents.

Other health-related programs are directed at reduction of smoking because the relationship between health problems and smoking is well known. It has been found that employee absenteeism rates are approximately 50 percent higher for smokers. Rates of early disability and mortality are approximately 300 percent higher. The combination of these and the secondary effects of smoking cost companies an extra $2,500 each year per smoker.[99] Because of these costs and the detrimental impact on productivity, some employers have adopted hard-line policies against smoking. Furthermore, there is empirical evidence that policies prohibiting smoking on company premises have caused employees to quit smoking. Such a policy at a telephone company led to the following results: "Overall, 21 percent of the respondents who were smoking at the time they heard about the policy had quit smoking; 42 percent of quitters said they stopped smoking because of the policy."[100] This decline was statistically significant; however, the support program that accompanied the policy did not appear to produce differences in quitting behavior.[101] Nonetheless, another empirical study that employed an experimental design, with experimental and control groups drawn from two companies, found increased quitting behavior to be associated with training, financial incentives, and competition.[102]

There are several other examples of company actions in this area. Cardinal Industries, which has a similar requirement, pays for smoking cessation programs. At Pullman Company PTC Aerospace, employees who smoke must pay an additional charge for health insurance that other employees do not have to pay. Litho Industries adopted a no-smoking policy for employees both on and off the job. Likewise, a number of fire and police departments have adopted comprehensive no-smoking policies.[103] The stressful nature of these emergency services and the prevalence of heart disease among firefighters probably explain why these departments were early adopters of no-smoking policies. The number of companies enforcing no-smoking policies has increased substantially according to surveys by the Bureau of National Affairs and the Administrative Management Society.[104] As resistance to no-smoking policies indicates, part of the investment component may be the expense of defending the policies in arbitration procedures or in court. Further, during the initial year after employees stop smoking, their levels of absenteeism and job tension increase while their job satisfaction declines. On the other hand, employers that give smokers breaks to leave the work area or the building may find that nonsmokers feel that they are treated unfairly unless they receive equal break time.[105]

Another investment in human resources is also related to health issues. Large numbers of companies have invested in fitness centers and physical conditioning programs. Many claim very positive returns for their investments. For example, Mutual Benefit Life Insurance found that after it provided a fitness center for its employees, the average number of workdays missed by the facility's users was 2.51 days and annual medical claims were $313. In contrast, nonusers averaged 4.25 missed workdays and medical claims of $1,086. In addition to the fitness centers, the company established an on-site health clinic. A return of two dollars for every dollar invested is claimed, without counting increased morale.[106] There also are claims of other fitness-related outcomes. These include better mental health, stress resistance, increased commitment, increased productivity, lower absenteeism, and lower turnover. Although the relationship between fitness and health benefits has been well established, there are other potential outcomes of fitness programs that have not been adequately examined. More research is needed to determine the relationship between fitness programs and productivity, commitment, turnover, and absenteeism.[107]

Some organizations, such as hospitals, may need to make other nontraditional investments, such as in programs that reduce the incidence of employee burnout. Such programs may involve support and close monitoring of the self-esteem of employees working in jobs having high potential for burnout. Because low self-esteem appears to be a cause of burnout, as well as a result, a downward spiral can occur without interventions to enhance burned-out employees' self-esteem.[108]

Finally, a more indirect health-related investment has been made by Sunbeam Oster Housewares, Inc. Sunbeam found that premature births were dramatically increasing its health care costs. During a two-year period, six premature births cost its health care program $1.2 million. As a result of finding that its employees were not well versed in prenatal care, Sunbeam established an on-site health clinic, required periodic checkups of pregnant employees, and made such employees attend an instructional program. The decline in health care costs was dramatic. Average medical costs per birth declined from $27,000 to $3,500 over a five-year period.[109] However, it is easy to visualize situations in which such programs could be viewed as an undesired intrusion into the privacy of employees.

Countercyclical Hiring

In addition to not laying off as many employees as technical production requirements might suggest, companies may pursue *countercyclical hiring* strategies of hiring a limited number of managers and professionals during economic downturns. In essence, companies would be stockpiling a limited number of high-quality key personnel for future use in pursuing strategies requiring certain personnel capabilities. As opposed to economic upturns when competitors are also attempting to obtain the same personnel, bargains in quality can be obtained during downturns. Several other benefits may result from countercyclical hiring. One benefit might be a more regular age distribution, which is lacking the spikes or troughs that occur with discontinuous hiring. As a result of dramatically increased health insurance costs, age distributions have become a concern to employers that have disproportionate numbers of older workforces. Aside from the benefits of countercyclical hiring, there are obvious costs, such as hiring employees when they are not needed and equity issues with the current workforce. There also are several implementation issues such as the ability to forecast future human resource demand accurately enough to pursue such a strategy.[110] Empirical studies of countercyclical hiring indicate that successful companies employ systematic approaches toward human resource management and are more likely to make investments in human capital by hiring during downturns.[111]

Summary

This chapter has discussed the factors that should be considered in making strategic human resource investment decisions and the specific investment approaches that are available to help accomplish the strategic objectives of organizations. Presentation of the investment considerations began with a discussion of managerial values, followed by an examination of the unique risk and return aspects of investments in human resources. Next, the economic rationale for investments in specific and general training was examined. Utility theory was also examined as a means for determining returns on investments in human resources. Alternatives to such investments, in the form of strategic outsourcing were also discussed.

Specific human resource investments in training and development were then considered, beginning with investments in the future employability of employees. As noted, declines in the viability of employment guarantees and no-layoff policies have increased the importance of individual security through the notion of future employability. In order to have the world-class human resources needed to pursue strategic objectives, organizations must provide employees with skills and development they will need to be employable in the future. Training investments constitute the bulk of investments in human resource investments. Nonetheless, the discussion of U.S. investments in training, relative to other leading industrial countries, indicated that the United States is lagging behind some of its competitors. On-the-job training was examined as an approach to investment in human resources. Management development programs also were examined from an investment perspective with specific attention to job rotational approaches. Other specific investment approaches also were discussed including the prevention of skill obsolescence and career plateauing.

Investments in employment practices also were examined in relation to the accomplishment of strategic objectives. Several practices that enhance retention and reduce the turnover of employees were identified. Costs of layoffs were discussed along with techniques for avoiding business cycle-based layoffs, alternatives to layoffs, and employment guarantees. There also was a discussion of the relationship between work effort and job insecurity. Additionally, nontraditional investment approaches were discussed, including countercyclical hiring, in which employers hire and stockpile high-quality candidates during economic downturns. Other nontraditional investments discussed included programs that help disabled workers return to work and investments in employee health through such programs as those directed at smoking cessation and employee fitness.

Endnotes

1. Dyer, Lee. "Bringing Human Resources into the Strategy Formulation Process," *Human Resource Management* 22, no. 3 (1983): 263.
2. Quinn, James B., Thomas L. Doorley, and Penny C. Paquette. "Beyond Products: Services-Based Strategy," *Harvard Business Review* 90, no. 2 (1990): 58–67.
3. Quinn, Doorley, and Paquette. "Beyond Products: Services-Based Strategy," p. 60.
4. Lawler, Edward E. III. *The Ultimate Advantage: Creating the High Involvement Organization*. San Francisco: Jossey-Bass Publishers, 1992, p. 21.
5. Bolt, James F. "Job Security: Its Time Has Come," *Harvard Business Review* 61, no. 6 (1983): 115–23; Peters, Tom. *Thriving on Chaos: Handbook for a Management Revolution*. New York: Harper and Row, 1987.
6. Jackson, Susan E., Randall S. Schuler, and J. Carlos Rivero. "Organizational Characteristics as Predictors of Personnel Practices," *Personnel Psychology* 42, no. 4 (1989): 727–86.
7. Beer, Michael, Bert Spector, Paul R. Lawrence, D. Quinn Mills, and Richard Walton. *Managing Human Assets*. New York: The Free Press, 1984.
8. Ivancevich, John M., David M. Schweiger, and Frank R. Power. "Strategies for Managing Human Resources During Mergers and Acquisitions," *Human Resource Planning* 10, no. 1 (1987): 19–35.
9. Kochan, Thomas A., John Paul MacDuffie, and Paul Osterman. "Employment Security at DEC: Sustaining Values Amid Environmental Change," *Human Resource Management* 27, no. 2 (1988): 121–43.
10. Chiang, Shin-Hwan, and Shih-Chen Chiang. "General Human Capital as a Shared Investment Under Asymmetric Information," *Canadian Journal of Economics* 23, no. 1, February 1990, pp. 176–88; Becker, Gary. *Human Capital: A Theoretical and Empirical Analysis, with Special Reference to Education*. New York: National Bureau of Economic Research, 1964; Mitchell, Daniel J. B. *Human Resource Management: An Economic Approach*. Boston: PWS-Kent Publishing Company, 1989; Doeringer, Peter B., and Michael J. Piore. *Internal Labor Markets and Manpower Analysis*. Lexington, MA: Heath Lexington Books, 1971.
11. Chiang and Chiang. "General Human Capital as a Shared Investment Under Asymmetric Information," p. 176.
12. Chiang and Chiang. "General Human Capital as a Shared Investment Under Asymmetric Information."
13. Chiang and Chiang. "General Human Capital as a Shared Investment Under Asymmetric Information"; Doeringer and Piore. *Internal Labor Markets and Manpower Analysis*; Mitchell. *Human Resource Management: An Economic Approach*.
14. Mitchell. *Human Resource Management: An Economic Approach*.
15. Boudreau, John W. "Utility Analysis," in Lee Dyer (Ed.). *Human Resource Management: Evolving Roles and Responsibilities*. Washington, DC: Bureau of National Affairs, 1988, pp. 125–86; Cascio, Wayne F. *Costing Human Resources: The Financial Impact of Behavior in Organizations*, 3rd ed. Boston: PWS-Kent Publishing Company, 1991.
16. Becker, Brian E., and Mark A. Huselid. "Direct Estimates of SD_y and the Implications for Utility Analysis," *Journal of Applied Psychology* 77, no. 3 (1992): 227–33.
17. Quinn, Doorley, and Paquette. "Beyond Products: Services-Based Strategy."

18. Greer, Charles R., Stuart A. Youngblood, and David A. Gray. "Human Resource Management Outsourcing: The Make or Buy Decision," *Academy of Management Executive* 13, no. 3 (1999): 85–96.
19. Kanter, Rosabeth M. *When Giants Learn to Dance: Mastering the Challenge of Strategy, Management, and Careers in the 1990s.* New York: Simon and Schuster, 1992.
20. Swoboda, Frank. "Boundaryless Ambition at General Electric," *Washington Post–National Weekly Edition* (March 7–13, 1994): 21.
21. Ibid.
22. Kanter. *When Giants Learn to Dance: Mastering the Challenge of Strategy, Management, and Careers in the 1990s*, pp. 321–22.
23. Ellig, Bruce R. "Employment and Employability: Foundation of the New Social Contract," *Human Resource Management* 37, no. 2 (1998): 173–75.
24. Hoerr, John. "Sharpening Minds for a Competitive Edge," *Business Week* (December 17, 1990): 78 (whole article pp. 72–78).
25. Hoerr. "Sharpening Minds for a Competitive Edge."
26. Ibid.
27. Ibid.
28. Dana Corporation. *Annual Report*, 1987.
29. Branch, Shelly. "The 100 Best Companies to Work for in America," *Fortune* (January 11, 1999): 118–19.
30. Becker. *Human Capital: A Theoretical and Empirical Analysis, with Special Reference to Education.*
31. Thurow, Lester C. "Education and Economic Equality," *Public Interest* 28, no. 3 (1972): 66–81.
32. Strober, Myra H. "Human Capital Theory: Implications for HR Managers," *Industrial Relations* 29, no. 2 (1990): 214–39.
33. Maranto, Cheryl L., and Robert C. Rodgers. "Does Work Experience Increase Productivity? A Test of the On-the-Job Training Hypothesis," *Journal of Human Resources* 19, no. 3 (1984): 341–57.
34. Schein, Edgar H. "Reassessing the 'Divine Rights' of Managers," *Sloan Management Review* 30, no. 2 (1989): 63–68; Drucker, Peter F. "The Coming of the New Organization," *Harvard Business Review* 66, no. 1 (1988): 45–53; Applegate, Lynda M., James I. Cash Jr., and D. Quinn Mills. "Information Technology and Tomorrow's Manager," *Harvard Business Review* 88, no. 6 (1988): 128–36; Semler, Ricardo. "Managing Without Managers," *Harvard Business Review* 67, no. 5 (1989): 76–84; Schein, Edgar H. "International Human Resource Management: New Directions, Perpetual Issues, and Missing Themes," *Human Resource Management* 25, no. 1 (1986): 169–76.
35. Saari, Lise M., Terry R. Johnson, Steven D. McLaughlin, and Denise M. Zimmerle. "A Survey of Management Training and Education Practices in U.S. Companies," *Personnel Psychology* 41, no. 4 (1988): 731–43.
36. Greenlaw, Paul S., and John P. Kohl. *Personnel Management: Managing Human Resources.* New York: Harper and Row, 1986; Derr, C. Brooklyn, Candace Jones, and Edmund L. Toomey. "Managing High-Potential Employees: Current Practices in Thirty-three U.S. Corporations," *Human Resource Management* 27, no. 3 (1988): 273–90.
37. Greenlaw and Kohl. *Personnel Management: Managing Human Resources.*
38. Derr, Jones, and Toomey. "Managing High-Potential Employees: Current Practices in Thirty-three U.S. Corporations"; Saari, Johnson, McLaughlin, and Zimmerle. "A Survey of Management Training and Education Practices in U.S. Companies."
39. Lawrie, John. "Selling Management Development to Managers," *Training and Development Journal* 43, no. 2 (1989): 54–57.
40. Saari, Johnson, McLaughlin, and Zimmerle. "A Survey of Management Training and Education Practices in U.S. Companies"; Keys, Bernard, and Joseph Wolfe. "Management Education and Development: Current Issues and Emerging Trends," *Journal of Management* 14, no. 2 (1988): 205–29.
41. Hewlett-Packard Corporation. *Hewlett-Packard Annual Report*, 1985.
42. Greenhaus, Jeffery H. *Career Management.* Chicago: The Dryden Press, 1987; Wexley, Kenneth N., and Gary P. Latham. *Developing and Training Human Resources in Organizations.* Glenview, IL: Scott, Foresman and Company, 1981.

43. Fossum, John A., Richard D. Arvey, Carol A. Paradise, and Nancy E. Robbins. "Modeling the Skills Obsolescence Process: A Psychological/Economic Integration," *Academy of Management Review* 1, no. 2 (1986): 362–74.

44. Greenhaus. *Career Management*; Wexley and Latham. *Developing and Training Human Resources in Organizations.*

45. Hewlett-Packard Corporation. *Hewlett Packard Annual Report*; Ward, Dan L. "Layoffs: What Does Flexibility Really Cost?", in Richard J. Niehaus and Karl F. Price (Eds.), *Creating the Competitive Edge through Human Resource Applications.* New York: Plenum Press, 1988, pp. 169–78.

46. Bowles, Valerie B., and Arthur R. Riles Jr. "Work Place Challenges for Managers in the Twenty-First Century," in Richard J. Niehaus and Karl F. Price (Eds.), *Creating the Competitive Edge through Human Resource Applications.* New York: Plenum Press, 1988, pp. 35–46; Gaertner, Karen N. "Managerial Careers and Organization-Wide Transformations," in Richard J. Niehaus and Karl F. Price (Eds.), *Creating the Competitive Edge through Human Resource Applications.* New York: Plenum Press, 1988, pp. 85–95. Ference, Thomas P., James F. Stoner, and E. Kirby Warren. "Managing the Career Plateau," *Academy of Management Review* 2, no. 4 (1977): 602–12.

47. Gaertner. "Managerial Careers and Organization-Wide Transformations."

48. Ibid.; Choa, Georgia T. "Exploration of the Conceptualization and Measurement of Career Plateau: A Comparative Analysis," *Journal of Management* 16, no. 1 (1990): 181–93.

49. Gaertner. "Managerial Careers and Organization-Wide Transformations"; Ference, Stoner, and Warren. "Managing the Career Plateau"; Elsass, Priscilla M., and David A. Ralston. "Individual Responses to the Stress of Career Plateauing," *Journal of Management* 15, no. 1 (1989): 35–47.

50. Hasen, Fay. "What Is the Cost of Employee Turnover?" *Compensation and Benefits Review* 29, no. 5 (1997): 17–18.

51. Sheridan, John E. "Organizational Culture and Employee Retention," *Academy of Management Journal* 35 (December 1992): 1036–56.

52. Stum, David L. "Five Ingredients for an Employee Retention Formula," *HR Focus* 75, no. 9 (1998): S9–S10; Middlebrook, John F. "Avoiding Brain Drain: How to Lock in Talent," *HR Focus* 76, no. 3 (1999): 9–10; Hom, Peter W., and Rodger W. Griffeth. *Employee Turnover.* Cincinnati: South-Western College Publishing, 1995.

53. "Traditional Retention Methods Aren't Deterring Employee Turnover," *HRMagazine* 43, no. 9 (1998): 20–22.

54. Hom, Peter W., Rodger W. Griffeth, and Leslie E. Palich. "Revisiting Met Expectations as a Reason Why Realistic Job Previews Work," *Personnel Psychology* 52, no. 1 (1999): 97–112; Hom and Griffeth. *Employee Turnover*; Hom, Peter W., Rodger W. Griffeth, L. E. Palich, and J. S. Bracker. "Realistic Job Previews: Two-Occupation Test of Mediating Processes," Tempe, AZ: College of Business, 1993.

55. "Traditional Retention Methods Aren't Deterring Employee Turnover," *HRMagazine*; Flannery, Thomas P., David Hofrichter, and Paul E. Platten. *People, Performance, and Pay: Dynamic Compensation for Changing Organizations.* New York: The Free Press, 1996; Branch. "The 100 Best Companies to Work For in America."

56. Wysocki, Bernard Jr. "Retaining Employees Turns Into a Hot Topic," *Wall Street Journal* (September 8, 1997): A1.

57. Sheridan. "Organizational Culture and Employee Retention"; Stum. "Five Ingredients for an Employee Retention Formula"; Middlebrook. "Avoiding Brain Drain: How to Lock in Talent"; Hom and Griffeth. *Employee Turnover.*

58. Branch. "The 100 Best Companies to Work for in America," pp. 122, 128.

59. Stum. "Five Ingredients for an Employee Retention Formula"; Middlebrook. "Avoiding Brain Drain: How to Lock in Talent"; Branch. "The 100 Best Companies to Work For in America."

60. Stum. "Five Ingredients for an Employee Retention Formula."

61. Collins, James C., and Jerry I. Porras. *Built to Last: Successful Habits of Visionary Companies.* New York: Harper Business, 1994, p. 48.

62. Cook, Barbara, Assistant Vice President, Burlington Northern Santa Fe, Comments to the Human Resource Roundtable, Texas Christian University, April 5, 2000. Tsumpis, Vice President

Information Technology Applications, Alcon Laboratories, Comments to the Human Resource Roundtable, Texas Christian University, April 5, 2000.

63. Dalton, Dan R., and William D. Todor. "Turnover, Transfer Absenteeism: An Interdependent Perspective," *Journal of Management* 19 (1993): 193–219; Stum. "Five Ingredients for an Employee Retention Formula"; Middlebrook. "Avoiding Brain Drain: How to Lock in Talent"; Hom and Griffeth. *Employee Turnover*; Stum. "Five Ingredients for an Employee Retention Formula."
64. Branch. "The 100 Best Companies to Work For in America."
65. Kochan, MacDuffie, and Osterman. "Employment Security at DEC: Sustaining Values Amid Environmental Change."
66. Branch. "The 100 Best Companies to Work for in America," pp. 118–44.
67. Bolt. "Job Security: Its Time Has Come"; Peters. *Thriving on Chaos: Handbook for a Management Revolution.*
68. Ward. "Layoffs: What Does Flexibility Really Cost?"
69. Greller, Martin M., and David M. Nee. *From Baby Boom to Baby Bust.* Reading, MA: Addison-Wesley, 1989; Perry, Lee T. "Least-Cost Alternatives to Layoffs in Declining Industries," *Organizational Dynamics* 14, no. 4 (1986): 48–61; Beer, Michael, Bert Spector, Paul R. Lawrence, D. Quinn Mills, and Richard Walton. *Managing Human Assets.* New York: The Free Press, 1984; Joseph T. McCune, Richard W. Beatty, and Raymond V. Montagno. "Downsizing: Practices in Manufacturing Firms," *Human Resource Management* 27, no. 2 (1988): 145–61. Dyer. "Bringing Human Resources into the Strategy Formulation Process."
70. Ward. "Layoffs: What Does Flexibility Really Cost?"
71. Rees, Albert. *The Economics of Trade Unions*, 3rd ed. Chicago: University of Chicago Press, 1989.
72. Ward. "Layoffs: What Does Flexibility Really Cost?"; McCune, Beatty, and Montagno. "Downsizing: Practices in Manufacturing Firms."
73. Bolt. "Job Security: Its Time Has Come."
74. Mills, D. Quinn. *The New Competitors.* New York: John Wiley and Sons, 1985; Bolt. "Job Security: Its Time Has Come."
75. Hoerr, John, and Wendy Zellner. "A Japanese Import That's Not Selling," *Business Week* (February 26, 1990): 86 (whole article on pp. 86–87).
76. Peters. *Thriving on Chaos: Handbook for a Management Revolution.*
77. Hewlett-Packard Corporation. *Hewlett-Packard Annual Report*, 1985.
78. Fay, Jon A., and James L. Medoff. "Labor and Output Over the Business Cycle: Some Direct Evidence," *American Economic Review* 75, no. 4 (1985): 638–55.
79. Bolt. "Job Security: Its Time Has Come"; Peters. *Thriving on Chaos: Handbook for a Management Revolution*; Greenhalgh, Leonard, Anne T. Lawrence, and Robert I. Sutton. "Determinants of Work Force Reduction Strategies in Declining Organizations," *Academy of Management Review* 13, no. 2 (1988): 241–54.
80. McCune, Beatty, and Montagno. "Downsizing: Practices in Manufacturing Firms."
81. Perry. "Least-Cost Alternatives to Layoffs in Declining Industries"; Bolt. "Job Security: Its Time Has Come."
82. Bolt. "Job Security: Its Time Has Come"; Peters. *Thriving on Chaos: Handbook for a Management Revolution.*
83. Davidson, Margaret. "Temporary Financial Executives: Who Are They and Who Uses Them?" *Financial Executive* 6, no. 2 (1990): 15–18; Mangum, Garth, Donald Mayall, and Kristin Nelson. "The Temporary Help Industry: A Response to the Dual Internal Labor Markets," *Industrial and Labor Relations Review* 28, no. 4 (1985): 599–611.
84. *Welcome to Walt Disney World: A Cast Member's Handbook*, 1988.
85. Perry. "Least-Cost Alternatives to Layoffs in Declining Industries."
86. Peters. *Thriving on Chaos: Handbook for a Management Revolution*, p. 417.
87. Peters. *Thriving on Chaos: Handbook for a Management Revolution.*
88. Ibid.

89. Kochan, MacDuffie, and Osterman. "Employment Security at DEC: Sustaining Values Amid Environmental Change."

90. Brockner, Joel, Steven Grover, Thomas F. Reed, and Rocki Lee Dewitt. "Layoffs, Job Insecurity, and Survivors' Work Effort: Evidence of an Inverted-U Relationship," *Academy of Management Journal* 35, no. 2 (1992): 413–25.

91. Landers, Peter. "Refusing to Move On, Mr. Sakai Opts to Buck Japanese-Style Layoff," *Wall Street Journal* (September 14, 1999): A1, A8.

92. Landers. "Refusing to Move On, Mr. Sakai Opts to Buck Japanese-Style Layoff," *Wall Street Journal*, pp. A1, A8.

93. Bowe, Frank. "Intercompany Action to Adapt Jobs for the Handicapped," *Harvard Business Review* 63, no. 1 (1985): 166–68.

94. Bowe. "Intercompany Action to Adapt Jobs for the Handicapped," p. 166.

95. Bowe. "Intercompany Action to Adapt Jobs for the Handicapped"; Pati, Gobal C., and John I. Adkins Jr. "Federal Officials Are Stepping Up Their Efforts to Enforce Affirmative Action Requirements," *Harvard Business Review* 58, no. 1 (1980): 14–22.

96. Pati and Adkins. "Federal Officials Are Stepping Up Their Efforts to Enforce Affirmative Action Requirements."

97. Pati, Gobal C., and Glen Morrison. "Enabling the Disabled," *Harvard Business Review* 60, no. 4 (1982): 152–68.

98. Pati and Morrison. "Enabling the Disabled."

99. Cascio, Wayne F. *Costing Human Resources: The Financial Impact of Behavior in Organizations*, 2nd ed. Boston: PWS–Kent Publishing Company, 1987.

100. Sorensen, Gloria, Nancy Rigotti, Amy Rosen, John Pinney, and Ray Prible. "Effects of a Worksite Nonsmoking Policy: Evidence for Increased Cessation," *American Journal of Public Health* 81, no. 2 (1991): 202 (whole article on pp. 202–4).

101. Sorensen, Rigotti, Rosen, Pinney, and Prible. "Effects of a Worksite Nonsmoking Policy: Evidence for Increased Cessation."

102. Jason, Leonard A., Shyamalanita Jayaraj, Caryn C. Blitz, Mark H. Michaels, and Lori E. Klett. "Incentives and Competition is a Workplace Smoking Cessation Intervention," *American Journal of Public Health* 80, no. 2 (1990): 205–6.

103. Geyelin, Milo. "The Job Is Yours—Unless You Smoke," *Wall Street Journal* (April 21, 1989): B1.

104. Ibid.

105. Manning, Michael R., Joyce S. Osland, and Asbjorn Osland. "Work-Related Consequences of Smoking Cessation," *Academy of Management Journal* 32, no. 3 (1989): 606–21; Nobile, Robert J. "Putting Out Fires with a No-Smoking Policy," *Personnel* 67, no. 3 (1990): 6–10.

106. Farrell, Christopher, Joseph Weber, and Michael Schroeder. "Why We Should Invest in Human Capital," *Business Week* (December 17, 1990): 88–90.

107. Falkenberg, Loren E. "Employee Fitness Programs: Their Impact on the Employee and the Organization," *Academy of Management Review* 12, no. 3 (1987): 511–22.

108. Rosse, Joseph G., R. Wayne Boss, Alan E. Johnson, and Deborah F. Crown. "Conceptualizing the Role of Self-Esteem in the Burnout Process," *Group and Organization Studies* 16, no. 4 (1991): 428–51.

109. Farrell, Weber, and Schroeder. "Why We Should Invest in Human Capital."

110. William E. Bright. "How One Company Manages Its Human Resources," *Harvard Business Review* 54, no. 1 (1976): 81–93; Greer, Charles R. "Countercyclical Hiring as a Staffing Strategy for Managerial and Professional Personnel: Some Considerations and Issues," *Academy of Management Review* 9, no. 2 (1984): 324–30; Greer, Charles R., and Yvonne Stedham. "Countercyclical Hiring as a Staffing Strategy for Managerial and Professional Personnel: An Empirical Investigation," *Journal of Management* 15, no. 3 (1989): 425–40.

111. Greer. "Countercyclical Hiring as a Staffing Strategy for Managerial and Professional Personnel: Some Considerations and Issues"; Greer and Stedham. "Countercyclical Hiring as a Staffing Strategy for Managerial and Professional Personnel: An Empirical Investigation."

CASE 1 Mergers and Acquisitions

In the past, the decision criteria for mergers and acquisitions were typically based on considerations such as the strategic fit of the merged organizations, financial criteria, and operational criteria. Mergers and acquisitions were often conducted without much regard for the human resource issues that would be faced when the organizations were joined.[1] As a result, several undesirable effects on the organizations' human resources commonly occurred. Nonetheless, competitive conditions favor mergers and acquisitions and they remain a frequent occurrence. Examples of mergers among some of the largest companies include the following: Honeywell and Allied Signal, British Petroleum and Amoco, Exxon and Mobil, Lockheed and Martin, Boeing and McDonnell Douglas, SBC and Pacific Telesis, America Online and Time Warner, Burlington Northern and Santa Fe, Union Pacific and Southern Pacific, Daimler-Benz and Chrysler, Ford and Volvo, and Bank of America and Nations Bank.

Layoffs often accompany mergers or acquisitions, particularly if the two organizations are from the same industry. In addition to layoffs related to redundancies, top managers of acquiring firms may terminate some competent employees because they do not fit in with the new culture of the merged organization or because their loyalty to the new management may be suspect. The desire for a good fit with the cultural objectives of the new organization and loyalty are understandable. However, the depletion of the stock of human resources deserves serious consideration, just as with physical resources. Unfortunately, the way that mergers and acquisitions have been carried out has often conveyed a lack of concern for human resources. A sense of this disregard is revealed in the following observation:

> Post combination integration strategies vary from such "love and marriage" tactics in truly collaborative mergers to much more hostile "rape and pillage" strategies in raids and financial takeovers. Yet, as a cursory scan of virtually any newspaper or popular business magazine readily reveals, the simple fact is that the latter are much more common than the former.[2]

The cumulative effects of these developments often cause employee morale and loyalty to decline, and feelings of betrayal may develop.[3] Nonetheless, such adverse consequences are not inevitable. A few companies, such as Cisco Systems, which has made over 50 acquisitions, are very adept in handling the human resource issues associated with these actions. An example of one of Cisco's practices is illustrative. At Cisco Systems, no one from an acquired firm is laid off without the personal approval of Cisco's CEO as well as the CEO of the firm that was acquired.[4]

Questions

1. Investigate the approach that Cisco Systems has used in its many successful acquisitions. What are some of the human resource practices that have made its acquisitions successful?
2. If human resources are a major source of competitive advantage and the key determinant of an organization's ability to pursue a given strategy, why have the human resource aspects of mergers and acquisitions been ignored or handled poorly in so many instances in the past?
3. Interview someone who has been through a merger or acquisition. Find out how they felt as an employee. Determine how they and their coworkers were affected. Ask about the effects on productivity, loyalty, and morale. Find out what human resource practices were used and obtain their evaluations of what was helpful or harmful.

References

1. Buono, Anthony F., and James L. Bowditch. *The Human Side of Mergers and Acquisitions: Managing Collisions Between People, Cultures, and Organizations.* San Francisco: Jossey-Bass Publishers, 1989.
2. Buono and Bowditch. *The Human Side of Mergers and Acquisitions*, p. 263.
3. Buono and Bowditch. *The Human Side of Mergers and Acquisitions.*
4. Branch, Shelly. "The 100 Best Companies to Work For in America," *Fortune* (January 11, 1999): 118–44; Thurm, Scott. "Joining the Fold: Under Cisco's System, Mergers Usually Work; That Defies the Odds," *Wall Street Journal* (March 1, 2000): A1.

CHAPTER 2

The Human Resource Environment

As indicated in the conceptual framework, following the development of an investment perspective for making strategic decisions about human resources, managers need to scan the environment before formulating strategy. This chapter examines the numerous factors making up the environment of human resources as well as emerging trends. Because of its complexity and importance, the legal environment of human resources is covered separately in Chapter 3.

Inarguably, the human resource environment is currently more turbulent than in any other period since World War II. During the last 10 years of the twentieth century, many political developments at home and abroad had massive impacts on human resources. Eastern European countries were freed from occupation by the Soviet Union, the Soviet Union was broken up into independent but unstable nations, civil wars broke out, and in less than one year East and West Germany were reunited. Almost overnight, previously communistic Eastern European countries became markets for western goods, suppliers of labor, and business competitors. The economic sphere of the European Community became a reality, as did the North American Free Trade Agreement (NAFTA).

Technology also had massive impacts as well. The Internet alone had an impact of epic proportions. Dot-com companies and existing businesses created thousands of e-business and e-commerce operations, employing some of the labor force's most talented workers. Companies providing infrastructure for the Internet, such as Cisco Systems, Oracle, Sun Microsystems, and Microsoft became some of the largest companies in the world based on their market capitalization.

Developments such as these affect business and human resources. It seems clear that the economic turbulence that characterized the last of the twentieth century will continue into the twenty-first century. Dynamic political and technological environments are likely as well. During such times of rapid change, the difficult processes of formulating viable competitive strategies and planning for their implementation become even more difficult as well as more important. Only some of the developments that occurred at the turn of the century could have been forecasted. Nonetheless, those organizations that scanned the environment, developed strategies, and planned alternatives for dealing with changing conditions probably fared better than those that did not.

This chapter will identify issues and trends relevant to strategy and human resources by following an environmental scanning framework. The framework for scanning is composed of the following categories: technology and organizational structure, worker values and attitudinal trends, managerial trends, demographic trends, trends in the utilization of human resources, and international developments. These trends and developments will be discussed in the following sections.

TECHNOLOGY AND ORGANIZATIONAL STRUCTURE

Broad Influences of Technology

Technology, particularly information technology, is having a major impact on the structure of organizations and on the nature of managerial work. Enterprise software systems have been implemented to integrate the major areas of business: manufacturing, sales, finance, supply-chain management, and human resources. These information systems have enabled companies to gain numerous benefits such as efficiency gains, quicker response times, better inventory control, enhanced coordination, and improved decision making. Companies now spend $23 billion a year on enterprise software such as Oracle, SAP, and PeopleSoft, compared with only $1 billion in 1990.[1] Information systems such as these and others have eliminated the need for many middle management positions. Because much of middle management involves coordination and dissemination of information, many of its functions have been computerized. With this removal of a level of the organizational hierarchy, a valuable training ground for top executives has been eliminated. Further, the context in which much work is currently being performed is changing. The era of the "smart machine" and the skilled professionals who operate such machines probably will produce conditions in which there is less need for supervision or a very different type of supervision. Human resource strategists will need to consider changes in the nature of managerial work that will result from the accumulation of knowledge power in nonmanagerial, technical positions.[2]

Managers who can be effective in such environments require new skills. Not only the number of managerial positions has changed, but also in many settings the nature of management has changed as well because of other developments. Thus, in information-based, lean and flat organizations, alternative job assignments and opportunities are needed for the development of tomorrow's high-level managers.[3]

Although the need for middle managers and low-skilled employees has been lessened by information technology, it is useful to reflect on these developments before concluding that the jobs of human beings are being eliminated. Sar Levitan has put the effects of these developments in perspective.

> There is nothing new about the prediction that labor will become less important as new technology replaces human labor with machines—this prediction has been heard repeatedly since the beginning of the industrial age. It can be asserted with some confidence, however, that this forecast is no more true today than it was a century ago.[4]

Another impact of increasing technology is that skill and managerial educational requirements tend to increase. Although managers in advanced technological environments cannot have detailed knowledge of all aspects of the technology with which their subordinates work, they must have a conceptual understanding in order to provide effective support and direction.[5]

Another impact of technology is that manufacturing is moving toward much shorter developmental cycles. New product development approaches based on concurrent or parallel engineering avoid the delays of sequential developmental processes. In parallel processes, engineering, design, purchasing, marketing, software, hardware, field support, and manufacturing specialists work together, beginning with the earliest product development phases.[6] The availability of highly trained specialists who have the skills to work effectively in such environments cannot be taken for granted. Training programs and developmental assignments must be planned to ensure the availability of such workers.

Influences of Human Resource Information Systems

As noted, firms have invested heavily in the implementation of enterprise or integrated software such as Oracle, SAP, and PeopleSoft. Such information systems include human resource information system (HRIS) components and provide immediate information to decision makers about the organization's human resource capabilities. Human resource departments and the activities they perform have been affected dramatically by these enterprise software systems, and executives can now include more human resource information in the equation when making strategic or operational decisions. In addition to their impact on strategic and operational decision making, such systems also have allowed firms to automate human resource processes of a transactional nature.[7] Such automation is described as follows:

> For example, managers and employees can now use personal computers or kiosks to complete many HR transactions. Employees can make simple changes to personal information, such as their home address or contribution to a 401(k) plan, without going through any sign-off loops. Line managers can complete routine tasks, such as appraisals and salary changes, automatically.[8]

The implementation of systems such as PeopleSoft and SAP also has led to the restructuring of human resource departments, jobs, and processes. Processes have been changed to conform to the requirements of information systems. Jobs also have been redesigned with fewer transactional activities because of computerization.[9]

Redeployment of Human Resource Staff to Operating Units

One of the outcomes of organizational decentralization has been that human resource generalists have been redeployed from human resource departments to individual operating units. Such decentralization provides better service to the units because the staff member is on site and typically reports to the unit's line management while retaining a dotted line or functional reporting relationship to the human resource department. Generalists, who can handle a relatively broad range of issues, are typically the staff members assigned to operating units. These individuals can access specialists in the human resource department when greater expertise is needed for various issues.

Because of the redundancies and costs associated with the deployment of human resource generalists to operating units, some observers have questioned the value of such assignments. Fred Foulkes has provided an interesting account of an exchange between the top human resource executives at two large companies. One argued that his Boston-based company had no human resource representatives at its Texas location where it had 400 employees. Instead, the company provided a toll-free number for its employees to call human resource representatives in Boston when they needed assistance with major issues, such as attempts at unionization or sexual harassment. In marked contrast, the other executive supported the deployment of human resource specialists to the operating units. He pointed out how difficult it would be for employees to have productive conversations with strangers on a toll-free line in Boston about such sensitive matters such as the autocratic behavior of their manager. Thus, although deployment to the operating units has costs, it also adds value that comes from having good human resource staff representatives on site who can sense the atmosphere and organizational climate. There is probably substantial value added by the deployment of trusted, sensitive, and compassionate staff members to the operating units.[10]

New Organizational Structures

Not only is the nature of work and management changing, but organizations also are changing as a result of advances in information technology. The distinctions between management and labor have become blurred. Workers are becoming increasingly responsible to act on matters that they become aware of through computerized information systems. Further, there is a shift from individual to joint accountability because more group members have the same information for decision making. Because of the knowledge power of skilled technology workers, the structure of many of today's organizations is poorly suited for the future. Regardless of the exact form, many organizations have become much less hierarchical. More work is being performed in task force teams and project-oriented work groups. Temporary organizations, such as task forces, require different managerial skills. Likewise, there is evidence that organizations are becoming more flexible, porous, and adaptive. In some, the organizational structure may become less pyramidal and more like a set of concentric circles.[11]

Changes entailing more real participation, de-emphasis of managerial status, new forms of superior–subordinate relations, and rotating leadership roles require different managerial skills. Power shifts from one part of the organization to another as tasks demand.[12] Most companies cannot take for granted the emergence of managers with the skills to operate in such environments. As a result, their numbers and skill requirements must be anticipated and developmental experiences planned so that the organization will have an adequate number on hand when the need emerges.

There are other views on the structure of future organizations. Aside from the structural changes noted, there are four new structural forms of interest: (1) *unbundled corporations*, (2) *network organizations*, (3) *cellular organizations*, and (4) *respondent organizations*. All four forms have the ability to adapt to rapidly changing conditions characteristic of the present and likely for the future.[13]

Unbundled Corporations

Essentially, *unbundled corporations* employ a portfolio or conglomerate approach toward their peripheral business units. As a result, units are retained or divested according to profitability and risk criteria. An example of an unbundled corporation is Johnson & Johnson, which has 190 autonomous operating companies in 51 countries. Johnson & Johnson has had over 100 consecutive years of profitability and has achieved exceptional growth.[14] The following provides an indication of its willingness to add or divest units based on their performance:

> Over the past 10 years, through ongoing mergers and acquisitions, we have added nearly 50 companies and product lines . . . More than one third of each year's sales come from new products introduced within the past five years and from existing products launched into new markets.[15]

In unbundled organizations, many of the traditional support services of bureaucracies are outsourced to consultants and vendors. For example, some traditional human resource management functions such as training are performed by vendors, along with some compensation and payroll functions. An advantage results from the potential to redeploy resources rapidly to more profitable alternatives. In addition, developing managers have more opportunities to exercise general managerial skills in running relatively autonomous business units that function as profit centers. For a small group of fortunate employees who form the core unit of the unbundled corporation, there is some job security. These units, which may be quite small, are composed of high-impact employees who coordinate the work of vendors, manage change, and manage the portfolio of business units.[16]

While the jobs of the core of permanent employees are more protected, there is lower commitment to the employees of the peripheral units. Essentially, some of the employment security of the core employees comes at the expense of the peripheral's employees. Other implications for human resource strategy are that some of the benefits of using temporary employees may be offset by the reduced control and inefficiencies of dealing with "employees" through a vendor/supplier relationship. Further, when scarce labor is involved, the wage savings of unbundling may be wiped out by the increased costs of components purchased from vendors who must employ such labor.[17]

Network Organizations or Virtual Corporations

Charles Snow, Raymond Miles, and Henry Coleman have used the term *network organizations* to describe organizations that are similar to unbundled corporations. (They refer to unbundled corporations, consisting of one corporate entity with multiple autonomous units, such as Johnson & Johnson, as *internal networks.*) One of the driving forces for the evolution or creation of network organizations is the need to outsource activities that other companies, consultants, or joint venture partners can perform better or more quickly. The term *virtual corporation* also has been used to describe similar organizations in which there is heavy reliance on outsourcing and a critical need for speed. Membership of the network may include companies from throughout the world. Like unbundled corporations, network organizations also have a permanent core member that performs a broker role. However, the noncore membership of the network may be stable or dynamic. With the *dynamic network* form, the core network member or broker may replace network components with some frequency. For example, a member of a dynamic network performing a manufacturing role may be replaced because its production facilities cannot handle a new product design preferred by customers. However, with the *stable network* form, the organization retains the component members for long periods of time.[18]

The managerial requirements in network organizations are somewhat unique and include (1) referral skills, such as needed for guiding problems to network components where there are solutions; (2) partnering skills, such as problem solving or negotiating for outcomes that are beneficial to all parties; and (3) relationship management, such as being attentive to customers' and partners' needs.[19]

Cellular Organizations

Another structural form is called the *cellular organization*, which has some similarities with classical guilds. Such organizations are typically groups of small technology-oriented companies that maintain affiliations over time. Employees of these companies are predominantly technical professionals. Subsets of the organization's companies join forces on various projects when their unique skills and capabilities are needed. One company takes the leadership role depending on the nature of the project. Individual companies also may join projects even when they only want to learn about a new technology that may be involved. The skills required of managers in cellular organizations are technical knowledge, cross-functional experience, international experience, collaborative leadership, self-management skills, and flexibility.[20]

Respondent Organizations

Another structural form, the *respondent organization*, is essentially an entrepreneurial corporation that exists by filling niches to supply customized services to unbundled corporations and bureaucracies. In such corporations, decision making is quick and likely retained at the level of the central entrepreneurial figure. Unfortunately, these corporations are risky and have high failure rates. The positive trade-offs, from the employee's perspective, are that although there is greater risk and less individual development from participative decision making, there should be opportunities to develop as a generalist and acquire new skills as well as the potential for financial gain.[21] Some of today's smaller Internet players are respondent corporations.

Stimulus for Entrepreneurial Businesses

Entrepreneurial firms, medium-sized companies, and small businesses are accounting for increasing numbers of jobs as employment accounted for by the largest U.S. corporations has declined.[22] Some of this growth in jobs may be related to their role in providing services or manufactured components for larger companies. In essence, some may be playing the role of respondent corporations. A study by Donald Hicks of job creations in the Dallas metropolitan area found that 61 percent came from new businesses whereas 25 percent came from existing small companies.[23] Some of the human resource knowledge base developed for large corporations may not be directly applicable to quickly responding, lean respondent corporations and smaller businesses. Nonetheless, recent literature describes small-business applications of such managerial innovations as open-book management and team building. Further, there has been a tendency for some innovative, smaller companies to decentralize the human resource management function by distributing greater personnel responsibilities to line managers.[24] A future challenge for the managers of these organizations will be to develop or adapt existing human resource practices for these settings. Interestingly, some human resource executives who lost their jobs as a result of corporate downsizing now operate successful consulting firms that supply human resource services to smaller businesses.

WORKER VALUES AND ATTITUDINAL TRENDS

Before examining worker attitudes and values, it is important to note that attributing less work-oriented values to a younger generation has been a long-standing tradition. As a result, popular views on the work values of younger employees may be biased. Seymour Lipset has observed the following:

> Beliefs about the work ethic vary over time and place. There is, however, a general inclination for older people to believe that things were better—or at least more moral, more decent—when they were young.[25]

There are a several arguments that can be used to support the contention that the work ethic in the United States is strong and that it has remained relatively stable. One argument is that employees have worked the same number of hours per week for over 45 years and that when commuting is included, they are spending more time in work-related activities. Thus, workers are involved in more hours of work-related activity and are spending less time in leisure. Another argument is that the overwhelming majority of U.S. workers enjoy their jobs, and as a result, work appeals to them. A final argument is that U.S. workers are second only to the Japanese in the proportion who keep working after they reach 65 years of age. The meager retirement benefits for Japanese workers may explain their tendency to remain employed.[26]

Lipset's warning and arguments notwithstanding, there have been some shifts in work values of importance to strategic management. Among the most important of these are values and attitudes of employees toward their employers. As discussed in the previous section, unbundled organizations typically display low loyalty to the employees of their peripheral units. This lack of loyalty seems to be reflected in the attitudes of the younger cohorts of today's employees as well. Terence Pare has observed the following about young college graduates: "They show no loyalty toward their corporate employers and expect none in return. It may be a perfect match."[27] Indeed, Daniel Yankelovich and Bernard Lefkowitz predicted some time ago that employee loyalty toward employers would decline.[28] There is ample evidence that levels of loyalty have probably declined on both sides, along with shifts in some other fundamental work-related values. However, decreased loyalty is probably not a unique characteristic of younger workers. In a survey, 57 percent of the respondents indicated that they were "less loyal to their employers than they were five years ago."[29] Reasons for declining loyalty include executives' receipt of large bonuses during cutbacks and perceived lack of concern on the part of management for the welfare of employees. Indeed, there has been a growth of cynicism in the workforce, probably resulting from such factors as excessive focus on the bottom line to the exclusion of other values and lofty executive salaries.[30]

An understanding of trends in other work values, particularly those of younger workers, is critical to understanding the future human resource environment. One study of work values analyzed data collected from a survey of high school students and young, newly hired male smelter workers and female telephone operators. The study found that high school students tended to place greater emphasis on extrinsic values than the recently hired employees. Conversely, the recently hired employees placed greater value on the intrinsic aspects of work. These employees had strong values of wanting to take pride in their work, being involved in their jobs, and performing meaningful work. The initial work experience of young employees, even in relatively low-level jobs, apparently has the potential to shift their work value foci from extrinsic to intrinsic work aspects. Interestingly, it is only after lengthy socialization in the work environment that there are work value changes from intrinsic to extrinsic.[31] The implications of these findings are that blaming young entrants to the labor market for an emphasis on extrinsically oriented work values may be counterproductive because the real cause for such values may be companies' mismanagement of the socialization process of young workers.

Further research indicates that younger U.S. workers are not more materialistic than workers from other countries. A comprehensive study compared work values of subjects from the United States, Germany, Holland, Israel, Korea, Taiwan, China, and Hungary. The U.S. sample was drawn from undergraduate and graduate business students mostly between the ages of 21 and 39, of which more than 90 percent were employed in full-time jobs from a broad range of occupations. The responses of the subjects, who were asked to rank 24 work values, revealed the following:

1. U.S. subjects ranked pay 15th, which was about the same for most other countries.
2. Having an interesting job was the most important value for U.S. students, as well as for subjects from Germany and Holland. Subjects from Israel, Korea, and Taiwan also ranked job interest as one of the top three work values. Subjects from China and Hungary viewed job interest less importantly, ranking it at eighth and seventh place, respectively.
3. The second-ranking work value for the U.S. subjects was achievement, which was also ranked first or second by subjects from all countries except Germany. Surprisingly, German subjects, who were small-business managers and employees or business students, ranked achievement in ninth place.
4. When compared to German subjects, U.S. subjects placed much higher value on advancement and responsibility, while German subjects placed much higher emphasis on benefits, security, and supervision.
5. A final difference of interest is that while U.S. subjects—along with subjects from Germany, Holland, Israel, and Taiwan—placed contribution to society in last or next to last place, subjects from China ranked it much higher, fourth place, apparently as a result of their collective culture.[32]

The implications for strategic management of these results are that U.S. workers are interested in the types of jobs that they perform and that they still have desirable work values. Younger workers who currently account for a major portion of the workforce and who will dominate it during the rest of the decade and beyond, feel entitled to meaningfulness and involvement. They want interesting work, to participate in decisions affecting them, autonomy, and opportunities to grow. Pay will remain important, but workers will probably not be as focused on pay as in the past.[33] These findings are consistent with the description of changing work values conveyed in the following:

> After a decade of excessive consumerism and blind ambition, American workers between the ages of 25 and 49 are beginning to emphasize public service and family life as measures of success . . .[34]

The trend toward greater interest in aspects of job satisfaction, such as autonomy and interesting work, are even reflected in the significant impact such factors have on workers' intentions to vote for unionization. Recent research also has demonstrated the significance of values as determinants of job choice decisions.[35]

The values of older workers also may be important to strategic management. When labor shortages persist, older workers will have to be persuaded to stay on the job or be drawn back into the labor force. One critical element to their return may be job satisfaction. Unfortunately, there is evidence of continuing bias against older workers in various aspects of the work relationship.[36] Although there is empirical evidence of a positive relationship between job satisfaction and age, the relationship is curvilinear and reflects a decline in job satisfaction among older workers, as a result of such factors as lost influence and unmet expectations.[37] Since downsizing organizations also have targeted older, higher-paid workers for voluntary early retirement programs as a means of cutting costs, older workers also may feel unappreciated. In planning for the environmental challenges of the future, strategic managers may need to develop approaches to prevent the decline of job satisfaction of older workers.

MANAGEMENT TRENDS

Several managerial trends are having an impact on human resources. Trends discussed in this section include work teams, virtual teams, open-book management, management of diversity, total quality management, reengineering, management of professionals, and managing in the aftermath of mergers and acquisitions.

Management of Diversity

Because of the increased heterogeneity of the workforce, which will be discussed later in this chapter, managers must be prepared to deal with the challenges associated with such demographic changes. Effective *management of diversity* can increase an organization's productivity through several avenues, one of which is increased problem-solving ability. Such productivity may result from increases in creativity that have been hypothesized to be related to heterogeneity. For example, bilingualism and biculturalism have been found be related to divergent thinking, which in turn has been hypothesized to be associated with creativity. Recently, it has been demonstrated that ethnic heterogeneity in small groups is associated with increased quality of ideas generated for solving problems. Increased heterogeneity also may bring another benefit—the prevention of the "groupthink" phenomenon that occurs only in cohesive groups. However, whether these benefits will be obtained is dependent on how well diversity is managed. Such factors as the amount of diversity, communications, ease of discussing differences, cultural awareness training, and awareness of background information on group members affect the quality of idea generation.[38]

Through such contributions, the management of diversity may enable companies to gain competitive advantages. In addition to diversity-related creativity and problem-solving advantages, companies also may be able to tap gender and racially diverse markets better with a more diverse workforce. They also may obtain better acceptance from these markets as a result of a good public image based on diversity. As an example, the Avon Corporation has had success with this strategy. Companies having good records in managing diversity may be able to attract better employees. Organizations that do a good job of managing diversity also tend to be more flexible because they have broadened their policies, are more open-minded, have less standardized operating methods, and have developed skills in dealing with resistance to change.[39]

Although prejudice still exists, there is evidence that progress has been made. For minorities and females, obtaining jobs with companies is less of a problem than it was in the past. Instead, any apprehension about minorities and females is more likely to be based on perceptions of their qualifications. These perceptions are affected by the fact that, on average, minorities and females have less training and education.[40] As Roosevelt Thomas has stated: "Companies are worried about productivity and well aware that minorities and women represent a disproportionate share of the undertrained and undereducated."[41] To the extent that companies generalize from classes to individuals and make unfounded attributions, they underestimate the value and contribution that minorities and females can make. Not surprisingly, the careers of minorities and females tend to plateau earlier than those of male nonminorities.

Two caveats on the implications of the diversity literature seem warranted. One is that some of the empirical literature recommends that researchers should seek to determine the optimal level of heterogeneity because there is a curvilinear relationship between heterogeneity and performance.[42] An example of such a recommendation is that "groups should pay careful attention to how much they increase diversity . . . too much diversity can lead to communication problems and unavoidable conflict."[43] Unfortunately, if one had knowledge of an optimal level of heterogeneity, the application of such information to increase performance might lead to specific consideration of race, ethnicity, or gender in making work assignments, which would appear to violate civil rights legislation. A second caveat is that much of the past research on racial diversity has focused on blacks and whites but has not devoted much attention to Hispanics. As will be discussed later in this chapter, Hispanics are the fastest growing segment of the workforce. Thus, managers need to be sensitive to diversity issues for all races and nationalities as well as gender and other forms of workforce diversity.[44]

Work Teams

Work teams have been of increasing interest to managers in a number of leading companies, such as Procter & Gamble, Eli Lilly, and Motorola. These companies have developed substantial expertise in the utilization of teams.[45] John R. Katzenback and Douglas K. Smith define *work teams* as "a small number of people with complementary skills who are committed to a common purpose, performance goals, and approach for which they hold themselves mutually accountable."[46] A number of benefits have been attributed to the use of work teams as an organizational form. These include improved decision making, improved performance, improved quality, and increased flexibility afforded by the ease with which they can be created and disbanded. The use of teams may also lead to reduced labor costs, lower employee turnover, greater service efficiency, facilitation of change resulting from reduced individual threat, and shorter product development cycles. Empirical analysis of the long-term performance of work teams involved in business simulations has provided some evidence of their effectiveness.[47]

In spite of the advantages, there also are disadvantages with the use of work teams as they are sometimes subject to the dysfunctional groupthink phenomenon and norms of production restriction. Further, as researchers Eric Sundstrom, Kenneth P. De Meuse, and David Futrell have pointed out, the literature on work teams provides mixed evidence on their effectiveness and identifies a large number of factors that potentially influence work team effectiveness. These include developmental aspects, the boundaries of the teams, and the organizational context.[48] There also are examples of difficulties with the implementation of teams such as Levi Strauss, where the introduction of teams led to declines in productivity and morale.[49]

Although work team effectiveness is a complex subject, effective work teams have some common characteristics. Such characteristics include relatively small size, dedication to a common purpose, commitment to common performance standards, willingness to be collectively accountable, equitable and effective work and role assignment procedures within the team, and complementary skills. Effective work teams also require compensation approaches that reward teamwork, such as gain sharing or team bonuses.[50]

Aside from their complexity and the potential disadvantages of teams, there is great interest in their potential contributions. For example, in design and production situations, *cross-functional work teams* have been found to be effective in reducing the time required from initial product design to eventual production through simultaneous engineering. Such teams, which typically include both design and production engineering personnel, as well as program managers who mediate differences, are ideally housed in the same area. Another benefit derived from these teams is the broadening experience that takes place within the teams across engineering specialties.[51]

An example of the use of work teams having a great deal of autonomy is provided by the experiences of Steelcase, Inc., which introduced work teams into its new Context plant. The plant's hourly employees are organized into some 47 work teams, several of which are cross-functional in nature. In addition to normal production work, these teams perform many activities that normally would have been managerial responsibilities, such as scheduling production, scheduling vacations, ordering materials, and purchasing new equipment. Performance evaluation and compensation reviews are still the responsibility of managerial personnel.[52]

Steelcase has derived a number of important benefits from its work groups. One is that the teams, which include machine operators, tend to make better machinery purchasing decisions than managers. Another benefit is savings in labor costs because the proportion of indirect labor costs is lower than other plants in the industry. For example, there is no need for the position of assistant foreman. An additional benefit is that the Context plant has experienced an annual turnover rate lower than one percent. Furthermore, communication has been facilitated as a result of the use of work teams. Finally, Steelcase has found that its workers have not become complacent because of the sense of ownership produced by the teams.[53] The performance effects of teams will be discussed in Chapter 8.

Virtual Teams

Virtual teams have members who work closely together even though they are based at different locations, including different countries, and may even be in different time zones. They typically have members from different functions and work across organizational boundaries as well. Advances in telecommunications, such as the Internet, e-mail, cell phones, and videoconferencing, have made virtual teams a possibility. In turn, market factors such as shorter product life cycles, rapidly shifting customer tastes, and international competitive pressures have provided the driving force for the use of technology to develop virtual teams.[54] A team at a Johnson & Johnson unit provides a good example of a virtual team. This team has been assigned the task of developing a new surgical product and bringing it into production. The team consists of representatives of various functions and has members in Arlington, Texas, and Juarez, Mexico, where production facilities are located. Team members communicate frequently with each other using e-mail, fax, and telephone, and the team leader also makes frequent trips between the different locations.

Human Resource Outsourcing

One of the most significant forces affecting human resource management has been the outsourcing of human resource functions. Human resource outsourcing is commonly understood as the permanent contracting out of activities that were previously performed in-house. The trend toward outsourcing has been extremely widespread, and recent surveys have found as many as 91 to 93 percent of responding companies engaging in outsourcing.[55]

The trend toward outsourcing has been caused by several strategic and operational influences. From a strategic perspective, some human resource departments have attempted to shift their focus and resources toward a more strategic role through the use of outsourcing. To accomplish this, human resource executives have used outsourcing to relieve their departments of some of the more mundane aspects of the function, such as those involving routine, low-value-added transactions. Outsourcing also has been used to help reduce bureaucracy and to encourage a more responsive and cost-sensitive culture by introducing external market forces into the organization through the bidding process. In addition, outsourcing has been used for political purposes, such as to reduce or control head count in human resources.[56]

Outsourcing has been pursued for several operational reasons as well, such as for greater efficiency or better service in the performance of functions. For example, companies almost universally outsource 401(k) plans because large financial services companies can provide almost flawless low-cost administration of the plans. Other examples include medical claims processing and the processing of benefit continuation under the Consolidated Omnibus Budget Reconciliation Act (COBRA). Outsourcing also has been seen as a vehicle for cutting costs. While cost reduction is an important consideration in many firms, the evidence indicates greater likelihood of successful outsourcing when it is pursued as part of a coordinated plan, such as for strategic focus and service quality, rather than solely on the basis of lower costs. In addition, outsourcing has been used to obtain specialized expertise that is not available in-house. During the past two decades, downsizing has often reduced the number of human resource specialists in human resource departments. This reduction in staff has required organizations to go to outside vendors to obtain specialized services, such as for test validation or in-depth assessments for leadership development.[57]

Open-Book Management

The practice of sharing financial and performance information is often referred to as *open-book management.* Essentially, the practice relies on the notion that empowered employees can make informed decisions and take informed actions on behalf of the firm. Because employees have the information and are empowered, they are almost compelled to take action. Jack Stack of Springfield Manufacturing has been credited for being the inventor of open-book management. Stack acquired a nearly bankrupt plant from International Harvester and was able to achieve a remarkable turnaround through the use of open-book management. One of his most critical changes in implementing open-book management was to help employees think of the firm as a business instead of an organization that reconditioned diesel engines. Interestingly, "He persuaded employees to view running the business as a game they could learn to play—and win."[58]

Open-book management is broader than many human resource practices as it combines a number of practices such as profit sharing, use of bonuses, scoreboarding (reporting results on scoreboards), and training employees to understand the business. It often places heavy emphasis on the use of games in which the objective is to defeat a problem instead of other employees. Typically, firms that practice open-book management develop simplified methods for reporting their financials to employees and train them to interpret various measures of performance. Open-book management usually combines generous bonuses beyond competitive base pay for a broad group of employees when the firm's goals are achieved.[59]

Such bonuses are carefully spelled out as indicated in the following:

> The bonus in open-book companies is an agreed-upon part—a significant part—of everyone's compensation package. It pays out only if the company or business unit hits certain goals, which are determined and spelled out in advance. The bonus is everybody's reward for boosting the company's performance—for succeeding in business . . . Right away you can see a couple of conditions that an open-book bonus plan must meet. For one thing, it has to be generous—generous enough to matter . . . A bonus plan that leaves out any group of regular employees runs counter to the basic ideas of open-book management. So does a plan with widely disparate rewards . . . A bonus is an addition to competitive base pay.[60]

Another positive feature of open-book management is that the sharing of such information instills a sense of trust among employees. In firms that do not practice open-book management, financial and performance information is often restricted to high-level executives. This restricted information flow conveys to other employees that they are not to be trusted with such information. As a result of its positive features, open-book management has the potential to enhance employee motivation.[61]

Examples of companies using open-book management include R.R. Donnelly and Sons, Carolina Safety Associates, and Terminex (North Carolina). The Bradshaw Group, Inc., in Richardson, Texas, provides an example of a small company that is practicing open-book management. The firm trains its employees to understand accounting and financial terms and shares ten percent of its firm's profits when profit goals are achieved.[62]

Total Quality Management

While not new, another continuing trend of importance to management strategists is *total quality management (TQM)*. TQM, pioneered by Edwards Deming, is a broad-based, systematic approach for achieving high levels of quality. Many leading companies such as Motorola, Cadillac, and Xerox, whose strategies require them to survive against the pressures of world-class competition, have implemented TQM. In a strategic context, TQM is probably most accurately categorized as a tactic for carrying out strategies requiring high levels of product or service quality. Essentially, TQM pulls together a number of well-known managerial principles into a coherent and systematic framework. Through the systematic interaction of these principles, TQM has the potential to lead to increased quality. TQM principles emphasize:

- Articulation of a strategic vision
- Objective and accurate measurements
- Benchmarking
- Widespread employee empowerment and team building
- Striving for continuous improvement
- Emphasis on a systems view of quality that conceptualizes quality-related activities as being highly interdependent
- Leadership committed to quality
- Great emphasis on customer satisfaction[63]

Interestingly, TQM programs have the potential to increase the importance of the human resource management function. Human resource management plays a major role in providing more systematic training, facilitating changes that empower employees, instituting team-based reward systems, and communicating to workers their role in quality.[64] David Bowen and Edward Lawler have described the relationship between TQM and human resource management as follows:

> The importance of the HR side of the quality equation provides HR departments with a golden opportunity. Quality can be the "business issue" that truly brings senior managers and HR execs together to move from *just* HRM to *strategic* HRM. A major role in the quality improvement effort puts HR in a position to contribute directly and visibly to the bottom line, to add value to the company's products and services in the same way that other functions, such as sales, accounting, and production, add value.[65]

Before the human resource function can make full contributions to TQM efforts, high quality must be assured within the function itself. Unfortunately, measurement of the function's contributions is often difficult because of their indirect effects. Nonetheless, as discussed in Chapter 9, valid measures of human resource effectiveness can be developed. One means by which this might be accomplished is through external benchmarking. *Benchmarking*, which is discussed in more depth in Chapter 9, provides a useful means of both evaluating the quality of human resource programs, activities, and impact as well as a means of identifying areas in which resources should be concentrated. The following quotation by David Ulrich, Wayne Brockbank, and Arthur Yeung describes this practice:

> Benchmarking HR practices provide the means of focusing attention on highest value-added HR activities—those practices which are more likely to be practiced

by successful companies. Rather than fall into the trap of trying to do everything well and please everyone with insufficient resources—which results in no one being satisfied—HR professionals could use benchmarking to focus limited resources on critical activities.[66]

Evaluation of the human resource function can also be accomplished by asking other mangers in the organization to evaluate the quality of services provided by the human resource management function.[67] One guide for evaluation is to place greatest emphasis on measuring the most critical human resource management attributes, with secondary emphasis on the precision with which these attributed can be measured. This point is evident in the following statement by Curt Reiman, Director of the Baldrige Award for the U.S. Department of Commerce: "A company doesn't earn money making measurements. The trick is to avoid great measurements of irrelevant things. You may have to live with approximate measurements of exactly the right things."[68] Along this same line, proponents of TQM also advocate the use of Pareto analysis.[69] The basis of Pareto analysis is that a small number of factors has a disproportionately large impact on outcomes, such as quality. Therefore, by correcting a few critical problems, disproportionate improvements in quality can be obtained.

One of the important impacts of TQM, from a human resource management perspective, is that it places great emphasis on training. TQM maintains that errors and mistakes, which detract from the quality of companies' products and services, are a predictable result of untrained workers, and therefore training must be provided. Consistent with the emphasis on measurement, in some companies that use TQM, training is evaluated with the use of control groups and experimental designs.[70]

In contrast to training, TQM is sharply at odds with conventional human resource practice in the area of performance evaluation. According to Deming, traditional performance evaluation systems are flawed because they are directed toward the individual instead of the team. Such systems also focus on assigning blame for past mistakes instead of pointing out direction for the future and may even detract from teamwork. Deming also argued that faulty systems and procedures are usually the cause of quality problems, not the performance of individual employees. TQM proponents also maintain that compensation should be directed toward teams instead of individuals. In addition to disagreement over performance evaluation, there also is controversy among TQM proponents over the appropriateness of team-based pay. Even some companies that have won the Baldrige Award for quality have not extended TQM into the areas of performance evaluation or compensation. Instead, companies implementing TQM have focused on problem areas that detract from quality, are relatively easy to fix, and do not involve much risk. For example, many companies focus their TQM efforts on improving training and communications. Fewer companies have shifted from more traditional compensation systems to team-based pay, abandoned their performance evaluation systems, or instituted self-managed teams. Motorola and Cadillac are exceptions in that they have instituted such teams.[71]

As with any managerial innovation, TQM is not without problems. One criticism is that TQM efforts can lead to goal displacement, in which TQM becomes an end instead of a means. In such cases, attention is diverted from productive activities to gaining approvals from committees, filling out forms, and other bureaucratic procedures. The well-publicized difficulties encountered by Florida Power & Light and the Wallace Company after they won the Baldrige Award for quality provide wonderfully ironic examples of this problem. Additionally—although not the fault of TQM—during economic difficulties, some companies have reduced the level of employee empowerment. Executives in these companies have blamed employee empowerment for slower decision making. However, this appears to be a short-sighted criticism since the critical decision implementation process is facilitated by employee empowerment. Nonetheless, even in Japan there has been second-guessing of employee empowerment and consensus decision approaches because of their slowness. As a result, some leading Japanese companies have turned to more top-down–oriented chief executive officers.[72] Another problem is incompatibility of some basic TQM concepts and downsizing strategies. Bernado De Sousa from Ciba-Geigy Ltd., has stated:

> Because the aim of TQM is to add value to all stakeholders in every activity, it must of necessity make a company more efficient . . . Increased productivity implies producing more with the same resources or, in a saturated market, producing the same amounts with fewer resources. In the latter case, which is the rule rather than the exception in the industrialized nations today, downsizing is the inevitable consequence.[73]

Although De Sousa claims that layoffs can be avoided, presumably by attrition, worker insecurity resulting from downsizing or layoffs would seem to undermine the TQM philosophy.

Integrated Manufacturing

Integrated manufacturing systems provide a new approach for streamlined manufacturing. Such systems are commonly composed of *advanced manufacturing technology (AMT)*, TQM, and *just-in-time (JIT)* inventory control methods. AMT is a manufacturing approach based on highly computerized technologies, such as *computer-aided manufacturing (CAM)*. JIT inventory control is a method for delivering manufacturing components to the production line at the shortest practical time before they are needed. When these technologies and managerial systems are combined, integrated manufacturing systems have the potential to provide greater dissemination of information, remove barriers associated with functional specialization, promote collaboration to solve quality problems, and develop congruence between goals of cost, quality, and desired production lead times.[74]

These systems require knowledge workers whose levels of technical and problem-solving skills are advanced beyond those needed for earlier forms of manufacturing and have major implications for human resource management.

Scott Snell and James Dean conducted an empirical analysis of the types of human resource practices associated with various components of integrated manufacturing systems. In companies in which there is greater emphasis on AMT and TQM, there is more selectivity in hiring, more comprehensive training, greater developmental use of performance appraisal, and greater emphasis on external pay equity. These results are consistent with companies' motivations to hire and maintain high-quality workforces and to preserve their investments in human resources.[75]

Reengineering

Reengineering, which is also called *process innovation*, *core process redesign*, and *business process reengineering*, has been practiced since the late 1980s, often by companies facing intense competitive pressures. Essentially, reengineering is directed at achieving large cost savings by eliminating unneeded activities and consolidating work. It also sometimes redirects work across traditional departmental boundaries in order to accomplish work more quickly in cross-functional teams. Accordingly, reporting relationships are sometimes changed along with reward structures. The type of service desired by customers is the key to the process.[76]

An example of reengineering is provided by its application at Texas Instruments. In this application, the driving force was the desire to reduce the time required for making customized semiconductor chips for a customer. In another example, the driving force was increased competition. In this case, GTE revamped its customer service process when it found that customers wanted to call only one number for repair service, to obtain answers to billing questions, or to obtain additional services. Prior to reengineering, customers having service problems called repair clerks, who then recorded the information and then forwarded it to repair personnel. These activities were subsequently combined into one job performed by employees called front-end technicians who also now operate testing and switching equipment relocated from repair personnel. As a result, the front-end technicians solve 30 percent of all service calls, and a smaller percentage of calls must be passed on to other repair personnel.[77] Another example involves a bank. In order to reduce its operating costs the Banca di America e di Italia (BAI) reengineered its retail banking operations with the goal of becoming a paperless bank. After reengineering activities involved in depositing checks, the number declined from 64 to 25. As a result of these and other changes, employees in each branch declined from seven to nine prior to reengineering to three to four afterwards. With these labor savings, the bank was able to open 50 new branches with its existing workforce.[78]

Often, reengineering requires cross-functional coordination and the crossing of organizational boundaries. Because it may disrupt existing power relationships and eliminate organizational jobs, it has high potential for conflict. Because the process often fails to obtain desired improvements and it has high potential for destructive consequences, organizations should not engage in reengineering unless they perceive a serious need. Furthermore, reengineering typically does not achieve the level of improvement desired. The conventional wisdom is that the organization's strategy should provide direction to the process by indicating the major business activities that should be reengineered. Activities unnecessary to these business needs are potential targets for elimination. As with any intervention of this nature, the organization's culture will have a major impact on its success. In many contemporary organizational cultures, the broad direction for reengineering should come from top management, while the specifics of reengineering should be the responsibility of those who perform work. In addition to the requirement for extensive time commitment from the chief executive, successful reengineering is more likely to take place where it is applied to a broad range of activities, training programs accompany work redesign, and there is extensive communication with employees.[79]

As a closing note on reengineering, it should be noted that some high-level executives are not convinced of the ultimate value of reengineering. They have observed the elimination of jobs and such a massive increase in the workload of remaining employees that they have serious concerns about the long-range, detrimental human impact of such programs. Because of such reactions, the use of reengineering may diminish somewhat in the future.

Management of Professionals

Because of their nature, professionals require a different form of management and provide a challenge for human resource management. Important characteristics of professionals are that they often have low organizational loyalty, require substantial autonomy, follow a code of ethics established by their profession, adhere to standards of the profession, and have a high need for intellectual and technical challenges.[80] The availability of managers who can manage the work of professionals cannot be taken for granted. The difficulties are well known, and there has been a long-standing controversy over whether such managers should be members of the relevant profession themselves or laypersons. The problems of failing to plan for the development of managers who can be effective in such settings are apparent. Mary Anne Von Glinow has stated:

> Maximizing a professional's productivity has led to the adoption or development of new methods of work organization that limit hierarchical levels of supervision, link pay and other rewards to performance, ease the tensions between the competing cultures of professionals and other employees, and give professionals greater participation in the decisions that affect their lives . . . These managerial challenges and their solutions are crucial to the success and long-term survival of every high tech firm. The changes . . . require different and sometimes counterintuitive management skills and practices.[81]

A human resource problem for the future will be to develop career paths for professionals. To move up in an organization, professionals have traditionally pursued an administrative track. Since they are often unprepared for management or administrative careers, they may not find such work satisfying. As a result, dual career ladders are sometimes provided, one in management and the other within the professional work.[82] Planning for career progressions for professionals will require greater attention to the development of alternative tracks that will satisfy the needs of both professionals and their employing organizations. Large public accounting firms provide a remarkable example of turnover problems among professionals. A study of one such firm found that retention rates, after 60 months with the firm, ranged from 6 to 29 percent.[83] A challenge for the future will be to develop career tracks for professionals that will enhance organizational loyalty.

Managing in the Aftermath of Mergers and Acquisitions

Although the level of merger and acquisition activity has lessened, mergers and acquisitions still are a permanent feature of the economy. Whether a merger or acquisition is successful depends on more than financial considerations. Success often depends on how well the two organizations' human resources are integrated. As a result, the degree to which human resource aspects of mergers and acquisitions are planned can be critical.[84] Bruckman and Peters have stated:

> The amount of time and energy needed to successfully merge two sophisticated organizations, however, is more likely to resemble the planning and execution of the invasion of Normandy, accompanied by the resultant clash of cultures from many elements attempting to work together toward one end.[85]

There is much evidence of the failure to work through human resource issues even when organizations are acquired for their human resources. It also has been argued that planning for the contingencies of a merger is critical because human resources will pay the price. If the company loses a takeover battle, there may be redundant employees and the new entity will have to resort to layoffs. Conversely, if a company is successful in fending off a takeover, personnel layoffs are generally required to pay the costs of the defensive actions.[86]

DEMOGRAPHIC TRENDS

Many of the major demographic trends for the future are relatively well known. Nonetheless, these massive changes in demography have important implications for human resource management. Major changes include an aging workforce, the baby boom age glut, the baby bust labor shortage, increased racial diversity, and greater feminization of the workforce. These developments, particularly the variations in growth across different age cohorts, will have major implications for the career potential of individual workers. Planning will be necessary to avoid age bulges, age gaps, and surpluses in job categories or job families.[87]

An Aging Workforce

As indications of aging trends, the median age for the U.S. population will increase from 42 in 1998 to 45 by the year 2008, while the median age for the labor force will increase from 39 in 1998 to 41 in 2009.[88] Some of the implications of aging are that the workforce will be more experienced, stable, and reliable. As a result, it should be more productive. However, an older workforce may lead to less flexibility as older workers may not adapt as quickly to a dynamic economy. Greater costs will also result from greater pension contributions that are likely to be associated with an aging workforce.[89] One implication of this trend is that as the workforce ages there should be correspondingly greater health care costs. Huge increases in health care costs have already occurred.[90] Companies' age distributions have already begun to affect their production costs and ability to compete. Interestingly, during the postwar period in which Japan's remarkable economic growth occurred, it had a relatively smaller proportion of retired people to support than other industrial countries.[91]

The Boomer Age Bulge

Projections of the labor force through the year 2008 reveal vast differences in the size of age cohorts. As Table 2-1 indicates, the intermediate age groups will decline. Participants in the 25-to-34 age group will decline 1.3 percent from 1998, while those in the 34-to-44 age group will decline by 6.9 percent. In contrast, participants in the youngest groups will increase. Those 16 to 19 will increase by 13.8 percent, while those 20 to 24 will increase by 16 percent. The largest increases come at the upper end of the age groups where the boomers are located. Labor force participants aged 45 to 54 will increase by 29.7 percent from 1998 levels, while those 55 to 64 will increase by a phenomenal 55.8 per-

TABLE 2-1 Civilian Labor Force

Age Category	*1998*	*2008*[a]	*Percentage Change*
16 to 19	8,256,000	9,396,000	+13.8
20 to 24	13,638,000	15,814,000	+16.0
25 to 34	32,813,000	32,398,000	−1.3
35 to 44	37,536,000	34,945,000	−6.9
45 to 54	28,368,000	36,790,000	+29.7
55 to 64	13,215,000	20,588,000	+55.8
65 and older	3,847,000	4,645,000	+20.7

[a] Projections.

Source: Labor force and labor force projections extracted from Howard N. Fullerton Jr. "Labor Force Projections to 2008: Steady Growth and Changing Composition," *Monthly Labor Review* 122, no. 11 (1999): 27.

cent. The implications of these projections are dramatic. There will be a shortage of workers aged 25 to 44, while there will be an abundance of more experienced workers with the largest age category in the labor force of ages 45 to 54.[92]

Labor Shortages

At the beginning of the twenty-first century, firms faced the tightest U.S. labor markets in 30 years. In some states, the unemployment rates for adults fell below three percent. The combination of an exceptionally strong economy and demographic trends produced the labor shortages that had been predicted solely from demographic trends. Employers were expected to respond to the shortage by hiring retired workers and creating more varied work schedules to accommodate their needs. Indeed, as the shortage developed, employers responded in many predicted ways like hiring disabled workers such as the mentally challenged and retired workers.[93] Barring an economic collapse, labor shortages also are predicted for the future:

> The traditional want ad will be replaced with "situation wanted" ads: Workers will place these ads on the Internet or other media and wait for companies to call them. They will have good reason to expect a call back. The U.S. Bureau of Labor Statistics projects 151 million jobs by 2006 and 141 people employees. As often happens today, many of those workers will be working two jobs.[94]

The lure of jobs with dot-com or e-business companies and the prospects for rapid accumulation of wealth has made the labor market even tighter for highly skilled workers who are willing to take risks and live with uncertainty. Nonetheless, the most admired companies in the United States such as Lucent Technologies, General Electric, Microsoft, and Dell Computer have high ratios of applicants to jobs. These companies are aggressive recruiters, but ratios of applicants to jobs as high as 81 at Southwest Airlines help reinforce the notion that good employees are attracted to companies that have good management even in tight labor markets.[95]

The Internet has created many of the jobs for highly skilled workers and has helped the labor market work more efficiently by providing information about jobs and applicants and facilitating match-ups. Internet recruiting has become so important that trade journals publish ratings of the top job sites such as Monster.com or Jobs.com. In addition to its advantages of speed and economy, Internet recruiting reaches the global labor market. Internet sites also offer the potential for tremendous volume. For example, GTE receives 20,000 to 30,000 résumés each year through e-mail. In addition, there is great specialization. For instance, one site specializes in job openings for morticians.[96]

In addition to recruiting efforts, companies have responded to labor shortages by hiring nontraditional workers. A number of companies have achieved excellent results by hiring disabled employees. For example, at Carolina Fine Snacks, 50 percent of the employees have various impairments including mental retardation and cerebral palsy. Nonetheless, after hiring these employees, the company's productivity climbed from 50 to 60 percent of capacity to over 90 percent, and turnover declined dramatically. Du Pont also has a long history of hiring disabled employees and five percent of its workers have disabilities.[97] Kroger has an excellent record of hiring mentally challenged individuals to work as grocery baggers and has been able to cope with tight labor markets with these reliable and loyal employees.

Older workers also have provided an excellent source of labor. Although many older workers are not interested in full-time work, they appear to be interested in "fill-in" work of a part-time nature if the jobs provide flexibility and are close to home. The Senior Employment Service in New York and Operation Able in Chicago provide examples of successful employment of older workers. Companies such as Cigna, Grumman, and Hewlett-Packard are already using innovative approaches in staffing with older workers, frequently hiring their own retirees. The Days Inn hotel chain has staffed 25 percent of its reservation workforce with older workers.[98]

Interestingly, the reserve of female workers that provided needed labor in the past has been depleted by their current involvement in the labor force. Liberalized policies that would allow greater immigration of skilled workers also are also being viewed as a remedy for shortages of labor.[99]

Unfortunately for unqualified workers, U.S. employers will need entry-level workers whose skills are on par with global standards. Peter Morrison has stated, "When today's first-graders reach adulthood they will compete within a global labor market and will need intellectual skills and levels of education and literacy never demanded of their predecessors."[100] Stated differently, "jobs that are currently in the middle of the skill distribution will be the least-skilled occupations of the future, and there will be very few net new jobs for the unskilled."[101] The U.S. Bureau of Labor Statistics has projected that 40 percent of the growth in jobs through 2008 will require at least an associate's degree.[102]

Greater Racial Diversity

The labor force will become much more diverse in the twenty-first century. The category consisting of Asians and others (Pacific Islanders, Native Americans, and Alaskan Natives) is projected to grow by over 40 percent through 2008, the fastest of all racial groups. Hispanic participation is expected to increase by 36.8 percent, and Hispanics will become the largest minority group in the labor force by 2008, accounting for 12.7 percent of the labor force. The participation of black workers is expected to grow more slowly, 19.5 percent. Growth in labor force participation of white workers will be the slowest, only 9.7 percent. As a result of these growth patterns, by the year 2008, over 29 percent of the workforce will be composed of nonwhites.[103] As noted earlier in this chapter's discussion of the management of diversity, organizations will need to plan to take advantage of diversity instead of forcing conformity. Likewise, organizations will need to be proactive in helping to create a work environment in which the creativity and innovativeness of diversity will flourish.[104]

Changing Occupational Distributions for Women

Females have constituted a growing portion of the workforce for several decades. However, this growth has slowed tremendously as women are predicted to constitute 48 percent of the workforce by 2008, only one percentage point more than in 1998. While the occupational distribution of women still differs from that of men, they have made great strides in several job categories. Women now account for 68.3 percent of the workers in training, human resources, and labor relations and for approximately 50 percent of accountants, although they are still underrepresented at the level of partner. Women have advanced most rapidly in cutting-edge industries because the need for pure intellectual horsepower overcomes inclinations for exclusion on the basis of gender. For example, they have fared well as information workers and as computer scientists. In the past 10 years, they also have made impressive inroads as engineers, sales engineers, and as support staff for technical sales.[105]

In order to attract talented women, many employers have work arrangements that better accommodate childbirth and, for women as well as men, the care of young children. Such approaches include part-time schedules, flextime, flexi-scheduling, and allowing employees to work part of the time at home. Experiences with the latter have been reported at both General Motors and Citibank for managerial and professional personnel. The trends toward greater flexibility are clear. Between 1991 and 1997, the proportion of the civilian labor force working on flextime increased from 15 percent to 27 percent.[106]

Dual-Career Couples

An issue related to increased feminization of the workforce is the number of dual-career families. The number of couples having two wage earners has increased rapidly, having passed the two-thirds point more than a decade ago. In order to accommodate such families, many employers offer support services such as "sick child" care programs and day care. Such services are believed to produce reductions in absenteeism, lower turnover, recruiting advantages, and a positive impact on productivity.[107] In order to help such dual-career couples, as well as single parents, employers now provide several forms of support. For example, referral services for child care are provided by one of the large public accounting firms as well as IBM. Other companies have set up child care facilities on company premises. Campbell Soup Company has had success with such a program. However, such programs are not automatic successes. Corning Glass and Merck encountered high costs and resentment from employees who did not need such services.[108]

TRENDS IN THE UTILIZATION OF HUMAN RESOURCES

The Internet, e-mail, fax machines, cable modems, digital subscriber lines, personal computers, other forms of telecommunications, and express mail make up a set of forces that have allowed many workers to work off-site by telecommuting. Some also have been able to relocate geographically while continuing to perform the same work for their employers via telecommunications technology. Workers are relocating in the United States in patterns that are very different from past migration flows.[109]

Telecommuting

Telecommuting, or *telecommunicating*, does not necessarily involve geographic relocation but simply involves working at home at least part of the time. In recent years, the number of workers who telecommute has increased dramatically, with estimates of more than 10 million working at least 20 percent of the time at home. An indication of this trend toward telecommuting is evident in the experience of U.S. West, where telecommuters now account for 16,000 of the company's 54,000 employees. Another example is Merrill Lynch's Private Client Technology Unit in which 19 percent of employees are telecommuters. Furthermore, the U.S. federal government also has a program for telecommuters called *flexiplace* that is used by employees of agencies such as the Internal Revenue Service.[110]

Telecommuting is thought to bring several individual benefits, including time savings from the avoidance of commuting as well as at-home child care, ease of working for multiple employers, access to jobs by disabled workers, and lifestyle advantages. There is a positive impact on the environment as well when fewer workers are on the highways. Organizational benefits include recruiting advantages, lower costs in using part-time workers, increased ability to use skilled professionals on an ad hoc basis, reduced likelihood of unionization, less need for office space, productivity improvements, better morale for those employees given the option of telecommuting, and employee retention. AT&T states that it is able to retain more of its employees because of telecommuting. Some observers have asserted that telecommuters work more efficiently.[111]

Nonetheless, there are potential problems with such arrangements, including control difficulties, career limitations related to lack of visibility, workers' concerns about missing opportunities, social isolation, less sense of belonging, and reduced loyalties to both employer and employee. There are also concerns about the security of confidential or competitive information when it is transmitted over telephone lines from to and from the telecommuter. Although encryption technology may reduce such threats, security is a concern for some companies. Telecommuters also need remote-office and information technology support. In addition, some managers find it difficult to trust their employees to work at home without their supervision.[112]

Relocation of Work

Telecommunication advances have allowed information workers to migrate from cities to rural areas and small towns. This migration has created what futurists Naisbitt and Aburdene call the *electronic heartland.* These workers have been attracted to the heartland because there is less crime, a lower cost of living, and quality-of-life benefits. Workers who are making this relocation include owners of home-based businesses, writers, artists, stock traders, composers, software developers, and engineers.[113]

Companies also are relocating their operations. In information systems and data processing, companies are relocating their facilities to areas where there are favorable costs. For example, a New York money center bank relocated its data processing operations to a nearby state where real estate and the cost of living are lower. Information is transmitted electronically back and forth with no delay in information system responsiveness while achieving substantial cost savings.

It is increasingly common for automobile rental companies and hotels to locate their reservations operations in areas of the country where there are wage advantages. For example, Hertz has its reservations and accounting operations in Oklahoma City. Thrifty and Avis both have reservations operations in Tulsa, and Budget's reservations operations are in Carrolton, Texas. Reservations operations for Hyatt Hotels are located in Omaha, Nebraska. These geographic areas offer wage advantages over many areas in the United States, and location is irrelevant to the nature of the work performed.

Recently, manufacturing companies have been relocating out of California because of the high costs of land and labor as well as the regulative environment. For example, California-based Applied Materials built a new $100 million facility in Texas because of such factors. Other examples include Weiser Lock, which closed a plant in California and moved it to Tucson where labor and cost of living are substantially lower. Similarly, Atlas Pacific Engineering relocated from northern California to Pueblo, Colorado, for lower labor and land costs.[114] Companies from service industries also are relocating. Bank of America, for example, relocated its credit card unit from Pasadena to Phoenix.[115] Additionally, the expense of operating in such high-cost areas as New York City has prompted some large companies to move their headquarters to less expensive areas. W. R. Grace announced its intentions to move its headquarters to Florida while JCPenney and Exxon–Mobil had already moved their headquarters from New York to the Dallas/Fort Worth area.[116]

Growing Use of Temporary and Contingent Workers

Another important human resource issue is the increasing use of *temporary* or *contingent workers.* Temporary employees are often used to provide a buffer of protection for the jobs of the core of permanent employees. Further, the use of such workers is increasing, and there is likely to be additional unbundling in the future. In contrast to core employees, contingent workers have short-term affiliations with employers. Examples include temporaries, subcontracted workers, part-time workers, consultants, life-of-the-project workers, and *leased employees.* Companies also are using more "leased" employees who are "rented" from a temporary help agency on a long-term basis. Not surprisingly, unions typically resist the use of temporary workers.[117]

Although there is growing use of higher-skilled temporary employees, the largest category of temporaries is still administrative support or clerical work. The second largest category is industrial help workers such as laborers, equipment cleaners, helpers, and handlers. Because demand for such industrial help workers is cyclical and seasonal, the advantages to the employer are obvious.[118] Temporary workers are even being used in the health care industry as registered nurses, practical nurses, and x-ray technicians.[119]

As indicated, the nature of temporary jobs is changing as there is a shift toward the higher skill levels. Temporary workers now include accountants, computer specialists, engineering personnel, financial executives, and technical writers. In information systems, temporary management services are being used for project management, installation of new systems, or during transition periods. Temporary management personnel and executives are sometimes early retirees from major computer companies or managers displaced as a result of restructuring.[120]

Factors Prompting Use of Temporary or Contingent Employees

A number of factors encourage the use of temporary or contingent employees. Because of economic uncertainty or turbulence, many employers are reluctant to hire permanent employees and have increased their use of contingent employees. Another factor is fluctuating workloads.[121] A client of Atlanta-based Norrell Corporation provides an example of adaptation to such fluctuations. The client organization has only 50 employees, while Norrell supplies it with 450 temporaries. Because the client needs most employees for only a seven-month cycle, it uses temporaries. Previously, the organization had 400 full-time employees and was overstaffed part of the time and understaffed the rest of the time.[122] Companies also can avoid paying overtime pay by using temporaries during peak demand periods. Growing and declining companies have been found to use more temporary employees. The use of temporaries who can be dismissed on short notice allows these companies to protect the core of permanent employees.[123] Nonetheless, in tight labor markets, it may be difficult to obtain qualified temporary employees.

Other factors prompting the use of contingent workers include avoidance of recruiting, hiring, and training expenses for workers who are to be used only a short time and avoidance of severance costs. The perverse effects of legislation also may have prompted the use of temporaries in some instances. For example, the Worker Adjustment and Retraining Notification Act (WARN), which was designed to provide advance notice of plant shutdowns to full-time employees, may encourage the use of temporary workers. Other advantages for employers in the use of such workers include flexibility, potential savings in labor costs, and acquiring labor needed during hiring freezes.[124]

In addition to benefits for employers, there are some benefits for temporary or contingent workers. These benefits include the flexibility to match lifestyle and family obligations with work and the ease of finding a job. For women, who constitute approximately two-thirds of the temporary workforce, the benefits also include exposure in the job market, opportunities to obtain work experience and work skills, and the opportunity to sample employment situations. Opportunities to reacquire work skills and confidence may have appeal for women who have withdrawn from the labor force for substantial lengths of time. Youthful workers also may be attracted by temporary work as opportunities to gain work experience.[125]

Factors Limiting the Use of Temporary or Contingent Employees

Although there are several advantages for employers in using temporary employees, there are also disadvantages. One disadvantage is the increased likelihood of missing affirmative action goals. Employers may not obtain desired numbers of female and minority employees in their permanent workforce if they curtail hiring and rely extensively on temporary workers. Another disadvantage is the need to train such workers. With temporary executives, disadvantages may include inordinate emphasis on short-term financial performance and absence of company loyalty. Disadvantages for temporary employees include lower opportunities to receive health insurance and retirement benefits, lower pay, and fewer training and educational opportunities. However, temporaries frequently have benefit coverage from spouses' employment.[126]

Employee Leasing

Employee leasing is different from the use of temporary workers because there is no implication that employees will be other than full-time, long-term employees. Often, when an employer makes the decision to lease employees, his or her employees then become employees of a leasing firm. The leasing firm then supplies these same employees to the original employer. As with the use of temporaries, there are some advantages with employee leasing. One primary reason for leasing is that small employers can obtain more economical health insurance by virtue of the leasing company's larger numbers of employees and inclusion under pooled rates. Another motivating factor is that all payroll and administrative services are performed by the leasing company, leaving the management of the small company free to focus on other aspects of the business.[127]

However, there are other disadvantages with the use of leased employees. One is that some of the advantages of small size, such as exclusion from coverage by various federal laws based on size limits, are lost because of the leasing company's larger size. The use of a leasing company also may not eliminate liability, as there may be a shared employment relationship. Another disadvantage is that a number of leasing companies have failed, leaving the employers using leased employees liable for workers' compensation.[128]

INTERNATIONAL DEVELOPMENTS

Global Competition

Companies competing on a global basis will need to use world-class labor to obtain the quality needed for some product markets. For example, the Dana Corporation uses its training programs to develop employees who can produce at the level of world competitive standards. One of Dana's accomplishments has been to develop some of its U.S. workers into world-class machinists.[129] One large food manufacturer has obtained specialized world-class information services by having programming done in Mexico and routing work done in England.

Moving foreign nationals across international boundaries is another approach for highly skilled individuals. However, the use of U.S. expatriate workers in overseas holdings may be declining. In some U.S. companies with large overseas holdings, the number of U.S. expatriate workers is relatively small. For example, during one year, Honeywell had 27,159 employees overseas but only approximately 200 were U.S. citizens.[130] Instead, there may be a growing tendency to bring foreign nationals to the United States for a few years' training with the parent company and having them take on the managerial or professional responsibilities in their countries. The legal restrictions involved in these actions may be critical. Some large organizations have human resource management specialists who have developed expertise in working through the legalities for such moves.

Global Sourcing of Labor

Innovative uses of labor on a global basis are evident. One example is a large U.S. insurance company in which claims are processed in Ireland. The combination of a common language, an educated labor force, a shortage of jobs, and relatively low wages make this an attractive option. As operations have been set up, claims data are sent from the United States using overnight airmail and electronic transmission. An interesting benefit of this relationship is that, in addition to the low cost of labor, there is a time differential advantage as work delivered overnight can be worked on several hours prior to the normal starting time of 8:00 A.M. on the East Coast. Additionally, U.S. companies sometimes have data entry performed offshore in order to take advantage of wage differentials. In some instances, data entry is performed by clerical workers who do not even speak English. For example, American Airlines has data entry performed in China and Barbados.[131]

Several Asian countries such as Korea, Singapore, Taiwan, Malaysia, and Indonesia are major U.S. trading and outsourcing partners. Nonetheless, the dramatic changes in Eastern Europe also have implications for labor supplies. Germany is especially intriguing. Although productivity in the eastern portion of Germany is lower because of the residual effects of communism, the prospects for rapid productivity growth are good because the labor force is literate, competent, mechanically adept, and has a strong work ethic. This transition to high productivity is in stark contrast to expectations of the labor force in many U.S. cities where illiteracy among workers is high.[132] Although the workforce from the former East Germany may be more skilled than those of some Eastern European countries, the labor forces of these countries are attractive in many respects and are now accessible to Western companies.

North American Free Trade Agreement

The North American Free Trade Agreement (NAFTA) between the United States, Canada, and Mexico eliminates tariffs on goods produced in these countries. Canada is the largest trading partner of the United States and Mexico is the second largest. The act is still controversial, with unions claiming that jobs have been lost, while employers and the U.S. Department of Commerce point to job creations. Regardless of the various claims, the effect on trade among the three countries is indisputable because there has been remarkable growth. Trade between the United States and Canada increased by 56 percent during the first four years alone. Even more impressive is that during the same period trade with Mexico increased by 113 percent. In addition, NAFTA has probably helped stimulate interest in broader trade agreements between countries in North and South America, such as the proposed Free Trade Area of the Americas that would include many nations.[133]

NAFTA and the possibility of further trade agreements have several interesting implications for human resource management. Many human resource managers become involved in their companies' operations in Canada and Mexico. For example, along the border region of Mexico and Texas, human resource managers commonly commute between El Paso, where they live, and Juarez, where their plants are located. These human resource managers are bilingual and knowledgeable about the cultural and legal environment of human resources in Mexico. Similar examples exist for Canada as well. Some of the future challenges for human resources will be to develop effective practices for their cross-border operations, such as equitable compensation systems and the ability to move key employees into their operations in all three countries. They also will need to help develop managers and key professionals who can work effectively in the cultures of the other countries.

European Community

Access to this huge market has major human resource implications for U.S. companies that have operations in European Community (EC) countries or do business with them. The relaxation of trade rules and the adoption of uniform standards within the EC have produced efficiencies in moving goods and workers across borders that have implications for U.S. operations in Europe. Nonetheless, the European labor environment remains highly unionized, and governmental regulations make it very difficulty to lay off or terminate employees. However, the EC may produce benefits for U.S. operations in Europe through more unified regulations affecting human resources. From another perspective, there also is the possibility of a unified response from a huge market that can affect domestic U.S. operations. For example, the EC was vehement in its attack on the Boeing and McDonnell Douglass merger because of the threat to the EC's Airbus. For some time, U.S. takeovers of European companies have been viewed as threats to the national identities of Italy, France, and Germany. However, in this instance, the resistance was to a purely U.S. merger.[134]

Summary

This chapter has overviewed several trends and developments that are likely to affect human resources in the twenty-first century. The impact of technology on employee skill requirements and jobs was considered along with the impact on organization structure. As a result of information technology, organizations are becoming less hierarchical and more adaptive and flexible. The emergence of unbundled corporations, network or virtual organizations, cellular organizations, respondent corporations, and the growth in entrepreneurial businesses were discussed. Some of these new organizational structures or forms that take contingent views toward organizational units and their workers are becoming more commonplace. The examination of worker values and attitudes revealed that employees also are becoming less loyal toward their employers, more concerned with having interesting jobs that allow them to grow, and more inclined to feel that they are entitled to participate in decisions affecting them.

Several important managerial trends were examined, including the need to manage an increasingly diverse workforce and to harness its capacity for creativity. The increased use of teams and the emergence of virtual teams was discussed. Team practices, such as rotating leadership responsibilities among team members based on the stage of product development cycles, were addressed. The increasing practice of human resource outsourcing was described as a major change in the management of human resources. In addition, there was discussion of the continued emphasis of TQM, which requires a number of changes in the human resource function, including a stronger service orientation. The implications of several other managerial trends were examined, including integrated manufacturing, process reengineering, and managing an increasing number of professionals. There also was a discussion of how organizations will need to prepare for and deal with the aftermath of mergers and acquisitions.

Several other trends also were examined, including demographic trends such as the aging workforce, the age gaps and bulges that have resulted from the baby boom and baby bust, the possibility of continuing labor shortages, greater racial diversity, changing occupational distributions for women, and dual-career couples.

Trends in the utilization of human resources were also examined, including telecommuting and the relocation of work. The implications of telecommuting and the migration of information workers to rural areas and small towns for cost-of-living and quality-of-life reasons were discussed. In addition, there was a discussion of the relocation of companies that are taking advantage of low costs in Midwestern, Southwestern, and mountain states. The trend toward increasing use of temporary or contingent workers, which has expanded to professionals, was discussed. The increased internationalization of business and global sourcing of labor also were examined along with the implications of NAFTA and the EC.

Endnotes

1. Kirkpatrick, David. "The E-Ware War: Competition Comes to Enterprise Software," *Fortune* (December 17, 1998): 102–12.
2. Drucker, Peter F. "The Coming of the New Organization," *Harvard Business Review* 66, no. 1 (1988): 45–53; Schein, Edgar H. "Reassessing the 'Divine Rights' of Managers," *Sloan Management Review* 30, no. 2 (1989): 63–68; Schein, Edgar H. "Increasing Organizational Effectiveness through Better Human Resource Planning and Development," *Sloan Management Review* 19, no. 1 (1977): 1–20.
3. Drucker. "The Coming of the New Organization."
4. Levitan, Sar. "Beyond 'Trendy' Forecasts: The Next 10 Years for Work," *The Futurist* 21, no. 6 (1987): 29.
5. Greller, Martin M., and David M. Nee. "Baby Boom and Baby Bust: Corporate Response to the Demographic Challenge of 1990–2010," in Richard J. Niehaus and Karl F. Price (Eds.), *Creating Competitive Edge through Human Resource Applications.* New York: Plenum Press, 1988, pp. 24–25; Schein, "Increasing Organizational Effectiveness through Better Human Resource Planning and Development."
6. Bussey, J. "Speeding Up: Manufacturers Strive to Slice Time Needed to Develop Products," *Wall Street Journal* (February 23, 1988): 1, 13; Port, Otis, Zachary Schiller, and Resa W. King. "A Smarter Way to Manufacture," *Business Week* (April 30, 1990): 110–17.
7. Greer, Charles R., Stuart A. Youngblood, and David A. Gray. "Human Resource Management Outsourcing: The Make or Buy Decision," *Academy of Management Executive* 13, no. 3 (1999): 85–96.
8. Jones, Melody. "Four Trends to Recon With," *HR Focus* 73, no.7 (1996): 22.

9. Greer, Youngblood, and Gray. "Human Resource Management Outsourcing: The Make or Buy Decision."
10. Foulkes, Fred K. "Future of Human Resources," in Ulrich, Dave, Michael R. Losey, and Gerry Lake (Eds.), *Tomorrow's HR Management: 48 Thought Leaders Call for Change.* New York: John Wiley and Sons, 1997, pp. 280–87.
11. Schein, "Reassessing the 'Divine Rights' of Managers"; Schein, Edgar H. "International Human Resource Management: New Directions, Perpetual Issues, and Missing Themes," *Human Resource Management* 25, no. 1 (1986): 169–76; Applegate, Lynda M., James I. Cash Jr., and D. Quinn Mills. "Information Technology and Tomorrow's Manager," *Harvard Business Review* 88, no. 6 (1988): 128–36; Drucker. "The Coming of the New Organization"; Peters, Tom. "Restoring American Competitiveness: Looking for New Models of Organizations," *Academy of Management Executive* 2, no. 2 (1988): 103–9; Semler, Ricardo. "Managing Without Managers," *Harvard Business Review* 67, no. 5 (1989): 76–84.
12. Schein. "International Human Resource Management: New Directions, Perpetual Issues, and Missing Themes."
13. Greller, Martin M., and David M. Nee. *From Baby Boom to Baby Bust.* Reading, MA: Addison-Wesley, 1989; Snow, Charles C., Raymond E. Miles, and Henry J. Coleman Jr. "Managing 21st Century Network Organizations," *Organizational Dynamics* 20, no. 3 (1992): 5–20.
14. Tanouye, Elyse. "Johnson & Johnson Stays Fit by Shuffling Its Mix of Businesses," *Wall Street Journal* (December 22, 1992): A1, A4; Greller and Nee. *From Baby Boom to Baby Bust.* Johnson & Johnson. *1999 Annual Report.*
15. Johnson & Johnson. *1999 Annual Report*, p. 5.
16. Greller and Nee. *From Baby Boom to Baby Bust.*
17. Greller and Nee. *From Baby Boom to Baby Bust;* Greller and Nee. "Baby Boom and Baby Bust: Corporate Response to the Demographic Challenge of 1990–2010."
18. Snow, Miles, and Coleman. "Managing 21st Century Network Organizations"; Miles, Raymond E., Charles C. Snow, John A. Mathews, Grant Miles, and Henry J. Coleman Jr. "Organizing in the Knowledge Age: Anticipating the Cellular Form," *Academy of Management Executive* 11, no. 4 (1997): 7–21. Allred, Brent B., Charles C. Snow, and Raymond E. Miles. "Characteristics of Managerial Careers in the 21st Century," *Academy of Management Executive* 10, no. 4 (1996): 17–27. Jones, Thomas M., and Norman E. Bowie. "Moral Hazards on the Road to the 'Virtual' Corporation," *Business Ethics Quarterly* 8, no. 2 (1998): 273–92.
19. Allred, Snow, and Miles. "Characteristics of Managerial Careers in the 21st Century."
20. Ibid.
21. Greller and Nee. *From Baby Boom to Baby Bust.*
22. Belous, Richard S. "How Human Resource Systems Adjust to the Shift Toward Contingent Workers," *Monthly Labor Review* 112, no. 3 (1989): 7–12.
23. Neumeier, Shalley. "Economic Intelligence: How Jobs Die—And Are Born," *Fortune* (July 26, 1993): 26.
24. Schuler, Randall S., and Drew L. Harris. "Deming Quality Improvement: Implications for Human Resource Management as Illustrated in a Small Company," *Human Resource Planning* 14, no. 3 (1991): 191–207; Darling, John R. "Team Building in the Small Business Firm," *Journal of Small Business Management* 28, no. 3 (1990): 86–91; Forward, Gordon E. "Wide-open Management at Chaparral Steel," *Harvard Business Review* 64, no. 3 (1986): 96–102; Rogers, T. J. "No Excuses Management," *Harvard Management Review* 90, no. 4 (1990): 84–98; Semler, Ricardo. "Managing Without Managers," *Harvard Business Review* 67, no. 5 (1989): 76–84.
25. Lipset, Seymour M. "The Work Ethic—Then and Now," *The Public Interest*, no. 98 (Winter 1990): 61.
26. Lipset. "The Work Ethic—Then and Now"; Harris, T. George, and Robert J. Trotter. "Work Smarter, Not Harder," *Psychology Today* 23, no. 2 (1989): 33; Skrzycki, Cindy. "Poll Finds Less Worker Emphasis on Materialism," *Washington Post* (January 10, 1989): C1, C4.
27. Pare, Terence P. "The Uncommitted Class of 1989," *Fortune* 119 (June 5, 1989): 199.
28. Yankelovich, Daniel, and Bernard Lefkowitz. "Work and American Expectations," *National Forum: Phi Kappa Phi Journal* 62, no. 2 (1982): 3–5.

29. Braham, James. "Dying Loyalty: Companies, Employees Both Less Faithful," *Industry Week* (June 1, 1987): 16–17.
30. Braham. "Dying Loyalty: Companies, Employees Both Less Faithful"; "Complain, Complain, Complain: Worker Cynicism on the Rise," *Management Review* 76, no. 6 (1987): 10–11; Kanter, Donald L., and Philip H. Mirvis. "Cynicism: The New American Malaise," *Business and Society Review* 77, no. 2 (1991): 57–61.
31. Pinfield, Lawrence T. "A Comparison of Pre- and Postemployment Work Values," *Journal of Management* 10, no. 3 (1984): 363–70.
32. Elizur, Dov, Ingwer Borg, Raymond Hunt, and Istvan M. Beck. "The Structure of Work Values: A Cross Cultural Comparison," *Journal of Organizational Behavior* 12 (1991): 21–38.
33. Offermann, Lynn R., and Marilyn K. Gowing. "Organizations of the Future: Changes and Challenges," *American Psychologist* 45, no. 2: 95–108; Yankelovich and Lefkowitz. "Work and American Expectations."
34. Skrzycki, Cindy. "Poll Finds Less Worker Emphasis on Materialism," *Washington Post* (January 10, 1989): C1.
35. Jarley, Paul, and Jack Fiorito. "Unionism and Changing Employee Views Toward Work," *Journal of Labor Research* 12, no. 3 (1991): 223–29; Judge, Timothy A., and Robert D. Bretz Jr. "Effects of Work Values on Job Choice Decisions," *Journal of Applied Psychology* 77, no. 3 (1992): 261–71.
36. Offermann and Gowing. "Organizations of the Future: Changes and Challenges."
37. Wagel, William H. "On the Horizon: HR in the 1990s," *Personnel* 67, no. 1 (1990): 11–16; Luthans, Fred, and Linda Thomas. "The Relationship Between Age and Job Satisfaction: Curvilinear Results From an Empirical Study," *Personnel Review* 18, no. 1 (1989): 23–26.
38. McLeod, Poppy L., and Sharon Alisa Lobel. "The Effects of Ethnic Diversity on Idea Generation in Small Groups," *Academy of Management Best Papers Proceedings* (1992): 227–31; Cox, Taylor H., and Stacy Blake. "Managing Cultural Diversity: Implications for Organizational Competitiveness," *Academy of Management Executive* 5, no. 3 (1991): 45–56.
39. Cox and Blake. "Managing Cultural Diversity: Implications for Organizational Competitiveness."
40. Thomas, R. Roosevelt. "From Affirmative Action to Affirming Diversity," *Harvard Business Review* 90, no. 2 (1990): 107–17.
41. Ibid., p. 108.
42. McLeod and Lobel. "The Effects of Ethnic Diversity on Idea Generation in Small Groups."
43. Ibid., p. 229.
44. Fullerton, Howard N. Jr. "Labor Force Projections to 2008: Steady Growth and Changing Composition," *Monthly Labor Review* 122, no. 11 (2000): 19–32.
45. Katzenbach, Jon R., and Douglas K. Smith. "Why Teams Matter," *The McKinsey Quarterly* no. 3 (1992): 3–27.
46. Ibid., p. 5.
47. Bergstrom, Robin P. "The Team's the Thing," *Production* 104, no. 5 (1992): 46–51; Dean, James W. Jr., and Gerald I. Susman. "Organizing for Manufacturable Design," *Harvard Business Review* 67 no. 1 (1989): 28–32; Sundstrom, Eric, Kenneth P. De Meuse, and David Futrell. "Work Teams: Applications and Effectiveness," *American Psychologist* 45, no. 2 (1990): 120–33; Katzenhbach and Smith. "Why Teams Matter"; Jackson, Susan E., and Eden B. Alvarez. "Working Through Diversity as a Strategic Imperative," in Susan E. Jackson and Associates (Eds.), *Diversity in the Workplace: Human Resources Initiatives.* New York: Guilford Press, 1993, pp. 13–29; Wolfe, Joseph, Donald D. Bowen, and C. Richard Roberts. "Team-Building Effects on Company Performance," *Simulation and Games* 20, no. 4 (1989): 388–408.
48. Sundstrom, De Meuse, and Futrell. "Work Teams: Applications and Effectiveness."
49. King, Ralph T. Jr. "Levi's Factory Workers Are Assigned to Teams and Morale Takes a Hit," *Wall Street Journal* (May 20, 1998): A1, A6.
50. Katzenbach and Smith. "Why Teams Matter"; Sisco, Rebecca. "Put Your Money Where Your Teams Are," *Training* 29, no. 7 (1992): 41–45.
51. Dean and Susman. "Organizing for Manufacturable Design."

52. Bergstrom. "The Team's the Thing."

53. Ibid.

54. Eom, Sean B., and Choong Kwon Lee. "Virtual Teams: An Information Age Opportunity for Mobilizing Hidden Manpower," *Advanced Management Journal* 64, no. 2 (1999): 12–15.

55. Harkins, Philip J., Stephen M. Brown, and Russell Sullivan. "Shining New Light on a Growing Trend," *HRMagazine* 40, no. 12 (1995): 75–79; Greer, Youngblood, and Gray. "Human Resource Management Outsourcing: The Make or Buy Decision."

56. Ibid.

57. Ibid.

58. Davis, Tim. "Open-Book Management: Its Promise and Pitfalls," *Organizational Dynamics* 25, no. 1 (1997): 6–19.

59. Case, John. *The Open-Book Experience: Lessons from Over 100 Companies Who Successfully Transformed Themselves.* Reading, MA: Perseus Books, 1998.

60. Ibid., pp. 95–96.

61. Case. *The Open-Book Experience: Lessons from Over 100 Companies Who Successfully Transformed Themselves*; Hall, Cheryl. "An Open-Book Policy," *Dallas Morning News* (June 28, 1998): 1H–2H.

62. Ibid.

63. Hart, Christopher, and Leonard Schlesinger. "TQM and the HR Professional: Applying the Baldrige Framework to Human Resources," *Human Resource Management* 30, no. 4 (1991): 433–54; Barrier, Michael. "Small Firms Put Quality First," *Nation's Business* (May 1992): 22–32; Blackburn, Richard, and Benson Rosen. "Total Quality and Human Resource Management: Lessons Learned from Baldrige Award-Winning Companies," *Academy of Management Executive* 7, no. 3 (1993): 49–66; Bowen, David E., and Edward E. Lawler, III. "Total Quality-Oriented Human Resources Management," *Organizational Dynamics* 20, no. 4 (1992): 29–41.

64. Blackburn and Rosen. "Total Quality and Human Resources Management: Lessons Learned from Baldrige Award-Winning Companies"; Hart and Schlesinger. "Total Quality Management and the Human Resource Professional: Applying the Baldrige Framework to Human Resources."

65. Bowen and Lawler. "Total Quality-Oriented Human Resources Management," p. 31.

66. Ulrich, Dave, Wayne Brockbank, and Arthur Yeung. "Beyond Belief: A Benchmark for Human Resources," *Human Resources Management* 28, no. 3 (1989): 312.

67. Bowen and Lawler. "Total Quality-Oriented Human Resources Management."

68. Barrier. "Small Firms Put Quality First," p. 25.

69. Bowen and Lawler. "Total Quality-Oriented Human Resources Management."

70. Blackburn and Rosen. "Total Quality and Human Resources Management: Lessons Learned from Baldrige Award-Winning Companies."

71. Bowen and Lawler. "Total Quality-Oriented Human Resources Management"; Duncan, Jack, and Joseph G. Van Matre. "The Gospel According to Deming: Is It Really New?" *Business Horizons* 33, no. 4 (1990): 33–39; Barrier. "Small Firms Put Quality First"; Blackburn and Rosen. "Total Quality and Human Resource Management: Lessons Learned from Baldrige Award-Winning Companies."

72. Harari, Oren. "Ten Reasons Why TQM Doesn't Work," *Management Review* 82, no. 1 (1993): 33–38; Blackburn and Rosen. "Total Quality and Human Resources Management: Lessons Learned from Baldrige Award-Winning Companies"; Harari, Oren. "The Eleventh Reason Why TQM Doesn't Work," *Management Review* 82, no. 5 (1993): 34–37; Niven, Daniel. "When Times Get Tough, What Happens to TQM," *Harvard Business Review* 71, no. 3 (1993): 20–34; Schlesinger, Jacob M., Michael Williams, and Craig Forman. "Japan Inc., Wracked by Recession, Takes Stock of Its Methods," *Wall Street Journal* (September 19, 1993): A1–A4.

73. Niven. "When Times Get Tough, What Happens to TQM," p. 32.

74. Snell, Scott A., and James W. Dean Jr. "Integrated Manufacturing and Human Resource Management: A Human Capital Perspective," *Academy of Management Journal* 35, no. 3 (1992): 467–504.

75. Snell and Dean. "Integrated Manufacturing and Human Resource Management: A Human Capital Perspective."

76. Stewart, Thomas A. "Reengineering: The New Management Tool," *Fortune* (August 23, 1993): 41–48; Moad, Jeff. "Does Reengineering Really Work?" *Datamation* (August 1, 1993): 22–28.
77. Stewart, Thomas A. "Reengineering: The New Management Tool," *Fortune* (August 23, 1993): 41–48; Moad. "Does Reengineering Really Work?"
78. Hall, Gene, Jim Rosenthal, and Judy Wade. "How to Make Reengineering Really Work," *Harvard Business Review* 71, no. 6 (1993): 119–31.
79. Stewart. "Reengineering: The New Management Tool"; Moad. "Does Reengineering Really Work?"; Hall, Rosenthal, and Wade. "How to Make Reengineering Really Work."
80. Von Glinow, Mary Anne. *The New Professionals: Managing Today's High-Tech Employees.* Cambridge, MA: Ballinger, 1988.
81. Von Glinow. *The New Professionals: Managing Today's High Tech Employees*, p. 27.
82. Von Glinow. *The New Professionals: Managing Today's High-Tech Employees.*
83. Barkman, Arnold I., John E. Sheridan, and Lawrence H. Peters. "Survival Models of Professional Staff Retention in Public Accounting Firms," *Journal of Managerial Issues* 4, no. 3 (1992): 339–53.
84. Bruckman, John C., and Scott C. Peters. "Mergers and Acquisitions: The Human Equation," *Employment Relations Today* 14, no. 1 (1987): 55–63.
85. Ibid., p. 57.
86. Bruckman and Peters. "Mergers and Acquisitions: The Human Equation."
87. Walker, James W. *Human Resource Planning.* New York: McGraw-Hill, 1980; Greller and Nee. "Baby Boom and Baby Bust: Corporate Response to the Demographic Challenge of 1990–2010"; Greller and Nee. *From Baby Boom to Baby Bust*; Johnston, William B., and Arnold H. Packer. *Workforce 2000: Work and Workers for the Twenty-first Century.* Indianapolis: Hudson Institute, 1987.
88. Fullerton. "Labor Force Projections to 2008: Steady Growth and Changing Composition."
89. Johnston and Packer. *Workforce 2000: Work and Workers for the Twenty-first Century.*
90. Jasinowski, Jerry, and Sharon Canner. *Meeting the Health Care Crisis.* Washington, DC: National Association of Manufacturers, 1989.
91. Rutledge, John, and Deborah Allen. *Rust to Riches.* New York: Harper and Row, 1989.
92. Fullerton, Howard W. "Evaluation of Labor Force Projections to 1990," *Monthly Labor Review* 115, no. 8 (1992): 3–14; Howard W. Fullerton. "New Labor Force Projections, Spanning 1988 to 2000," *Monthly Labor Review* 112, no. 11 (1989): 3–12.
93. Greller and Nee. "Baby Boom and Baby Bust: Corporate Response to the Demographic Challenge of 1990–2010"; American Association of Retired Persons. *The Aging Work Force: Managing an Aging Work Force*, 1990; Machan, Dyan. "Cultivating the Gray," *Forbes* (September 14, 1989): 127–28; Morrison, Peter A. "Applied Demography: Its Growing Scope and Future Direction," *The Futurist* 24, no. 2 (1990): 9–15; Fest, Glen. "Ready, Willing and Able," *Fort Worth Star-Telegram* (May 9, 2000): 1C–3C; Mergenhagen, Paula. "Enabling Disabled Workers," *American Demographics* 19 (July 1997): 36–42; "No End in Sight for Tight Labor Markets, Upward Pressure on Wages," *Compensation and Benefits Review* 31, no. 5 (1999): 23–26.
94. Challenger, John A. "There Is No Future for the Workplace," *The Futurist* 32, no. 7 (1998): 16.
95. "Employees Flee for Online Opportunities," *Industrial Distribution* 89, no. 2 (2000): 21, 25; "Raising the Bar," *Fortune* 141, no. 4 (2000): 113–16; Martel, Jennifer, and Laura A. Kelter. "The Job Market Remains Strong in 1999," *Monthly Labor Review* 123, no. 2 (2000): 3–23.
96. "Internet Recruiting Expert Defines Top Five Features Employers Must Consider in Choosing an Internet Job Site," *PR Newswire* (July 17, 1998); "Recruiting on the Internet," *Printing World* (May 10, 1999): 54; "Finding Workers Online Grows More Popular," *The Journal Record* (December 6, 1999).
97. Mergenhagen. "Enabling Disabled Workers."
98. Machan, Dyan. "Cultivating the Gray."
99. Greller and Nee. "Baby Boom and Baby Bust: Corporate Response to the Demographic Challenge of 1990–2010"; Murray, Alan. "Bush Sees Labor Shortage, Looks Abroad," *Wall Street Journal* (February 7, 1990); Johnston and Packer. *Workforce 2000: Work and Workers for the Twenty-first Century.*

100. Morrison. "Applied Demography: Its Growing Scope and Future Direction," p. 11.

101. Johnston and Packer. *Workforce 2000: Work and Workers for the Twenty-first Century*, p. 100.

102. Braddock, Douglas. "Occupational Employment Projections to 2008," *Monthly Labor Review* 122, no. 11 (1999): 51–80.

103. Fullerton. "Labor Force Projections to 2008: Steady Growth and Changing Composition."

104. Jackson, Susan E., and Randall S. Schuler. "Human Resource Planning: Challenges for Industrial/Organizational Psychologists," *American Psychologist* 45, no. 2 (1990): 223–39.

105. Challenger. "There Is No Future for the Workplace"; Caudron, Shari. "The Female Profession," *Training and Development* 53, no. 5 (1999): 54–55; Fullerton. "Labor Force Projections to 2008: Steady Growth and Changing Composition," "Women Partners on the Rise," *Journal of Accountancy* 188, no. 6 (1999): 20; Johnston and Packer. *Workforce 2000: Work and Workers for the Twenty-first Century*; Naisbitt, John, and Patricia Aburdene. *Megatrends 2000: Ten New Directions for the 1990's*. New York: William Morrow and Company, 1990.

106. Schrenk, Lorenz P. "Environmental Scanning," in Lee Dyer (Ed.), *Human Resource Management: Evolving Roles and Responsibilities*. Washington, DC: Bureau of National Affairs, 1988, pp. 1-88–1-124; Kovach, Kenneth A., and John A. Pearce II. "HR Strategic Mandates for the 1990s," *Personnel* 67, no. 4 (1990): 50–55; Redwood, Anthony. "Human Resources Management in the 1990s," *Business Horizons* 33, no. 1 (1990): 74–80; Stautberg, Susan S. "Status Report: The Corporation and Trends in Family Issues," *Human Resource Management* 26, no. 2 (1987): 277–90; Challenger. "There Is No Future for the Workplace."

107. Morrison. "Applied Demography: Its Growing Scope and Future Direction."

108. Stautberg. "Status Report: The Corporation and Trends in Family Issues."

109. Naisbitt and Aburdene. *Megatrends 2000: Ten New Directions for the 1990s*; Wilde, Candee. "Telework Programs—High-Speed Access Technologies Like Cable Modems and DSL Give Telecommuting a Lift," *InternetWeek* (April 17, 2000): 40.

110. Morant, Dave. "Liability, Bosses Are Big Drags on Spread of Telecommuting," *Omaha World-Herald* (January 16, 2000): 11; Wilde. "Telework Programs—High-Speed Access Technologies Like Cable Modems and DSL Give Telecommuting a Lift"; Kunde, Diana. "Managers Key to Telecommuting," *The London Free Press* (January 26, 2000): D10.

111. Metzger, Robert O., and Mary Ann Von Glinow. "Off-Site Workers: At Home and Abroad," *California Management Review* 30, no. 3 (1988): 101–9; Morant. "Liability, Bosses Are Big Drags on Spread of Telecommuting"; Wilde. "Telework Programs—High-Speed Access Technologies Like Cable Modems and DSL Give Telecommuting a Lift."

112. Metzger and Von Glinow. "Off-Site Workers: At Home and Abroad"; Morant. "Liability, Bosses Are Big Drags on Spread of Telecommuting"; Bruzzese, Anita. "Companies Often Ignore Telecommuting Option Ninety-Three Percent of Human Resource Managers Surveyed Say Their Companies Provide No Work-at-Home Training to Employees," *Des Moines Register* (April 16, 2000): 2; Challenger. "There Is No Future for the Workplace."

113. Naisbitt and Aburdene. *Megatrends 2000: Ten New Directions for the 1990s.*

114. Stern, Richard L., and John H. Taylor. "Is the Golden State Losing It?" *Forbes* 146, no. 10 (October, 1990): 86–90.

115. Kerwin, Kathleen, and Ronald Grover. "California Steamin': Business Makes Tracks From L.A.," *Business Week* (May 13, 1991): 44–45.

116. Barsky, Neil. "Grace Will Move Most of Its Staff Out of New York," *Wall Street Journal* (January 9, 1991): B1.

117. Barrier, Michael. "Temporary Assignment," *Nation's Business* 77, no. 10 (October 1989): 34–36; Mangum, Garth, Donald Mayall, and Kristin Nelson. "The Temporary Help Industry: A Response to the Dual Internal Labor Markets," *Industrial and Labor Relations Review* 28, no. 4 (1985): 599–611; Belous, Richard S. "How Human Resource Systems Adjust to the Shift Toward Contingent Workers," *Monthly Labor Review* 112, no. 3 (1989): 7–12; Moberly, Robert B. "Temporary, Part-Time, and Other Atypical Employment Relationships in the United States," *Labor Law Journal* 38, no. 11 (1987): 689–96.

118. Howe, Wayne J. "Temporary Help Workers: Who They Are, What Jobs They Hold," *Monthly Labor Review* 109, no. 11 (1986): 45–47.

119. Barrier. "Temporary Assignments"; Mangum, Mayall, and Nelson. "The Temporary Help Industry: A Response to the Dual Internal Labor Markets."

120. Personick, Valerie A. "Industry Output and Employment: A Slower Trend for the Nineties," *Monthly Labor Review* 111, no. 11 (1989): 25–41; Davidson, Margaret. "Temporary Financial Executives: Who Are They and Who Uses Them?" *Financial Executive* 6, no. 2 (1990): 15–18; Ludlum, David A. "Now It's Temporary Managers," *Computerworld* (September 5, 1988): 92. Mangum, Mayall, and Nelson. "The Temporary Help Industry: A Response to the Dual Internal Labor Markets."

121. Mitchell, Daniel J. B., and Mahmood A. Zaidi. "Macroeconomic Conditions and HRM-IR Practice," *Industrial Relations* 29, no. 2 (1990): 164–88; Barrier. "Temporary Assignments"; Howe. "Temporary Help Workers: Who They Are, What Jobs They Hold"; Moberly. "Temporary, Part-Time, and Other Atypical Employment Relationships in the United States."

122. Barrier. "Temporary Assignments."

123. Darrow, Terri L. "Temporary Expertise Develops Into a Permanent Solution," *Management Review* 78, no. 11 (1989): 50–52; Mangum, Mayall, and Nelson. "The Temporary Help Industry: A Response to the Dual Internal Labor Markets."

124. Howe. "Temporary Help Workers: Who They Are, What Jobs They Hold"; Barrier. "Temporary Assignments"; Rothstein, Mark A., Andria S. Knapp, and Lance Liebman. *Cases and Materials on Employment Law* (2nd ed.). Westbury, NY: The Foundation Press, 1991; Colosi, Marco L. "WARN: Hazardous to HR Health?" *Personnel* 66, no. 4 (1989): 59–67; Barrier. "Temporary Assignment"; Darrow. "Temporary Expertise Develops Into a Permanent Solution."

125. Belous. "How Human Resource Systems Adjust to the Shift Toward Contingent Workers"; Mangum, Mayall, and Nelson. "The Temporary Help Industry: A Response to the Dual Internal Labor Markets"; Howe. "Temporary Help Workers: Who They Are, What Jobs They Hold."

126. Belous. "How Human Resource Systems Adjust to the Shift Toward Contingent Workers"; Davidson. "Temporary Financial Executives: Who Are They and Who Uses Them?"; Darrow. "Temporary Expertise Develops Into a Permanent Solution"; Moberly. "Temporary, Part-Time, and Other Atypical Employment Relationships in the United States."

127. Resnick, Rosalind. "Leasing Workers," *Nation's Business* (November 1992): 20–28.

128. Resnick. "Leasing Workers."

129. Dana Corporation. *Annual Report*, 1987.

130. Honeywell Corporation. *Annual Report*, 1985.

131. Metzger, Robert O., and Mary Ann Von Glinow. "Off-Site Workers: At Home and Abroad," *California Management Review* 30, no. 3 (1988): 101–9.

132. Flint, Jerry. "Letter from Germany," *Forbes* (October 29, 1990): 72–76.

133. McClenahen, John S. "NAFTA Works: And Not Just by Moving Production to Mexico," *Industry Week* 249, no. 1 (January 10, 2000): 5–6; U.S. Department of State. "Background Notes: Mexico, August 1999," Released by the Bureau of Western Hemisphere Affairs, U.S. Department of State, 1999; Fox, Adrienne. "Losing Ground on Free Trade," *Investor's Business Daily* (September 26, 1997): A1; Bagsarian, Tom. "NAFTA at 5: A Boon for Customers," *New Steel* 15, no. 10 (1999): 18–22.

134. Cerruti, James L., and Joseph Holtzman. "Business Strategy in the New European Landscape," *Journal of Business Strategy* 10, no. 6 (1990): 18–23; Goette, Eckart E. "Europe 1992: Update for Business Planners," *Journal of Business Strategy* 10, no. 2 (1990): 10–13; Devinney, Timothy M., and William C. Hightower. *European Markets after 1992.* Lexington, MA: Lexington Books, 1991; Oster, Patrick, Bill Javetski, and Gail E. Schares. "It's 1993—and Europe Can Pop a Few Corks After All," *Business Week* (January 11, 1993): 48.

CASE 2

U.S. Automobile Manufacturing in the Twenty-First Century

In 1989, economists John Rutledge and Deborah Allen predicted a resurgence of U.S. manufacturing before the new century. They predicted that resurgence would be stimulated by increased investment in the capital base of machinery and tools by which products are manufactured. When they made their prediction, many U.S. manufacturers were using outdated tools and machines, compared with those of global competitors. As a result, some U.S. products were not competitive in price or quality.

Factors expected to drive the resurgence of manufacturing included a low rate of inflation and the demographic influences associated with the baby boom. U.S. manufacturing investment stagnated during earlier periods of high inflation, which reached 14 percent in 1980. High inflation caused investors to purchase tangible assets, such as hotels and office buildings, as inflation hedges. Since stocks and bonds do not provide this same hedge, they became less attractive investments and funding for the plant and equipment needed for production of goods became more difficult to obtain. The attack on inflation during the 1980s and tax reform made tangible assets less attractive as inflation hedges and tax shields. Stocks and bonds then became relatively more attractive.[1]

One foundation for the economists' prediction was aging of the baby boomers. When the economists made their predictions, the baby boomers had reached their mid-forties and were predicted to start to save more. The savings of this huge age cohort were expected to serve as major sources of funding for the new plant and equipment needed to make U.S. manufacturing competitive in world markets.[2] The oldest of the baby boomers were in their mid-fifties in 2000 and will be in their mid-sixties in 2010. As pointed out in Chapter 2, this is a huge age cohort and is expected to push the median age of the U.S. labor force to 45 in 2008. As a result of the baby boomers and past layoffs based on inverse seniority, some U.S. manufacturing firms in the year 2000 had workforces with an average age in the mid-fifties.

Employment in manufacturing was fairly stable in the 1990s while manufacturing productivity increased. With increased productivity, fewer workers were needed to manufacture the same amount of goods. (The health of the industry is not necessarily indicated by whether there is a growing or declining level of employment.) Furthermore, some manufacturing employment shifted to the services sector as a result of outsourcing. (Employees of firms supplying services, such as information services, for manufacturing companies are not counted in manufacturing employment.[3])

Interestingly, in automobile manufacturing the capital requirements for assembly plants has declined as indicated in the following:

> We could be seeing a radical transformation in where and how cars are built, predicts David Cole, director of the Office for the Study of Automotive Transportation at the University of Michigan in Ann Arbor. But will we? Assembly plants can now be built for around US$400 million, instead of the $1 billion they historically cost. These "disposable plants" could, at least in theory, be readily written off, making site selection decisions extremely flexible and short-term. "We've learned a lot about plant design and about designing with less redundancy," explains Cole.[4]

In addition, experts on the automobile industry say that labor costs are increasing in Mexico and that it actually costs more to build a plant in Mexico.

> "Mexico is still generally a cheaper place to do business, but not as cheap as it used to be. Labor, for example, is getting more expensive . . . The labor force in northern Mexico is getting increasingly sophisticated, and wages have gone up." . . . Building a plant in Mexico also entails a number of unexpected costs . . . "Simple materials like concrete may be cheaper, but overall, I can build a plant cheaper in South Carolina than I can in Mexico" . . . That's because there are few to no local suppliers for more sophisticated building systems like air conditioning, and because the energy and water constraints mean the plant has to be built for greater efficiencies than would be necessary in the United States.[5]

Interestingly, the labor costs of producing automobiles in Canada are lower than in the United States and productivity is substantially higher. Additional developments in the automobile industry are that the manufacturers would like to sell automobiles over the Internet, which they predict would reduce the average price of automobiles by approximately $1,000. However, there is stiff resistance from the dealers who have been able to obtain legal restrictions making direct sales more difficult for manufacturers. Finally, the United Auto Workers (UAW) has lifetime employment agreements with the automobile manufacturers.[6]

Questions

1. Consider all of the information provided in this case and your knowledge of current economic and business conditions. What human resource issues should managers in the automobile industry be prepared for in the future?
2. How might the employee skills, management practices, and automobile manufacturing companies change in the future? How would you expect the managerial trends discussed in Chapter 2 to affect human resource practices and policies in future automobile manufacturing?
3. Describe how the human resource and managerial environments of automobile manufacturing firms in the twenty-first century differ from the same environments in the 1970s. (You may need to do some reading or interview someone who

can provide a historical perspective.) Try to explain these differences with respect to the effects of technology, organizational structure, worker values, managerial trends, demographic trends, and trends in the utilization of human resources.

4. Explain how the North American Free Trade Agreement may affect the U.S. automobile manufacturing workforce in the United States by the year 2010.

References

1. Rutledge, John, and Deborah Allen. *Rust to Riches.* New York: Harper and Row, 1989.
2. Ibid.
3. Masur, Sandra. "The North American Free Trade Agreement: Why It's in the Interest of U.S. Business," *Columbia Journal of World Business* 26, no. 2 (1991): 99–103; Flint. "The Myth of U.S. Manufacturing's Decline," *Forbes* (January 18, 1993): 40–42.
4. Aron, Laurie Joan. "Automotive Industry: Searching for Speed," *Site Selection* 45, no. 1 (2000): 129.
5. Ibid.
6. Aron. "Automotive Industry: Searching for Speed"; Ball, Jeffrey. "Auto Dealers, Fearing That Detroit Will Hog the Web, Fight Back," *Wall Street Journal* (May 10, 2000): A1–A12.

CHAPTER 3

The Human Resource Legal Environment

The third component of the conceptual framework for this book is the legal environment of human resources. Because of its increasing coverage and complexity, the legal environment has more strategic importance than ever before. All managers making input into strategic decisions, not just those involved in human resources, must be familiar with the laws that regulate employer conduct in dealing with employees. Because the coverage of such laws and regulations has become so pervasive, they must be considered as input in overall strategy formulation and have probably increased the involvement of human resource management in the process. There is also growing recognition of the strategic importance of having good human resource management programs in order to limit the financial outlays of litigation initiated by disgruntled employees and job applicants. Further, as the following quotation by Francine Hall and Elizabeth Hall indicates, practices ensuring legal compliance can sometimes provide a source of strategic advantage.[1]

> While few firms have missions that are inconsistent with the ADA [Americans with Disabilities Act of 1990], many have yet to seize the opportunity to link compliance with purpose . . . There are many examples of how select companies have tied their human resource initiatives to their strategic advantage. Johnson and Johnson, Stride-Rite, and others have become examples of the "family friendly" movement. McDonald's has been a forerunner by embracing the ADA and modeling the employment of learning-disabled young adults. Most families (the target market for McDonald's) can identify with the need to give a child a chance.[2]

Author's note: In preparing this chapter, the author drew on a large number of articles and books. A few sources were particularly helpful and were cited several times. These sources, which would be excellent reference books for practitioners, are Robert Jacobs and Cora Koch's *Legal Compliance Guide to Personnel Management*, David Twomey's *Equal Employment Opportunity Law*, Patrick Cibon and James Castagnera's *Labor and Employment Law*, Commerce Clearing House's *Labor Law Course*, and Mark Rothstein, Andria Knapp, and Lance Liebman's *Cases and Materials on Employment Law*.

The importance of the human resource legal environment can be demonstrated with a few examples. For instance, in order to respond more quickly to the needs of its customers, a company might consider a decentralization strategy in which traditional functional responsibilities are reassigned to line units. In this example, the human resource function might be decentralized by reassigning corporate-level human resource responsibilities, such as recruitment and staffing, to the line units. However, with passage of the Americans with Disabilities Act of 1990 the company may wish to avoid increased liability from violations of disabled applicants' rights, which might be more likely when line managers have sole responsibility for recruitment and staffing. In this example, the legal environment might cause the company to modify its approach to decentralization.

Similarly, the advance notification requirements of the Worker Adjustment and Retraining Notification Act (WARN) passed in 1988,[3] which are covered in the Chapter 6 discussion of strategy implementation, may affect the timing of a company's strategic decision to withdraw from a line of business. More strategic implications of the legal environment, specifically those involving economy and managerial flexibility, will be discussed at the end of the chapter after coverage of the various federal laws. In this chapter, the federal regulatory environment will receive the most emphasis, although some areas of state law also will be covered. Areas of the legal environment to be discussed include equal employment opportunity, compensation, employee relations, labor relations, and emerging issues. Table 3-1 provides a summary of federal laws relevant to human resource management.

EQUAL EMPLOYMENT OPPORTUNITY

Continued emphasis on equal employment opportunity and affirmative action appears to be a reality for the foreseeable future and is an issue of importance for strategic management. The following section will provide a review of equal employment opportunity legislation, beginning with civil rights legislation.

Civil Rights Legislation

Title VII of the Civil Rights Act of 1964 provides the basic requirements for equal employment opportunity. As amended by the Equal Employment Opportunity Act of 1972, Title VII prohibits the following discriminatory practices:

> It shall be an unlawful employment practice for an employer—(1) to fail or refuse to hire or to discharge any individual, or otherwise to discriminate against any individual with respect to his compensation, terms, conditions, or privileges of employment, because of such individual's race, color, religion, sex, or national origin; or (2) to limit, segregate, or classify his employees or applicants for employ-

TABLE 3-1 Federal Laws Affecting Human Resource Management

Law or Executive Order	*Impact*	*Coverage*
Railway Labor Act of 1926 (RLA)	Provides employees with rights to unionize and engage in collective bargaining	Railroads and airlines
Davis Bacon Act of 1931	Sets minimum (prevailing) wage standards	Employers having construction contracts with the federal government
National Labor Relations Act of 1935 (NLRA) as amended by the Labor Management Relations Act of 1947 (LMRA) and the Labor Management Reporting and Disclosure Act of 1959 (LMDRA)	Provides employees with rights to unionize and engage in collective bargaining; specifies employer and union unfair labor practices; provides for the National Labor Relations Board (NLRB) to administer the act	Private sector employers engaged in interstate commerce (nonretail establishments having $50,000 or more input or output across state lines or retail establishments having $500,000 or more in annual sales) and unions
Walsh-Healy Public Contracts Act of 1936	Sets minimum (prevailing) wage standards	Employers having contracts with the federal government
Fair Labor Standards Act of 1938 (FSLA)	Sets minimum wage standards and governs underage employment	Employers having at least $500,000 in annual sales; for lesser amounts, coverage applies to employees engaged in interstate commerce
Portal-to-Portal Act of 1947	Specifies work-related activities for which wages must be paid	Same as Fair Labor Standards Act
Equal Pay Act of 1963	Requires equal pay for equal work regardless of gender	Same as Fair Labor Standards Act
Civil Rights Act of 1964 as amended by the Equal Employment Opportunity Act of 1972 and the Civil Rights Act of 1991	Prohibits employment discrimination on the basis of race, color, religion, sex, or national origin	Employers having at least 15 employees
Age Discrimination in Employment Act of 1967 as amended in 1978 and in 1986 (ADEA) and by the Older Workers Benefit Protection Act of 1990	Prohibits discrimination on the basis of age for individuals 40 and older with exceptions for executives, police, firefighters, and some governmental officials	Employers having at least 20 employees
Occupational Safety and Health Act of 1970 (OSHA)	Requires employers to provide a workplace free from recognized hazards	Applies to all employers with no minimum size exclusions

(continued)

TABLE 3-1 *(continued)*

Law or Executive Order	*Impact*	*Coverage*
Employee Retirement Income Security Act of 1974 (ERISA)	Governs funding and administration of pension plans	Employers offering health, pension, severance, or welfare-related benefits
Pregnancy Discrimination Act of 1978 (amendment to Civil Rights Act)	Prohibits employment discrimination on the basis of pregnancy	Employers having at least 15 employees
Consolidated Omnibus Budget Reconciliation Act of 1985 (COBRA)	Requires employers to continue health benefits for employees who have terminated their employment relationship at 102% of the employer's cost for 18 to 36 months	Employers having at least 20 employees
Americans with Disabilities Act of 1990 (ADA) (provides more comprehensive coverage than the Rehabilitation Act of 1973)	Prevents employment discrimination of disabled individuals and requires employers to make reasonable accommodation	Employers having 15 or more employees
Immigration Reform and Control Act of 1986 (IRCA)	Requires employers to determine that job applicants are legally qualified to be employed	
Worker Adjustment and Retraining Notification Act (WARN) (1988)	Requires 60 days' advance notice of plant closures and large-scale layoffs	Employers having 100 or more employees
Family and Medical Leave Act of 1993 (FMLA)	Requires unpaid leave for birth and adoption of children; care of seriously ill children, spouses, or parents; or serious health problems of the employee	Employers having 50 or more employees
Health Insurance Portability and Accountability Act of 1996 (HIPAA)	Requires portability of health insurance when employees take jobs at other companies	

Note: Some laws are listed individually although they may be amendments of other laws.

Sources: The material in this table summarizes material presented in this chapter and in Chapter 6. Sources are identified in the chapters where the laws are discussed.

> ment in any way which would deprive or tend to deprive any individual of employment opportunities or otherwise adversely affect his status as an employee, because of such individual's race, color, religion, sex, or national origin.[4]

In addition to employers having at least 15 employees, the act also applies to employment agencies and labor organizations. In addition to specifying these unlawful practices, the Civil Rights Act of 1964 established the Equal Employment Opportunity Commission (EEOC) to administer and enforce the legislation.[5] In 1972, the act was amended by the Equal Employment Opportunity Act, which, among other changes, expanded the enforcement powers of the EEOC by allowing it to go to court to bring charges of discrimination.[6]

This legislation prohibits two forms of discrimination. The first form of discrimination is called *disparate treatment*. With this type of discrimination, the employer intentionally discriminates against individuals on the basis of one of the prohibited criteria, such as by not hiring them because of their race. The legislation also prohibits employment practices having an indirect but *adverse impact* on protected groups, which is called *disparate impact* discrimination. In contrast to the other form, a discriminatory intent is not required to establish that discrimination has occurred. The term *adverse impact* is frequently used synonymously with the term *disparate impact*.[7]

An example of disparate impact discrimination is an employer's use of an invalid selection test having no ability to predict successful job performance. In addition to the test's lack of validity, it rejects a disproportionate number of applicants from protected groups. The test's adverse impact and lack of validity constitutes a form of disparate impact discrimination. This interpretation of Title VII was established in the landmark U.S. Supreme Court decision, *Griggs v. Duke Power Co.*, which prohibited the use of selection tests having an adverse impact but no relationship with job performance.[8] Specifically, the court stated:

> The Act proscribes not only overt discrimination but also practices that are fair in form, but discriminatory in operation. The touchstone is business necessity. If an employment practice which operates to exclude Negroes cannot be shown to be related to job performance, the practice is prohibited.[9]

However, if such a test is valid or job-related (i.e., it predicts applicants' performance on the job), it can be used. This is true even if it has an adverse impact by rejecting a disproportionate number of applicants from protected groups. As a result of provisions of the Civil Rights Act of 1991, however, if a plaintiff can demonstrate that the employer is unwilling to use an alternate selection procedure having less adverse impact, the employer's use of the test may constitute a violation of the law. Additionally, although tests appear to trigger more concerns over disparate impact, the need to establish the validity of tests also extends to other selection procedures, such as the use of educational criteria for selection purposes, since they may also have a disparate impact.[10]

In addition to validity-based exceptions to prohibitions against the use of procedures having a disparate impact, there are other exceptions. Employers can use selection criteria having a disparate impact by demonstrating a *business necessity*. For example, a public transportation agency's decision not to hire methadone users was upheld, even for jobs in which safety was not an issue.[11] *Bona fide occupational qualifications* (BFOQ) also may provide highly restricted exceptions to prohibitions against disparate treatment. As an example, actors and models can be selected on the basis of their gender. Further, although race BFOQs are prohibited, in some narrowly defined instances, applicants have been selected on the basis of race. These have been justified for reasons of business necessity and have involved actors and police undercover roles. As a result of the Civil Rights Act of 1991, the status of this special exemption is now in question.[12]

In order to enforce the law, the EEOC, along with other enforcement agencies, adopted the *Uniform Guidelines on Employee Selection Procedures*, which cover such issues as the validation of selection procedures.[13] For the most part, these guidelines essentially call for sound validation procedures that employers should follow anyway in the absence of legislation. Any doubts about the employer's obligation to follow the guidelines were resolved in 1975 in a second landmark U.S. Supreme Court decision involving *Albemarle Paper Co. v. Moody*.[14] In this case, the employer had not conducted a suitable job analysis and its test validation was deficient.[15] In this ruling, the Supreme Court made it clear that employers should follow the guidelines. The Court's emphasis on job analysis in this decision points out the underlying importance of job analysis to test validation, performance evaluation, and job evaluation.

One of the technical details explained in the guidelines is the definition of adverse impact. Specifically, the guidelines define adverse impact as:

> A selection rate for any race, sex, or ethnic group which is less than four-fifths (4/5) (or eighty percent) of the rate for the group with the highest rate will generally be regarded by the Federal enforcement agencies as evidence of adverse impact.[16]

There are problems with such definitions of adverse impact since ratios computed on the basis of small numbers of employees can cause unstable results. In such cases, statistical significance tests would be more appropriate. Interestingly, it appears that courts are able to deal with these limitations. As Richard Arvey and Robert H. Faley have observed, "courts, judges, and lawyers are now demonstrating considerable statistical sophistication in employment discrimination cases." [17]

As a result of congressional disappointment with a number of U.S. Supreme Court decisions in 1989, which were felt to decrease the impact of existing civil rights legislation, the Civil Rights Act of 1991 was passed. Several provisions of the act represent significant changes in the regulatory environment. Disparate impact is now part of the statute, along with a burden of proof procedure that requires stronger employer justification of selection practices. The consequences of these changes are that employers have greater motivation to perform competent job analysis, specify important dimensions of job performance, and validate selection procedures.[18] Because there are several common approaches to job analysis, guides to their strengths and weakness, such as one prepared by Hubert Feild and Robert Gatewood,[19] may be helpful in this regard.

Some observers have predicted that employers may resort to hiring by quota in order to eliminate any disparate impact on protected groups. There have been anecdotal reports of quota-based overt reverse discrimination in retention decisions in which companies have been acquired.[20] In any event, "bottom line" defenses, at which such efforts may be directed, are questionable. The inadequacy of such defenses has been pointed out in the Supreme Court's *Connecticut v. Teal* decision.[21]

The Civil Rights Act of 1991 also prevents the *race-norming* of test scores. An example of such a practice could involve test score cutoff scores. With this example of race-norming, members of a protected group are hired if their scores are above the 80th percentile of scores from applicants in the protected group. Applicants from unprotected groups would be hired if their scores are above the 80th percentile of scores obtained by unprotected group members. Such a practice is likely to expose employers to reverse discrimination liabilities. Other important components of the Civil Rights Act of 1991 are the provision for punitive as well as compensatory damages for intentional discrimination; employers' defenses in so-called mixed-motive discrimination cases in which selection decisions have drawn on both legal and illegal criteria; and the timing of charges against discriminatory seniority systems.[22] The Civil Rights Act of 1991 also has strategic implications for U.S.-based multinational corporations having U.S. employees in their foreign operations. As a result of the 1991 amendment, the Civil Rights Act now applies extraterritorially to these employees.[23]

In addition to this legislation, employers doing business with the federal government must comply with the equal employment opportunity requirements specified in Executive Order 11246, its amendments, and Executive Order 11141. These executive orders prohibit employment discrimination based on race, color, religion, sex, or national origin. Smaller employers having contracts of at least $10,000 are prohibited from discriminating while employers having at least 50 employees and federal contracts of at least $50,000 or more must file written *affirmative action plans*. These plans must be filed with the Office of Federal Contract Compliance Programs (OFCCP), which enforces the executive orders. As a part of the preparation of an affirmative action plan, the employer must conduct a *utilization analysis* of members of protected groups within the company, at both entry-level and higher-level positions. These utilization levels must then be compared with an *availability analysis* of minorities and females in the company's relevant labor markets. Where minorities and females are underrepresented according to the utilization analysis, the employer must negotiate acceptable goals and timetables with the OFCCP. Aside from the affirmative action plan requirements of the OFCCP, courts may require employers found guilty of egregious Title VII violations to pursue affirmative action plans.[24]

Unfortunately, although the Civil Rights Act was passed many years ago and progress has been made, there is still justification for the continuance of affirmative action programs. Discriminatory behaviors in some of the country's largest companies provide evidence of the need for protection against discrimination and advancement of minorities and women. Recent examples include crude workplace humor and racial slurs directed against black employees at

American Eagle, the American Airlines commuter; racial discrimination against black employees at Dillard's; high-level executives' use of derogatory terms for black employees at Texaco; and discrimination against women in jobs and promotions at Publix Super Markets.[25]

Age Discrimination

The Age Discrimination in Employment Act (ADEA), which covers private sector employers having at least 20 employees, prohibits discrimination against employees and job applicants over age 40. The act also covers governmental employers at the state and local level. The ADEA was passed in 1967 and amended in 1978 and 1986. The original legislation protected individuals of ages 40 to 65, while the 1978 amendments increased the upper limit of the protected age category to 70. In 1986, the ADEA was amended to eliminate the upper limit of the protected age category, making it illegal to discriminate against anyone 40 years of age or older. Exceptions to these prohibitions include executives, who can be required to retire at age 65; firefighters and police officers; and elected governmental officials and policy-level appointees. In addition to ethical motivations for complying with the provisions of the ADEA, another reason for compliance is that the financial costs for violating the act can be severe. For willful violations of the act, employers may be liable for double the amount of actual damages.[26]

In order to cope with the removal of upper age limits in the legislation, employers are advised to adopt objective performance standards, preferably in writing. By using such standards as a basis for treatment of all employees, regardless of age, any decrease in performance can be documented and properly attributed to legitimate aspects of performance rather than age. Another suggestion is to ensure that periodic performance evaluations are conducted for all employees, including employees age 40 and older. A further suggestion is to train employees' supervisors and managers not to use age in making employment decisions. As discussed later, in this era of downsizing, managers need to exercise care in administering voluntary early retirement programs so as to not violate the ADEA. Finally, managers should attempt to maintain high levels of job satisfaction and self-esteem among older employees. They should take time to communicate to older workers that they are valued and appreciated. Giving older workers the opportunity to mentor younger employees also can help build morale. Declines in satisfaction and self-esteem have been found to be associated with perceptions of age discrimination.[27]

In addition to the amendments to the ADEA already noted, the Older Workers Benefit Protection Act amended the act again in 1990. This act prevents employers from providing lower levels of benefits to older workers, unless it can be demonstrated that the provision of equal benefits for older workers is more costly. The act also addresses the coercive circumstances in which older workers sometimes waive their rights to pursue age discrimination claims. Along with company downsizing strategies, there has been an increase in the number of companies using such waivers to reduce the number of older employees in their workforces. This procedure commonly involves offering early retirement settlements to older workers in return for waivers of such employees' rights to pursue age discrimination claims under the ADEA.[28] Unfortunately, the conditions under which these waivers are obtained may be described as follows: "The employee in such an instance is usually given two options: sign the waiver and receive the benefits or suffer a dismissal due to the elimination of the job through what is commonly called 'company reorganization efforts.' "[29] As a result of this amendment to the ADEA, specific procedures are required for the legitimate use of such waivers in downsizing strategies. The amendment requires that an average employee must be able to understand the wording and that waived rights must be specified. Also, postagreement rights cannot be waived, and consideration beyond the employee's current pension and compensation entitlements must be provided. Employees also must be provided with written advice to obtain assistance from an attorney. Additionally, the employee is permitted to revoke the waiver within a seven-day period, and a time period of 21 days is provided for employees' consideration of the offer. A consideration period of 45 days and other conditions apply when exit incentives are involved.[30]

Sexual Harassment

President Clinton's incident with former State of Arkansas employee, Paula Jones, provides evidence that sexual harassment is a problem even at the highest levels of organizations. Top executives in companies also have been involved in incidents of sexual harassment. Charges of sexual harassment resulted in the resignation of a Morgan Stanley Dean Witter banker whose annual compensation was approximately $7 million.[31] Similar charges resulted in the removal of the chief executive officer (CEO) at Astra Pharmaceuticals (now merged with Zeneca). The following excerpt describes the culture at Astra:

> It was the final night of Astra USA Inc. national sales meeting last June, and pairs of employees were dancing in the ballroom of a suburban Boston hotel. Astra President and Chief Executive Officer Lars Bildman, then 49, was entwined with a 25-year-old sales representative, Pamela L. Zortman. Two onlookers noticed that Bildman, extremely drunk, was running his hands along her back and nibbling at her neck . . . *Business Week* found a dozen cases of women who claimed they were either fondled or solicited for sexual favors by Bildman or other executives. Many women described evenings in which they were expected to escort senior executives to bars and dancing clubs. Others received frequent invitations to join the often inebriated managers in their hotel suites for more intimate late-night gatherings.[32]

Even the FBI has not been immune from such problems, as there have been allegations about the sexual harassment of female agents.[33] Although discrimination according to sex was first prohibited by Title VII of the Civil Rights Act of 1964, courts did not begin to treat sexual harassment as a violation of the act until the late 1970s, followed shortly by its codification in 1980 in the Equal Employment Opportunity Commission's *Guidelines on Discrimination Because of Sex.*[34] Sexual harassment is specified in the EEOC guidelines as follows:

> Unwelcome sexual advances, requests for sexual favors, and other verbal or physical conduct of a sexual nature constitute sexual harassment when (1) submission to such conduct is made either explicitly or implicitly a term or condition of an individual's employment, (2) submission to or rejection of such conduct by an individual is used as a basis for employment decisions affecting such individual, or (3) such conduct has the purpose or effect of unreasonably interfering with an individual's work performance or creating an intimidating, hostile, or offensive working environment.[35]

Quid Pro Quo and Hostile Environment

In the *Meritor Savings Bank v. Vinson* decision, the U.S. Supreme Court agreed that sexual harassment constitutes gender discrimination, which is prohibited by Title VII.[36] An important component of the EEOC's specification of sexual harassment is that it places emphasis on the "unwelcome" nature of sexual advances, not simply whether such advances are voluntary. The first two specifications of sexual harassment, also called sexual blackmail or *quid pro quo* actions, require little explanation. However, the definition of an "intimidating, hostile, or offensive work environment" needs further explanation. Aside from physical contact, such as touching and pinching, lesser actions such as using sexually vulgar language, telling dirty jokes, and placing sexually demeaning pictures on walls and lockers have been found to contribute to such environments. One of the critical determinants of such an environment is whether a "reasonable" person would have been offended, although the term is subject to varying interpretations. In order to reduce the likelihood of charges of sexual harassment, companies need to educate their employees of both genders that actions as seemingly harmless as telling an off-color joke can be viewed as contributing to a hostile or offensive environment. Employees have to be aware that their actions may be offensive to others and have to modify their behavior or face disciplinary action.[37]

Unfortunately, a cause of sexual harassment is that many men do not perceive such behaviors to be offensive while many women do. This could be a costly difference in perceptions because sexual remarks were the basis for approximately 50 percent of the sexual harassment claims examined in a study. Interestingly, hostile environment cases have accounted for the bulk of sexual harassment, as one study found of 75 percent due solely to a hostile environment and another 19 percent resulting from a combination of hostile environment and *quid pro quo* harassment.[38]

Employer Liability in the Absence of Knowledge of Harassment

Another problem area for employers was identified in the *Meritor Savings Bank v. Vinson* decision. According to this decision, employers may incur liability even without knowledge that sexual harassment is occurring, as long as they should have known about such conduct.[39] Recently, the U.S. Supreme Court decided two more cases in which managers were unaware of their subordinates' behavior. In *Faragher v. City of Boca Raton*, two female lifeguards were subjected to a hostile environment because of offensive comments and touching by male supervisors. Even though Faragher and her female coworker did not file a complaint and higher-level managers were unaware of the incidents, the court ruled that the women could sue the city. In *Burlington Industries, Inc. v. Ellerth,* a male supervisor told a female subordinate that her work situation would improve if she went along with his sexual advances. As in the *Faragher* case, the female employee did not notify upper management of the harassment. Furthermore, the employee's refusal of the advances did not adversely affect her job situation as the supervisor even helped her gain a promotion. As in *Faragher*, the court ruled that the female employee could sue the employer for harassment. However, Burlington Industries could avoid liability as a result of the fact that there was no adverse employment action, by demonstrating that it took reasonable measures to prevent and correct sexual harassment, and by showing that the female employee unreasonably ignored complaint procedures.[40]

Liability for the Actions of Coworkers and Customers

In addition to being responsible for the actions of their supervisory and managerial personnel, employers also are liable for the actions of the coworkers. Furthermore, employers may be liable even for the actions of customers. In the latter circumstance, as demonstrated in the *EEOC v. Sage Realty Corp.* decision, the employer may incur sexual harassment liabilities for such actions as requiring employees to wear provocative attire.[41]

E-Mail and the Internet

Advances in communications technology have produced another form of hostile environment sexual harassment. The circulation of bawdy jokes or pornographic material through e-mail or the Internet can create a hostile environment form of sexual harassment. While a couple of inappropriate jokes are unlikely to be interpreted as a hostile environment, the repeated circulation of such material can constitute harassment and create liability for the employer. Employers need to inform employees that such use of e-mail is inappropriate and that disciplinary action will be taken to address such behavior. Recently, the *New York Times* terminated 22 employees for violations of its e-mail policies. The *Times* claimed that employees either sent or forwarded raunchy jokes or sexual images to each other. Employees have complained that the disciplinary action was too severe but have little recourse to their terminations.[42] Clearly, this is an area in which management should take disciplinary measures to halt the creation of a hostile environment. Such intermediate disciplinary actions can stop the behaviors before the company reaches the point of terminating valued employees.

Office Romances

Aside from the prohibited behaviors involved in sexual harassment, office romances are common human relationships among consenting adults. Such relationships will probably increase in the future as workplaces become even more balanced in their proportions of male and female employees. Such romances are usually not job-related and therefore are none of the employer's business. Nonetheless, when a supervisory relationship is involved, or the romance involves two high-level managerial equals, such relationships can create morale problems, conflicts of interests, biases in power alliances, and greater likelihood that problems of sexual harassment will arise. The probability of such romances evolving into claims of sexual harassment are increased by the fact that in the bulk of such relationships (74 percent), the male is higher in the organization's hierarchy than the female. In more than 25 percent of these romances, the male is her supervisor.[43]

Some companies have resorted to the use of "love contracts" to provide before-the-fact evidence that the relationship was consensual and to help defend against charges of retaliation if the romance cools off at a later time.[44] While such a contract may not be enforceable, it does the following:

> A love contract: 1. restates the voluntary nature of the relationship, 2. affirms that the parties will use the company's sexual harassment policies if a problem persists, and 3. affirms that is [if] a problem arises, the parties will use alternative dispute resolution.[45]

Some of the best overall guidance to pass on to supervisory personnel may be that offered by a seasoned manager with whom the author has worked: "Remember that today's willing participant in an office romance is tomorrow's litigant."

Precautions

Employers should take several precautions against sexual harassment. Some of these actions may also be helpful for reducing employer liability in the event that sexual harassment charges are filed. Specifically, the employer should:

1. Institute a policy prohibiting sexual harassment. Nonetheless, employers should realize that such policies are not, by themselves, adequate shields against liability.
2. Communicate the policy to all employees.
3. Train employees as to behaviors that will likely be viewed as sexual harassment.
4. Implement a complaint procedure for reporting allegations of sexual harassment. This procedure should bypass the employee's immediate supervisor because the harasser often occupies this position.
5. Investigate, in a timely manner, all claims of sexual harassment.
6. Repudiate the behavior after verifying the truthfulness of the allegation.
7. Take timely and appropriate disciplinary action against the harasser.
8. Set a consistent pattern of appropriate disciplinary action over time.

9. Ensure that there is no retaliation against an employee making a compliant. Unfortunately, retaliation, which is also a violation of Title VII, has been a common problem for women making such complaints. The fact that supervisors are usually the harassers compounds the problem. One study has found them to be the harassers in approximately 79 percent of the cases.

Aside from these suggestions derived from court decisions and practitioner advice, a recent empirical analysis of federal sexual harassment cases provides support for several of them. Specifically, the study found that complainants were more likely to prevail in instances of severe harassment, where they had witnesses or documentation, where they informed the employer of the problem before initiating litigation, and where the employer failed to act.[46] Another earlier study by the same researchers analyzed charges of sexual harassment filed with a state human rights agency. As in the more recent study, complainants were more successful when the sexual harassment was severe, there were witnesses, and the employee informed management of the problem prior to pursuing the issue through outside agencies.[47]

Dealing with Incidents

Even with the best training program, there is always a strong likelihood that someone will behave in a manner that is offensive to another employee. The literature points out that if the behavior constitutes an isolated event and not a pattern (and presumably not too extreme), the employer may not incur liability. The likelihood of liability may also be reduced if the employer quickly repudiates the behavior and takes disciplinary action against the harasser. Needless to say, before taking disciplinary action, the employer must make sure that the accused has an opportunity to present his or her side of the incident, and that the other elements of due process have been preserved. Of course, due to the sensitive nature of sexual harassment, it is essential to handle such matters with confidentiality.[48]

Unfortunately, the legal protections against the serious problems of sexual harassment also have the potential to cause other harm. Some allegations of sexual harassment will be false and have the potential to damage innocent individuals unless managers exercise appropriate diligence in ascertaining the truth. Furthermore, the employer should take care to preserve the rights and reputation of the accused. Taking premature disciplinary action against an innocent accused employee only compounds the problem.

Pregnancy Discrimination

As indicated in Chapter 2, by the year 2008, 48 percent of the workforce will be women.[49] These women were expected to have 2.3 million babies in the year 2000. As a result of the increasing number of employees who will be having babies, it is important that employers and management strategists understand these female employees' legal protections. The primary legislation in this area is the Pregnancy Discrimination Act, which was passed in 1978 as an amendment to Title VII. The act applies to employers having at least 15 employees and provides several protections. Employers are not allowed to reject job applicants or refuse to promote employees for reasons of pregnancy, demote or otherwise penalize pregnant workers, and terminate an employee based on pregnancy. Further, when employers provide health insurance, medical leave, post-leave reinstatement, and disability benefits, they cannot deny such benefits when pregnancy is the medical condition. Another provision of the act is that employers cannot require pregnant employees to take leave at a date determined by the employer. A number of states have similar legislation.[50]

Empirical research has found that the most prevalent form of discrimination specifically directed against pregnancy occurs when employers do not reinstate female employees after they return from medical leave for childbirth. Employers are significantly more likely to fill the jobs of women on leave for childbirth than for employees on leave for other medical reasons.[51] As will be addressed later, the Family and Medical Leave Act of 1993 provides such protections and should eliminate these problems, except for employees working for employers too small to be covered by the act.[52]

Disability Discrimination

The Americans with Disabilities Act of 1990 (ADA) covers employers of 15 or more employees in both the private and public sectors. The ADA goes beyond the Rehabilitation Act of 1973, setting broad prohibitions against discrimination in the employment of disabled workers. It also requires *reasonable accommodation* of such individuals in the workplace and has very broad implications for employers. The Equal Employment Opportunity Commission (EEOC) administers the act and has issued regulations and guidance for compliance with the law.[53] Key provisions of Title I of the act specify the following:

> Section 102. (a) GENERAL RULE. No covered entity shall discriminate against a qualified individual with a disability because of the disability of such individual in regard to job application procedures, the hiring, advancement, or discharge of employees, employee compensation, job training, and other terms, conditions, and privileges of employment.
>
> Section 102. (b) CONSTRUCTION. As used in subsection (a), the term "discriminate" includes . . . (5) (A) not making reasonable accommodations to the known physical or mental limitations of an otherwise qualified individual with a disability who is an applicant or employee, unless such covered entity can demonstrate that the accommodation would impose an undue hardship on the operation of the business of such covered entity. . . .

The act protects three types of disabilities: (1) workers who currently have disabilities, (2) workers who formerly had disabilities, and (3) workers who are perceived by others to have disabilities. If qualified individuals with a disability can perform the essential functions of the job, the employer cannot discriminate against them. Further, if these otherwise qualified individuals can perform the essential functions only after reasonable accommodations, the employer is required to make such accommodations unless it would pose an undue hardship. Although accommodations are not required where there is undue hardship, there is a great deal of uncertainty about this provision. Factors such as the costs of accommodation, number of employees in the facility, employer's financial resources, administrative factors, and impact on production processes are considered in determining undue hardship. However, large employers will probably find that only extreme accommodations will meet the definition of undue hardships. Thus, the undue hardship provision is not expected to provide a very useful defense for large employers.[54]

The second classification of disabilities pertains to diseases, such as cancer, heart disease, or mental illness, from which the worker has recovered. This prevents the employer from discriminating against such workers because of concerns about recurrence of the illness. The third classification prevents employers from discriminating against workers affected by such conditions as human immunodeficiency virus (HIV). Although the ADA does not define HIV or acquired immune deficiency syndrome (AIDS) as disabilities, several court decisions have found them to be disabilities. Additionally, in proposed EEOC regulations, HIV and AIDS have been mentioned as disabling impairments. Current drug users are not protected by ADA. However, former users no longer using illegal drugs, who have finished rehabilitation programs or are currently completing such programs, are protected.[55]

Other forms of equal employment opportunity legislation are clearer about coverage because they pertain to relatively unambiguous characteristics, such as gender, age, and race. On the other hand, the determination of who is a *qualified individual with a disability* (QUID), is a likely subject for litigation. Additionally, there are complications in determining whether an applicant fits the QUID definition because of differences across jobs in their essential functions. Because of the necessity to make individualized assessments of each employee's ability to perform essential job functions and the ambiguity involved in making reasonable accommodations, employers are advised to appoint ADA review officers, who can provide expertise and facilitate compliance.[56]

Employers obtained some assistance in determining the applicability of the ADA in 1999 with three U.S. Supreme Court rulings: *Sutton v. United Airlines, Murphy v. UPS*, and *Albertson's v. Kirkingburg*. In the *Sutton v. United Airlines* case, twin sisters applied for employment as pilots with United Airlines. They were rejected because of myopia (20/200) too severe for United's standard of 20/100. However, their disability of myopia was completely correctable to 20/20 with eyeglasses or contact lenses. The sisters claimed that they had been wrongfully discriminated against because of their disability and, as a result, the employer had violated the ADA.[57] Nonetheless, the court supported United's standard and "concluded that the two sisters are not disabled as defined by the law, and therefore could not invoke the law to sue." [58] Essentially, the court determined that the ADA does not apply to correctable impairments. The court reached similar conclusions in the *Murphy* case involving a truck mechanic who was terminated for high blood pressure and in the *Kirkingburg* case involving a truck driver who was terminated for blindness in one eye even though he had an excellent driving record.[59]

One interesting feature of the law is that it prevents employers from using selection procedures that reject applicants because of their disabilities rather than their ability to do the work. For example, giving a blind applicant a paper and pencil test would eliminate him or her from further consideration although the person could possibly perform the major activities of the actual job. In this regard, work sample tests may be used more frequently in the future because of their direct assessment of such abilities.[60]

The types of accommodations required by the ADA not only include modification of facilities and adaptation of machines, but also extend to making changes in jobs and adapting work schedules. Interestingly, the current movement toward work teams may help since disabilities could be offset by other members' abilities within the teams. However, it is unknown whether this extent of accommodation will be required under the ADA. Fortunately, disabled workers can perform many jobs after relatively low-cost accommodations. It has been reported that one-half of these accommodations can be done for $50 or less and two-thirds for under $500. In preparing for compliance with the ADA, employers must conduct adequate job analysis in order to identify the essential elements of their jobs. These functions are then included in written job descriptions against which to measure applicants' abilities to perform the jobs. To be used as a defense against charges of discrimination, employers must have these job descriptions, containing the essential functions in written form, prior to the initiation of recruiting efforts.[61]

Another ADA selection rule is that employers cannot inquire about job applicants' disabilities. Instead, they must direct their efforts toward assessment of whether applicants can perform the essential functions of jobs. A positive aspect in this area is that increasing education may prove to be effective in helping to eradicate discrimination against the disabled. This is because such discrimination generally results from ignorance, not hostility. A practical bit of advice for selection decisions is to place the most emphasis on other relevant qualifications to perform the job, as opposed to the disability.[62]

An interesting dilemma in making reasonable accommodations is that the ADA requires employers to keep information on disabilities confidential except for managerial personnel who are directing work accommodations. First aid personnel and governmental compliance officials can also be told of the disability. Unfortunately, under some conditions, when coworkers are unaware of the disability, accommodation may be perceived as favoritism. For example, accommodation for Crohn's disease may involve allowing the affected employee to take restroom breaks when needed, in contrast to restrictions for other employees. Obviously, if the employee voluntarily tells coworkers of the condition, associated problems can be avoided. However, employers cannot force or coerce employees to inform coworkers of their disabilities. For the employer's protection, it is advisable to obtain a signed statement from the disabled employee that he or she is aware of confidentiality rights but is voluntarily informing coworkers of the disability. Periodic educational programs, which inform employees about the ADA and its dual obligations of reasonable accommodation and confidentiality, may help head off perceptions of favoritism.[63]

Under the ADA, any medical examinations or inquiries must occur only after applicants are given a conditional or tentative job offer. The medical exam must be a regular component of the preemployment procedures for the job in question. Further, any medical conditions used to reject applicants must meet the job-relatedness standard. Under the ADA, tests for illegal drug use are not defined as medical examinations. To control health insurance costs that may increase as a result of ignoring unrelated disabilities in the selection process, employers may wish to adopt wider exclusions of preexisting conditions. It should be remembered that while the ADA protects disabled job applicants from discrimination, it also protects current employees. This is critical because the majority of disabilities arise among employees who are already on the job. Frequently, these disabilities are a result of the aging process and the associated incidence of such diseases as diabetes and cancer.[64]

Religious Discrimination

As indicated earlier, Title VII prevents discrimination on the basis of religion. In order to avoid such discrimination, employers must be prepared to take reasonable actions to accommodate employees' requests. For example, as established in the Supreme Court's decision in *Ansonia Board of Education v. Philbrook*, if an employee makes a request to take days off from work for religious observance, the employer must attempt a *reasonable accommodation*. In the *Ansonia* case, the employer's offer of unpaid leave was a reasonable accommodation. In situations in which the employer cannot make such accommodation, it need not do so if it would incur undue hardship. Additionally, the employer is not required to select from alternative methods of accommodation suggested by the employee.[65]

In the Supreme Court's decision in *Trans World Airlines, Inc. v. Hardison*, an employee wanted to take off Saturdays for religious observance. Before obtaining a transfer, the employee had been able to take off Saturdays because he had sufficient seniority to do so. After the transfer, he had insufficient seniority to do so. The company then asked the union to allow the employee to switch assignments, but the union refused to violate its seniority-based assignment contract provisions. The employee then requested that the employer allow him to work four-day weeks by filling in with another employee, which the employer refused because of a detrimental impact on other work functions and the premium pay required. The Court ruled that because TWA would have incurred undue hardships with all alternatives, it was not required to make such accommodations. It also ruled that the employer is not required to make changes in work assignments of other employees if seniority-based contractual rights would be violated. Where special dress or grooming is involved in religious beliefs, employers can limit these practices when they pose safety risks or cannot be tolerated due to a business necessity (e.g., facial hair is prohibited by sanitation rules in restaurants).[66]

Employers may reduce the likelihood of religious discrimination problems by adopting seniority systems for assignment of work on weekends. They can also minimize such problems by permitting employees to obtain days off for religious observance through trades with other employees. Other preventative measures include adopting and enforcing a policy against religious harassment and providing a procedure for the filing of grievances on religious discrimination. Employers should maintain detailed documentation on employee requests and reasons why they could not be granted.[67]

There are some circumstances in which employers are able to take religion into consideration because it is a bona fide occupational qualification, such as when hiring for a church-affiliated religious school. Additionally, under Title VII, religious institutions are provided some latitude for religion-based employment discrimination that other organizations are not allowed. Interestingly, religious discrimination is usually not a problem with the generally recognized religions. Instead, problems often arise from obscure religions or individuals' definitions of religions.[68] Teresa Brady provides a glimpse into the bizarre issues that can be encountered in this area:

> Brown alleged that he was the victim of religious discrimination when he was fired due to his personal, religious belief that "Kozy Kitten People/Cat Food" was contributing significantly to his state of well-being and therefore to his overall work performance by increasing his energy. Brown failed to establish a religious belief that is generally accepted in society as a religion.[69]

Sexual Orientation

Although there is no federal law that prohibits employment discrimination on the basis of sexual orientation, there is a trend among the states to adopt such legislation, and 11 states now prohibit such discrimination in the private sector. In addition, hundreds of county governments and cities have adopted similar prohibitions against such discrimination. Where such laws have been passed, religious organizations have usually been exempted from coverage. The federal courts have ruled that the Title VII protections against hostile environment sexual harassment do not apply to homosexuals because the law protects against only gender-based discrimination, not sexual orientation.[70]

In addition to governments, hundreds of companies such as Exxon–Mobil, SAS Institute Inc., and Coors Brewing have adopted practices against discrimination according to sexual orientation. Furthermore, starting in the 1980s, companies such as Ben and Jerry's, Levi Strauss, and Lotus Development Corporation started to provide benefits to the domestic partners of their employees. This practice tended to be more prevalent in industries facing tight labor markets. However, recent research indicates that the practice has not become widespread, although there has been a slow upward trend. One of the difficulties faced by companies offering such benefits is that, in the absence of a legal marriage, the company has to deal with the issue of the legitimacy of the relationship in order to prevent employees from providing such benefits to uncovered friends. A survey of 829 human resource professionals found that 86 percent of their companies do not provide such benefits. Aside from the issue of sexual orientation, the number of unmarried couples in general has increased: There were 1.6 million in 1980 compared with 4.2 million in 1998.[71]

COMPENSATION

U.S. employers must be concerned about a number of regulations affecting wages and benefits. These regulations, along with workforce skills and their supply in the labor force, affect the employer's cost of doing business in the United States and therefore may impact an employer's plant location strategies. Labor costs were a major issue in the debate over the proposed North American Free Trade Agreement.

Wages and Benefits

Federal legislation in this area includes the Fair Labor Standards Act (FLSA) first passed in 1938, which, as amended, sets minimum wages and governs the employment of underage workers. This legislation has numerous special provisions for specific industry and employee classifications. Under the FLSA, exempt employees do not have to be paid overtime wages for work over 40 hours per week. *Exempt employees* are executives, professionals, and outside salespersons. The FSLA applies to employers having at least $500,000 in annual sales and smaller employers having employees engaged in interstate commerce. Those employers covered by the FSLA must also comply with the Equal Pay Act of 1963. The Equal Pay Act mandates that men and women must be paid equal amounts of pay for equal work. Legitimate exceptions to this requirement are those pay differences resulting from variations in seniority, merit, production quality, and production quantity.[72]

The Employee Retirement Income Security Act of 1974 (ERISA) governs the funding and administration of pension plans. It applies to all employers that offer health, pension, severance, or welfare-related benefits. ERISA is a very complex law that mandates actuarially determined funding levels for defined benefit pension plans. *Defined benefit plans* are those that promise a benefit at the time of retirement. An example is a plan promising 2 percent of one's highest pay for every year worked for the company. In addition to administration and funding requirements, the legislation established the Pension Benefits Guaranty Corporation that insures pension benefits, much like the Federal Deposit Insurance Corporation.[73]

Both federal and state laws are involved in unemployment compensation. At the federal level, the Unemployment Tax Act specifies compliance standards for federal funding to the states for unemployment claims. Also at the federal level, the Social Security Act controls the funding aspects of the system. Employers having a payroll of at least $1,500 each quarter and one or more employees for one or more days in any of 20 weeks per year are subject to the requirement to pay unemployment taxes. However, there is an extensive list of exceptions. The states specify different requirements for eligibility, although federal regulations set minimum standards. A key issue for employers is that the number of claims filed by their former employees determines their unemployment compensation tax rate. Because employment claims can also be an avenue for wrongful discharge or discrimination-based litigation, employers should monitor carefully any claims and contest those where appropriate.[74]

There also are several other laws affecting compensation that cannot be covered in depth in this discussion because of space limitations. These include workers' compensation laws, which provide benefits for disabled workers at the state level. Because workers' compensation legislation and systems vary across the states, differentials in system efficiencies and administrative costs affect the attractiveness of states as potential business sites. In the past, such systems have been notoriously inefficient and subject to abuse. Additionally, other federal laws affecting compensation include two Depression Era laws: the Davis Bacon Act of 1931, which sets minimum (prevailing) wage standards for construction contractors doing business with the federal government, and the Walsh-Healy Public Contracts Act of 1936, which sets minimum (prevailing) wage standards for employers having contracts with the federal government. Additionally, the federal Portal-to-Portal Act of 1947 specifies the work-related activities for which employers are required to pay.[75]

Health Care Benefits

The Health Insurance Portability and Accountability Act of 1996 (HIPAA) provides portability of health insurance when employees take jobs at other companies. The earlier Consolidated Omnibus Budget Reconciliation Act of 1985 (COBRA) allowed employees and their dependents to continue health care coverage after termination of employment for a period of 18 to 36 months. Employees or their dependents retained coverage by paying for health insurance at a rate of 102% of the cost to their former employer. COBRA applies to employers having at least 20 employees.[76] One of the purposes for the HIPAA was to enable employees, and their dependents, who have medical problems to be able to change employers while retaining coverage for the problem. Prior to the passage of the HIPAA, such problems would commonly be excluded from health insurance coverage with the new employer as a preexisting condition. Nonetheless, the HIPAA is complex, and there are many provisions affecting the terms and degree to which coverage is portable. Among these provisions are requirements for health insurance providers to serve small employers, guarantee renewals of policies, and allow group-to-individual portability such as when an employee leaves the employer but wishes to retain coverage as an individual.[77]

Family and Medical Leave

One area of recent legislation is particularly relevant to increasing feminization of the workforce. With some 80 percent of American female workers of child-bearing age, maternity leaves and guarantees of job availability upon return are important. Although the U.S. legislative requirements lagged those of many European countries, even before passage of the Family and Medical Leave Act of 1993 (FMLA), several high-standards U.S. companies provided such leaves. For example, Time, Inc. and AT&T allowed liberal unpaid leave periods for parents after childbirth or adoption.[78] Companies allowing employees to take lengthy unpaid parental or family care leaves included Johnson & Johnson, Aetna Life and Casualty, Allstate Insurance, Arthur Andersen, Atlantic Richfield, Champion International, Corning, Inc., Du Pont, Gannett, Hallmark Cards, John Hancock Mutual Life, Levi Strauss, Merck, Pacific Gas & Electric, Polaroid, Procter & Gamble, Travelers, U.S. Sprint, and Wells Fargo Bank.[79]

Even prior to passage of the FMLA, a state law in California required employers to provide unpaid maternity leave.[80] The obvious implications of such legislation are that companies will need to plan for temporary vacancies created by employees on maternity leave. Although support programs such as child care and maternity leave carry an economic cost, some observers argued that they are necessary to preserve workers' effectiveness.

> A good support system is the single most important aid if a woman is to remain an effective employee. . . . there are going to be even more single women in the workforce who will require corporations to meet the needs of their dual agenda—career progress and family harmony. In addition, the number of two-paycheck families will continue to rise, with the concomitant problems of division of responsibilities as each partner struggles with the demands of work and family.[81]

With the passage of the FMLA in 1993, the law mandated the leave components of such support systems. Specifically, the act requires that employers provide unpaid leave to employees making such requests for the following reasons: (1) to provide care for newborn children, newly placed adopted children, and for foster care; (2) to provide care for seriously ill spouses, children, or parents; or (3) the employee's own serious health problems that prevent job performance. When such requests are foreseeable, employees must make them 30 days in advance of the desired leave. Employers also are entitled to medical certifications of the existence of serious health conditions if they so request. Once employees go on such leaves, employers are required to continue health care coverage; when they return, they are entitled to equivalent jobs, pay, and benefits. An exception to this provision is that, for the employer's highest-paid employees (top 10 percent), the employer does not have to hold the position until the employee returns under conditions in which substantial economic damage can be demonstrated.[82]

The leave requirement is limited to a maximum of 12 weeks per 12-month period. Such leave may also be of an intermittent nature when it is for illness of the employee or his or her family members. With regard to coverage, the FMLA applies to employers having 50 or more employees within a 75-mile area and provides rights to employees who have worked at least one year for the employer and have worked 1,250 or more hours in the past 12 months. Under the provisions of the FMLA, the definition of children also includes mentally or physically disabled individuals of age 18 or over who must have others care for them.[83] Additionally, the act "allows employers to require employees to use up available vacation, personal, or sick leave time before the unpaid leave begins." [84]

EMPLOYEE RELATIONS

Legal influences in the area of employee relations include the evolving area of negligent hiring, the employment of immigrants, employment-at-will, drug testing, and safety.

Negligent Hiring

Negligent hiring has become an increasingly attractive area for employee litigation, as employers are being found liable for acts of violence committed by their employees. Such liability has typically been incurred in situations in which the employee had access to customers in isolated circumstances or had easy access to their property. For example, an apartment complex owner hired a resident manager who subsequently raped a tenant in her apartment. The employee turned out to have had a history of violence. Although the employer was unaware of the employee's violent background, the tenant sued and the employer was found liable for negligent hiring. In some circumstances, the employer's liability may even extend beyond actions occurring during the course of business.[85] Another similar incident occurred when a convenience store chain hired a clerk who had previously been imprisoned for murder. Because of the isolated nature of the work, customers and other employees were vulnerable to the employee's violent nature. In this case, the employee murdered a store coworker, and the employer was found be negligent for failing to check on the employee's background. As a result, the employer agreed to a settle the case by paying the deceased employee's family $4.95 million.[86] Conversely, in another case involving a radio station, the employer was not liable. In this case, the employee, one of the station's entertainers, lured an underage listener into sexual acts. The court ruled that the station was not liable, although it had conducted an inadequate background check. The court reasoned that an even exhaustive examination of the employee's background would not have revealed similar conduct from the past.[87]

Such situations have constituted a Catch-22 for employers because of privacy protections, defamation suits that made it difficult to obtain meaningful information on job applicants from previous employers, and the difficulty of obtaining information on the criminal records of applicants. Fortunately, there may be less likelihood of defamation suits in the future because there is a legislative trend among the states to shield employers from liability when they provide information about an individual's work performance. However, it is sometimes difficult for employers to check for violent criminal backgrounds because some states, such as North Carolina and Massachusetts, have prohibited private sector employers from obtaining such information. Furthermore, employers cannot use arrest information in making employment decisions and may not be able to use convictions unless they are job related.[88]

Although negligent hiring situations pose substantial difficulties for employers, past court rulings provide some guidance for action. For example, for negligence to occur, the actions of the employer must have been unreasonable. It is also critical that the employer must have known, or should have known, about the vicious or violent nature of the employee. Further, greater precautions and a more intensive background investigation are in order when the employee will have close and unsupervised contact with customers or other employees. Examples of jobs falling within this category might be maintenance workers having special access, as noted earlier, bus drivers, and child care workers. In addition to exercising greater care where customers and fellow employees may be more vulnerable, the employer should investigate gaps in an applicant's employment record. Efforts to obtain such information should be documented because, even when unsuccessful, they provide evidence of a reasonable background search.[89] As indicated earlier, criminal information cannot be used for selection decisions unless it is job related. The rationale for this prohibition is described in the following:

> The leading court cases in this area have held that if an employer's rule against hiring applicants with criminal records has an adverse impact on minorities, the practice violates Title VII unless it is justified by "business necessity."[90]

Nonetheless, circumstances in which customers or employees may be vulnerable to the violent actions of another employee may constitute business necessity. Further, it appears that it will become easier for employers to check on applicants' criminal records as a result of enabling legislative and better computerized information systems. However, such availability of information may be a two-edged sword, as at least one court has found that "where criminal records were *easily available*, the failure of the employer to check his employee's criminal records can be used as evidence of his negligence."[91] Thus, negligent hiring appears to be another minefield for employers. In order to avoid financial losses, employers must exercise greater diligence in investigating the backgrounds of job applicants.

Immigration

The Immigration Reform and Control Act of 1986 (IRCA) directs employers to determine that applicants are legally qualified to be employed in the United States before hiring them. In attempting to determine legal status, employers should be careful to avoid discrimination on the basis of national origin. Nor should they reject applicants because they look like aliens. This can be done by first making *conditional offers of employment* to applicants and then asking for their documentation to determine legal qualification for employment. In making employment decisions, employers should not favor citizens over noncitizens having appropriate work authorization, although citizenship can sometimes be legally required under some situations by governmental employers and defense contractors. Further, employers having fewer than four employees are not prevented from discriminating against noncitizens. There are also several special business visas that authorize aliens to work in the United States. One of particular interest to companies having operations in other countries is the L-1 visa. This visa permits such companies to transfer foreign managers or specialists, employed in their foreign operations, into the United States. In addition to the IRCA, the Immigration Act of 1990 also authorizes a visa for certain highly educated workers.[92]

Employment at Will

An issue of increasing importance to employers is the vitality of the employment-at-will doctrine, as a number of exceptions to the doctrine have developed in recent years.[93] Current estimates indicate that approximately two-thirds of U.S. employees work under employment-at-will conditions in which they can readily be terminated from employment.[94] The *employment-at-will doctrine* states that "an employer can legally dismiss an employee for a good reason, a bad reason, or no reason at all, so long as the dismissal does not violate the provisions of a specific statute, such as the National Labor Relations Act or the Civil Rights Act of 1964."[95]

Because employees working under employment-at-will conditions outnumber those afforded protections against arbitrary discharge, it is easier to identify employees having protection against arbitrary discharge. These employees include those covered by collective bargaining agreements. Another such group is governmental employees at the local, state, and federal levels who often work under civil service rules. Such rules mandate due process disciplinary procedures with some form of appeal procedure, often culminating in a hearing before an impartial arbitrator or hearing officer. Frequently, governmental employees may have these protections as a result of collectively bargained agreements. University faculty members are often covered by contractual agreements or legislation, which also prevent arbitrary termination. Additionally, the National Labor Relations Act provides protection against discharge where the action is directed against preventing employees from organizing a union. There is also statutory protection against discharge when it results from retaliation against whistle-blowers or workers who file charges under such laws as the Fair Labor Standards Act or the Occupational Safety and Health Act. Finally, where discharges result from discrimination against an employee's race, color, national origin, religion, gender, age, or disabilities, other statutory protections exit. Beyond these groups and special conditions, the remaining employees work under the employment-at-will doctrine.[96] Even for employees subject to employment at will, some exceptions to the doctrine have evolved. These include situations in which the termination is in *opposition to public policy.* Examples include terminating an employee for refusing to commit perjury, declining to become involved in bribery, and refusing submit to a polygraph test when such refusal is protected under the Employee Polygraph Protection Act of 1988.[97] Violations of state public policies have also been used for such public policy exemptions, as indicated in the specific example of the *Wagenseller v. Scottsdale Memorial Hospital* case.[98]

> On a company river outing, a nurse refused to "moon" her fellow employees while singing "Moon River" as her boss requested. She was fired as a result. Noting the state's indecent-exposure laws as a statement of public policy, the Arizona Supreme Court approved her right to sue for wrongful discharge as a public policy exception to the state's at-will employment rule.[99]

Another exception to the employment-at-will doctrine is *abusive discharge.* An example of abusive discharge is a situation in which an employee is fired for refusing to date her boss. An additional exception is where there is an *implied covenant of good faith.* An example of a breach of covenant is an employer's discharging sales employees to evade obligations to pay earned commissions. Also, statements in personnel handbooks categorizing employees as permanent employees have been interpreted as *implicit contracts.*[100] As a result of litigation on this issue, employers have learned to be careful about such statements and now often include disclaimers in handbooks that explicitly specify employment-at-will status.[101]

Limitations on an employer's ability to discharge employees at will have also evolved in the form of a statute in the state of Montana. The state of Montana has adopted legislation that sets a standard of good cause for employee terminations. Under Montana's Wrongful Discharge From Employment Act, discharges of nonprobationary employees will be considered as wrongful unless there is just cause.[102] In addition, several other states have considered similar legislation that would require just cause for terminations. Such developments have caused some observers to conclude that the employment-at-will doctrine has been weakened.[103] Nonetheless, an empirical analysis of California's experience, where there are substantial inroads into the employment-at-will doctrine, concluded the following: "Quantitative analysis of the California experience indicates that the erosion of employment at will has not proceeded nearly as far as is commonly believed."[104] Such laws, the emergence of exceptions to the employment-at-will doctrine, increased litigation over terminations, and large judgments in favor of employees have caught the attention of human resource managers. Nonetheless, there is some evidence that large judgments have involved high-level managerial personnel and are not prevalent among discharged hourly employees.[105]

Finally, companies should consider the impact of employment-at-will policies on potential job applicants' perceptions of the organization as an attractive employer. Catherine Schwoerer and Benson Rosen have found that such policies, when compared with policies providing due process grievance and appeals procedures, are associated with significantly lower perceptions of employer attractiveness.[106]

Drug Testing

Drug testing has been a common practice in companies and governmental agencies for many years, particularly as a preemployment screening process and to test for cause such as in the case of accidents.[107] Such testing is almost universal in the largest companies. "Almost 98 percent of *Fortune* 200 companies have drug-testing policies. As more employers implement drug-testing policies, it seems to have an effect on drug use in the workplace." [108] Some of the reasons for increased testing include favorable court decisions, federal requirements in transportation and defense industries, and initiatives by insurance companies.[109]

Although the widespread use of testing indicates that companies apparently perceive benefits from drug-testing programs, there is criticism of the foundation for testing:

> But a new report by the American Civil Liberties Union (ACLU) questions the benefits usually associated with drug testing, challenges the process's cost-effectiveness, contests its overall value, and touts less-intrusive alternatives . . . The ACLU cites analysis by a committee of the National Academy of Sciences (NAS), which found that most workers who use illicit drugs never use them at work, and when they use drugs on their own time, they do so in a way that does not affect their work performance.[110]

Because industrial studies of the effectiveness of drug-testing programs typically have not employed experimental designs, their impact on desired outcomes cannot be confirmed. Nonetheless, John Osterloh and Charles Becker's comprehensive literature review found anecdotal evidence of program success. Such successes included reports of reduced accident rates in the railway industry; reduced absenteeism, accidents, and disciplinary actions at General Motors;

and drastic reductions in drug incidence in the U.S. Navy.[111] While some of the studies on the impact of drug testing and anecdotal evidence are subject to criticism, there is little question about the trends in the results of drug testing as the percentage of positive results in preemployment drug testing as well as in the testing of current employees have shown substantial declines.[112] The following excerpt indicates the magnitude of this decline:

> SmithKline Beecham Corp., one of the primary testing agencies based in Philadelphia, has an interesting study. In 1987, its statistical information showed that in employment-related testing, 18.1 percent of those tested showed positive drug use. In 1997, only 5 percent of approximately 5 million employment-related tests came back positive.[113]

One explanation in the past for the decline of positive results in preemployment testing has been that drug users have become aware of companies' testing programs and no longer apply for employment at their companies. However, with increasing use of drug testing, such self-selection does not appear to provide a plausible explanation for the declines.

Basically, there are three drug-testing approaches for private sector employers. The most prevalent involves the testing of job applicants. The popularity of this *preemployment approach* to testing appears to be a result of its effectiveness and the employer's lower exposure to liability. A second approach, for which there is some legal support, involves testing employees when there is *probable cause* to suspect drug use, such as when there has been an accident. *Reasonable suspicion* of drug use may also fall under this category, as when supervisors observe symptoms of drug intoxication. A third approach, which involves *random testing* of all employees, is not as widely used as the first two approaches. Disadvantages with this approach include the uncertainty of its legal standing, its cost, and substantial administrative requirements. When random testing is conducted, it is typically used for employees in environments in which safety is an important consideration. Not surprisingly, random testing is more defensible under such considerations. In fact, private and public sector employees covered by public safety requirements of the U.S. Department of Transportation are required to conduct random drug tests for safety purposes.[114] Nonetheless, laws in the states are not uniform on drug testing, and in some states, such as California, random drug testing is restricted to the following:

> In California, for example, there's tension between privacy rights of employees and rights of employers to test. The California state constitution contains an individual right to privacy which has been applied fairly rigorously to drug testing, so it's hard to implement random testing in California. Unless it's a safety position or there are some real signs that drug use is going on, employers in that state don't have the right to test current employees. Random testing is a risk in many states [for similar reasons].[115]

In many companies where there are substantial safety hazards, drug testing is required by regulations of the U.S. Department of Defense, U.S. Department of Transportation, and other governmental agencies. Accordingly, there is extensive drug testing in the transportation industry, as an American Management Association survey found that 89 percent of the companies in this industry conduct drug testing.[116]

Drug testing of federal governmental employees is explicitly regulated. Executive Order 12,564 specifies that drug testing of federal employees can take place under four conditions. These include situations of reasonable suspicion, accident investigation, preemployment screening, and as a condition of drug rehabilitation.[117] State and local governments also test employees under similar circumstances. Nonetheless, both public and private employers should take note of the difficulties of establishing reasonable suspicion as justification for drug testing. In two recent court decisions involving governmental employees, observations of erratic or abnormal behavior were rejected as a basis for reasonable suspicion. These rulings noted the absence of a strong link between drug impairment and erratic behavior. They also noted commonplace alternative explanations for such behavior, other than drug use.[118]

In order to minimize legal and managerial problems, drug-testing programs should conform to a number of requirements. Clearly, steps leading up to the implementation of such programs are critical. One very important requirement is that there should be a well-documented need for testing. Employees should also perceive this need since acceptance of testing programs is expected to correlate with the perceived need for testing, such as in dangerous working conditions.[119] As a result, employees are probably more accepting of both preemployment testing and cause-based testing but are probably much more resistant to universal random testing.

Another requirement for drug-testing programs is that the testing should involve a two-step process. The first step should be a *screening test*. All positive results should then be subjected to a *confirmatory test*. Confirmatory tests are typically much more expensive. Privacy issues also are a consideration in such programs and, in an employment context, direct observation of the collection of specimens is probably invasive and unnecessary. However, the collection of specimens must be conducted with several precautions to preserve the integrity of the chain of custody. Other requirements include uniform application. For example, if preemployment testing is used, all applicants must be tested. Further, when testing is conducted for cause, there must be uniform application without regard to race or gender. There also should be mechanisms for employee challenges, and a provision for employee assistance programs for those found to be using drugs.[120]

Employee acceptance is an extremely important requirement for effective drug-testing programs. Because of its importance, the likelihood of litigation or adverse arbitration decisions should be reduced as a result of negotiating agreements with employees on drug-testing policies. Such agreements should specify the testing procedures, steps to be taken in collecting specimens, and the consequences of positive results.[121] In addition to litigation in which private and public sector employees are represented by a union, or in the public sector in which civil service rules apply, arbitrators rule on grievances concerning such issues. Arbitrators tend to look for many of these components of drug-testing programs before they will uphold employers' actions.

In summary, drug testing involves complicated technical issues and is subject to variations in accuracy. However, as indicated earlier, some drug-testing programs have probably produced positive outcomes, such as reductions in accidents.[122] Further, as indicated earlier, employers working under regulations of the U.S. Department of Transportation have no choice in the matter of random drug testing. Nonetheless, a wide array of factors makes drug testing a complex matter. These complexities include the financial risk of exposure to liability, the potential negative impacts on employee trust, and the potential negative impact on morale. As a result, the strategic management team must consider carefully, the broad implications of drug testing before proceeding.

Safety

The Occupational Safety and Health Act of 1970 (OSHA) requires employers "to provide employees a place of employment free from recognized hazards that are causing, or are likely to cause death or serious harm to employees."[123] OSHA has a massive set of specific safety standards with which employers are required to comply. Unlike most federal employee relations legislation, there is no minimum size exclusion for small employers. Under OSHA, employers are required to maintain safety records and are responsible for employees' compliance with safety standards. Further, employers are subject to unannounced inspections by OSHA authorities, although some have been successful in requiring search warrants for entry. Additionally, OSHA has the power to level meaningful fines for violations of safety standards. Some of the more controversial aspects of OSHA have been its standards that require massive financial outlays for compliance without evidence that meaningful reductions in health hazards will be forthcoming. This situation has changed somewhat. OSHA's standards for acceptable levels of exposure to substances, such as airborne toxic materials, must now meet both technological and economic feasibility standards.[124] Nonetheless, there is no requirement that "the cost of a standard bears a reasonable relationship to its benefits."[125]

LABOR RELATIONS AND COLLECTIVE BARGAINING

The National Labor Relations Act (NLRA), also called the Wagner Act, was passed in 1935. Section 7 of this act gave employees the right to form unions and engage in collective bargaining. In order to enforce these rights, section 8(a) of the act prohibited five *employer unfair labor practices*: (1) interfering with employees attempting to unionize or engage in collective bargaining, (2) dominating a union, (3) discriminating on the basis of union status, (4) retaliating against workers charging violations of the act, and (5) refusing to bargain. In order to enforce the law, the act created the National Labor Relations Board (NLRB). Essentially, the first of the unfair labor practices is a general provision, which is particularly relevant to employer conduct when employees are attempting to unionize. This provision is intended to prevent employers from using coercive tactics, such as discharging workers who are attempting to unionize. The second unfair labor practice prevents *company unions*. (In a company union, the company might handpick the leaders, provide financial support, and dominate the union in other ways.) Interestingly, worker committees that act on issues similar to those involved in collective bargaining may be viewed as company unions and therefore constitute an unfair labor practice. The third unfair labor practice prevents the employer from treating employees in the bargaining unit differently, depending on whether or not they are members of the union. The fourth and fifth unfair labor practices are self-explanatory.[126]

Following the passage of the NLRA in 1935, unionization increased dramatically, almost quadrupling by 1948. By 1946, a record of 4,985 strikes had occurred, and Congress recognized that unfair labor practices on the union side also needed to be curbed.[127] The Labor Management Relations Act of 1947 (LMRA), also called the Taft-Hartley Act, amended the National Labor Relations Act and sought to restore a balance between the power of unions and employers. Section 8(b) of the act specified a series of *union unfair labor practices*: (1) restraining or coercing employees who are pursuing their rights to bargain collectively, (2) discriminating on the basis of union membership, (3) refusing to bargain, (4) conducting prohibited strikes, (5) charging excessive fees, and (6) requiring employers to provide compensation for services that are not performed. The first of these practices prevents unions from coercing employees who do not want to unionize. The second prevents the union from forcing the employer to terminate an employee, except in cases in which he or she refuses to pay union dues where there is a *union shop agreement*. (With union shops, an individual must join the union after becoming employed.) It also prevents the union from attempting to induce the employer to favor union members in hiring and outlaws the *closed shop*. (With closed shops, an individual must be a member of the union before being hired.) The third union unfair labor practice does not have much meaning because unions want to bargain. The fourth unfair practice basically outlaws *secondary boycotts*, which involve application of coercive economic power to neutral third parties to labor disputes. The fifth unfair labor practice allows unions to charge dues or initiation fees that are reasonable in light of industry practice and the wage level of the job. The sixth provision was intended ostensibly to prevent featherbedding practices, such as requiring overstaffing for certain jobs, but has been largely ineffective.[128]

Another provision of the act is the so-called *right-to-work* provision, which allows states to decide whether union shop agreements are legal. Further, the act also requires unions and employers to *bargain in good faith* over mandatory issues, such as wages, hours, and other working conditions. Additionally, the Taft-Hartley Act added provisions whereby employees may decertify unions and established a procedure for the resolution of strikes constituting national emergencies.[129]

Because of continuing problems of union corruption and of lack of democratic procedures in the governance of unions, the Labor Management Reporting and Disclosure Act (LMRDA), called the Landrum-Griffin Act, was passed in 1959 and also amended the NLRA. Important provisions of the LMRDA include financial reporting and disclosure requirements for union officers and labor relations consultants, requirements on unions to conduct regular elections, and prohibitions of hot cargo agreements. In *hot cargo agreements*, union members refuse to handle materials or components that have previously been processed by nonunion workers or by a company with which the union has a dispute. The act also added a prohibition of recognitional picketing, under certain circumstances, as a seventh union unfair practice. Where *recognitional picketing* takes place, expedited representation election procedures may be invoked. Additionally, the NLRA was amended again in 1974. Unions representing employees of health care institutions are now required to provide 10 days' advance notice of a strike.[130]

Many practitioners refer to combinations of these three pieces of legislation as the act. Employees not covered by the act include supervisors, agricultural workers, domestic servants, employees of parents or spouses, independent contractors, governmental workers, and railroad and airline employees. Further, only the labor relations activities of those private sector employers involved in interstate commerce come under the jurisdiction of the NLRB. Threshold values for NLRB jurisdiction are defined for nonretail companies as $50,000 or more annual input or output across states lines, or in retailing as $500,0000 or more in annual sales. Additionally, employers not covered by the act include governments, airlines, and railroads. The Railway Labor Act of 1926 covers airlines and railroads.[131]

In addition to these federal acts, labor relations are also governed by NLRB policies and decisions, as well as court decisions. Unfortunately for unions, the law has not provided effective protection for employees attempting to unionize. Essentially, employers who commit unfair labor practices must provide "*make whole*" remedies to employees whose rights they have violated. For example, an employer might terminate an employee who is attempting to form a union. Upon establishing that the employer has actually committed such an unfair labor practice, the employer would probably be required to reinstate the employee and pay back wages the employee lost while he or she was unemployed. Unfortunately, there is typically a lengthy time period before the remedy is implemented. If the employer's conduct is particularly egregious and a fair representation election cannot be held, the NLRB may order the employer to bargain with the union. Even where the employer commits no unfair labor practices and the union wins the representation election, many unions are never successful in negotiating a contract. Even though the employer is required to bargain in good faith, the sanctions for failure to bargain are not strong. This is another weakness in the law that is particularly troublesome to unions.[132] Another influence of the legal environment on strategy may be seen in the replacement of strikers. In the past, Democratic politicians have proposed legal prohibitions of the permanent replacement of strikers.[133] This right of employers has been an enduring principle of labor relations going back to its affirmation by the U.S. Supreme Court in 1938.[134] It is a certainty that such proposed legislation will generate very strong resistance from the business community.

EMERGING ISSUES

Employment Practices Liability Insurance

Because of the complexity of the regulatory environment of human resources and the potential liability, some employers have attempted to manage their risk by purchasing employment practices liability insurance (EPLI). Over time, as insurers have gained experience, they have tended to broaden the coverage of EPLI policies, although the particular exclusions must be examined carefully. Interestingly, large employers generally are able to purchase EPLI at discounted rates because it is presumed that they are more likely to be in compliance with regulations because of more sophisticated human resource departments. Some of the factors that underwriters use to determine insurance rates are the same that are associated with human resource effectiveness. For example, underwriters examine employee turnover rates, company policies on sexual harassment, and employment handbooks. It is interesting to speculate as to whether EPLI rates will someday provide top management with a proxy measure of the quality of their human resource departments.[135]

Genetic Testing

The topic of genetic testing in the workplace faces significant obstacles because it could be used to discriminate among applicants for employment. Through genetic testing of applicants, employers could reject those whose genetic backgrounds make them more susceptible to future illnesses and could thereby reduce their health insurance costs. Because of its discriminatory consequences, there is a trend by states to outlaw such procedures for employment selection.[136]

STRATEGIC IMPACT OF THE LEGAL ENVIRONMENT

Whether the increasingly complex and comprehensive regulatory environment of human resources will weaken the competitiveness of U.S. companies in the international marketplace is yet to be determined. Obviously, the legal environment is a major consideration of strategic managers because of the potential exposure to liability, plant location concerns, productivity influences, and other impacts on cost structures. In the future, strategic managers may need to become more proactive in the design of legislation so that the laudable social goals can be obtained simultaneously with organizational growth and efficiency. Without managerial flexibility, some assurance of what the "rules of the game" are, and predictable means of determining when the employer is in compliance with legislation, U.S. companies are not likely to be as productive and efficient as they should be. Conversely, with higher levels of productivity and efficiency, companies are likely produce a larger economic pie to share with all employees. Given strong economic performance, they should have less difficulty in providing equal opportunity employment opportunities. In the absence of these efficiencies and economic growth, companies will be faced with the difficult situation of allocating or rationing employment opportunities to a smaller set of individuals.

A controversial but comprehensive analysis of the economic and legal effects of equal employment opportunity regulation has been conducted by Richard Epstein.[137] The major conclusion of his analysis is that substantial economic inefficiency is associated with such regulation. While few of his recommendations for reform are likely to be implemented in the foreseeable future, strategic managers and planners may gain insights from a review of his analysis of the impact of current legislation. Peter Brimelow and Leslie Spencer also have described similar concerns about the legislative environment of human resources as follows:

> Ironically, just as socialism has collapsed across the globe, the leading capitalist power has adopted a peculiarly American neosocialism, putting politics (and lawyers) in command of its workplace, albeit on the pretext of equity rather than efficiency.[138]

While there are costs to equal employment opportunity legislation, as Brimelow and Spencer have pointed out, there are also costs with the alternative of failing to advance members of society who have been subject to prior discrimination. Unfortunately, some of the new legislation appears to have left areas of ambiguity that create greater uncertainty for employers. When employment procedures are made uncertain by ill-conceived legislation and likely targets for even greater litigation are created, rational employers are not likely to be as aggressive in their hiring, as when the legislation is unambiguous and thoughtful of the practical issues involved in running an economically viable business.

Summary

This chapter described the legal environment of human resources, beginning with the equal employment opportunity protections of the Civil Rights Act of 1964, which prohibit discrimination on the basis of race, color, religion, sex, or national origin. Disparate treatment and disparate impact forms of discrimination were explained, along with the implications for human resource selection procedures such as those involving the use of tests. The enforcement role of the EEOC in administering the act also was discussed along with the role of the OFCCP. Changes incorporated in the Civil Rights Act of 1991 also were covered, including prohibitions against race-norming of test scores, punitive damages for intentional discrimination, and extraterritorial civil rights coverage of expatriate employees of U.S. companies. Prohibitions against discrimination on the basis of age (Age Discrimination in Employment Act), sexual harassment, pregnancy (Pregnancy Discrimination Act), disabilities (Americans with Disabilities Act), and religion were also reviewed. The legal status of discrimination directed at sexual orientation also was discussed.

The regulatory environment governing the administration of compensation and benefit programs also was described. Legislation and regulations included in this discussion were the Fair Labor Standards Act, the Employee Retirement Income Security Act, the Equal Pay Act, the Health Insurance Portability and Accountability Act, and the Family and Medical Leave Act.

Other relatively recent legal developments also were discussed including the establishment of employer liability for negligent hiring, rules governing the employment of immigrants as established by the Immigration Reform and Control Act, exceptions to the employment-at-will doctrine, and drug testing. In addition, the safety requirements of the Occupational Safety and Health Act and the labor relations regulations of the National Labor Relations Act, the Labor Management Relations Act, and the Labor Management Reporting and Disclosure Act were also discussed. The emerging issues of employment practices liability insurance and genetic testing also were examined. Finally, because of the increased complexity of recent legislation governing human resource management, the economic impact of the legislative environment was examined in terms of decreased managerial flexibility and the uncertainties created by ambiguities in determining compliance.

Endnotes

1. Hall, Francine S., and Elizabeth L. Hall. "The ADA: Going Beyond the Law," *Academy of Management Executive* 8, no. 1 (1994): 17–26.
2. Ibid., p. 18.
3. Jacobs, Roger B., with Cora S. Koch. *Legal Compliance Guide to Personnel Management*. Englewood Cliffs, NJ: Prentice Hall, 1993.
4. Civil Rights Act of 1964 as amended by the Equal Employment Opportunity Act of 1972.
5. Cibon, Patrick J., and James O. Castagnera. *Labor and Employment Law*, 2nd ed. Boston: PWS-Kent Publishing Company, 1993.
6. Miner, Mary G., and John B. Miner. *Employee Selection Within the Law*. Washington, DC: Bureau of National Affairs, 1978.
7. Twomey, David P. *Equal Employment Opportunity Law*, 3rd ed. Cincinnati: South-Western Publishing Company, 1994; Arvey, Richard D., and Robert H. Faley. *Fairness in Selecting*

Employees, 2nd ed. Reading, MA: Addison-Wesley Publishing Company, 1988; Greenlaw, Paul S. *Proving Title VII Discrimination* 42, no. 7 (1991): 407–17.

8. *Griggs v. Duke Power Co.*, 401 U.S. 424 (1971).
9. Ibid.
10. Twomey. *Equal Employment Opportunity Law.*
11. Greenlaw, Paul S. "Proving Title VII Discrimination," *Labor Law Journal* 42, no. 7 (1991): 407–17.
12. Player, Mack A. *Federal Law of Employment Discrimination in a Nutshell*, 3rd ed. St. Paul: West Publishing Company, 1992.
13. Ledvinka, James. *Federal Regulation of Personnel and Human Resource Management.* Boston: Kent Publishing Company, 1982.
14. *Albemarle Paper Co. v. Moody*, 422 U.S. 405 (1975).
15. Rothstein, Mark A., Andria S. Knapp, and Lance Liebman. *Cases and Materials on Employment Law*, 2nd ed. Westbury, New York: Foundation Press, 1991.
16. Equal Employment Opportunity Commission. *1978 Uniform Guidelines on Employee Selection Procedures.*
17. Arvey and Faley. *Fairness in Selecting Employees*, p. 80.
18. Robinson, Robert K., Billie Morgan Allen, David E. Terpstra, and Ercan G. Nasif. "Equal Employment Requirements for Employers: A Closer Review of the Effects of the Civil Rights Act of 1991," *Labor Law Journal* 43, no. 11, 1992.
19. Feild, Hubert S., and Robert D. Gatewood. "Matching Talent With the Task," *Personnel Administrator* 32, no. 4 (1987): 113–26.
20. Robinson, Allen, Terpstra, and Nasif. "Equal Employment Requirements for Employers: A Closer Review of the Effects of the Civil Rights Act of 1991"; Brimelow, Peter, and Leslie Spencer. "When Quotas Replace Merit, Everybody Suffers," *Forbes* (February 15, 1993): 80–102.
21. *Connecticut v. Teal*, 457 U.S. 440 (1982); Robinson, Allen, Terpstra, and Nasif. "Equal Employment Requirements for Employers: A Closer Review of the Effects of the Civil Rights Act of 1991."
22. Robinson, Allen, Terpstra, and Nasif. "Equal Employment Requirements for Employers: A Closer Review of the Effects of the Civil Rights Act of 1991."
23. Cibon and Castagnera. *Labor and Employment Law.*
24. Levin-Epstein, Michael D. *Primer of Equal Employment Opportunity*, 4th ed. Washington, DC: Bureau of National Affairs, Inc., 1987; Ledvinka. *Federal Regulation of Personnel and Human Resource Management;* Twomey. *Equal Employment Opportunity Law.*
25. McCartney, Scott. "Tension in the Air: What Some Call Racist at American Eagle, Others Say Was in Jest," *Wall Street Journal* (April 20, 1999): A1, A8; Lee, Louise. "Dillard's Is Meeting With Minorities to Talk of Diversity," *Wall Street Journal* (April 8, 1998): B6; Hammonds, Keith H. "Texaco Was Just the Beginning," *Business Week* (December 16, 1996): 34–35. "Publix Settles Discrimination Suit," *Dallas Morning News*, (January 1, 1997): 2F.
26. Cibon and Castagnera. *Labor and Employment Law*; Dube, Lawrence, E. Jr. "Removing the Cap—Eliminating Mandatory Retirement Under the ADEA," *Employment Relations Today* 15, no. 3 (1988): 199–204. Player. *Federal Law of Employment Discrimination in a Nutshell*; Twomey. *Equal Employment Opportunity Law.*
27. Dube. "Removing the Cap—Eliminating Mandatory Retirement Under the ADEA"; Player. *Federal Law of Employment Discrimination*; Hassell, Barbara L., and Pamela L. Perrewe. "An Examination of the Relationship Between Older Workers' Perceptions of Age Discrimination and Employee Psychological State," *Journal of Managerial Issues* 5, no. 1 (1993): 109–20. Steinhauser, Sheldon. "Is Your Corporate Culture in Need of an Overhaul?" *HRMagazine* 43, no. 8 (1998): 86–91.
28. Twomey. *Equal Employment Opportunity Law*; Mitchell, Charles E. "Waiver of Rights Under the Age Discrimination In Employment Act: Implications of the Older Workers Benefit Protection Act of 1990," *Labor Law Journal* 43, no. 11 (1992): 735–44.
29. Mitchell. "Waiver of Rights Under the Age Discrimination In Employment Act: Implications of the Older Workers Benefit Protection Act of 1990," p. 735.

30. Player. *Federal Law of Employment Discrimination in a Nutshell*; Mitchell. "Waiver of Rights Under the Age Discrimination In Employment Act: Implications of the Older Workers Benefit Protection Act of 1990."
31. Gasparino, Charles, and Ann Davis. "Margan Stanley Case Illustrates Less Tolerance In Bias Claims," *Wall Street Journal* (September 14, 1999): C1, C14.
32. Maremont, Mark. "Abuse of Power," *Business Week* (May 13, 1986): 86–87.
33. American Broadcasting Company. *ABC News* (October 11, 1993).
34. Twomey. *Equal Employment Opportunity Law*.
35. Equal Employment Opportunity Commission. *Guidelines on Discrimination Because of Sex*, Section 1604.11, November 10, 1980.
36. *Meritor Savings Bank v. Vinson*, 106 S. Ct. 2399 (1986); Koen, Clifford M. Jr. "Sexual Harassment Claims Stem From a Hostile Work Environment," *Personnel Journal* 69, no. 8 (1990): 90–99.
37. Greenlaw, Paul S., and John P. Kohl. "Proving Title VII Sexual Harassment: The Courts' View," *Labor Law Journal* 43, no. 3 (1992): 164–71; Koen. "Sexual Harassment Claims Stem From a Hostile Work Environment."
38. Bass, Stuart L. "The 'Reasonable Woman' Standard: The Ninth Circuit Decrees Sexes Perceive Differently," *Labor Law Journal* 43, no. 7 (1992): 449–55. Slonaker, William M., and Ann C. Wendt. "No Job Is Safe from Discrimination," *HRMagazine* 36, no. 10 (1991): 69–72; Koen. "Sexual Harassment Claims Stem From a Hostile Work Environment."
39. Koen. "Sexual Harassment Claims Stem From a Hostile Work Environment"; Woods and Flynn. "Heading Off Sexual Harassment."
40. Felsenthal, Edward. "Beach Dispute May Bring a Pivotal Harassment Ruling," *Wall Street Journal* (January 7, 1998): B1, B6; Segal, Jonathan A. "Prevent Now or Pay Later," *HRMagazine* 43, no. 11 (1998): 145–49; Vinson and Elkins L.L.P. "Labor and Employment Update: Appropriate Management Response to New Sexual Harassment Cases" [undated].
41. *EEOC v. Sage Realty Corp.*, 507 F. Supp. 599 (S.D.N.Y. 1981); Rothstein, Knapp, and Liebman. *Cases and Materials on Employment Law*; Twomey. *Equal Employment Opportunity Law*.
42. Minerd, Jeff. "Preventing E-Mail Lawsuits," *Futurist* 33, no. 6 (1999): 6–7; Carrns, Ann. "Prying Times: Those Bawdy E-Mails Were Good for a Laugh—Until the Ax Fell," *Wall Street Journal* (February 4, 2000): A1, A8.
43. Collins, Eliza G. C. "Managers and Lovers," *Harvard Business Review* 61, no. 5 (1983): 142–53; Quinn, Robert E., and Patricia L. Lees. "Attraction and Harassment: Dynamics of Sexual Politics in the Workplace," *Organizational Dynamics* 13, no. 2 (1984): 35–46.
44. Flynn, Gillian. " 'Love Contracts' Help Fend Off Harassment Suits," *Workforce* 78, no. 3 (1999): 106–8.
45. Ibid., p. 106.
46. Terpstra, David E., and Douglas D. Baker. "Outcomes of Federal Court Decisions on Sexual Harassment," *Academy of Management Journal* 35, no. 1 (1992): 181–90.
47. Terpstra, David E., and Douglas D. Baker. "Outcomes of Sexual Harassment Charges," *Academy of Management Journal* 31, no. 1 (1988): 185–94.
48. Hames, David S. "An Actionable Condition of Work-Related Sexual Harassment," *Labor Law Journal* 43, no. 7 (1992): 430–39; Koen. "Sexual Harassment Claims Stem From a Hostile Work Environment."
49. Fullerton, Howard N. Jr. "Labor Force Projections to 2008: Steady Growth and Changing Composition," *Monthly Labor Review* 122, no. 11 (1999): 19–32.
50. Slonaker, William M., and Ann C. Wendt. "Pregnancy Discrimination: An Empirical Analysis of a Continuing Problem," *Labor Law Journal* 42, no. 6 (1991): 343–50; Levin-Epstein. *Primer of Equal Employment Opportunity*.
51. Slonaker and Wendt. "Pregnancy Discrimination: An Empirical Analysis of a Continuing Problem."
52. U.S. Department of Labor. *Your Rights Under the Family and Medical Leave Act of 1993*. Washington, DC: U.S. Department of Labor, Employment Standards Administration, Wage and Hour Division; Barnet, Tim, Winston N. McVea Jr., and Patricia A. Lanier. "An Overview of the Family and Medical Leave Act of 1993," *Labor Law Journal* 44, no. 7 (1993): 429–33.

53. Postol, Lawrence P., and David D. Kadue. "An Employer's Guide to the Americans With Disabilities Act," *Labor Law Journal* 42, no. 6 (1991): 323–42; Kohl, John P., and Paul S. Greenlaw. "The Americans with Disabilities Act of 1990: Implications for Managers," *Sloan Management Review* 33, no. 3 (1992): 87–90; Bureau of National Affairs. "ADA Americans With Disabilities Act of 1990," *Labor Relations Reporter* 134, no. 11 (1990): S5–S12; Mello, Jeffrey. "Employing and Accommodating Workers With Disabilities: Mandates and Guidelines for Labor Relations," *Labor Law Journal* 44, no. 3 (1993): 162–70.
54. Postol and Kadue. "An Employer's Guide to the Americans With Disabilities Act."
55. Mello. "Employing and Accommodating Workers with Disabilities: Mandates and Guidelines for Labor Relations"; Krugel, Charles A. "AIDS and the ADA: Maneuvering Through a Legal Minefield," *Labor Law Journal* 44, no. 7 (1993): 408–21; Postol and Kadue. "An Employer's Guide to the Americans With Disabilities Act."
56. Snyder, David A. "Qualified Individuals with Disabilities: Defining the ADA's Protected Class," *Labor Law Journal* 44, no. 2 (1993): 101–9; Postol and Kadue. "An Employer's Guide to the Americans With Disabilities Act."
57. Levin, Amanda. "Supreme Court Limits Employer Liabilities," *National Underwriter* 103, no. 4 (1999): 10, 40; Carelli, Richard. "High Court Limits Scope of Disabilities Act," *The Miami Herald, International Edition* (June 23, 1999): 5A.
58. Carelli. "High Court Limits Scope of Disabilities Act," p. 5A.
59. Ibid.
60. Mello. "Employing and Accommodating Workers with Disabilities: Mandates and Guidelines for Labor Relations."
61. Ibid.
62. Ibid.; Postol and Kadue. "An Employer's Guide to the Americans With Disabilities Act."
63. Frierson, James G. "An Employer's Dilemma: The ADA's Provisions on Reasonable Accommodation and Confidentiality," *Labor Law Journal* 43, no. 5 (1992): 308–12.
64. Postol and Kadue. "An Employer's Guide to the Americans With Disabilities Act"; Krugel. "AIDS and the ADA: Maneuvering Through a Legal Minefield"; Frierson. "An Employer's Dilemma: The ADA's Provisions on Reasonable Accommodation and Confidentiality."
65. Brady, Teresa. "The Legal Issues Surrounding Religious Discrimination in the Workplace," *Labor Law Journal* 44, no. 4 (1993): 246–51; *Ansonia Board of Education v. Philbrook*, 479 U.S. 60 (1986); Wermiel, Stephen. "High Court Allows Employers Leeway in Accommodating Workers' Religions," *Wall Street Journal* (November 18, 1986): 7; Sculnick, Michael W. "Reasonable Accommodation of Religious Observances," *Employment Relations Today* 14, no. 1 (1987): 9–15.
66. Brady. "The Legal Issues Surrounding Religious Discrimination in the Workplace"; *Trans World Airlines, Inc. v. Hardison*, 432 U.S. 63 (1977).
67. Brady. "The Legal Issues Surrounding Religious Discrimination in the Workplace."
68. Ibid.
69. Ibid., p. 246.
70. Nelson, Richard R. "State Labor Legislation Enacted in 1999," *Monthly Labor Review* 123, no. 1 (2000): 3–19; "Laws Prohibiting Discrimination. Eleven States Bar Discrimination in Private Employment Based on Sexual Orientation," *The CQ Researcher* 10, no. 14 (April 14, 2000): 308; Web site: **www.qrd.org/browse/sexual.orientation.nondiscrimination.list;** Leonard, Arthur S. "Sexual Orientation and the Workplace: A Rapidly Developing Field," *Labor Law Journal* 44, no. 9 (1993): 574–83.
71. Wells, Susan J. "A Benefit Built for 2," *HRMagazine* 44, no. 8 (1999): 68–74; Koenig, David. "Oil Giant Limits Partner Benefits," *Fort Worth Star-Telegram* (December 7, 1999): 12C.
72. Jacobs and Koch. *Legal Compliance Guide to Personnel Management*; Rothstein, Knapp, and Liebman. *Cases and Materials on Employment Law*; Steingold, Fred S. *The Employer's Legal Handbook*, 2nd ed. Berkeley, CA: Nolo Press, 1997.
73. Jacobs and Koch. *Legal Compliance Guide to Personnel Management.*
74. Ibid.
75. Rothstein, Knapp, and Liebman. *Cases and Materials on Employment Law*; Milkovich, George T., and Jerry M. Newman. *Compensation*, 2nd ed. Plano, TX: Business Publications, Inc., 1987.

76. Paetzold, Ramona L. "Consolidated Omnibus Budget Reconciliation Act of 1985 (COBRA)," in Lawrence H. Peters, Charles R. Greer, and Stuart A. Youngblood (Eds.). *The Blackwell Encyclopedic Dictionary of Human Resource Management*. Oxford, UK: Blackwell Publishers, Ltd., 1997, p. 57; Jacobs and Koch. *Legal Compliance Guide to Personnel Management.*
77. Sunoo, Brenda Paik. "Carrying the Weight of the HIPAA-potamus," *Workforce* 77, no. 11 (1998): 58–60.
78. Stautberg. "Status Report: The Corporation and Trends in Family Issues."
79. Morgan, Hall, and Kerry Tucker. *Companies That Care*. New York: Simon and Schuster/Fireside, 1991.
80. Cook, Alice H. "Public Policies to Help Dual-Earner Families Meet the Demands of the Work World," *Industrial and Labor Relations Review* 42, no. 2 (1989): 201–15; Stautberg. "Status Report: The Corporation and Trends in Family Issues."
81. Stautberg. "Status Report: The Corporation and Trends in Family Issues," p. 288.
82. U.S. Department of Labor. *Your Rights Under the Family and Medical Leave Act of 1993*; Barnet, McVea, and Lanier. "An Overview of the Family and Medical Leave Act of 1993."
83. Barnet, McVea, and Lanier. "An Overview of the Family and Medical Leave Act of 1993."
84. Ibid., p. 430.
85. Susser, Peter A., and David H. Jett. "Negligent Hiring: What You Don't Know Can Hurt You," *Employment Relations Today* 14, no. 3 (1987): 279–86; Miller, Gary D., and James W. Fenton Jr. "Negligent Hiring and Criminal Record Information: A Muddled Area of Employment Law," *Labor Law Journal* 42, no. 3 (1991): 186–92.
86. Clausing, Jeri. "Children to Receive Millions," *Fort Worth Star-Telegram* (October 3, 1992): 23A, 26A.
87. Peltin, Steve. "How to Reduce Workplace Violence," *National Underwriter* (August 2, 1999): 9, 22.
88. Nelson. "State Labor Legislation Enacted in 1999"; Susser and Jett. "Negligent Hiring: What You Don't Know Can Hurt You"; Miller and Fenton. "Negligent Hiring and Criminal Record Information: A Muddled Area of Employment Law."
89. Susser and Jett. "Negligent Hiring: What You Don't Know Can Hurt You"; Miller and Fenton. "Negligent Hiring and Criminal Record Information: A Muddled Area of Employment Law."
90. Susser and Jett. "Negligent Hiring: What You Don't Know Can Hurt You," p. 285.
91. Miller and Fenton. "Negligent Hiring and Criminal Record Information: A Muddled Area of Employment Law," p. 189.
92. Lake, Monte B., and Lynnette R. Conway. "Avoiding Discriminatory Immigration-Related Employment Practices," *Employment Relations Today* 15, no. 1 (1988): 49–55; Levin-Epstein. *Primer of Equal Employment Opportunity*; Twomey. *Equal Employment Opportunity Law*.
93. Krueger, Alan B. "The Evolution of Unjust-Dismissal Legislation in the United States," *Industrial and Labor Relations Review* 44, no. 4 (1991): 644–60.
94. Mandelbaum, Leonard B. "Employment at Will: Is the Model Termination Act the Answer?" *Labor Law Journal* 44, no. 5 (1993): 275–85.
95. Krueger. "The Evolution of Unjust-Dismissal Legislation in the United States," p. 644.
96. Mandelbaum. "Employment at Will: Is the Model Termination Act the Answer?"; Hauserman, Nancy R., and Cheryl L. Maranto. "The Union Substitution Hypothesis Revisited: Do Judicially Created Exceptions to the Termination-At-Will Doctrine Hurt Unions?" *Marquette Law Review* 72, no. 3 (1989): 317–48.
97. Twomey. *Equal Employment Opportunity Law*; Naeve, Robert A. *Wrongful Termination*. Walnut Creek, CA: Borgman Associates, 1990; Krueger. "The Evolution of Unjust-Dismissal Legislation in the United States"; Mandelbaum. "Employment at Will: Is the Model Termination Act the Answer?"
98. *Wagenseller v. Scottsdale Memorial Hospital*, 147 Ariz. 370, 710 P.2d 1025 (1985); Mackey, Daniel M. *Employment at Will and Employer Liability*. New York: American Management Association, 1986, p. 41.
99. Mackey. *Employment at Will and Employer Liability*.

100. Naeve. *Wrongful Termination*; Krueger. "The Evolution of Unjust-Dismissal Legislation in the United States"; Mandelbaum. "Employment at Will: Is the Model Termination Act the Answer?"; Twomey. *Equal Employment Opportunity Law*.

101. Stieber, Jack, and Richard N. Block. "Comment on Alan B. Krueger, 'The Evolution of Unjust-Dismissal Legislation in the United States,' " *Industrial and Labor Relations Review* 45, no. 4 (1992): 792–99; Mandelbaum. "Employment at Will: Is the Model Termination Act the Answer?"; Mackey. *Employment at Will and Employer Liability*.

102. Bierman, Leonard, and Stuart A. Youngblood. "Interpreting Montana's Pathbreaking Wrongful Discharge From Employment Act: A Preliminary Analysis," *Montana Law Review* 53, no. 1 (1992): 53–74; Krueger. "The Evolution of Unjust-Dismissal Legislation in the United States."

103. Krueger. "The Evolution of Unjust-Dismissal Legislation in the United States."

104. Maltby, Lewis L. "The Decline of Employment At Will—A Quantitative Analysis," *Labor Law Journal* 41, no. 1 (1990): 51–54.

105. Krueger. "The Evolution of Unjust-Dismissal Legislation in the United States"; Mandelbaum. "Employment at Will: Is the Model Termination Act the Answer?" Stieber and Block. "Comment on Alan B. Krueger, 'The Evolution of Unjust-Dismissal Legislation in the United States.' "

106. Schwoerer, Catherine, and Benson Rosen. "Effects of Employment-at-Will Policies and Compensation Policies on Corporate Image and Job Pursuit Intentions," *Journal of Applied Psychology* 74, no. 4 (1989): 653–56.

107. Hanson, David J. "Drug Abuse Testing Programs Gaining Acceptance in Workplace," *Chemical and Engineering News* 64 (June 2, 1986): 7–14; "Motorola Plans Drug Test for All," *Fort Worth Star-Telegram* (May 22, 1990): 2-1.

108. Flynn, Gillian. "How to Prescribe Drug Testing," *Workforce* 78, no. 1 (1999): 107.

109. American Management Association. "Fewer People Fail as Workplace Drug Testing Increases."

110. Gips, Michael A. "Drug Testing Assailed," *Security Management* 43, no. 12 (1999): 16.

111. Osterloh, John D., and Charles E. Becker. "Chemical Dependency and Drug Testing in the Workplace," *Western Journal of Medicine* 152, no. 5 (1990): 506–13.

112. American Management Association. "Fewer People Fail as Workplace Drug Testing Increases," *HR Focus* 70, no. 6 (1993): 24.

113. Flynn, Gillian. "How to Prescribe Drug Testing," *Workforce* 78, no. 1 (1999): 107.

114. Osterloh and Becker. "Chemical Dependency and Drug Testing in the Workplace"; Weiss, Donald H. *Fair, Square, and Legal*. New York: AMACOM, 1991; Rothstein, Knapp, and Liebman. *Cases and Materials on Employment Law*.

115. Flynn, Gillian. "How to Prescribe Drug Testing," *Workforce* 78, no. 1 (1999): 107.

116. American Management Association. "Fewer People Fail as Workplace Drug Testing Increases"; Greenberg, Eric R. "Test-Positive Rates Drop as More Companies Screen Employees," *HR Focus* 69, no. 6 (1992): 7.

117. Rothstein, Knapp, and Liebman. *Cases and Materials on Employment Law*.

118. Liem, Stephen A. "The Fourth Amendment and Drug Testing in the Workplace: Current U.S. Court Decisions," *Labor Law Journal* 43, no. 1 (1992): 50–57.

119. Osterloh and Becker. "Chemical Dependency and Drug Testing in the Workplace"; Gray and Brown. "Issues in Drug Testing for the Private Sector."

120. Rothstein, Knapp, and Liebman. *Cases and Materials on Employment Law*; Gray and Brown. "Issues in Drug Testing for the Private Sector"; Osterloh and Becker. "Chemical Dependency and Drug Testing in the Workplace."

121. Osterloh and Becker. "Chemical Dependency and Drug Testing in the Workplace"; Weiss. *Fair, Square, and Legal*.

122. Osterloh and Becker. "Chemical Dependency and Drug Testing in the Workplace"; Weiss. *Fair, Square, and Legal*.

123. Jacobs and Koch. *Legal Compliance Guide to Personnel Management*, p. 303.

124. Jacobs and Koch. *Legal Compliance Guide to Personnel Management*; Ledvinka. *Federal Regulation of Personnel and Human Resource Management*; Cibon and Castagnera. *Labor and Employment Law*.

125. Cibon and Castagnera. *Labor and Employment Law*, p. 445.
126. Commerce Clearing House. *Labor Law Course*, 26th ed. Chicago: Commerce Clearing House, Inc., 1987; Weiss. *Fair, Square, and Legal.*
127. Taylor, Benjamin, and Fred Witney. *Labor Relations Law*, 5th ed. Englewood Cliffs, NJ: Prentice-Hall, Inc., 1987.
128. Commerce Clearing House. *Labor Law Course*; Taylor and Witney. *Labor Relations Law.*
129. Commerce Clearing House. *Labor Law Course.*
130. Ibid.
131. Cibon and Castagnera. *Labor and Employment Law.*
132. Cibon and Castagnera. *Labor and Employment Law.*
133. "Promises, Promises, Promises," *Fort Worth Star-Telegram* (January 10, 1993): AA1.
134. Cibon and Castagnera. *Labor and Employment Law.*
135. Zellner, Harriet. "Discriminating Risk," *Best's Review* 100, no. 6 (1999): 117–18; Mueller, Brian, "Everyone Is a Prospect for EPL Insurance," *American Agent and Broker* 71, no. 5 (1999): 36–42; Skinner, David C., William T. Edwards, and Gregory L. Gravlee. "Selecting Employment Practices Liability Insurance," *HRMagazine* 43, no. 10 (1998): 146–52.
136. Nelson. "State Labor Legislation Enacted in 1999."
137. Epstein, Richard A. *Forbidden Grounds: The Case Against Employment Discrimination Laws.* Cambridge, MA: Harvard University Press, 1992.
138. Brimelow and Spencer. "When Quotas Replace Merit, Everybody Suffers," p. 80.

CASE 3
The Legal Environment as an Incentive for Smallness

In the past, many large companies found that they were not competitive when faced with challenges from smaller companies that responded more quickly to market opportunities and environmental changes. As a result, some downsized and restructured in order to gain some of the advantages of smaller, more entrepreneurial firms. The inherent properties of smallness, such as flexibility, streamlined decision-making processes, and closer customer contact, make it more likely that small companies can adapt more quickly to changes in their environments. An example of efficiencies of smallness is provided by findings that the highest sales per employee ratios are found in companies having less than 20 employees. Not surprisingly, small companies and businesses are becoming an increasingly important source of jobs. Outsourced work from large companies and the emergence of network or unbundled organizations are other important reasons for the growth of employment accounted by small firms.[1]

U.S. politicians may have become more aware of the jobs created by small businesses. Some also may be aware of the impact of more human resource regulations on small businesses. Such awareness is probably reflected in the threshold employment levels for federal regulation. For example, threshold employment levels are 20 for the Age Discrimination in Employment Act, 20 for the Consolidated Omnibus Budget Reconciliation Act of 1985 (COBRA), 15 for the Civil Rights Act of 1964, 15 for the Pregnancy Discrimination Act, and 15 for the Americans with Disabilities Act of 1990. (It should be noted that some states have similar laws with lower employment thresholds.)

Entrepreneurs are well aware of the greater responsiveness and efficiencies they are able to obtain with small organizations. These benefits may encourage them to keep their organizations relatively small. On the other hand, expanding human resource regulations also may have had an impact on the strategies of entrepreneurs. Entrepreneurs need look no further than the daily newspaper to find examples of greater regulation in this area. The Americans with Disabilities Act of 1990 provides some of the latest illustrations. For example, Weight Watchers was sued because of the "company's refusal to offer sign language at its meetings."[2]

Regardless of whether such suits against employers are successful, they probably convince some small business entrepreneurs that federal laws represent a threat. As a result, entrepreneurs may view the threshold employment levels of federal laws as an important determinant of their strategies. Some may not want to increase employment to the point where they are covered by federal employment laws.[3] Aside from a strategy to limit employment or substitute capital for labor, an entrepreneur may pursue a growth strategy by adding several small independent entities rather than pursuing a growth strategy within one company. There is precedent for the latter strategy as some unionized construction contractors have established independent companies that operate on a nonunion basis. Furthermore, small companies can outsource activities, such as payroll and accounting functions, in order to keep their employment levels down.

Interestingly, in the high-technology sector, small companies are making use of flexible assembly lines and flexible manufacturing techniques in order to meet the changing needs of current markets. Such technologies require highly skilled employees.[4] Employees having such skills typically have greater mobility than less skilled workers. In the absence of legal protections from unfair actions by their employers, the mobility of such employees may guarantee at least a minimum level of fair treatment, as employers will have a strong incentive to preserve their investments in such employees.

Questions

1. Examine the viability of strategies based on keeping employment levels below the threshold levels for coverage by federal employment laws. What are the positive and negative consequences of such strategies?

2. As a result of exclusion of small businesses from coverage by some federal laws, the employees of such businesses have fewer rights than employees of larger companies. Discuss the potential effects of this discrepancy.
3. It may be argued that employment thresholds for legal coverage provide Congressional acknowledgment that employment laws restrict competitiveness and productivity. If this is true, why is the legal regulation of human resource management expanding? Conversely, how could laws such as the Family and Medical Leave Act of 1993 and the Worker Adjustment and Retraining and Notification Act increase productivity?

References

1. Kanter, Rosabeth M. *When Giants Learn to Dance: Mastering the Challenge of Strategy, Management, and Careers in the 1990s*. New York: Simon and Schuster, 1989; "Ain't Necessarily So," *The Economist* (September 11, 1993): A22–23; Snow, Charles C., Raymond E. Miles, and Henry J. Coleman Jr. "Managing 21st Century Network Organizations," *Organizational Dynamics* 20, no. 3 (1992): 5–20; Phillips, Bruce D. "The Increasing Role of Small Firms in the High-Technology Sector: Evidence from the 1980s," *Business Economics* 26, no. 1 (1991): 40–47.
2. Mahlburg, Bob. "Disability Suit Hits Diet Firm," *Fort Worth Star-Telegram* (May 8, 1994): A1.
3. Personal observations reported by John Thompson, Texas Christian University, 1993.
4. Phillips. "The Increasing Role of Small Firms in the High-Technology Sector: Evidence from the 1980s."

CHAPTER 4

Strategy Formulation

The fourth component in the conceptual framework, strategy formulation, provides direction to the organization. Effective organizational strategies are required for the organization to accomplish its mission while being guided by an investment perspective. After scanning the environment for opportunities and threats and the introspective process of evaluating strengths and weaknesses, the organization is ready for strategy formulation. As noted in the Preface, human resource planning also may provide input for strategy formulation, although it is sequenced in the conceptual framework after strategy formulation.

This chapter will first discuss the importance of human resource management to strategy formulation. Following this discussion, the theoretical foundation for strategic human resource management will be presented, along with strategic concepts and definitions. International strategy, a topic of rapidly growing importance, will then be discussed. The chapter will then examine the contributions that human resources can make to corporate strategy and the interaction between strategy and human resources. After this discussion, strategy-driven role behaviors, types of human resource activities, types of firms, network organizations, and organizational learning will be examined. Following these strategic topics, the integration of strategy with human resource planning will be explored. Finally, personal requirements of strategically oriented roles will be discussed. Although the material presented in this chapter is often expressed in a human resource context, the strategic principles have broad application to all managers.

IMPORTANCE OF HUMAN RESOURCES TO STRATEGY

Human resource management has become more important to general management, largely as a result of its role in providing competitive advantage, the rush to competitiveness, and an awareness of the demands of the technologically advanced environment of the future.[1] Strategist Michael Porter has found that human resource management is a key to obtaining competitive advantage.[2] In a growing number of organizations, human resources are now viewed as a source of competitive advantage. There is greater recognition that distinctive competencies are obtained through highly developed employee skills, distinctive organizational cultures, management processes, and systems. This is in contrast to traditional emphasis on transferable resources, such as equipment that can be purchased by competitors. Increasingly, it is being recognized that competitive advantage can be obtained with a high-quality workforce, which enables organizations to compete on the basis of market responsiveness, product and service quality, differentiated products, and technological innovation, instead of reliance on low costs.[3] An example of human resource–based competitive advantage is provided by John Deere's efforts to automate its factories. As a result of the development of exceptional talent and expertise in factory automation, the company established a technology division.[4] Another example is provided by ARCO's increased emphasis on human resource management issues in its executive development program.[5] Examples such as these indicate the broader responsibilities and importance of today's more strategically oriented human resource management.

Aside from its role in providing competitive advantage through a quality workforce, the necessity of controlling labor costs also has elevated the role of human resource management. As a result of intense pressure to control costs, general managers have gained a greater awareness of the impact of inefficient use of human resources. Managers need look no further than underutilized workers, lack of trust, resistance to change, antagonistic labor–management relations, motivational problems, and restrictive work practices to find causes of lower productivity. Interestingly, resources allocated toward better utilization of human resources may prove to be more cost efficient than investments in plant and equipment. Because of potential cost efficiencies, improved human resource management can play a key role in the organization's competitive strategy and in the development of distinctive competencies.[6]

Economic turbulence also has increased the importance of the strategic role of human resource management. Turbulence, globalization, technology, dramatically changing demographics, and differences in workforce values have created almost unprecedented environmental uncertainty. Strategic human resource management and the subprocess of human resource planning are increasingly being seen as means of buffering environmental uncertainty. Not surprisingly, human resource management is becoming integrated into the strategy formulation and planning process.[7] As human resource management becomes a more important component of a company's competitive strategy, general management has an incentive to ensure alignment and consistency between strategy and human resource practices and policies.[8] The first alignment challenge comes with finding the answer to the following question: "What kinds of people will be needed to lead the organization in the years to come?" [9] The expectation is that people and practices, which are aligned with future strategic needs, produce superior organizational performance. While the evidence on this point is mixed, some recent empirical studies have found higher performance to be related to integrated, strategic human resource management.[10] There has also been recognition of contributions of human resource management to company success in international endeavors. Such success is more likely when international involvement is rewarded and international business training is provided. It is also more likely when managerial selection and promotion criteria incorporate international experience.[11] Nonetheless, before such contributions can be made, a coherent human resource strategy must be developed and linked to the organization's overall strategy.

THEORETICAL FOUNDATIONS

Strategic Concepts and Definitions

The term *strategic human resource management* has become a widely used in the management literature. In general, the goal of strategic human resource management is the effective application of such resources to meet organizations' strategic requirements and objectives. When defining the term, practitioners tend to emphasize its implementation role,[12] as revealed in the following definitions:

> Getting the strategy of the business implemented effectively . . . getting everybody from the top of the human organization to the bottom doing things that make the business successful." [13]

A more comprehensive academic definition of strategic human resource management specifies the following:

> Strategic human resources management is largely about integration and adaption. Its concern is to ensure that: (1) human resources (HR) management is fully integrated with the strategy and the strategic needs of the firm; (2) HR policies cohere both across policy areas and across hierarchies; and (3) HR practices are adjusted, accepted, and used by line managers and employees as part of their everyday work.[14]

Patrick Wright and Gary McMahan have offered a similar definition of strategic human resource management.[15] Their definition is "the pattern of planned human resource deployments and activities intended to enable an organization to achieve its goals." [16]

Given these definitions of strategic human resource management, a comprehensive theoretical framework can now be used to organize knowledge of how human resource practices are affected by strategic considerations. Such a theoretical framework has been developed by Patrick Wright and Gary McMahan and is presented in Figure 4-1. This framework presents six theoretical influences, four of which provide explanations for practices resulting from

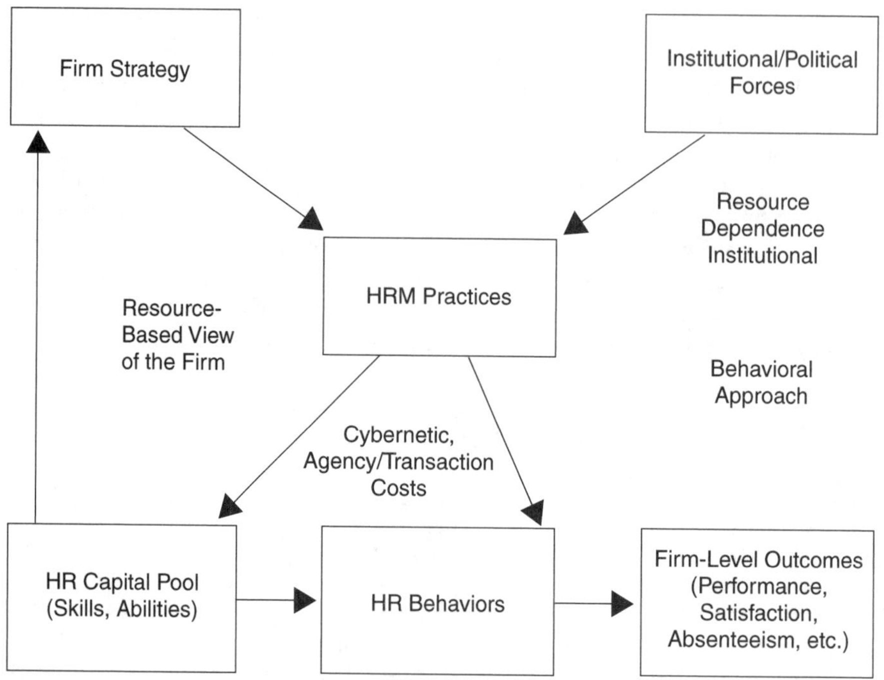

FIGURE 4-1 Strategic Human Resource Management: A Theoretical Framework

Source: Patrick M. Wright and Gary C. McMahan. "Theoretical Perspectives for Strategic Human Resource Management," *Journal of Management* 18, no. 2 (1992): 299. Reprinted with permission of *Journal of Management*.

strategy considerations. The first, the *resources-based view*, explains practices that provide competitive advantage, such as the unique allocation of the firm's resources, organizational culture, and distinctive competence. For example, a firm might allocate its resources to produce superior selection procedures and compensation systems in order to obtain distinctive competence. The second influence, a *behavioral view*, based on contingency theory, explains practices designed to control and influence attitudes and behaviors. It stresses the instrumentality of such practices in achieving strategic objectives. The third draws on *cybernetics systems*. This view explains the adoption or abandonment of practices resulting from feedback on contributions to strategy. When viewed from this perspective, training programs might be adopted to help the organization pursue a strategy and would be updated according to feedback. The fourth, an *agency/transaction cost view*, explains why companies use control systems, such as performance evaluation and reward systems. In the absence of performance evaluation systems linked to reward systems, strategies might not be pursued.[17]

The other two theories provide explanations for personnel practices that are not driven by strategy considerations. *Resource dependence and power theo-*

ries explain practices caused by power and political influences such as legislation, unionization, control of resources, and expectations of social responsibility. The final influence, *institutional theory*, explains that practices, such as the use of inappropriate performance evaluation dimensions, may exist because of organizational inertia rather than conscious or rational decision making.[18]

Strategy

The contemporary literature provides a number of different definitions of *strategic management*. James Brian Quinn's definition of strategy focuses on the integration of goals, policies, and action sequences: "A strategy is the *pattern* or *plan* that *integrates* an organization's *major* goals, policies, and action sequences into a *cohesive* whole." [19] Thus, strategy deals with providing direction, coordinating, and providing a decisional framework. Another role of strategy deals with the allocation of resources. The following definition by William Henn focuses on this aspect of strategy: "Strategy is the concentration of resources on selected opportunities for competitive advantage." [20] Strategist Kenichi Ohmae has made a similar point, "Merely allocating resources in the same way as your competitors will yield no competitive advantage." [21] Henn's and Ohmae's definitions focus on making hard decisions to take resources from less promising product lines, projects, and the like, and concentrating them in areas where the company can obtain a strategic advantage. By failing to be selective about opportunities and failing to make tough decisions about the company's distribution of resources, they are spread too thinly across all product lines. As a result, companies that fail to concentrate their resources are at a disadvantage.[22] Thus, strategy performs directional, coordinating, decision-making, and resource allocation functions.

Strategic Planning

Definitions of *strategic planning*, also called the *strategy formulation process*,[23] differ in their emphasis on rationality and formality. The following is James Craft's description of *rational/comprehensive* strategic planning:

> The rational/comprehensive process, frequently advocated in strategic planning texts and apparently by many practitioners, emphasizes purposeful activity through a logical formulation of goals, examination of alternatives, and delineation of plans prior to actions. It tends to have a long-term orientation and focuses on measurable forces affecting the firm, as well as on quantitative activities and procedures.[24]

The process of formal rational/comprehensive strategic planning is typically composed of the following steps:

1. Development of organizational philosophy and mission statement
2. Environmental scanning
3. Analysis of strengths, weaknesses, opportunities, and threats (SWOT analysis)
4. Formulation of strategic objectives

5. Generation of alternative strategies for achieving objectives
6. Evaluation and selection of strategies

This series of steps makes no mention of the political aspects of strategic planning. Nonetheless, the formality of the process and its emphasis on logic and quantitative processes should not obscure the fact that strategic planning is conducted by a dominant coalition. Because of the political nature of the process, some aspects of a plan will be negotiated.[25]

In contrast to formal/comprehensive strategic planning, *informal/incremental* strategic planning emphasizes the emergent and temporal nature of strategy and has a shorter-term orientation.[26] According to Quinn, to a certain extent the managed or logical incremental approach represents an adaptive process, making changes and adjustments to strategy on the basis of new information. Such planning is not "muddling through," "disjointed," or "unconscious." Further, managed or logical incremental planning is not inconsistent with formal planning, but instead leads to quicker implementation and reduces the likelihood of catastrophic errors that might result from rigid adherence to formal rational/comprehensive planning.[27] Logical incrementalism is consistent with adapting to input from organizational subunits and functional areas as information becomes available. This appears to be the case as more of the responsibilities of strategic planning are being shared with line mangers.[28]

Although the two types of strategic planning differ, their use is not mutually exclusive as companies tend to employ both approaches. It is probably more useful to think of strategic planning as a balance between rational/comprehensive and incremental planning or a matter of degree.[29] Regardless of the degree of formality versus incrementalism, strategic planning serves a number of vital functions, which are presented in Table 4-1.[30]

Competitive Strategy in Business Units

To this point, the discussion of strategic planning has been primarily focused at the corporate level. Nonetheless, competitive strategies at the business level are

TABLE 4-1 Functions of Strategic Planning

1. Periodic forward scanning
2. Analysis based on longer time frame
3. Communication about goals and resource allocation
4. Framework for short-term plan evaluation and integration
5. Institutionalization of longer-term time horizons necessary for investments such as in research and development
6. Decisional criteria framework for short-term decision making

Source: Adapted from James B. Quinn. "Strategic Change: Logical Incrementalism," *Sloan Management Review* 30, no. 4 (1989): 45–55.

very relevant to human resources and the development of human resource strategies. Michael Porter's framework provides a good basis for understanding competitive strategies at the business level. Porter has argued that there are five forces that affect the potential profitability of an industry: These forces, which have some foundation in the economic reasoning of the economist Alfred Marshall, include the ease with which new competitors can enter an industry, customers' bargaining power, suppliers' bargaining power, the strength of rivalry among the industry's competing firms, and the availability of substitutes for the industry's goods or services. In turn, there are several specific characteristics by which each of these forces can be evaluated. For example, the strength of barriers to entry into an industry is determined by such influences as economies of scale, capital costs, and governmental regulation. These forces provide the basis for the development of an analytical tool called the *value chain*, which provides insights into how firms assess their capabilities to compete and make decisions regarding their competitive strategies. Examples of primary activities in the value chain include operations, outbound logistics, and service, while examples of support activities include human resources and technology.[31]

The combined understanding of an industry's attractiveness and an awareness of the firm's capabilities to compete allows firms to chose a strategy for competing in the industry. Essentially, there are three generic strategies for competing in an industry: *low-cost leadership, differentiation* (distinctive products or services), and *niche* or *focus* variations that apply low-cost leadership or differentiation in a narrow or focused segment of the industry. Such business competitive strategies are important to human resource strategy formulation because different human resource practices are consistent with different competitive strategies.[32] Raymond Miles and Charles Snow's adaptive model of business strategy provides insights into how firms adapt themselves for better alignment with their competitive environments. Their model is addressed later in this chapter.

Planning in Strategic Business Units

Human resource management can play an important role in strategic planning at the level of the strategic business unit and, as noted, is one of the links in value chain analysis. This role may be examined in the context of human resource input in the development of strategic alternatives. For example, a strategic business unit's marketing group may identify an opportunity during its planning processes. Marketing planners then develop alternative strategies for exploiting the opportunity. As a part of the planning process, representatives from the functional areas such as production, finance, and human resources make inputs on the strengths, weaknesses, and resource requirements. Human resource management would be expected to provide an analysis of the staffing implications of each alternative. The product of these planning processes is then submitted to the corporate top management team for approval and funding. In some corporations, the vice president for human resources would also be a member of the executive committee making the final decisions on these planning proposals. This representation of human resources by the human resource vice president or senior human resource official would constitute a separate role.[33]

Human Resource Strategy

To this point, the discussion of strategy and strategic planning has focused on the general concept of strategic human resource management and the relatively broad concepts of corporate level and strategic business unit considerations. The next focal point is *human resource strategy*, which has been defined by Randall Schuler as follows: "HR strategies are essentially plans and programs to address and solve fundamental strategic issues related to human resources management."[34] Human resource strategy focuses on the alignment of the organization's human resource practices, policies, and programs with corporate and strategic business unit plans. Consistent human resource policies and practices are important concerns of general management as well as the human resource function.[35]

Differences in human resource management policies and practices across industries demonstrate that policies and personnel practices vary according to the environment in which companies operate. However, industrial categories do not explain all such differences because variations in company strategies also determine human resource policies and practices. Companies generally try to avoid excessive emphasis on achieving a fit between their strategies and human resource policies and practices. Excessive concern with fit can be detrimental, since there must be transition periods during which mismatches will occur. Likewise, too much fit between a company's human resources and its strategies may unnecessarily restrict the range of employee skills, detract from innovation, and limit the capacity to change.[36]

Human Resource Planning or Staffing Planning

Human resource planning provides input into higher-level strategic planning processes. One benefit of such planning is that, regardless of the accuracy of forecasts involved, the very act of developing forecasts forces managers to reassess the fundamental assumptions under which the organization operates. Other contributions of human resource planning are that it signals the need for change and serves to guide the activities within human resource management toward greater compatibility with the organization. The process of *human resource planning*, in sequential order, includes environmental scanning and an interface with strategic planning, forecasting human resource demand, inventorying the organization's current stock of human resources, forecasting both internal and external supplies of labor, comparing supply and demand forecasts, developing plans for dealing with shortages and surpluses, and feeding back these results in a strategic planning interface.[37] The actual human resource planning process is covered in greater detail in Chapter 5.

INTERNATIONAL STRATEGY

Companies use different strategies to produce products and services that enable them to compete in the global marketplace. These strategies include multinational strategies, global strategies, transnational strategies, strategic alliances, and hybrid strategies. Nonetheless, as noted in Chapter 2, world-class workforces are required with all of these strategies. Human resource management must be able to identify sources of such labor and plan its use. Even with alliances, human resource management input is critical for both strategy formulation and implementation.[38]

Multinational, Global, and Transnational Strategies

International strategies may be described as multinational, global, transnational, or mixtures of basic strategies. With a *multinational strategy*, companies operate in countries chosen for their individual profit potential. All activities related to design, production, and marketing are then performed in each of these countries. (These are called *value-chain* activities.) *Multidomestic strategies* customize the product and its marketing to the unique preferences of each country. In contrast, *global strategies* produce standardized products, with different activities such as design and production being located in different countries, depending on labor costs, skills, or other strategic advantages. With *transnational strategies*, companies compete in the global marketplace through the use of networks and strategic alliances.[39]

Multinational or multidomestic strategies provide a power advantage in dealing with unionized workers, because labor difficulties or other production problems only shut down production and revenue flows from one country's operations or a small set of countries. However, they do not produce the economies of scale of global strategies. With global strategies, economies of scale are obtained by maintaining only a few different product models. As a result, lower costs and higher quality are obtained. Japanese automobile manufacturers provide an example of a successful application of this strategy. A disadvantage with this approach is that standardization does not address all customers' preferences. Likewise, greater coordination is required, and marketing may be less effective. A human resource implication of the global strategy is that there is concentration of resources and talent on a smaller set of activities. Thus, with the global strategy, it is important to locate each of the value-chain activities where there is world-class labor, in terms of cost or skills. Another human resource implication is that with a global strategy, a company would probably be particularly vulnerable to strikes or labor relations problems at any link in the value chain, since the whole process is dependent on each link. However, with more than one source of manufacturing facilities, the company can shift production to other operating plants.[40]

Strategic Alliances

Companies are increasing their use of *strategic alliances* with foreign companies. Such alliances allow companies to combine their distinctive competencies in order to gain an advantage in producing or marketing a product. Frequently, U.S. companies reduce their labor requirements by forming alliances with foreign firms. However, the history of U.S. companies' experiences with strategic alliances indicates that the arrangement may be fraught with perils. According to David Lei and John Slocum, alliances can be extremely dangerous for companies that outsource manufacturing. The allure of low-cost production, without the costs of investing in product development and new manufacturing technologies, is particularly seductive. Unfortunately, U.S. companies pursuing this strategy have typically ended up being "deskilled" or "hollowed out" in critical skill areas. Although in the short run financial benefits of entering into an alliance may be impressive, in the long run the alliance partner doing the manufacturing typically becomes the dominant player in the market. This occurs as a result of the U.S. partner's diminished manufacturing knowledge and the manufacturing partner's capture of knowledge of the other company's core competencies.[41] Lei and Slocum have concluded the following:

> Collaboration may unintentionally open up a firm's entire spectrum of core competencies, technologies, and skills to encroachment and learning by its partners . . . Alliances can be used as an indirect strategic weapon to slowly "deskill" a partner who does not understand the risks inherent in such arrangements.[42]

A prime example where this has occurred is the consumer electronics industry in which U.S. companies such as General Electric, RCA, and Zenith held dominant positions in all skill areas of the industry. Twenty years after their entry into alliances, virtually no consumer electronics are manufactured in the United States, while alliance partners have become dominant in the industry. More significantly, their alliance partners have used the knowledge gained from these U.S. companies to develop core competencies and take the lead in other areas such as miniature lasers and sensor systems. The greatest danger of transferring such skills occurs in situations in which there is frequent interaction and exchange between the organizations' engineering and technical employees. Companies that have outsourced manufacturing in alliances frequently no longer have the skills to compete in manufacturing and may be relegated to marketing the alliance partner's products. Further, because of the integrated design, production, and marketing processes required for today's short product development cycles, the pace of the dependent company's decline may quicken.[43]

Lei and Slocum have concluded that the importance of domestic manufacturing may have been underestimated. For example, companies that have licensed foreign companies to use their manufacturing technologies have placed themselves at future disadvantage. As Lei and Slocum pointed out, "As technology becomes a greater source of competitive advantage, licensing decisions can often radically shift the firm's competitive posture in that industry." [44]

Human resource managers need to know how to decrease the likelihood of these undesirable outcomes. Measures that may prevent alliances from working to the eventual disadvantage of the company include: (1) understanding the real aspirations of the alliance partner, (2) keeping in mind the original purposes of the alliance so that objectives are not redefined to the company's disadvantage, (3) avoiding a false sense assurance provided by legal control since the real key is knowledge transfer, and (4) keeping alliance interface managers in place over long periods of time so that subtle nuances are understood.[45] Because the latter is often in opposition to the length of job rotation cycles in management development programs, human resource managers may need to lengthen such cycles.

Sustainable Global Competitive Advantage

Interestingly, predictions by some observers that the United States would become an information economy while underdeveloped countries would take on the less skilled manufacturing roles appear to have been off the mark. These predictions have underestimated the intellectual resources of such countries and the limited capital investments required for entry into the information industry. For example, the city of Bangalore, India, has high-quality computer programming talent that U.S. companies and companies from other countries are using for development of highly complex computer software. The Indian programmers have the reputation of exceptional ability and the persistence to be able to develop very complex programs. Further, their lower salaries compared to U.S. standards makes them a highly sought out source of world-class labor.[46] Strategists would do well to avoid a premature dismissal of other countries' long-run capabilities and focus on the factors that provide companies with real and *sustainable competitive advantage* in the global economy.

Likewise, there are other strategy-related human resource implications of globalization. With greater globalization of markets, it will become more difficult for companies that do no human resource planning to compete with companies from other countries that have taken advantage of such strategy and planning contributions. For example, Volkswagen has attributed some of its managerial successes to its human resources. Volkswagen maintains a long-term approach, which is evident in its training programs that prepare workers for highly automated production systems. Also tied in with its human resource and planning efforts is Volkswagen's extensive involvement in apprenticeship training programs. During one year, 4,500 apprentices were employed by Volkswagen and guaranteed permanent jobs after completion of training, even though unemployment levels in Germany were relatively high.[47] Volkswagen's stock of skilled workers may provide it with a sustainable competitive advantage over its rivals. Nonetheless, Germany's current high wage rates have offset this advantage to some extent.

Globally Competent Managers

A growing area of strategic importance is the recruitment, selection, and development of globally competent managers. Nancy Adler and Susan Bartholomew have studied the human resource requirements for "transnationally competent managers" who have global understandings of business and broad cultural knowledge. Such managers have the flexibility to live in different cultural environments, can interact simultaneously with individuals from several different cultures, and have an egalitarian view of colleagues from other countries. A staffing goal would be to have a rich mixture of such managers from different countries, fluent in several languages, who use world-class standards for performance benchmarks. In order to acquire such managers, human resource managers must hire world-class individuals from throughout the world; develop them through transnational assignments; prepare them for organizational learning roles, such as in strategic alliances; and remove any glass ceiling limitations on promotions based on home country considerations. Unfortunately, Adler and Bartholomew found that most human resource operations in U.S. and Canadian multinational corporations do not meet these requirements.[48]

Location of Production Facilities

Decisions regarding the location of production facilities and related questions of labor cost and labor productivity provide particularly intriguing strategy-related questions. Although companies may have achieved production success with their human resource practices in one country, whether they can achieve success in other countries with the uniform application of human resource practices is subject to debate. For example, a recent study of the multinational corporation, Alcan, examined its production operations in Canada and Britain. The study found major differences in the extent to which best practices, such as flexible work practices and lean staffing, could be implemented in production facilities. As an example, managers in Britain had greater flexibility to make changes while fewer could be introduced in Canada because of the influence of seniority.[49]

Furthermore, there are growing questions about whether old notions of control and hierarchical structure are appropriate for international operations. As noted in the discussion of network organizations in Chapter 2, production can occur anyplace in the world. (Network organizations are discussed in greater detail later in this chapter.) Interestingly, some of the complications of international operations may be simplified by greater use of outsourcing. BP Amoco has contracted to outsource a substantial amount of its international human resource management activities, including payroll, benefits, and other administrative functions.[50] Nokia also handles some aspects of its international operations with outsourcing.

Production location decisions today frequently involve considerations of various sites in Asia. While many Asian countries went through a setback that will linger for several years, the expansion of markets and location of production facilities in Asia, particularly in China, has enormous implications. The growth of private entrepreneurship and manufacturing in China has been truly phenomenal. Private sector production in China now makes up 60 percent of the country's gross domestic product (GDP) compared to zero percent in 1979.[51] Furthermore, the list of international companies with manufacturing operations in China constitutes a virtual who's who of international business.

In addition to these developments, the competitive environment that companies now face in Europe is different than that which existed prior to the establishment of the European Union, the European Monetary Union, and euro currency. U.S. and other non–European Community companies have used mergers, joint ventures, and strategic alliances as means of gaining access to European markets. An example of such a joint venture is the Whirlpool and Philips arrangement in which Whirlpool appliances carry the Philips brand in European markets.[52] Another strategic issue involves the entry of several Eastern European countries that are negotiating for entry into the European Union.[53] Such memberships are important strategic human resource issues because they determine the ease of utilizing human resources across borders, as well as the markets for companies' products.[54] At this point, there is uncertainty about many of the human resource implications of these developments.

From a more regionalized perspective, the North American Free Trade Agreement (NAFTA) has added more flexibility in the location of production facilities. Prior to NAFTA, U.S. automobile manufacturers located assembly plants in Mexico in order to have access to the Mexican market. A NAFTA time schedule phases out tariffs on U.S. automobiles imported into Mexico as long as 62.5 percent of their costs come from North American production.[55] On one hand, because NAFTA will allow automobiles to be imported from U.S. plants without tariffs, there is less incentive to shift production facilities to Mexico. On the other hand, lower labor costs in Mexico as well as Canada argue for establishing plants in Mexico and Canada to take advantage of their lower labor costs. (As noted in Case 2, plant construction costs are higher in Mexico.) It is likely that many jobs requiring high skills will be created and retained in the United States, while a substantial number requiring lower skills will be shifted to Mexico until its workforce develops such skills.

From this discussion of international aspects of strategy, it is evident that companies' human resource strategies and policies cannot be developed in isolation to those of global competitors. Having human resource strategies or policies superior to those of domestic competitors is no longer sufficient. Companies must scan the regulatory environments of countries in which they wish to manufacture and sell their products in order to determine the human resource implications. Further, before they decide to locate production facilities in other countries, they also must understand the impact of cultural differences on issues as basic as the compensation mix.[56]

HUMAN RESOURCE CONTRIBUTIONS TO STRATEGY

Human resources can make contributions to strategy and strategic planning in a number of ways. Systems such as performance appraisal, staffing, training, and compensation enable managers to implement the organization's strategic plan. Human resource planning also links strategic management and business planning with these systems.[57] Most models of strategic human resource management view the function as having an implementation role, and it has been less common to find companies using unique human resource capabilities as a primary input in strategy formulation.[58] Nonetheless, more companies are drawing on human resource management in the strategy formulation process. Situations in which human resource capabilities serve as a driving force in strategy formulation occur where there are unique capabilities, such as noted earlier with the example of John Deere's creation of a technology division. Another example is Arthur Andersen's unique human resource capabilities in training. The accounting firm's Saint Charles, Illinois, training facility, which resembles a college campus, provides it with a competitive advantage.[59] Thousands of Arthur Andersen employees receive uniform training by the firm's own highly regarded instructional staff at this facility each year. Because of its facilities and in-house instructors, the firm can react quickly to the changing demands of its clients.

Additionally, recognition of the human resource cost implications of strategies can be brought into the strategy formulation process when human resource management plays an important role. This has not typically been the case in the past, until such costs have become extreme. To be sure, goal displacement or losing track of the objective is an outcome to be avoided when human resource capabilities are a primary driver in strategy formulation.[60] However, such dysfunctional side effects can be avoided with periodic reviews of the process.

Environmental Scanning and Competitive Intelligence

Human resource management has a role in *environmental scanning*, just like the finance and marketing functions. Scanning activities are particularly important in periods of rapidly changing technology and dynamic market environments. Typically, such scanning efforts focus on trends three to five years into the future and cover developments in demographics, technology, social issues, economics, and the regulatory environment.[61] An example of trends of interest to human resource scanners might be the reactions of competitors to greater access to Mexican labor markets resulting from NAFTA and whether Japanese auto manufacturers can find a way to assemble cars in Mexico and ship them duty-free into the United States.[62] Another example would be the Battelle Memorial Institute's development of inexpensive biodegradable plastics. Biodegradable plastics have cost as much as $250 per pound, while Battelle's new plastics range from $1 to $2 per pound.[63] Other examples of trends of interest to human resource scanners were covered in Chapter 2.

One interesting way in which the human resource management function can make additional contributions is in the area of *competitive intelligence* as the function can be an important source of such information. For example, because human resource managers receive résumés from employees at competing firms within the industry, they know who is moving. They also know the skills and types of individuals headhunters and competitors are recruiting. The types of individuals applying for jobs and trends in their applications can provide information that will help identify the direction being pursued by a competitor.[64] More specifically, human resources can provide the following *corporate intelligence*:

> From public information and legitimate recruiting and interview activities, you ought to be able to construct organization charts, staffing levels and group missions for the various organizational components of each of your major competitors. Your knowledge of how brands are sorted among sales divisions and who reports to whom can give important clues as to a competitor's strategic priorities. You may even know the track record and characteristic behavior of the executives.[65]

Regardless of the form of linkage between human resources and the strategic planning process, human resource managers must predict the type of people that will be needed to support the strategy.[66]

Implementation of Resource Reallocation Decisions

Although strategy implementation is discussed in Chapters 6 and 7, a major role of human resource management is to assess the feasibility of implementing a strategy and to provide such input in the strategy formulation process. Because the essence of strategy is to concentrate resources so that the organization can gain advantage over its competitors, this means that some units, divisions, or product lines must be denied resources. As a result of the denial of resources, human resource management must prevent the demoralization of those not receiving resources. Often, areas not receiving resources are still critical, at least in the short run, to the success and prosperity of the company. For example, those business areas in which there are opportunities and in which the company has strengths (the star areas) will be provided more resources. These resources would come from areas in which industry opportunities are expected to decline in the future, but in which the company now has strength and is making money (cash cows). Resources also would come from those areas characterized by both unattractive industry opportunities and low company strength (dogs). As resources are taken away from the cash cows and dogs, the manner in which employees from these areas are treated is critical to successful implementation of the strategy. For example, will those in areas facing eventual elimination be allowed to transfer out to the star areas? How will retrenchment or downsizing be handled?[67]

Lead Time for Dealing with Labor Shortages and Surpluses

Another potential contribution of human resource management comes from the lead time produced by human resource planning. The greater lead time provides alternatives for dealing with shortages or surpluses of labor. Additionally, if the organization has included the use of temporary and contingent employees in its staffing strategy, such employees provide a mechanism for strategic maneuvering, because this type of labor can sometimes be considered as a variable cost. As a result, employers have more degrees of freedom and flexibility to exercise options.[68] Unfortunately, human resource management does not yet have a strategic role in many organizations and, as a result, adequate lead time is not provided in many companies. A survey of the human resource managers of Midwestern manufacturing companies, facing financial problems or threats from intense competition, revealed that 94 percent of them had fewer than 60 days to plan downsizing. As a result, other alternatives were seldom considered in these companies.[69]

STRATEGY-DRIVEN ROLE BEHAVIORS AND PRACTICES

Competitive strategies require different human resource practices and different role behaviors. The role behaviors needed of employees throughout an organization provide a rationale for the linkage between competitive strategies and human resource practices. For example, the competitive strategies of (1) innovation, (2) quality enhancement, and (3) cost reduction can be used to explain how different employee behaviors are needed for successful implementation of different strategies. These behaviors are roles that go beyond skills, knowledge, and abilities.[70]

Essentially, for successful implementation of an innovative strategy, employees probably need to be cooperative—because of the interdependencies involved, highly creative, oriented toward the long term, risk takers, and comfortable with ambiguity. Companies pursuing such strategies include Johnson & Johnson, 3M, and Hewlett-Packard. With quality-enhancement strategies, employees need to place emphasis on production or service processes, risk reduction, and predictability. Examples of companies pursuing quality-enhancement strategies include L.L. Bean, Toyota, and Corning Glass. In contrast, for successful implementation of cost-reduction strategies, employees should be focused on the short term, risk averse, predictable, results oriented, and comfortable working by themselves.[71]

For each of the different sets of strategies and role behaviors, different human resource practices are required. General categories of such human resource practices include planning, staffing, appraisal, compensation, and training and development. It has been hypothesized that under *innovation strategies*, the appropriate role behaviors will be more likely to obtained with (1) group-oriented, long-term appraisal systems; (2) generalized skill development and broad career paths; (3) compensation approaches accentuating internal equity; and (4) flexible compensation packages including stock ownership. For *quality-enhancement strategies*, it has been hypothesized that human resource practices should include (1) employment security guarantees, (2) extensive training programs, and (3) participative decision making. With *cost reduction*, it has been hypothesized that desired role behaviors are more likely with (1) performance appraisal systems emphasizing results in the short term, (2) virtually no training programs, (3) very specialized jobs, (4) narrow and specialized career paths, and (5) procedures for continual tracking of wage rates in the labor market.[72]

STRATEGIC HUMAN RESOURCE ACTIVITY TYPOLOGY

The role of individual human resource activities may be better understood through the application of a conceptual typology developed by Alan Speaker, senior vice president at Synhrgy HR Technologies. The typology categorizes human resource activities in a 2 × 2 matrix according to two dimensions: (1) the extent to which such activities are relational or transactional and (2) whether they have high or low strategic value. At one end of the transactional and relationship continuum are transactional activities that are mostly administrative and impersonal. The performance of these activities does not require a high level of interpersonal skill, and many of these activities can be computerized. At the other end of the continuum are activities that require high levels of interpersonal skill, political awareness, and sensitivity. For the strategic-value dimension, at one end of the continuum are activities that have direct business impact on the firm's ability to implement its competitive strategies. At the other end of the continuum are activities that have a more indirect or less strategic impact. The model is presented in Figure 4-2. Although there has been no survey of practitioners indicating agreement as to the placement of activities in specific quadrants, Figure 4-2 provides some examples. It should be noted that the strategic value of the activities may vary according to the specific circumstances faced by each firm.

Examples of activities in the low strategic value/transactional quadrant include such tasks as payroll, benefits administration, employee records, and relocation administration. These activities do not have immediate impact on the firm's ability to implement various strategies, such as those emphasizing new product innovation, exceptional product quality, or low costs. Nonetheless, such activities are important to employees who become very concerned when their paychecks are not in the right amount or they are having difficulties with benefits such as medical claims. These activities must be performed accurately, in a

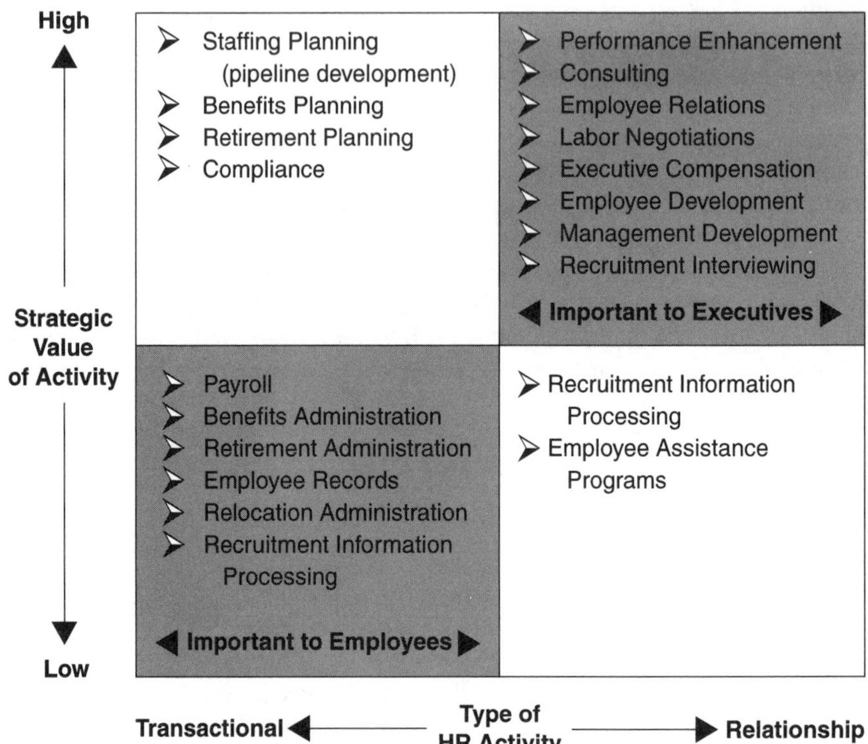

FIGURE 4-2 Strategic Typology of Human Resource Activities

Source: Slight modification of model developed by Alan W. Speaker, Synhrgy HR Technologies, Alpharetta, GA, 2000.

timely manner, and with cost efficiency. The firm's executives do not view these activities as strategically important and do not become concerned with them unless there is a problem. However, when such activities are performed poorly, human resource executives quickly get into trouble. Human resource departments must ensure that the activities in this quadrant are performed well before they can take on more strategic roles. In many instances, these activities are good candidates for outsourcing, which enables human resource departments to shift their focus and staff resources to a more strategic venue.[73] Baron and Kreps make a similar recommendation in that they argue that activities of low strategic importance and low social interdependence should be outsourced and that the decision criteria for such decisions are cost and flexibility.[74]

The evolving wisdom of strategic human resources argues that the function can make its greatest contributions in the upper right quadrant. Human resource executives see an imperative to move their departments toward greater contributions in this area. Activities in the high strategic value/relationship quadrant have a more direct impact on the firm's ability to successfully implement its competitive strategy. For example, if the firm has poor relations with its unionized workers and this produces restrictive work rules and resistance to more flexible work arrangements, then the firm is likely to have difficulty implementing a low-cost strategy. Likewise, if the firm does not have a good executive compensation program, then it is likely to have more political infighting and will encounter greater difficulty in getting its executives to cooperate for the good of the company. Given such conditions, the firm is unlikely to succeed with a differentiation strategy requiring superior customer service. Because excellence in these activities can provide firms with a source of competitive advantage and some are based on trusting relationships developed over time, they are unlikely to be outsourced. In contrast to executives, the firm's other employees are less likely to attach as much importance to these activities.

Several planning-related or design activities fall within the high strategic value/transactional quadrant. These activities potentially affect the firm's ability to implement strategies in the future. For example, staffing planning or human resource planning probably falls within this category. As will be explained in Chapter 5, such planning is necessary to ensure the availability of key people to implement the firm's strategies in the future. Compliance with governmental regulations is another activity of high strategic value of a transactional nature. For example, firms need to evaluate and monitor their staffing practices and analyze the upward mobility of their female and minority employees to ensure equal employment opportunity. If firms fail to comply with these regulations, the financial liabilities incurred can prevent them from successful implementation of their strategies.

The last quadrant, low strategic value/relationship, may include activities such as employee assistance programs. These activities or programs require substantial relationship skills such as trust, confidentiality, and genuine concern for employees' welfare. However, except for the long-term preservation of the firm's investments in valuable employees, positive contributions to employee morale, and good corporate citizenship, such an activity has little immediate impact on the firm's ability to implement its strategies.

CLASSIFYING HUMAN RESOURCE TYPES

Greater understanding of industrial and strategic differences can be obtained by examining different classifications of *strategic types*. Interestingly, principles of enlightened management suggest that companies should develop their employees, strive toward providing employment security, and seek to have supplies of internal candidates prepared for promotion when vacancies occur. Nonetheless, some companies do not manage their human resources in accordance with these principles, nor is there any indication that they should. In fact, promises of job security, committing too much of the company's resources to human resource programs, and placing too much emphasis on employees' feelings about strategic decisions can make them uncompetitive.[75] An analysis of one company's experience with employment security policies following the plunge of its stock revealed the following: "One discovery . . . was that the provisions of employment security did not automatically motivate employees to learn new skills, change jobs, or relocate to the extent demanded by the crisis." [76] Examples such as this demonstrate that the application of human resource management principles must be tempered by industry differences.

Systematic differences in utilization of human resource practices may be explained by a typology of career systems developed by Jeffrey Sonnenfeld and Maury Peiperl. Companies in this typology are classified as (1) *clubs*, (2) *baseball teams*, (3) *academies*, and (4) *fortresses*. This typology has been overlaid on an earlier typology of strategies developed by Raymond Miles and Charles Snow. In the Miles and Snow typology, the corresponding four basic types of strategies are, respectively: (1) *defenders* (low-cost producers), (2) *prospectors* (product differentiators and innovators), (3) *analyzers* (imitators of successful prospectors and focused operations), and (4) *reactors* (companies with dysfunctional strategies). Figure 4-3 presents the Sonnenfeld and Peiperl model.[77]

The personnel policies followed by companies in each of these categories provide marked contrasts. For economy of presentation in the following discussion, the characteristics of companies in the Miles and Snow categories are covered within the Sonnenfeld and Peiperl categories.

Club. When the strategy is to be the *low-cost* producer, the focus is on cost control. With cost control as the guiding principle, predictability and a short-term focus are valued.[78] Companies in this category compete by increasing their efficiency in controlling costs, maintaining quality, and providing customer service. Types of companies in the club category include airlines, banks, utilities, and governmental agencies. Club personnel policies emphasize development and training, as employees are hired in only at entry level, talent is developed within the organization, and higher-level vacancies are filled by promotions from within. There is an expectation that employees will remain with the company for a long period and there is low turnover. In terms of "make" or "buy," these companies "make" their own higher-level employees. A company well known for its managerial excellence in this category is Lincoln Electric.[79]

Baseball Team. Companies in this category pursue an *innovation* strategy. As such, they design and produce new products and routinely redeploy resources from discontinued products to the development of new ones. Hewlett-Packard is an example of a successful company in this category. In Sonnenfeld and

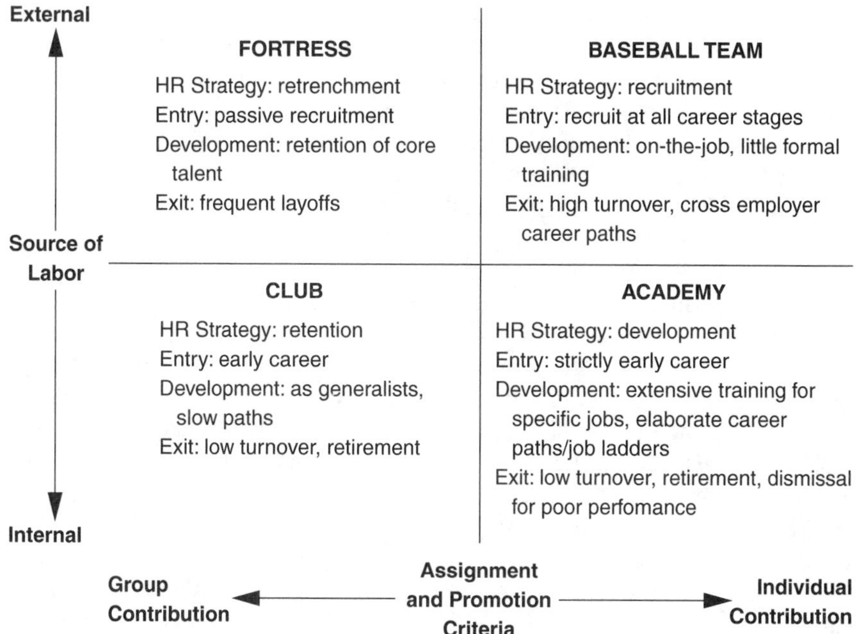

FIGURE 4-3 Strategic Staffing Policies

Source: Modification of figure from Jeffrey A. Sonnenfeld and Maury A. Peiperl. "Staffing Policy as a Strategic Response: A Typology of Career Systems," *Academy of Management Review* 13, no. 4 (1988): 591. Reprinted with permission of *Academy of Management Review*.

Peiperl's framework, investment banks, broadcasting companies, software developers, entertainment companies, and biological research companies fit this category. Companies in this category also can be professional firms such as law firms, advertising agencies, consulting firms, and accounting firms. When innovation is the strategy, those organizational conditions that foster risk taking, cooperation, creativity, and a long-term perspective are valued. Accordingly, companies pursuing an innovation strategy invest in training their employees and managers. In addition to providing more training, they also tend to train their employees in skills that apply beyond their present jobs. These differences highlight the benefits of integrating strategic planning and human resource planning.[80]

The baseball team brings in talent at any level within the organization and does not place much emphasis on development. Instead, there is a "buy" approach to talent. Nonetheless, there also may be development through rapid assignment changes. However, career paths often involve interorganizational moves as individuals take jobs with other companies as they develop and command greater compensation, responsibility, and professional stature. Promotion policies are often "up or out" as those passed over for promotion are terminated. Not surprisingly, in such companies, performance appraisals are more results oriented.[81] The trading of baseball players from one team to another provides a good example of career paths and the high talent and high turnover of the organizations in this category. Another example of career progression in this category might be the local television reporter who moves up to a national news network. Empirical evidence of distinctive "make" or "buy" patterns of human resource management practices has been established in a study of MBA students who have accepted offers of employment.[82]

Closer examination of the baseball team quadrant indicates some potential contradictions. Sonnenfeld and Peiperl's category of baseball teams does not correspond completely with Miles and Snow's prospector category because certified public accounting (CPA) firms and law firms probably do not operate at the same level of innovation as prospectors such as Hewlett-Packard. Firms emphasizing innovation, the prospectors in Miles and Snow's typology, have also been found to place a heavier emphasis on training than less innovative companies. There is also a need for lower turnover in such firms because the loss of personnel can be extremely disruptive.[83] Great disruption results from turnover in these firms because their quick rate of learning often leaves organizational knowledge unrecorded. Explanation for this apparent contradiction may require more complex descriptions of baseball teams in Sonnenfeld and Peiperl's typology. Even without considering prospectors, within the baseball team quadrant itself, law firms and CPA firms do indeed have high turnover, but typically it is confined mainly to the lower levels. The employees at the higher levels, partners, have very low turnover as they are frequently able to reap the financial rewards of managing the efforts of junior professionals.

Academy. Academies are somewhat of a hybrid in that they are both product innovators and competitors in long-run production roles. They attempt to exploit niches in the marketplace. Types of companies in this category include manufacturers of electronics, pharmaceuticals, consumer products, and automobiles. Texas Instruments is an example of a successful academy. The personnel policies of the academy, which follows a *focused* strategy, fall between the two extremes of clubs and baseball teams. In this category, there is substantial emphasis on development but some outsiders are hired to fill higher-level positions. These companies both "make" and "buy" human resources. There are extensive career paths within the companies themselves. Performance appraisal tends to emphasize process.[84] Although the personnel policies of these companies differ, they are consistent with their companies' overall strategies.

Fortress. Companies in this category are in highly competitive markets and are at the mercy of their environments. Examples of the types of companies in this category include those in hotels, retailing, publishing, textiles, and natural resources.[85] Because companies in this category are essentially reactive, there are few systematic strategic implications.

NETWORK ORGANIZATIONS AND STRATEGY

Network organizations were discussed in Chapter 2 as an important development in the human resource environment. Such organizations have developed as a result of advances in communications technology, desires for workforce flexibility, and intensified worldwide competition brought about by financial and economic deregulation. *Network organizations* readily acquire or divest their organizational units based on their return on assets and outsource activities that other companies or venture partners can produce at a lower cost in less time. Outsourcing enables network organizations to maintain an optimal size and lower economic risk of ventures into new markets. Essentially, network organizations retain for themselves only those activities in which they have expertise. Several different firms may be involved in a network, with the activities of product design, manufacturing, and distribution being performed by the specialist in each area.[86]

There are differences between network organizations in their degree of permanence and externality. They can even operate internally within giant companies, such as General Motors. In the case of internal networks, efficiencies are sought through the use of market-priced transactions between network components. For external networks, at one end of the spectrum are dynamic networks that have lead companies that basically act as brokers, outsourcing virtually all activities to a changing set of companies. Lewis Galoob toys, with only 100 employees, provides an example of such a network that outsources manufacturing, design, development, distribution, and collection of accounts receivable. At the other end of the external spectrum are stable networks in which one company remains as the central core as an investor and outsources to subsidiaries and other independent companies. BMW provides an example of the latter. As a result of computer, satellite, and telecommunications technology, company components of the network that perform outsourced activities may be located throughout the world.[87]

One strategic implication of network organizations is that lead firms will have needs for employees who have the entrepreneurial skills required for the broker activities of establishing the network. Project management experience across functional areas may help develop the kinds of skills needed. Additionally, the internal entrepreneurship approaches of firms such as Texas Instruments may also develop the entrepreneurial skills needed to establish networks. Further, because the establishment and operation of networks require contracting skills, managers of construction engineering and negotiators may prove to be good sources of network operators. As these skills indicate, while network lead companies and brokers have fewer permanent employees than more conventional companies, they will have to invest heavily in the training of their permanent core of very highly skilled employees.[88]

ORGANIZATIONAL LEARNING

As noted earlier, one of the problems of international alliances is that one partner may learn more and benefit more from the alliance than its partner. Companies sometimes become deskilled as a result of the alliance. This has been a problem for U.S. companies, particularly in alliances with Japanese and Korean companies. The problem is especially important because competitive advantage is increasingly being obtained from the invisible assets of *organizational knowledge* and information.[89] This knowledge or know-how is also referred to as *intellectual capital.* Increasingly, intellectual capital is being viewed as a source of competitive advantage. Further, a rate of *organizational learning* faster than competitors is important to maintaining such an advantage. One of the challenges related to intellectual capital is that most companies lack experience in managing it. Nonetheless, less hierarchy, fewer rules, and an absence of barriers to free exchange of information within organizations appear to be important to effective management of intellectual capital. One reason why intellectual capital has not received enough emphasis is that it is difficult to measure.[90] This is not surprising because intellectual capital may be described as "the sum of everything everybody in your company knows that gives you a competitive edge in the marketplace." [91] Nonetheless, a crude back door approximation can be obtained by calculating Tobin's q, which is "the ratio between a company's market value (stock price times shares outstanding) and the replacement value of its physical assets)." [92]

From a more theoretical perspective, one of the major roles of human resource management is to provide control. Such control may focus on behavior, such as through use of performance appraisals; outputs, such as accomplishment of goals; and inputs, such as through the selection and training of employees.[93] Because of the difficulty in measuring intellectual capital, organizations will be unable to use controls that require precise measures of organizational learning. It might be speculated that input controls would be appropriate because they avoid the necessity of having precise measures of learning. By selecting employees motivated toward learning and self-control, less emphasis on other controls may be required.

Organizational Learning in International Alliances

Because organizations' abilities to learn from alliance partners are affected by human resource practices and activities, it is critical to the company's own welfare that they are complementary to learning. Several human resource management practices can facilitate organizational learning. These include:

- Communicating the strategic goals of the alliance widely within the organization, such as the void of organizational knowledge that necessitated the alliance
- Forcing the focus of decisions beyond temporary short-run gains to the long-range consequences of outsourced manufacturing capabilities
- Rewarding organizational learning through career progressions based partially on acquisition of knowledge
- Not allowing the alliance partner to control human resource management functions, such as staffing the venture
- Maintaining some slack in staffing on site so that there can be an adequate focus on learning
- Providing managers and staff members who have language skills and training in the culture
- Making longer alliance assignments
- Monitoring the human resource assignments of the alliance partner, such as where personnel are assigned after they rotate out of the venture[94]

INTEGRATION OF STRATEGY AND HUMAN RESOURCE PLANNING

The integration of business strategy and human resource strategy and planning is particularly important for long-range planning efforts. Furthermore, with the recognition of the potential contributions of human resource planning, line managers have taken on greater responsibilities for these planning efforts.[95] The following provides a vivid description of why there should be greater integration of the processes:

> Because there is a greater understanding that an organization's work force cannot be turned around on a dime, long-term human resource planning is gaining currency. It is an activity that demands integration of the skills and knowledge of the human resource planner and all the other executives responsible for strategic planning.[96]

Evolution of Strategy and Human Resource Planning Integration

There are probably four stages in the evolution of linkages between strategic business planning and human resource management. The first stage is called an *administrative linkage*, although there is no real linkage. Senior executives operate as if qualified personnel are always available in the labor market, and the human resource unit is relegated to a paperwork-processing role. The second stage involves a *one-way linkage* in which the human resource function becomes involved only in implementation. In the third stage, there is a *two-way linkage*. This involves a reciprocal relationship in which the human resource function helps implement strategic business plans and also provides input to strategy formulation. The final stage is called an *integrative linkage*. This stage goes beyond the reciprocal relationship to an equal involvement with other functional areas of business in the development of strategic business plans, including issues outside of the human resource area. Interestingly, a fully integrated linkage may be described as informal.[97]

Determinants of Integration

The strategy and human resource planning linkage is affected by a number of influences, including environmental factors such as intense competition, which often requires productivity enhancements and workforce downsizing; technological change, which requires different employee skills; and changes in the composition of the workforce. Less integration is likely in stable environments. Another influence is level of diversification, as greater integration occurs in companies with one dominant core business as opposed to diversified companies. At the opposite end of the continuum, where an organization's divisions are in different core businesses, a decentralized structure would be likely. Greater integration also occurs where the top human resource executive has equal status with the heads of the other functional areas and has credible line experience. More integration also occurs out of necessity where there are severe skill shortages. Greater integration also occurs where compensation systems reward executives' performance. Likewise, it occurs where line managers perceive that human resource planning can help them implement strategies that will further the goals of the company.[98] One way in which the benefits of human resource planning can be demonstrated is provided by the following practical advice from the Director of Human Resource Planning and Development at Corning Glass: "Identify the issues that are making it tougher on line managers, then explain how good HR planning can help solve some of those problems." [99]

As noted earlier, changing demands for skills also has the potential to affect the degree of integration between strategic planning and human resource planning. With the decline in proportion of employment accounted for by manufacturing and growth of services, there has been a changing demand for employee skills. In the service industry, there is concurrent creation and consumption of the service by the consumer. As a result, service workers must be more involved in controlling quality, make appropriate adjustments when standards are not met, and must be responsible for more of their own supervision. Such changes dictate that service workers be more involved and committed to the organization. In order to create institutional climates and processes, which provide information and power sharing necessary for employees to operate in this manner, companies must plan ahead and make major changes in organizational direction.[100] Nonetheless, there is considerable confusion about manufacturing and its importance in the United States. Although a smaller proportion of the labor force may be employed in manufacturing in the future because of greater automation, computerization, robotics, and new technologies, the importance of manufacturing to the United States should not be underestimated.[101]

As indicated, the changing composition of the workforce also may cause greater integration between strategy and human resource planning. Human resource planning efforts, which forecast diversity can help organizations identify the proactive efforts needed to take advantage of the unique perspectives that diverse employees bring to the workplace. In the future there will be substantially more women, minorities, and immigrants in the U.S. labor force. There will be older workers who will be attracted back into the workforce, perhaps with the aid of innovative scheduling approaches and other inducements. Further, as a result of the Americans with Disabilities Act (ADA), there will probably more disabled employees on the job. Finally, there will be more diversity involved with coordinating activities that result from the global sourcing of labor.[102]

Mergers and acquisitions may also cause stronger planning and strategy linkages in the future. Their dismal record, in terms of both financial performance and adverse effects on employees, may be improved when human resource issues are planned out before the merger. In companies having recent merger or acquisition experience, human resource managers report that the top-level managerial talent of the firm to be acquired is the most important human resource criterion to be considered prior to a merger.[103] Nonetheless, the reported failures to consider these very issues prior to mergers or acquisitions indicate that there has been a failure to integrate human resource planning with the strategic planning process.

Conversely, integration is less likely where senior management incorrectly assumes that there are qualified employees in the external labor market and specifies that areas such as finance and marketing should have sole responsibility for strategic planning. Human resource executives who lack a strategic perspective of the business also impede integration.[104] Several benefits of linkage and integration are presented in Table 4-2.

TABLE 4-2 Benefits of Integrating Human Resource Planning with Strategic Planning

1. Generates more diverse solutions to complex organizational problems
2. Ensures consideration of human resources in organizational goal-setting processes
3. Ensures consideration of human resources in assessment of organization's abilities to accomplish goals and implement strategies
4. Reciprocal integration prevents strategy formulation based on personnel rigidities/preferences
5. Facilitates concurrent consideration of strategic plans and managerial succession

Sources: Adapted from Cynthia A. Lengnick-Hall and Mark L. Lengnick-Hall. "Strategic Human Resources Management: A Review of the Literature and a Proposed Typology," *Academy of Management Review* 13, no. 3 (1988): 454–70; James A. Craft. "Human Resource Planning and Strategy," in Lee Dyer (Ed.), *Human Resource Management: Evolving Roles and Responsibilities*. Washington, DC: Bureau of National Affairs, 1988, pp. 47–87.

Conditions Under Which Integration May Not Be Appropriate

Strategic integration is appropriate only after the human resource management function has progressed through earlier forms of development. In fact, Baird and Meshoulam state that a partial determinant of the effectiveness of an organization's human resource management is the degree to which it matches the organization's developmental stage. For example, without managerial comprehension of such processes as environmental scanning, strategy development, and managerial succession, the resources devoted to strategic integration efforts will be wasted. Additionally, a sophisticated compensation program may fail because the information and administrative systems required for its implementation may be undeveloped. It also follows that the stage of development in human resource management should match the stage of development of the parent organization.[105]

The five stages of organizational development are as follows:

1. *Initiation*, the start-up or entrepreneurial stage characterized by informality
2. *Functional growth*, the stage at which functional specialization and a more formalized structure develops
3. *Controlled growth*, the stage at which professional management is brought in, product lines are expanded, and productivity and cost control are emphasized
4. *Functional integration*, the stage in which coordination is increased to deal with interdependencies between functions and there is an increase in strategic emphasis
5. *Strategic integration*, the ultimate stage of development in which there is workforce flexibility and adaptability, extensive use of teamwork, broad sharing of human resource responsibilities, and human resource input into strategic decision-making processes

Table 4-3 presents describes the developmental range of several strategic aspects of human resource management, including management's realization of potential contributions of human resources, control and structure of the human resource function itself, human resource program offerings, skills of the human resource staff, information technology, and environmental scanning and awareness.[106]

THE HUMAN RESOURCE MANAGER AND STRATEGIC PLANNING

The human resource function sometimes fails to play a major role in the organization's strategy formulation process because of the planning inadequacies of human resource executives.[107] However, planning difficulties are not unique to such executives. Indeed, managers from all functional areas have problems with strategic planning. This section will review these general problems and will address the specific implications for human resource management.

TABLE 4-3 Strategic Components of Human Resource Management Relevant to Internal Fit

1. *Management Awareness.* Ranges from a focus on administrative needs, such as hiring and firing, to a full integration of human resource considerations in all management decision making.
2. *Management of the Function.* Includes the structure of the human resource function and the planning, allocation, and control of its resources. The structure may vary from very loose or nonexistent through matrixed and decentralized.
3. *Portfolio of Programs.* Ranges from simple salary administration and record-keeping programs to very complex and sophisticated flexible compensation, environmental scanning, and long-range planning programs.
4. *Personnel Skills.* Personnel professionals need appropriate skills. Basic programs and simple information systems require basic skills. The addition of complex programs and growth in size requires more advanced, differentiated, and specialized skills.
5. *Information Technology.* Information tools range from manual record keeping to sophisticated distributed systems with modeling capabilities. Information technologies range from the absence of formal analytical tools to advanced forecasting and simulation based on statistical tools.
6. *Awareness of the Environment.* In the initial stage, because of pressures involved in start-up, management does not systematically assess and react to the environment. At the strategic integration stage, management is very aware of the internal and external environments and their impact. They remain flexible and adjust to opportunities and risks that arise.

Source: Extracted from Lloyd Baird and Ilan Meshoulam. "Managing Two Fits of Strategic Human Resource Management," *Academy of Management Review* 13, no. 1 (1988): 122–23. Reprinted with permission of *Academy of Management Review*.

Planning Problems

It is well known that managers are action oriented, often preferring the action of decision-making or problem-solving interactions. In contrast, part of the planning process is done in isolation. There is a lack of feedback or knowledge of results for prolonged periods of time. Further, it is difficult to justify the time needed for planning in relation to more immediate problems that press for solutions. Thus, in spite of its value, many managers do not like to plan. In addition to these general planning problems, there are further problems with strategic planning because it often results in reallocations of resources that determine power and status. Effects of the desire to retain the status quo, through resistance to change, are evident in symptoms such as excessive defense of existing resource allocations, information hoarding, and excessive control of the planning process through manipulation of agendas. Attempts to maintain the status quo also may be evident in symptoms such as padding budgetary requirements.[108]

Other causes of problems in the strategic planning process include mismatches between the tasks of planning and individual managers' skills. Strategic planning requires thinking in terms of the organization as a whole and relationships between the organization and the numerous factors that affect it within its environment. The ability to see patterns at the macro level is more important than processing bits of information to find the solutions to micro-level problems. One of the symptoms of such mismatches is a propensity to slip back into operational issues and the inability to complete tasks. A final problem is lack of top-level executive commitment to the strategic planning process. Symptoms of this problem include managers' attempts to read between the lines to determine top managements' real views on the importance of the process. Compounding these difficulties is the typical absence of rewards for superior planning performance.[109]

Requirements for Strategic Human Resource Managers

Human resource executives sometimes lack the qualifications to take an important role in the company's strategic planning processes. Requirements for those who can operate in strategic human resource management go beyond the requirements of functional competence. Research into the role characteristics reveals the following personal qualifications for such involvement:

> (a) Information management skills—statistics, analysis, and research; (b) Planning skills—the knowledge of planning and planning methodologies plus statistics techniques; (c) Management skills—skills in the various business functions and environmental analysis; (d) Integration skills—competency at managing organizational interfaces, and skill in assessing the organization plus setting priorities; and (e) Change management skills—the skills of anticipating the future, facilitating changes, and developing organizational activities.[110]

Aside from selecting human resource executives on the basis of these qualifications, weaknesses with current personnel can be overcome even where there are cognitive skill mismatches. For example, pairing planners with offsetting skills and using planning teams may minimize the effect of individual cognitive weaknesses. The tasks of planning can also be broken up into phases, some of which can be performed by those whose cognitive skills are not well suited to strategy formulation. For instance, greater responsibilities for information gathering might be assigned to those whose strengths are not consistent with strategic thinking.[111] Using teams to offset weaknesses seems to have appeal: "Although the 'universal manager' may have lost credibility, the 'universal management team configuration' seems to have gained popularity."[112]

Summary

More organizations are recognizing that their human resources provide a source of competitive advantage. This recognition, along with increased environmental uncertainty, greater pressure to control costs, and increased governmental regulation, have elevated the strategic role of human resource management. As a result, there is growing involvement of human resource management in strategy formulation. Where human resources are an organization's source of competitive advantage, human resource management has a critical role of providing "up-front" input in the corporate level strategic planning process. Human resource planning provides another important linkage with organizational strategy by providing input on the availability of critical labor and by adding lead time to deal with shortages and surpluses of employees. Other strategic inputs of the human resource function include environmental scanning and competitive intelligence.

At the next level of strategy formulation, human resource strategies help align personnel practices, policies, and programs with strategy so that desired employee roles and behaviors will support different strategies (e.g., innovation, quality enhancement, cost reduction). A typology of activities indicates how human resource activities vary in their contributions to strategy implementation. Sonnenfeld and Peiperl's typology provides an explanation of differences in human resource strategies, their relationship to organizational strategies, and differences in personnel practices and policies across industries. Unbundled or network organizations also are of importance to the discussion of human resource strategy because they provide new challenges. While some traditional human resource functions may be unnecessary in such organizations, their core of permanent employees will require extraordinary levels of training and skill development.

Another critical aspect of strategy formulation is international human resource strategy. Aside from deciding such issues as whether to pursue multinational or global strategies, companies must resolve the human resource problem of becoming deskilled as a result of international alliances. In the past, U.S. companies have not learned as quickly as many of their international alliance partners and have been weakened as a result of this deficiency. Decisions over the location of production facilities now involve a much broader range of alternatives from all over the world. As a result, human resource practices and policies are critical to international strategies and organizational learning. The relationship between companies' international strategies and human resource planning should be understood because there can be major differences in the human resource management implications.

In spite of recent developments, in most companies, there is still need for a stronger integration of human resource planning with organizational strategy formulation. Factors that influence the level of integration include industry differences, shifts in economic activity, changing technology, and changing demographics. Several examples of integration of the processes were provided in this chapter, along with the barriers that have often limited such integration in the past. Finally, human resource managers must develop the personal skills needed to contribute to the strategy formulation process.

Endnotes

1. Miles, Raymond E., and Charles C. Snow. "Designing Strategic Human Resources Systems," *Organizational Dynamics* 13, no. 1 (1984): 36–52; Beer, Michael, Bert Spector, Paul R. Lawrence,

D. Quinn Mills, and Richard E. Walton. *Managing Human Assets*. New York: The Free Press, 1984; Jackson, Susan E., and Randall S. Schuler. "Human Resource Planning: Challenges for Industrial/Organizational Psychologists," *American Psychologist* 45, no. 2 (1990): 223–39; Mills, Daniel Q. "Planning with People in Mind," *Harvard Business Review* 63, no. 4 (1985): 97–105; Porter, Michael E. *Competitive Advantage: Creating and Sustaining Superior Performance*. New York: The Free Press, 1985; Schuler, Randall S., and Ian C. MacMillan. "Gaining Competitive Advantage through Human Resource Management Practices," *Human Resource Management* 23, no. 3 (1984): 241–55; Ulrich, David. "Human Resource Planning as a Competitive Edge," *Human Resource Planning* 9, no. 2 (1986): 41–50.

2. Porter, Michael E. *Competitive Advantage: Creating and Sustaining Superior Performance*.
3. Quinn, James B., Thomas L. Doorley, and Penny C. Paquette. "Beyond Products: Services-Based Strategy," *Harvard Business Review* 90, no. 2 (1990): 58–67; Ulrich, Dave. "Strategic Human Resource Planning: Why and How?" *Human Resource Planning* 10, no. 1 (1987): 37–56; Kochan, Thomas A., Rosemary Batt, and Lee Dyer. "International Human Resource Studies: A Framework for Future Research," in David Lewin, O. S. Mitchell, and Peter D. Sherer (Eds.), *Research Frontiers in Industrial Relations and Human Resources*. Madison, WI: Industrial Relations Research Association, 1992, pp. 309–37.
4. Dyer, Lee. "Bringing Human Resources into the Strategy Formulation Process," *Human Resource Management* 22, no. 3 (1983): 257–71.
5. ARCO. *ARCO Annual Report*, 1986.
6. Beer, Spector, Lawrence, Mills, and Walton. *Managing Human Assets*; Rodgers, T. J. "No Excuses Management," *Harvard Business Review* 90, no. 4 (1990): 84–98; Fombrun, Charles, and Noel Tichy. "Strategic Planning and Human Resource Management: At Rainbow's End," in R. B. Lamb (Ed.), *Competitive Strategic Management*. Upper Saddle River, NJ: Prentice-Hall, 1984, pp. 319–32.
7. Jackson and Schuler. "Human Resource Planning: Challenges for Industrial/Organizational Psychologists"; Tichy, Noel M., Charles J. Fombrun, and Mary Anne Devanna. "Strategic Human Resource Management," *Sloan Management Review* 23, no. 2 (1982): 47–61; Miles and Snow. "Designing Strategic Human Resources Systems."
8. Beer, Spector, Lawrence, Mills, and Walton. *Managing Human Assets*.
9. Miller, Edwin L., Schon Beechler, Bhal Bhatt, and Raghu Nath. "The Relationship Between the Global Strategic Planning Process and the Human Resource Management Function," *Human Resource Planning* 9, no. 1 (1986): 12.
10. Fisher, Cynthia D. "Current and Recurrent Challenges in HRM," *Journal of Management* 15, no. 2 (1989): 157–80; Cook, Deborah S., and Gerald R. Ferris. "Strategic Human Resource Management and Firm Effectiveness in Industries Experiencing Decline," *Human Resource Management* 25, no. 3 (1986): 441–58.
11. Gomez-Mejia, Luis R. "The Role of Human Resources Strategy in Export Performance: A Longitudinal Study," *Strategic Management Journal* 9, no. 5 (1988): 493–505.
12. Schuler, Randall S. "Strategic Human Resources Management: Linking the People With the Strategic Needs of the Business," *Organizational Dynamics* 21, no. 1 (1992): 18–32.
13. Ibid., p. 18.
14. Ibid.
15. Wright, Patrick M., and Gary C. McMahan. "Theoretical Perspectives for Strategic Human Resource Management," *Journal of Management* 18, no. 2 (1992): 295–320.
16. Ibid., p. 298.
17. Wright and McMahan. "Theoretical Perspectives for Strategic Human Resource Management."
18. Ibid.
19. Quinn, James B. *Strategies for Change: Logical Incrementalism*. Homewood, IL: Richard D. Irwin, 1980, p. 7.
20. Henn, William R. "What the Strategist Asks from Human Resources," *Human Resource Planning* 8, no. 4 (1985): 195 (whole article on pp. 193–200).
21. Ohmae, Kenichi. *The Mind of the Strategist*. New York: Penguin Books, 1988, p. 42.
22. Henn. "What the Strategist Asks from Human Resources."

23. Higgins, James M., and Julian W. Vincze. *Strategic Management: Text and Cases*. Chicago: Dryden Press, 1989.
24. Craft, James A. "Human Resource Planning and Strategy," in Lee Dyer (Ed.), *Human Resource Management: Evolving Roles and Responsibilities*. Washington, DC: Bureau of National Affairs, 1988, p. 53.
25. Higgins, James M., and Julian W. Vincze. *Strategic Management: Text and Cases*. Chicago: Dryden Press, 1989; Walker, James W. *Human Resource Planning*. New York: McGraw-Hill, 1980; Craft. "Human Resource Planning and Strategy."
26. Craft. "Human Resource Planning and Strategy."
27. Quinn, James B. "Retrospective Commentary," *Sloan Management Review* 30, no. 4 (1989): 55–60.
28. Henn. "What the Strategist Asks from Human Resources."
29. Craft. "Human Resource Planning and Strategy"; Quinn, James B. "Retrospective Commentary."
30. Quinn, James B. "Strategic Change: Logical Incrementalism," *Sloan Management Review* 30, no. 4 (1989): 45–55.
31. Pitts, Robert A., and David Lei. *Strategic Management: Building and Sustaining Competitive Advantage*, 2nd ed. Cincinnati, OH: South-Western College Publishing, 2000.
32. Ibid.; Porter, Michael E. *Competitive Advantage: Creating and Sustaining Superior Performance*. New York: The Free Press, 1985.
33. Zabriskie, Noel, and Alan Huellmantel. "Implementing Strategies for Human Resources," *Long Range Planning* 22, no. 114 (1989): 70–77.
34. Schuler. "Strategic Human Resources Management: Linking the People with the Strategic Needs of the Business," p. 24.
35. Craft. "Human Resource Planning and Strategy"; Beer, Spector, Lawrence, Mills, and Walton. *Managing Human Assets*.
36. Sonnenfeld, Jeffrey, and Maury A. Peiperl. "Staffing Policy as a Strategic Response: A Typology of Career Systems," *Academy of Management Review* 13, no. 4 (1988): 588–600; Lengnick-Hall, Cynthia A., and Mark L. Lengnick-Hall. "Strategic Human Resources Management: A Review of the Literature and a Proposed Typology," *Academy of Management Review* 13, no. 3 (1988): 454–70.
37. Walker, James W. *Human Resource Planning*. New York: McGraw-Hill, 1980; Milkovich, George L., and Thomas A. Mahoney. "Human Resources Planning and PAIR Policy," in Dale Yoder and Herbert G. Heneman Jr. (Eds.), *Planning and Auditing PAIR*. Washington, DC: Bureau of National Affairs, 1976, pp. 2-1–2-29; Middlemist, R. Dennis, Michael Hitt, and Charles R. Greer. *Personnel Management: Jobs, People, and Logic*. Upper Saddle River, NJ: Prentice-Hall, 1983; Niehaus, Richard J. "Models for Human Resource Decisions," *Human Resource Planning* 11, no. 2 (1988): 95–107.
38. Pucik, Vladimir. "Strategic Alliances, Organizational Learning, and Competitive Advantage: The HRM Agenda," *Human Resource Management* 27, no. 1 (1988): 77–93.
39. Yip, George S. "Global Strategy . . . in a World of Nations?" *Sloan Management Review* 30, no. 4 (1989): 29–41; Adler, Nancy J., and Susan Bartholomew. "Managing Globally Competent People," *Academy of Management Executive* 6, no. 3 (1992): 52–65.
40. Yip. "Global Strategy . . . in a World of Nations?"
41. Lei, David, and John W. Slocum Jr. "Global Strategy, Competence-Building and Strategic Alliances," *California Management Review* 34, no. 2 (1992): 81–97.
42. Ibid., p. 82.
43. Lei and Slocum. "Global Strategy, Competence-Building and Strategic Alliances."
44. Lei, David, and John W. Slocum Jr. "Global Strategic Alliances: Payoffs and Pitfalls," *Organizational Dynamics* 19, no. 3 (1991): 49 (whole article on pp. 44–62).
45. Lei and Slocum. "Global Strategy, Competence-Building and Strategic Alliances."
46. National Public Radio. *Morning Edition*, January 4, 1993.
47. Phillips, Dennis. "How VW Builds Worker Loyalty Worldwide," *Management Review* 76, no. 6 (1987): 37–40.

48. Adler and Bartholomew. "Managing Globally Competent People."
49. Belanger, Jaques, Paul Edwards, and Martyn Wright. "Best HR Practice and the Multinational Company," *Human Resource Management Journal* 9, no. 3 (1999): 53–70.
50. Flynn, Julia, and Bhushan Bahree. "PB Is Close to a Human-Resources Pact of $750 Million With U.S. Start-Up," *Wall Street Journal* (November 24, 1999): A14.
51. Doebele, Justin. "Chinese Capitalism Gets a Face: Yes, Entrepreneurs Can Get Rich in Bejing," *Forbes* (November 29, 1999): 175–80.
52. Kaikati, Jack B. "Europe 1992—Mind Your Strategic P's and Q's," *Sloan Management Review* 31, no. 1 (1989): 85–92.
53. Web site: europa.eu.int/abc-en.htm.
54. Cerruti, James L., and Joseph Holtzman. "Business Strategy in the New European Landscape," *Journal of Business Strategy* 10, no. 5 (1990): 18–23.
55. "The Agreement's Key Provisions," *Wall Street Journal* (November 18, 1993): A14.
56. Townsend, Anthony M., K. Dow Scott, and Seven E. Markham. "An Examination of Country and Culture-Based Differences in Compensation Practices," *Journal of International Business Studies* 21, no. 4 (1990): 667–78.
57. Wyatt, Larry L. "Adding Value: Future Challenges," *Human Resource Planning* 8, no. 4 (1985): 229–32.
58. Lengnick-Hall and Lengnick-Hall. "Strategic Human Resources Management: A Review of the Literature and a Proposed Typology."
59. Porter, Michael E. *Competitive Advantage: Creating and Sustaining Superior Performance*.
60. Dyer. "Bringing Human Resources into the Strategy Formulation Process"; Lengnick-Hall and Lengnick-Hall. "Strategic Human Resources Management: A Review of the Literature and a Proposed Typology."
61. Schrenk, Lorenz P. "Environmental Scanning," in Lee Dyer (Ed.), *Human Resource Management: Evolving Roles & Responsibilities*. Washington, DC: Bureau of National Affairs, 1988, pp. 88–124; Zabriskie and Huellmantel. "Implementing Strategies for Human Resources."
62. Magnusson, Paul, and Stephen Baker. "The Mexico Pact: Worth the Price?" *Business Week* (May 27, 1991): 32–35.
63. Smith, Emily T. "Plastics That Break Down—Without Breaking the Bank," *Business Week* (May 27, 1991): 111.
64. Henn. "What the Strategist Asks from Human Resources."
65. Ibid., p. 195.
66. Zabriskie and Huellmantel. "Implementing Strategies for Human Resources."
67. Henn. "What the Strategist Asks from Human Resources."
68. Jackson and Schuler. "Human Resource Planning: Challenges for Industrial/Organizational Psychologists"; Belous, Richard S. "How Human Resource Systems Adjust to the Shift Toward Contingent Workers," *Monthly Labor Review* 112, no. 3 (1989): 7–12.
69. McCune, Joseph T., Richard W. Beatty, and Raymond V. Montagno. "Downsizing: Practices in Manufacturing Firms," *Human Resource Management* 27, no. 2 (1988): 145–61.
70. Schuler, Randall S., and Susan E. Jackson. "Linking Competitive Strategies with Human Resource Management Practices," *Academy of Management Executive* 1, no. 3 (1987): 207–19.
71. Ibid.; Porter. *Competitive Advantage*.
72. Ibid.
73. Speaker, Alan W. Unpublished model from correspondence with the author, May 2000.
74. Baron, James. N., and David. M. Kreps. *Strategic Human Resources: Frameworks for General Managers*. New York: John Wiley and Sons, 1999.
75. Lengnick-Hall and Lengnick-Hall. "Strategic Human Resources Management: A Review of the Literature and a Proposed Typology."
76. Kochan, Thomas A., John Paul MacDuffie, and Paul Osterman. "Employment Security at DEC: Sustaining Values Amid Environmental Change," *Human Resource Management* 27, no. 2 (1988): 139.

77. Miles and Snow. "Designing Strategic Human Resources Systems"; Sonnenfeld and Peiperl. "Staffing Policy as a Strategic Response."
78. Jackson and Schuler. "Human Resource Planning: Challenges for Industrial/Organizational Psychologists."
79. Sonnenfeld and Peiperl. "Staffing Policy as a Strategic Response: A Typology of Career Systems"; Miles and Snow. "Designing Strategic Human Resources Systems."
80. Jackson and Schuler. "Human Resource Planning: Challenges for Industrial/Organizational Psychologists"; Sonnenfeld and Peiperl. "Staffing Policy as a Strategic Response: A Typology of Career Systems"; Miles and Snow. "Designing Strategic Human Resources Systems"; Jackson, Susan E., Randall S. Schuler, and J. Carlos Rivero. "Organizational Characteristics as Predictors of Personnel Practices," *Personnel Psychology* 42, no. 2 (1989): 727–86.
81. Miles and Snow. "Designing Strategic Human Resources Systems"; Sonnenfeld and Peiperl. "Staffing Policy as a Strategic Response: A Typology of Career Systems."
82. Rousseau, Denise M. "New Hire Perceptions of Their Own and Their Employer's Obligations: A Study of Psychological Contracts," *Journal of Organizational Behavior* 11, no. 5 (1990): 389–400.
83. Jackson, Schuler, and Rivero. "Organizational Characteristics as Predictors of Personnel Practices."
84. Sonnenfeld and Peiperl. "Staffing Policy as a Strategic Response: A Typology of Career Systems"; Miles and Snow. "Designing Strategic Human Resources Systems."
85. Miles and Snow. "Designing Strategic Human Resources Systems"; Sonnenfeld and Peiperl. "Staffing Policy as a Strategic Response: A Typology of Career Systems."
86. Snow, Charles C., Raymond E. Miles, and Henry J. Coleman Jr. "Managing 21st Century Network Organizations," *Organizational Dynamics* 20, no. 3 (1992): 5–20.
87. Ibid.
88. Ibid.
89. Pucik. "Strategic Alliances, Organizational Learning, and Competitive Advantage: The HRM Agenda."
90. Stewart, Thomas A. "Brainpower," *Fortune* (June 3, 1991): 44–60.
91. Ibid., p. 44.
92. Ibid., p. 50.
93. Snell, Scott A. "Control Theory in Strategic Human Resource Management: The Mediating Effect of Administrative Information," *Academy of Management Journal* 35, no. 2 (1992): 292–327.
94. Pucik. "Strategic Alliances, Organizational Learning, and Competitive Advantage: the HRM Agenda."
95. Ulrich. "Human Resource Planning as a Competitive Edge."
96. Jackson and Schuler. "Human Resource Planning: Challenges for Industrial/Organizational Psychologists," p. 233.
97. Golden, Karen A., and Vasudevan Ramanujam. "Between a Dream and a Nightmare: On the Integration of the Human Resource Management and Strategic Business Planning Processes," *Human Resource Management* 24, no. 4 (1985): 429–52.
98. Ibid.; Buller, Paul F. "Successful Partnerships: HR and Strategic Planning at Eight Top Firms," *Organizational Dynamics* 17, no. 2 (1988): 27–43; Thompson, James D. *Organizations in Action.* New York: McGraw-Hill, 1967; Craft. "Human Resources Planning and Strategy."
99. McManis, Gerald L., and Michael S. Leibman. "Integrating Human Resource and Business Planning," *Personnel Administrator* 33, no. 6 (1988): 36 (whole article on pp. 32–35).
100. Jackson and Schuler. "Human Resource Planning: Challenges for Industrial/Organizational Psychologists"; Jackson, Schuler, and Rivero. "Organizational Characteristics as Predictors of Personnel Practices."
101. Flint, Jerry. "The Myth of U.S. Manufacturing's Decline," *Forbes* (January 19, 1993): 40–42.
102. Jackson and Schuler. "Human Resource Planning: Challenges for Industrial/Organizational Psychologist"; Johnston, William B., and Arnold H. Packer. "Work and Workers in the Year 2000," in *Workforce 2000: Work and Workers for the Twenty-first Century*. Indianapolis: Hudson Institute, 1987, pp. 75–103; American Association of Retired Persons. *The Aging Work Force: Managing an*

Aging Work Force. Washington, DC: Author, 1990; Machan, Dyan. "Cultivating the Gray," *Forbes* (September 14, 1989), pp. 127–28; Morrison, Peter A. "Applied Demography: Its Growing Scope and Future Direction," *The Futurist* 24, no. 2 (1990): 9–15; Bureau of National Affairs. "ADA: Americans with Disabilities Act of 1990," *Labor Relations Reporter* 134, no. 11 (suppl) (1990): 5–12.

103. Schweiger, David A., and Yaakov Weber. "Strategies for Managing Human Resources During Mergers and Acquisitions: An Empirical Investigation," *Human Resource Planning* 12, no. 2 (1989): 69–86.
104. Craft. "Human Resource Planning and Strategy"; Baird, Lloyd, and Ilan Meshoulam. "Managing Two Fits of Strategic Human Resource Management," *Academy of Management Review* 13, no. 1 (1988): 116–28.
105. Baird and Meshoulam. "Managing Two Fits of Strategic Human Resource Management."
106. Ibid.
107. Burack, Elmer H. "Linking Corporate Business and Human Resource Planning: Strategic Issues and Concerns," *Human Resource Planning* 8, no. 3 (1985): 133–45.
108. Bedeian, Arthur G. *Management*, 2nd ed. Chicago: Dryden Press, 1989; Lenz, R. T., and Marjorie A. Lyles. "Managing Human Problems in Strategic Planning Systems," *Journal of Business Strategy* 6, no. 4 (1986): 57–66.
109. Lenz and Lyles. "Managing Human Problems in Strategic Planning Systems."
110. Baird and Meshoulam. "Managing Two Fits of Strategic Human Resource Management," pp. 126–27.
111. Lenz and Lyles. "Managing Human Problems in Strategic Planning Systems."
112. Lengnick-Hall and Lengnick-Hall. "Strategic Human Resources Management: A Review of the Literature and a Proposed Typology," p. 459.

CASE 4
Integrating Strategy and Human Resource Management

The experiences of several organizations provide good examples of the integration of strategy and human resource management. One such example is provided by the experiences of People's Bank, a financial services company headquartered in Bridgeport, Connecticut. Massive changes began to take place in the business environment of banking with deregulation and relaxation of ceilings on interest. Money markets began to drain off funds that ordinarily went into banks' deposits, forcing them to rely on more expensive sources of funds. Further, the money center banks began to compete in the same middle markets as regional banks. People's, which was a small regional bank, responded by changing its strategy from a product orientation to one directed toward markets. With a product orientation, products are developed and then markets are sought out in which to sell the product. Conversely, a market orientation involves an opposite approach in that market demands are determined and then products developed to serve the market. As a result of these changes, People's transformed itself into a diversified financial services company with 139 branches and a fully integrated banking services and stock trading presence on the Internet.[1]

Because of major changes in People's strategy, there was a recognition that new organizational structures would be needed to accommodate the changes. The organization was decentralized, hierarchical levels removed, strategic business units formed, and new senior vice presidencies created within a matrix structure. The bank then conducted a study of the types of employees that would be needed with the new strategy's skill and organizational requirements. Major changes were undertaken as a result of the audit. For example, the performance appraisal system was revised. The revised system emphasized goal setting, linked individual goal accomplishment and rewards with the attainment of the bank's objectives, and placed greater emphasis in performance appraisal on marketing and sales. Further, human resource planning was more fully integrated with the strategic planning process through synchronization of its scanning processes with the bank's overall environmental scanning process.[2]

The experiences of the U.S. Navy provide another example of the integration of strategy and human resource management. As a result of its linkage of strategic planning with human resource management, the Navy was able to pursue a proactive strategy that provided lower labor costs. In the Navy's case, its human resource planners analyzed the labor cost savings of a strategy involving its civilian employees that would substitute local wage policies for national wage policies. By developing human resource forecasts to determine labor market reactions to these changes, planners could determine whether sufficient labor supplies would be available with the cost-saving strategy. In this example, the planners also examined the impact of the reduction of private sector middle management positions and found that higher-quality employees could be hired.[3]

Ingersoll-Rand's experiences with one of its divisions also provide a good example of the outcome of a strong linkage between strategy and human resource management. Ingersoll-Rand's rock-drilling division was experiencing rapid growth and had shortages of labor. It also needed to train its employees to work with new technology and wanted to control labor costs. The outcome of integrating its human resource capabilities with its strategic planning process was that the company implemented a number of programs, including gain sharing and employee involvement teams. It also had employees participate in decisions on the purchase of new technology and made a major commitment to technological training.[4]

A final example of the integration of strategy and human resources is provided by Maid Bess, a manufacturer of uniforms. The company faced intense competition from foreign manufacturers, and control of labor costs became very critical. Because of its labor intensity, the company closely integrated human resource management with the strategic planning process. As an outcome of the integrated strategic planning process, the company's executive vice president designed a compensation program that incorporated bonuses that enhanced productivity, increased employee wages, and reduced turnover.[5]

Questions

1. Based on these descriptions of the experiences of People's Bank, Ingersoll-Rand, and Maid Bess, what is the unifying theme of the role played by human resource management?
2. How does the strategic role of human resource management in the U.S. Navy case differ from the others?
3. What were the environmental influences stimulating the actions described for each of these organizations?
4. What managerial trends are indicated in the experiences of these organizations?
5. The Ingersoll-Rand case indicates that its solutions to the problems it faced were based largely on employee empowerment approaches. Explain how employee empowerment can provide a viable source of competitive advantage to be considered in strategic decision making.

References

1. People's Bank. Company Press Release, "People's Announces Three Strategic Initiatives—New Key Areas Will Enhance the Organization's Agility and Effectiveness" (May 10, 2000); Coleman, Sharon M., Martin Leshner, and C. Chase Hewes. "Human Resources Planning: A Tool for Strategic Change," *The Bankers Magazine* 169, no. 6 (1986): 39–44.
2. Coleman, Leshner, and Hewes. "Human Resources Planning: A Tool for Strategic Change."
3. Atwater, D. M., E. S. Brees III, and R. J. Niehaus. "Analyzing Organizational Strategic Change Using Proactive Labor Market Forecasts," in Richard J. Niehaus and Karl F. Price (Eds.), *Creating the Competitive Edge through Human Resource Applications*. New York: Plenum Press, 1988, pp. 119–36.
4. McManis, Gerald L., and Michael S. Leibman. "Integrating Human Resource and Business Planning," *Personnel Administrator* 33, no. 6 (1988): 32–35.
5. Ibid.

CHAPTER 5

Human Resource Planning

As indicated in the conceptual framework presented in the Preface, the conventional wisdom has been that organizations conduct human resource or workforce planning after strategy formulation as a means of implementation. However, as also indicated in the framework, where human resource planning is fully integrated with strategy and has a reciprocal relationship, it provides input in the formulation process. In such an evolving role, human resource planning may identify competitive advantages of the organization's human resources or it may be used to assess the feasibility of various strategic alternatives, in terms of human resource capabilities. This chapter will begin with a discussion of the growing strategic role of human resource planning. Next, it will explore the topic by providing an overview of human resource planning and the managerial issues involved. It will then examine factors that influence the selection of forecasting techniques, discuss specific supply-and-demand forecasting techniques, and provide examples of their application.

THE STRATEGIC ROLE OF HUMAN RESOURCE PLANNING

Human resource planning is linked in several ways with strategy formulation and implementation. One such linkage is its developmental role.

Developmental Planning for Strategic Leadership

A management development expert observed that there is currently more interest in succession planning today than there has been during the past 30 years. Because of the rapidly changing environments in which companies must compete, there is concern that there will be a shortage of individuals with the requisite skills and talents who can lead companies in the twenty-first century. Given the significant costs of leadership failures at the highest organizational levels, it is important to have qualified replacements for high-level executives. Succession planning, a form of human resource planning discussed later, is an important part of the solution to the successorship problem. Such planning, as well as other forms of human resource planning, is becoming more critical to the successful formulation and implementation of strategies. Succession planning is quite challenging in today's rapidly changing environment because the skills that will be needed in the future are not well defined. Nonetheless, the potential strategic contributions of succession planning are substantial.[1]

Assessment of Strategic Alternatives

As organizations' human resources are utilized more frequently as sources of competitive advantage, human resource planning and forecasting will become more central to the strategic planning process. It will be essential for human resource executives or other executives to be able to forecast the future availability of employees having knowledge in such critical areas as technology. Companies that are developing a critical mass of employees who are knowledgeable or skilled in a particular technology may gain a potential source of competitive advantage. Similarly, information regarding critical employee knowledge bases provides important input for strategy formulation. Conversely, given a particular strategic alternative, it is useful for human resource executives, as well as other executives, to be able to forecast the human resources necessary to carry out various strategies.

Adding Value

The literature often states that human resource planning is becoming more important to organizations. While some observers have noted the difficulties of planning during turbulent periods and have downplayed the current role of human resource planning, there is some indication that other organizations are placing major emphasis on succession planning for top-level executives, as well as other forms of planning. Reasons cited for human resource planning include shifting demographics, the proportion of total costs accounted for by labor costs, and the competitive pressures of the global economy.[2]

In addition, a large study of 968 organizations by Mark Huselid found human resource planning to be positively related to the intensity of the organizations' research and development efforts.[3] There also is some empirical evidence that strategic planning is positively related to financial performance. Although various studies provide mixed evidence on this relationship, methodological problems appear to be responsible for some inconsistencies in results.[4] More specifically, it also has been hypothesized that human resource planning is related to profitability. Although there is good reason to expect such planning efforts to increase profitability, methodological limitations also have prevented the empirical validation of this hypothesis. Establishing such an empirical relationship is very difficult because of the many potential indirect effects of human resource planning and the time required for its effects to be manifested in profitability. Nonetheless, recent empirical research has found a positive relationship between succession planning for chief executive officers' and company profitability.[5]

Unfortunately, it is typically difficult to quantify value added in human resource management. The results of some human resource programs and policies undoubtedly have major impacts on morale and motivation, although they are not easily translated into dollars and cents. However, many human resource programs probably do not add value and do not conform to the investment perspective advocated in this book. Fortunately, as indicated in Chapters 1 and 9, some progress has been made in the area of measurement with such techniques as utility analysis.[6]

Contribution to Strategic Human Resource Management

Aside from anecdotal evidence on the strategic importance of human resource planning, surveys of company practices also provide an indication of its increasing importance for strategic applications. A survey asked human resource executives from 137 companies to indicate the reasons why their companies engaged in human resource forecasting, which is a major component of human resource planning. The top three reasons were for developing their human resources (77.6 percent), for avoiding personnel shortages (73.1 percent), and to obtain information for decisions (73.1 percent). A second set of reasons for human resource forecasting included the following: affirmative action efforts (63.6 percent), budgeting (62.1 percent), and career planning (59.7 percent). As noted earlier, forecasts are probably needed for the development of estimates of when affirmative action goals can be reached.[7] Similarly, another survey has found an association between the development of affirmative action strategies and human resource planning.[8]

Strategic Salary Planning

As noted earlier, survey results indicate that over 60 percent of companies conduct human resource planning for budgetary purposes. A related budgetary issue is strategic salary planning. Interestingly, compensation systems are one of the few business systems that have remained relatively static. Nonetheless, for effective implementation, such systems must change if they are incompatible with organizational strategies. While the importance of having compensation systems that are compatible with organizational goals is well known, in reality such compatibility is often not obtained. Strategic salary planning goes beyond ensuring compatibility and draws on the rationale of the essence of strategy.[9] Fundamentally, strategic management rejects the notion of allocating resources in the manner of competitors and instead advocates concentration of resources.[10] This rationale for strategic salary planning is demonstrated in the following:

> Realistically, few employers can justify above-average workers in all positions. An organization's business strategy leads to a staffing strategy and that, in turn, pro-

vides a basis for developing the compensation strategy. It may be that "world-class" experts are needed in just a few key positions. If the organization's success is dependent, for example, on its marketing expertise, this may justify higher pay levels in this function.[11]

Thus, strategic salary planning, which is based on input from human resource plans, provides another example of the strategic role of human resource planning.

OVERVIEW OF HUMAN RESOURCE PLANNING

Although a brief definition of *human resource planning* was provided in Chapter 4, a more comprehensive definition is appropriate for in-depth treatment of the process. Human resource planning encompasses the following steps:

1. Interfacing with strategic planning and scanning the environment
2. Taking an inventory of the company's current human resources
3. Forecasting the demand for human resources
4. Forecasting the supply of human resources both from within the organization and in the external labor market
5. Comparing forecasts of demand and supply
6. Planning the actions needed to deal with anticipated shortages or overages
7. Feeding back such information into the strategic planning process[12] (Step 4 could precede step 3.)

This chapter will place emphasis on the actual process of human resource forecasting.

Planning in a Context of Change

Because the major themes of this book deal with the strategic aspects of human resource management, a longer-range time perspective has been adopted. Since strategy and planning are essentially forward-looking activities, they are critical responsibilities of general managers. Although planning and strategy are sometimes neglected because of the press of current demands, at times these planning activities also take on an unwarranted sense of importance and can distract managers from the real goals of the organization. The rational and proactive nature of the process, uncluttered by the very real problems of implementation, may cause the planners to forget that they are dealing with changing phenomena.

The dangers of having a plan chiseled in granite and lesser forms of inflexibility are well known. The rapidity of and scope of environmental changes that can affect human resource strategy and plans are formidable and should not be forgotten. For example, Cisco Systems' annual sales grew from \$1.2 billion in 1994 to \$13 billion in 1999, during which time the company made 41 acquisitions. In addition, the company planned to make as many as 25 more acquisitions in 2000. While Cisco's number of acquisitions is remarkable, its success in assimilating acquired firms has been one of the keys to its success. Cisco's flexible planned approach for assimilating new employees from acquisitions contrasts with the experiences of many other companies that have mishandled acquisitions, often because of failures to plan for human resource issues. In addition, the company's early application of the Internet to its human resource function also points out the fundamental role of change at Cisco.[13] Admittedly, Cisco's example of growth is extreme, but it illustrates how flexibility is required in many environments.

Responsibility for Human Resource Planning

In early practice, human resource planning was often the responsibility of a specialist in the human resource area. This planning was sometimes conducted with little involvement of others in the organization. Not surprisingly, when planning was conducted in this manner, the data supplied for use in forecasting were often inaccurate. Managers were asked to take the time to supply information for something that they did not understand. Because they did not see how forecasts could help their job performance, the value of forecasts was not appreciated. These earlier experiences reveal that when the planning process is complex and cumbersome, as is more likely on a centralized basis, its value to managers is not as readily apparent. Further, when planning is concentrated in a single corporate planning unit, other management personnel may be demotivated by their exclusion from the strategic planning process. The weaknesses of centralized planning are even more apparent in large companies having diverse operating divisions. In these companies, decentralized human resource planning seems much more appropriate.[14]

Fortunately, the thrust of human resource planning has changed. There is evidence of much greater line management involvement in human resource planning and thus greater strategic impact. Surveys of planning practices reveal that greater emphasis is being placed on the use of simple forecasting techniques with line management involvement as opposed to heavy reliance on centralized planning and forecasting practices based on sophisticated quantitative forecasting techniques.[15] Even with extensive line management "ownership" of the process and recognition of its value, extensive staff involvement is still required to facilitate the process. Martin Greller and David Nee have pointed out the requirement for balancing of responsibilities between line and staff in the following two statements: "(1) The manager knows what needs to be done and has control of the day-to-day assignments that allow real development to occur. (2) Human resource planning requires that someone pay consistent attention to the process, year in and year out, not just when there is a crisis." [16]

Failure to Plan for Human Resources

There are a number of examples in which the failure to plan for human resources has had a major adverse effect on organizations. For example, General Electric once encountered difficulties because of a mismatch between the skills of its engineering staff and the work that needed to be done. At the time, General Electric had 30,000 electromechanical engineers whose skills were becoming largely irrelevant because the company's needs were shifting toward the skills possessed by electronics engineers. Eventually, the company recognized that its difficulties were caused by a failure to plan in earlier years. Problems such as these prompted General Electric's chairman to urge his managers to conduct human resource planning. A multinational corporation that planned a technologically advanced smelter for construction in Brazil provides a similar example. Because the company did not assess the availability of the computer technicians and service workers in the geographic area, it had to make expensive changes in its plans in order to match the plant with the available labor supply.[17] Public accounting firms provide another example. Some of the difficulties in public accounting firms have been attributed to the failure to plan for the succession of top managers. Part of this failure of planning appears to be related to the unique nature of the partnership form of these organizations.[18]

The public sector has not been immune from these problems. An example of a failure to plan is provided by the construction of an expensive, state-of-the-art jail facility in Fort Worth, Texas, as a solution to severe problems of inmate overcrowding. Well into the actual construction phase of the project, officials were shocked to learn that the facility, which had incorporated recent innovations in design, would be much more expensive to operate than they had assumed because the design required high staffing levels. Since labor costs are the most important cost in operating a jail, the effects of this oversight were profound.[19]

Other causes for failure to plan or failures in planning are related to inadequacies in broader strategic management processes. A survey has indicated that the most common problem in human resource planning is a lack of precision in business operating plans.[20] An example is provided by the following statement from the vice president of personnel for the Quaker Oats Company: "Little is gained by grafting a HR plan to an unreliable business plan." [21] Quinn Mills has reported a similar response from an executive:

> "I've told my staff to quit talking to me about human resource planning," said one executive. "We can't plan for people because we do a miserable job of business planning. And I don't want another nest of strategic planners in the company." [22]

Although the literature had advocated that companies should place increased emphasis on human resource planning, there was still a lack of enthusiasm for the process by practitioners for many years. Nonetheless, by the late 1970s, human resource planning activity appeared to have increased. Some observers of the turning point cited a reactive response to the need to comply with equal employment opportunity legislation and greater recognition of the contribution of human resources to the performance and profitability of companies.[23] In order to comply with affirmative action goals and timetables, some planning is a practical necessity. The experiences with the jail project just described can be contrasted with the experiences of the U.S. Navy's shipyards operations in which a total workforce of 80,000 was reduced to 72,000. Because of forecasting, alternative actions enabled the Navy to achieve these reductions while having to release only 58 employees.[24] Similarly, survey results reveal that companies doing extensive human resource planning have been able to minimize layoffs during a recession.[25]

MANAGERIAL ISSUES IN PLANNING

Several important managerial issues are critical to human resource planning. Among the most important are the personal implications for planners as well as acceptance by the organization and challenges to planning efforts.

Personal Implications

Aside from the reasons noted earlier for human resource planning and the associated benefits, there is another pragmatic reason of individual importance to managers. This reason is related to the fact that the planning process will have normally required the human resource manager to communicate with other managers, senior executives, and staff members about the future human resource environment and the associated staffing issues. It will also have forced the human resource manager and other managers with planning responsibilities to have thought through these staffing issues and to have examined their operating assumptions. Although there are limitations and abuses of planning and there has been resistance to human resource planning in the past, there are benefits as well. An important benefit from the planner's perspective is that senior management will be more comfortable with the knowledge that the manager has a plan.[26] As such, senior managers have greater confidence that the manager has thought through the implications of potential demand and supply relationships and there is less chance that the company will be unprepared in the future.

Changing Receptivity Toward Planning

As noted in this chapter, a paradox of planning is that it is difficult to conduct when it is most needed. The turbulent business environment in which companies currently operate is obviously a difficult time in which to plan. Nonetheless, there is substantive evidence that companies have increased their emphasis on human resource planning. It is evident that some corporate-wide planning objectives require centralized, sophisticated human resource planning processes. However, as noted earlier, there has been a trend toward the use of simple planning and forecasting techniques on a decentralized basis by line managers. This trend has developed at a time when planning has been difficult and long-term planning horizons seem to some like a relic of a foregone era. As the human resource function's role shifts from direct involvement to greater indirect and shared involvement, it will need to take on a more strategic role in environmental scanning and more responsibility for assisting in the development of pools of talent for the new jobs of the future. Further, the human resource function will need to help redesign organizations to meet the demands of the future, such as being able to respond to customer preferences more quickly, provide higher quality, make faster decisions, and be more cost competitive.[27] The interplay of the current trend toward organizational restructuring and redesign will have to be integrated with strategic human resource planning efforts.

Implications of the European Experience

It is interesting to speculate whether the growing restrictions in the United States on employers' abilities to lay off employees also will serve as an additional incentive for human resource planning. In the future, if layoffs in the United States become more restricted by legislation, as in Europe, U.S. companies may place greater emphasis on human resource planning as a means of avoiding employee surpluses. This may be an interesting hypothesis to consider, as some European companies had developed sophisticated human resource planning programs prior to the 1980s. Expertise in human resource planning also is evident in the recent planning success of one of the companies now making up Astrazeneca Pharmaceuticals.[28] C. J. Verhoeven, a Dutch researcher, has pointed out the importance of employment security policies as a factor encouraging human resource planning:

> In some countries—for instance, in the Netherlands—the commitment of many organizations toward their personnel is high, which means that protection from dismissal exists as well as good career opportunities, good work circumstances, and the like. This is partly in contrast to the United States, where people can be fired on short notice in many organizations.[29]

Guvenc Alpander has provided a similar perspective on Dutch firms in an example of the Philips Company's human resource planning efforts for a new plant. Because of its responsibilities to an immobile workforce, Philips assumed employment responsibilities from 20 to 30 years into the future. Consequently, Philips forecasters attempted to link the plant's technology to its workforce for the next 20 years.[30] Whether such firms will be able to maintain commitments to their employees in the future remains to be seen, because many European firms have experienced strong pressures to downsize.

Verhoeven also has identified concerns over irregular age distributions, such as disproportionate numbers of younger or older employees, as a reason for human resource planning.[31] Although there is little in the literature on the effects of irregular age distributions in the United States, as noted in an earlier chapter, some companies with disproportionately older workforces have incurred higher health care costs. Their health care outlays have challenged their cost competitiveness. Such challenges will probably grow in importance and will consume more of the planning time and attention of general managers.

It is interesting to speculate on whether European countries will reduce restrictions on terminations and layoffs as in the United States. Some European observers have noted their desire to obtain productivity gains made possible by the greater workforce flexibility enjoyed by U.S. firms.

SELECTING FORECASTING TECHNIQUES

Several factors influence the techniques used to forecast either the supply or demand for human resources.

Purpose of Planning

One such factor is related to the purpose of human resource forecasting.[32] If the purpose is to forecast the supply of human resources in order to identify and eliminate bottlenecks in the career paths of promising managers, replacement charts or Markov analysis may be used. Conversely, if the purpose is to forecast the future age distribution of a company's workforce in order to estimate its likely health care costs, it would be better to use some form of renewal analysis in which specific numbers of employees in various individual jobs, job categories, or job families would be relatively unimportant. In the former case, detailed data would be required on movements through the various jobs; in the latter case, the data requirements might be limited to employment data, age distributions, turnover, and retirement trends.

Organizational Characteristics

Several other factors influence the selection of forecasting techniques. One such factor is the size of the organization. For example, minimum numbers of incumbents in the various positions are necessary to develop reliable probabilities of transitions from one position to another. Nonetheless, companies having as few as 2,000 employees have developed effective human resource forecasting models. Size also is related to the sophistication of forecasting techniques, with larger companies tending toward greater sophistication, although industry and planning horizons also affect the relationship. Human resource forecasting also varies in sophistication across divisions within large companies. Another factor in selection of forecasting techniques is the complexity of the organization. With greater complexity there are more differences in model parameters and fewer common assumptions that can be applied. Further, another factor is that with longer-range forecasting horizons, there is a tendency to use more sophisticated forecasting techniques.[33]

Industry Characteristics

The type of industry also affects technique utilization, as companies in regulated industries tend to use more sophisticated forecasting techniques. These industries are normally subject to less change and, as a result, forecasts can be quite accurate. Not surprisingly, forecasts in utilities, insurance companies, and railroads have often been highly accurate. This accuracy could be contrasted with an industry, such as high-fashion women's clothing, in which forecasts can be off by a wide order of magnitude. Regardless of the planning technique employed, a *paradox of planning* in general is that it is probably the most difficult to conduct in circumstances in which it is most needed. Because human resource planning is undertaken to reduce uncertainty, the resultant need for planning is greatest in industries facing the greatest environmental change.[34]

Environmental Turbulence

Some general trends in the use of various human resource forecasting techniques are also evident. Consistent with the decentralization theme mentioned previously, a survey of forecasting techniques by Quinn Mills indicates that the most prevalently employed techniques are relatively unsophisticated ones that can be readily understood and used by line managers.[35] Many of these relationships also are explained by forecasters' perceptions of the level of uncertainty in the environment. Thomas Stone and Jack Fiorito have developed a *perceived uncertainty model*, which explains the selection of forecasting techniques. Their model's predictions are consistent with Mills' findings as it predicts lower utilization of sophisticated techniques such as Markov analysis, operations research, and computer simulation, under conditions of moderately high and high perceived uncertainty. Essentially, their model indicates that sophisticated techniques cannot be used effectively in such environments because they require greater stability for accurate predictions. Such conditions describe the current environment of many companies and may explain the trend toward use of less sophisticated techniques. The results of empirical research by Huselid, noted earlier, are consistent with Stone and Fiorito's predictions. Huselid found that companies with moderate levels of workforce volatility are more inclined to engage in human resource planning. Interestingly, those with low workforce volatility probably perceive less need for such planning whereas those with high volatility probably find it ineffective.[36]

The trend toward increasing economic turbulence began during the 1980s and has continued into the twenty-first century. The level of turbulence also has posed difficulties for economic forecasters. Interestingly, economic forecasting, which thrived during the 1950s and 1960s when conditions were much more stable, began to lose credibility during the 1980s. By the 1990s, many companies, such as Eastman Kodak, Citibank, Xerox, and Equitable Life had eliminated their economic forecasting staffs.[37] This loss of credibility is illustrated in the results of studies by Stephen McNees:

> Stephen McNees . . . has made a specialty of comparing economic forecasters' predictions against what has actually come to pass. His data show that the forecasters have made huge errors around virtually every major recent turning point of the economy—recessions as well as recoveries . . .[38]

In spite of the decline in credibility of macro-level economic forecasting, many economic forecasters have made a successful transition to more micro-level applications, such as forecasting the behavior of industries or specific companies.[39] Thus, although the value of macro-level forecasting may have declined, more micro-oriented applications, such as human resource forecasting, currently have greater credibility and value.

Other Considerations

The sheer number of forecasting techniques also can pose problems for those who must make decisions on which techniques to use. Several factors should be considered in making these decisions, including time horizon, level of technical or mathematical sophistication required of the forecaster, cost, whether appropriate data are available, the stability of the data on which forecasts will be based, and level of detailed data required. Other factors include accuracy, whether the technique is effective at identifying turning points, whether the forecast output includes a measure of central tendency, and an indication of the breadth of potential outcomes. One precaution regarding forecasting horizons is that the desire to extend the forecast far out into the future should be tempered with a recognition that with long-range time horizons, the process will become more complex and time consuming. The costs may also increase disproportionately to the forecast's value. A general recommendation for improving forecasting, which appears to have a great deal of validity, is to use a combination of techniques in order to offset their different disadvantages.[40] The basis of this recommendation is revealed in the following account:

> The research on combining forecasts to achieve improvements (particularly in accuracy) is extensive, persuasive, and consistent. The results of combined forecasts greatly surpass most individual projections, techniques, and analyses by experts . . . combining forecasts—particularly with techniques that are dissimilar—offers the manager an assured way of improving quality.[41]

David Georgoff and Robert Murdick have prepared a general guide to the selection of forecasting techniques. Their guide covers 20 different techniques and includes a set of questions to which the forecaster provides answers for guidance in selecting the most appropriate technique.[42] The following sections provide greater detail on several techniques that have potential applicability in human resource planning and forecasting. Because demand and supply forecasting are interchangeable in the planning sequence, and supply forecasting may be easier to understand, the discussion will begin on the supply side.

FORECASTING THE SUPPLY OF HUMAN RESOURCES

Techniques used to forecast supplies of human resources may be classified as either *quantitative* or *qualitative*, although the distinction is sometimes unclear.

Further, some forecasting techniques may be used to forecast both the supply and demand of human resources. Thus, classifications of techniques as either supply or demand, as well as quantitative or qualitative, must be arbitrary to some extent. With these limitations in mind, the category of quantitative techniques includes Markov analysis or network flow models, attrition analysis models, computer simulation, operations research techniques, and renewal models. The category of qualitative supply forecasting techniques includes replacement charts or succession planning and supervisory estimates. Occasionally, human resource inventories will be categorized as planning or forecasting techniques. However, they are not really forecasting techniques even though inventories provide the database from which forecasts of internal supplies of human resources are derived.[43] This section will describe replacement charts, succession planning, Markov analysis, renewal models, and computer simulation. In addition, the current utilization of these techniques will be discussed.

Replacement Charts

Replacement charts describe a company's organizational structure in terms of individuals occupying various managerial and professional positions. For each position incumbent, potential replacements are identified along with such information as their individual potential for advancement and numbers of years' experience needed before being qualified for the next higher position. The individual's age also may be included for estimating retirement dates.[44] For each replacement, the potential replacements for that individual also are listed with similar information. Thus, the replacement chart, which is likely to be computerized, provides a description of how vacancies can be filled from the internal labor market. It also shows the associated cascading effects.

In determining the time when potential managerial replacements will be ready to take on higher-level responsibilities, an assessment of their current skills must be conducted and matched against those required for higher-level positions. There are two organizational dimensions that should guide such assessments: (1) the hierarchical or vertical level of various jobs and (2) where the job falls in a continuum from basically individual contributions to managing the efforts of others. Thus, the assessment should include not only the skills that will be required for vertical moves, but also the skills to move horizontally, typically toward the broader orientation and responsibilities of general management. Movement upward often entails a shift toward the managerial end of the continuum. Beginning with the individual contributor end of the continuum and moving toward the managerial end, employees would be assessed against skill requirements for the following tracks: technical development, technical application, technical management, operations management, and business management.[45]

Another aspect of the utilization of replacement charts to forecast supplies of human resources involves the assessment of the organization's current employees' abilities and qualifications to take on future positions. Before the number of qualified replacements for a current or future position can be determined, there must be a means of comparing potential replacement candidates with the position's requirements. Robert Gatewood and Wayne Rockmore have provided an extensive description of an electric utility's systems and procedures that have enabled the company to evaluate this matching activity. One important component of the company's system is its human resource inventory, which is based on supervisory estimates of individual employees' capabilities of performing various job tasks. In this company, supervisory evaluations of their subordinates' capabilities are obtained with a lengthy questionnaire. The job requirements, in terms of tasks and employees' characteristics and capabilities to perform these tasks, are combined in a document called a talent bank, which is similar to a replacement chart. Self-assessments, instruments administered by the human resource staff, information from the talent bank, and assessment center data are used to guide the training and developmental efforts needed to prepare employees for future and current needs. An interesting side benefit of the company's system is that career paths have become better understood and the company now does a better job in career counseling.[46]

Emerson Electric provides a good example of replacement planning for managers. The company, which has had 165 consecutive quarters of growth in its net income, has 117,000 employees in 60 divisions. While this example is displayed in physical format, it could be easily computerized. The example also indicates the confidentiality with which such information is treated and the security measures that are applied to the end result of the process.[47]

> If there is an Exhibit A for Mr. Knight's [the CEO] management style, it is the "Organization Room," an unmarked chamber at Emerson's headquarters to which only a few people have a key. On the walls, floor to ceiling, are 1,400 2- by 4-inch refrigerator magnets, one for every manager at the company. Each magnet displays, in tiny print and color coding, date of hire, date of birth, international experience, a photograph, and postgraduate degrees. Separate organizational charts reduce elaborate personnel evaluations—entire career histories, really—to a single dot of color: orange for outstanding, green for above-average, red for underperforming. When a key job becomes open, Mr. Knight slips into the room and studies the walls, yanking down the magnets of a handful of candidates.[48]

Succession Planning

Although similar to replacement planning and the use of replacement charts, *succession planning* tends to be directed toward a longer-range time horizon and is more focused on development. It is also more concerned with the development of pools of potential replacements, as opposed to individuals. Succession planning involves more elaborate planning for skill development of potential replacements, is more systematic in the assessment of potential replacements and their developmental needs, and generally applies to higher levels of managerial positions.[49] For example, at Air Products and Chemicals, Inc., which has annual sales in excess of $1 billion, the succession plan involves only approximately 300 key jobs.[50]

A paper company now owned by Kimberly-Clark provides a good example of succession planning. Succession planning in this case involved the assessment of managers occupying positions as plant managers. As a result of succession planning and associated developmental efforts, the division was able to solve productivity problems. Prior to these efforts, the division suffered from problems related to employee dissatisfaction, autocratic management styles, and the aftermath of downsizing. The assessment procedures, conducted by an outside consulting firm, involved administration of a battery of tests and personality assessments by psychologists. Following the assessment, managers were provided detailed individual feedback on areas in which they needed further development. One of the keys to success in this succession planning effort was the emphasis placed on detailed specification of the skills and requirements needed for performance as plant managers.[51]

In some companies, succession planning also incorporates developmental planning for high-potential managers while they are still in lower-level positions. This is especially prevalent for minorities and women who are likely to become long-range successors. Additionally, succession planning also may be concerned with the future requirements of executive positions since the necessary personal skills and characteristics may differ substantially from current requirements. Given the growing interdependencies across functional areas in many companies, one promising approach for developing potential successors for positions of the future may be to assign them leadership responsibilities in cross-functional teams. Nonetheless, current executives may be hesitant to make selection decisions on projections of future skill requirements that are difficult to quantify.[52] A related difficulty is revealed in the following account:

> It becomes extremely difficult for top management to have confidence that they are selecting successors with this new profile when there are no data they can trust. Before, when executives were selecting successors in their own image, the data were less important, since they could use their own intuition, a sense that "he's one of us." (And he usually was a he.)[53]

To the extent that succession planning is participatory and plans are incorporated into career development sessions, there may be reduced turnover of valued managers. For those informed that they are next in line for a position, there may be a motivational effect as well as an enhanced likelihood that they will remain with the organization.[54]

While there are important benefits of succession planning, there are increasing concerns about the ability of traditional succession planning to produce qualified successors, particularly on a position-by-position basis. Improvements to the process involve 360-degree feedback, more self-initiated programs, and developmental assignments across functions and units. Of course, events such as acquisitions and mergers also can make such plans meaningless and increase the level of top management turnover.[55] In this regard, James Walsh has found that "59 percent of each company's top management team departs within 5 years of a merger." [56] In cases wherein change in the strategic direction of the organization is needed, succession plans become less important. The rationale is that organizations are more likely to obtain such changes in strategy with outsider successor executives. Such executives are less likely to be subject to the influences of escalating commitment and are more inclined to have a different vision. Empirical research is consistent with this reasoning and supports the notion that outsiders are more likely than insiders to change an organization's strategy.[57]

Fortunately, some of the complexity of the details of succession planning can be handled with computer software. For example, there are software packages that have been designed for succession planning, such as Succession Plus, which is available in Oracle versions.[58]

Markov Analysis

In the past, some researchers observed that companies tended to have greater expertise and placed greater emphasis on forecasting the demand for human resources than for their supply. However, the application of *Markov analysis* to human resource forecasting changed the situation by providing a practical and versatile technique for forecasting internal supply. As such, the techniques can serve the strategic purpose of evaluating the availability of human resources required for different strategies. Markov models have an advantage of being relatively simple to understand, although they can be quantitatively sophisticated.[59]

In setting up Markov models (see Figure 5-1), the forecaster must account for all possible moves or flows of employees in an organization. Such moves include moves into the organization, moves from one job to another, and exit moves. Moves between jobs can be upward moves in hierarchical level as well as moves across functions. Essentially, Markov models begin with distributions of the number of employees in various job categories at a starting point in time. These distributions are then transformed by a *transition probability matrix* into a forecasted distribution of employees across these same job categories one period later. The transition probabilities in each row of the matrix must total to 1. The diagonal set of transitional probabilities, after excluding the column representing exit moves, represents the proportion of employees remaining in the same job from Time 1 to Time 2. Markov models cannot take into account more than one move per time period.[60]

For purposes of illustration, the Markov model in Figure 5-1 contains only five different jobs and an exit move. Although not reflected in this example, the jobs also could be arrayed in terms of their hierarchical level, with Job 1 being lower in the job hierarchy than Job 2, and so on. The forecasted distribution of employees for period 2 is obtained by multiplying the initial distribution of

Transition Matrix

Distribution of Employees in Time 1	**Job 1**	27	.66	.11	.09	.03	.02	.09
	Job 2	41	.15	.60	.08	.06	.01	.10
	Job 3	55	.03	.08	.55	.13	.10	.11
	Job 4	64	.00	.09	.18	.54	.03	.16
	Job 5	73	.00	.08	.10	.17	.45	.20
			26	44	55	57	41	37
			Job 1	**Job 2**	**Job 3**	**Job 4**	**Job 5**	**Exit**

Distribution of Employees in Time 2

FIGURE 5-1 Markov Model for Forecasting Supply

Note: Numbers of employees in each job in Time 2 are rounded off to the nearest whole number.

employees by each column of transition probabilities. The number of employees for each job in the forecasted distribution is the sum of each of these levels of employment as multiplied by the column's transition probabilities.[61] Although any time period can be used, time periods of one year are relevant for many applications.

The transition probabilities for Markov models are typically derived from historical data on the movements of employees between jobs, as well as exit moves from the organization. For example, transition probabilities from Job 1 to Job 2 might be determined by computing the percentage of employees in Job 1 who make such a move over a one-year time period. An important consideration for the use of Markov models is that with small numbers of job incumbents, the transition probabilities become unstable. For example, if there are only two employees in a job and one leaves, a transition probability based on the number remaining would be only .50. This could be a very misleading transition probability.[62]

Another problem is that the probabilities derived from such percentages may not be stable if based on only the moves in one single year. Accordingly, the forecaster may want to compute an average percentage of employees making such moves over several years (e.g., from three to five years) in order to obtain a more stable transition probability. The positive aspect of the trade-off is that, with probabilities based on percentages derived from several years of data, they are less subject to spurious influences. Unfortunately, the downside is that the impact of recent trends will be muted to the extent that such recent data are averaged in with data from earlier years. With transition probabilities based on only one or two years of historical data, however, employee movements between jobs will track more quickly and recent trends will be more heavily represented in the forecast.

Human resource forecasters can obtain the proper balance between slower and quicker tracking transition probabilities through a process of trial and error. For example, a forecaster may attempt to forecast the movements of employees between jobs that occurred *last* year. He or she could experiment with transition probabilities based on movements for one year prior to that, an average of the two previous years, an average of the three previous years, and so on, and compare these forecasts with what actually happened. In this manner, the forecaster can determine the particular number of years that produces transition probabilities that will result in the most accurate forecast. Of course, any use of historical data assumes that certain conditions of the past will remain in the future, which may not be true.

In addition to forecasts of an organization's internal supply of human resources one year into the future, Markov analysis can be used for longer-range forecasts. Heneman and Sandver have pointed out that, through applications of matrix algebra, forecasts for multiple years into the future can be developed. Additionally, they have explained that such forecasts can incorporate new hires in the various jobs for individual years.[63] Iterative approaches provide an alternative for extending Markov analysis forecasts several years into the future. With an iterative approach, the forecasted distribution of employees across job categories is used as the input for the next year's employee distribution, which is then used with the transition probabilities to derive the next forecasted distribution. This process is then repeated for a forecast of another year into the future and can be performed on computerized spreadsheets. Forecasters must bear in mind that the validity of the transition probabilities will probably be lower as the forecast is extended further into the future since more conditions are likely to change.

Aside from use in forecasting, Markov analysis also can be used for audits of the human resource function to determine whether there are any irregularities in the flow of employees through an organization's different positions. This can be done by constructing separate Markov transition matrices for minorities and females and comparing their similarity. Likewise, Markov analysis may have applicability in the development of affirmative action goals because it can be used to forecast the internal supply of minorities and females that will be available in various positions at some point in the future. Additionally, the technique may be useful for identifying career paths and mobility patterns that may be helpful in career planning and development. Researchers also have demonstrated the feasibility of using a combination of Markov analysis and human resource accounting to forecast and depreciate the future value of an acquired firm's human resources.[64]

Although Markov models are classified here as a supply forecasting technique, they also can be used in conjunction with specifications of future demand. For example, a large computer manufacturer with many years of forecasting experience uses demand specifications with Markov models.[65] Forecasters combine Markov analysis with demand scenarios, by beginning with a specification of the desired future distribution of employees in various job categories, typically in higher-level positions. By working backward, the forecaster then determines the magnitude of the transition probabilities that will be needed to create the flow of employees from the existing distribution into the desired future distribution. Promotion rates and termination rates are examples of human resource policies that would be adjusted to obtain the desired flow of human resources through the company to achieve the desired future distribution of employees. Transition rates also can be changed to reflect changes in such policies. By running the models with different transition rates, corresponding to policy changes, the impact on human resource flows between jobs and hierarchical levels can be determined.[66]

Another example of an application of Markov analysis is provided by the experiences of the Weyerhaeuser Company. In this example, the model was first developed during a growth phase of the company. The model was used to forecast the number of employees in a specialty, on a corporate-wide basis, that would be available from the company's internal labor supply. In the event that internal supplies were forecasted to fall short of demand, accelerated programs were instituted to provide the training needed to qualify current employees to take on the responsibilities for the positions in which shortages were anticipated. During this phase, the model was used for decisions on a daily basis. Following this period, there was a recession that changed the situation from shortages to surpluses of employees and the company needed to reduce the number of employees by 700. Fortunately, information from the model helped decision makers discover that the solution to the problem could come from attrition of current employees. By modeling human resource flows through Markov analysis, Weyerhaeuser was able to reduce its employee surplus within 15 months through attrition rather than layoffs. In subsequent years, the company used the technique to examine flows of exempt personnel within its separate divisions. A weakness of Markov analysis was revealed when small numbers of employees in the various job categories prevented effective utilization of the technique.[67]

Renewal Models

Another category of human resource forecasting techniques consists of *renewal models*. These models reflect the movement or flow of employees through companies as they are "pulled" upward to fill vacancies in higher-level job categories. An advantage of renewal models is that they involve simple mathematics and are readily understood by managers. Renewal models, in their simplest form, can use age cohorts of employees as the focus of analysis. As the level of incumbent employees in an age group is projected forward into the future, the group is "aged" by one year. When greater rates of change are expected, shorter time periods may be used. The "aged" cohort is then adjusted for losses of employees due to various forms of attrition. Rates of attrition can be obtained from historical data and typically differ across the age cohorts. Typically, attrition would be relatively high with younger workers, such as recent college graduates and for age cohorts close to retirement.[68]

In addition to "aging" employee cohorts and adjusting age cohorts for attrition, renewal models also may be configured in accordance with the job classification hierarchy and also may reflect the hiring of new employees and promotions of current employees into different job categories. The numbers of employees in each job category may be adjusted during the process to reflect needs for growth or contraction, which is dictated by the company's strategic plan. Starting with the top of the job hierarchy, the human resource planner can work downward through each job category, in a stepwise manner, to determine the number of employees that must be promoted from the lower classifications and the flow policies that will be needed to supply such numbers. For example, in addition to promotion rates, needs for external hiring can be identified, as well as needs for training programs for specific job categories predicted to have shortages.[69]

Renewal models also can be run with different specifications of promotion rates so that their differential impacts can be determined. The models also can be run with different attrition rates and other planning assumptions. Additionally, renewal models can be applied to specific populations, such as minorities and females, so that a company's future affirmative action status may be forecasted.[70]

Computer Simulation

It is sometimes stated that *computer simulations* are the most useful forecasting techniques for guiding business decisions. Simulations have the advantage of allowing the forecaster to create a number of different future scenarios by altering the values of the simulation's parameters. Through this process, the forecaster can determine variations in forecasted values according to different formulations of future conditions and can plan alternative courses of actions to reduce uncertainty and manage risk. Further, computer simulations allow planners and forecasters to assess the sensitivity of the simulation model's parameters to alternative specifications. By running *sensitivity analyses*, forecasters can gain an understanding of the impact of inaccurate assumptions. With the rapidly increasing power of personal computers and advances in software, computer simulations are likely to grow in importance as human resource planning and forecasting techniques.[71]

An example of a strategic application of a combination of computer simulation and *attrition analysis* to forecast supplies of human resources is provided by the experiences of two public school districts in British Columbia. In this application, the current inventory of teachers was projected into the future after reductions for attrition. Attrition estimates were based on historical rates, which differed according to age cohorts and by school district.[72] The following account describes the outcomes of this planning effort:

> The most important outcome of these applications of manpower planning was that the analysis encouraged school administrators to think strategically about the manpower resources they managed. By using specific procedures to estimate the supply and demand for teachers, those factors which influenced the district's ability to balance supply and demand became more visible and explicit . . . A second aspect of this strategic orientation to manpower management was that school administrators concentrated on the importance of the relative rates of manpower flows into, through, and out of their organizations.[73]

Utilization of Supply Forecasting Techniques

A survey mentioned earlier also determined utilization rates for various supply forecasting techniques. The results of this survey are presented in Table 5-1 in terms of the percentage of companies using such supply forecasting techniques. As indicated in Table 5-1, the two most frequently used techniques are replacement charts or succession planning techniques (66.7 percent) and human resource inventories (66.7 percent). At the other end of the spectrum, only 7.6 of the companies used regression analysis while 6.1 percent used Markov analysis/network flow models. The small proportion of companies using Markov analysis/network flow models is consistent with the trend, reported earlier, toward simpler, less sophisticated techniques that can be used by line managers.[74]

Nonetheless, many companies have human resource forecasters, often possessing doctoral degrees, who do sophisticated, large-scale organization-wide forecasts of their organizations' internal supplies of human resources. These forecasts are not necessarily replaceable by the trend toward greater human resource planning at the managerial level and typically serve separate functions.

TABLE 5-1 Supply Forecasting Techniques

	Percentage of Companies Using Technique
Succession Planning or Replacement Charts	66.7
Human Resource Inventories	66.7
Supervisor Estimates	48.5
Rules of Thumb or Nonstatistical Formulas	27.3
Computer Simulation	12.1
Renewal Models	9.1
Regression Analysis	7.6
Markov or Network Flow Models	6.1
Exponential Smoothing or Trend Extrapolation	6.1
Operations Research Techniques	4.5

Source: Extracted from Charles R. Greer, Dana L. Jackson, and Jack Fiorito. "Adapting Human Resource Planning in a Changing Business Environment," *Human Resource Management* 28, no. 1 (1989): 110. Copyright © 1989 by John Wiley & Sons, Inc. Reprinted by permission of John Wiley & Sons, Inc.

For these applications, Markov models are probably still very important forecasting techniques. In addition, although 7.6 percent of the responding companies reported the use of regression analysis for forecasts of human resource supplies, the technique's direct applicability as a supply forecasting technique is not readily apparent and its use in this application may be overstated.

FORECASTING THE DEMAND FOR HUMAN RESOURCES

There are a number of practical difficulties in forecasting the demand for human resources. As a result, companies report dissatisfaction in this area and acknowledge that demand forecasting is the weakest link in their human resource or workforce planning efforts. For example, a common constraint on the value of forecasts, based on extrapolations of current labor and output relationships, is ignorance of whether current manning levels are appropriate. The massive reductions in labor utilization by companies facing intense competition have highlighted this problem. With the strategic moves toward leaner organizations, there have been labor cuts beyond those prompted by the efficiencies of new technology. Interestingly, along this same line, some companies implementing *total quality management* (TQM) programs have found that they need fewer employees. Similarly, the process of reeingineering, which is often associated with the adoption of new technology and the utilization of new computer systems, can reduce the number of employees required to perform work. Thus, human resource planners must use appropriate *learning curve parameters*, which reflect expected productivity improvements, in order to avoid overestimating the demand for human resources.[75]

Table 5-2 presents labor productivity data from the U.S. manufacturing sector as well as the entire business category. As the data indicate, in manufacturing, productivity increased substantially from an index value of 93.0 in 1990 to 140, in the first quarter of 2000. In contrast, the productivity gains were more modest in the entire business sector, which includes services. In this sector, the productivity index increased over the same time period from 95.1 to 116.6. Data for specific industries, where even greater differences are evident, are presented in Table 5-3. For example, productivity in electronic components increased from an index of 100.0 in 1987 to 222.0 in 1996, while there was a decline over the same period for eating and drinking establishments. In that labor-intensive service industry, the index declined from 100.0 in 1987 to 93.7 in 1997. In another labor-intensive service industry, hotels and motels, there was only a slight increase in productivity, 100.0 in 1987 to 107.9 in 1997. Furthermore, it should be noted that these are highly aggregated productivity averages. At greater levels of industry specificity, there may be even larger variances in productivity and learning curves.

Additionally, in forecasting demand, forecasters must choose predictor variables (independent variables) that are linked with variations in the underly-

TABLE 5-2 Trends in U.S. Labor Productivity

Year	*Manufacturing Output per Hour*	*Business Output per Hour*
1990	93.0	95.1
1991	95.1	96.2
1992	100.0	100.0
1993	102.2	100.5
1994	105.3	101.8
1995	109.4	102.5
1996	113.8	105.4
1997	119.6	107.4
1998	125.9	110.5
1999	134.0	114.0
2000	140.0[a]	116.6[a]

[a]Indicates data are for first quarter only.

Source: Data extracted from the Web site of the Bureau of Labor Statistics, U.S. Department of Labor, *www.bls.gov/blshome.htm*; base year is 1992. Public domain material.

TABLE 5-3 Trends in U.S. Labor Productivity in Selected Industries

	Services Output per Hour			*Manufacturing Output per Hour*		
	Commercial Banks	**Eating & Drinking Places**	**Hotels & Motels**	**Petroleum Refining**	**Electronic Components**	**Blast Furnaces & Steel Mills**
1987	100.0	100.0	100.0	100.0	100.0	100.0
1988	105.3	102.8	97.6	105.3	98.1	112.5
1989	109.6	102.2	95.0	109.6	105.4	108.4
1990	109.2	104.0	96.1	109.2	115.5	109.0
1991	106.6	103.1	99.1	106.6	138.9	106.5
1992	111.3	102.5	107.8	111.3	169.9	116.5
1993	120.1	101.7	106.2	120.1	187.4	136.5
1994	123.8	98.9	109.6	123.8	198.4	146.4
1995	132.3	97.6	110.1	132.3	211.1	148.6
1996	142.0	95.2	109.7	142.0	222.0	165.7
1997	—	93.7	107.9	—	—	—

Note: — indicates data not available.

Source: Data extracted from the Web site of the Bureau of Labor Statistics, U.S. Department of Labor, *www.bls.gov/blshome.htm*, May 4, 1999. Base year is 1987. Public domain material.

ing level of business activity.[76] This requirement for forecasting is evident in the experiences of a computer manufacturer that utilizes computerized productivity models to predict the demand for human resources. These models, which are based on statistical correlations between workload and staffing levels, enable the company to forecast the demand for human resources in its manufacturing divisions, as well as in marketing and services. In some other departments, where such relationships are less systematic, more qualitative techniques are used.[77]

An interesting forecasting example is provided by the case of maintenance workers. In forecasting the demand for maintenance workers, the reliability of the equipment to be repaired is an important predictor variable. With equipment that is to be maintained, forecasters can use such factors as the mean time between failure of components as indicators of the number of maintenance workers needed. In the case of maintenance work, these estimates of the demand for maintenance workers can be considered in conjunction with decisions to purchase equipment. In cases in which a stable employment level of maintenance is desired, purchases of equipment can be phased over time so that expected failures will not occur all at once, necessitating higher levels of maintenance workers. With phased purchasing, all equipment does not need maintenance at the same time and lower levels of maintenance workers who have a steady amount of work to perform can be maintained.[78]

It also should be noted that with some potential predictors of demand, a doubling of business activity might not necessarily translate into a doubling of the need for employees in a particular job category.[79] For example, the number of kilowatt hours generated by an electric power plant could double while there is no greater need for safety inspectors or billing clerks.

As indicated earlier, some forecasting techniques have both supply and demand applications. Replacement charts and renewal models have demand implications because they also indicate vacancies when replacements are promoted into vacancies at higher levels. Computer simulations also may be used for both supply and demand forecasting. These techniques have already been covered in detail and will not be addressed in this section. This section will briefly describe the qualitative techniques of heuristics, rules of thumb, and the Delphi technique. It will focus more extensively on the quantitative techniques involving management science and operations research applications and regression analysis.

Heuristics, Rules of Thumb, and the Delphi Technique

Rules of thumb are simple guidelines that are used to predict demand for human resources. For example, a retailing chain may have developed a heuristic that specifies that for every 12 new stores, another regional manager will be hired. *Heuristics* are conceptual frameworks, often expressed as diagrams, which help human resource forecasters organize relevant conceptual relationships and trace through the outcomes of various personnel action alternatives. Using the retail chain example, forecasters might consider the strategic plans for the number of new stores the next year, then apply the heuristic to forecast the number of regional managers that will be needed. One common qualitative approach for forecasting the demand for human resources is the *"bottom-up" approach* in which unit managers estimate their specific human resource needs for the next period. These estimates are then combined into aggregate forecasts for the whole company.[80] The *Delphi technique*, an iterative judgment refinement technique based on the collection of expert opinion, is sometimes categorized as a qualitative demand forecasting technique. This technique can approach the accuracy of quantitative techniques and does not require a historical database. Nonetheless, the Delphi technique is used for such purposes by only a very small number of organizations.[81]

Operations Research and Management Science Techniques

Techniques such as *linear programming, integer programming*, and *network optimization techniques* are generally considered as operations research or management science techniques. Such techniques can be used to determine optimal personnel flows through organizations. These flows can be managed through specification of time-in-grade requirements for promotions, rates of turnover, and the like. Managed flows can produce desired stocks of personnel in various positions or ranks at points in the future. A further extension of linear programming, called *goal programming*, allows human resource planners to take into consideration sequential and multiple managerial goals or constraints, such as maximum head counts, budgetary limitations, and so on. Goal programming has been used in human resource planning models that also can factor in equal employment opportunity considerations.[82]

The use of such planning techniques runs counter to the trend toward more reliance on less sophisticated approaches. However, such techniques are still very important in that they affect the service capability and profitability of major corporations and governmental organizations. Human resource planning systems based on these techniques require mathematical sophistication and complex computer programs. They also are expensive to develop. Nonetheless, they are often key systems in large organizations, which produce savings of millions of dollars in labor costs. Such systems are developed by human resource planning specialists. Although they are developed and maintained on a centralized basis, they may be used on computerized networks by line managers for applications such as the development of optimal workforce schedules.[83]

The United Airlines Station Manpower Planning System provides an example of the application of such techniques. This system has been used to develop work schedules for several thousand United employees who work as customer service agents and reservation sales representatives. While the system is used primarily for short-range planning, it does enable managers to forecast the number of employees needed to maintain desired service levels a few weeks and months into the future. It also allows industrial relations specialists to formulate the costs of various negotiated configurations of contract settlements. The system has been used to optimize the utilization of customer service agents at its airport operations. Through the specification of optimal staffing levels, sufficient numbers of agents are available to handle customer demand, but not so many that employees are underutilized. Managers and schedulers at each airport are able to use the computerized system to develop work schedules that take into account the unique demands of operations and employee preferences. Additionally, the system provides an optimal schedule standard for the minimization of labor costs. Managers of United's airline ticket reservations centers also make similar use of the system.[84]

Aside from the benefits already noted for this computerized simulation system, the complexity of airline operations necessitates the use of such systems. Several modules in United's system are needed to handle this complexity. Specifically, forecasts of demand for reservations representatives are determined on the basis of historical data through application of regression analysis and moving averages. The system's demand module takes a queuing approach to build in management's specification of customers' acceptable waiting times and employs a Poisson distribution to simulate the frequency and spacing of incoming calls for reservations. A similar approach, drawing on aircraft arrival trends and passenger loads, is used to forecast the demand for customer service agents. Aside from the system's demand forecasting module, there are modules that deal with starting times, scheduling, days off, and reports. Specific techniques employed in some of these modules include linear programming, continuous linear programming, and network assignment models.[85]

A practical managerial problem of user resistance was encountered when United's system was being implemented. Because the developers of the system needed to bring it on line quickly in order to meet the demands of business, potential users were not sufficiently involved in the system's development. As a result, the users perceived that the system did not meet all of their needs. This resistance was overcome by involving the potential users in refinements of the system and by making it more flexible to their locations' specific needs. Benefits of the system have included approximately $6 million in annual labor costs savings, increased employee satisfaction with scheduling, and better customer service.[86] The overall impact of the system is captured in the following quotation from a United manager: "Just as the (customer) lines begin to build, someone shows up for work; and just as you begin to think you're overstaffed, people start going home."[87]

Regression Analysis

Regression analysis is a robust statistical technique having applicability to forecasting demand for human resources. Although its greatest applicability may be for centralized human resource forecasting at the corporate level by planning specialists, its wide availability as a feature of computerized spreadsheets makes it a potential technique for widespread adoption by line managers as well. *Multiple regression analysis* allows the forecaster to control for several potential influences on the number of employees needed in a particular specialty.

An example of the use of regression analysis for predicting demand is provided by an application at the New York Power Authority (an electric power utility). In this application, regression analysis was used to predict such dependent variables as the overall staffing level and staffing levels for various categories of employees (e.g., professionals, managers, technicians, craft workers, service and maintenance workers). The predictor or independent variables used in the models include such variables as the number of kilowatt-hours produced, operating revenues, sales, and the capital budget. A limitation of this application is that the variables are only of a general nature. Therefore, they are inappropriate for predicting the demand for specific jobs, such as the various professional or managerial specialties. Another aspect of this application of regression analysis is the stability of the utility's environment. Because utilities typically have stable environments, assumptions of stable relationships between the predictor variables and the dependent variable are more likely to be valid than in many environments characterized by turbulence.[88]

Utilization of Demand Forecasting Techniques

The survey of techniques cited earlier also examined the utilization rates for demand forecasting techniques. The percentage of companies utilizing the various techniques are reported in Table 5-4, which indicates that the simple techniques of supervisor estimates (69.7 percent) and replacement charts or succession planning techniques (65.2 percent) are the most heavily utilized techniques. At the other end of the distribution are regression analysis (9.1 percent), and the

TABLE 5-4 Demand Forecasting Techniques

	Percentage of Companies Using Technique
Supervisor Estimates	69.7
Succession Planning or Replacement Charts	65.2
Rules of Thumb or Nonstatistical Formulas	37.9
Computer Simulation	18.2
Exponential Smoothing or Trend Extrapolation	12.1
Regression Analysis	9.1
Delphi Technique	3.0

Source: Extracted from Charles R. Greer, Dana L. Jackson, and Jack Fiorito. "Adapting Human Resource Planning in a Changing Business Environment," *Human Resource Management* 28, no. 1 (1989): 110. Copyright © 1989 by John Wiley & Sons, Inc. Reprinted by permission of John Wiley & Sons, Inc.

Delphi technique (3.0 percent). While the study found that there has been a decline in the utilization of regression analysis from earlier periods because of the reliance of line managers on simpler techniques, corporate-level specialists in human resource planning, who do large scale organization-wide forecasting, probably make extensive use of regression analysis.[89]

Summary

This chapter has reviewed the changing environment that has increased both the strategic importance and the difficulty of human resource planning. Organizations are concerned about having an adequate supply of successors for their top-level positions who will have the experiences and skills needed to provide leadership in this century. With the recognition of human resources as a source of competitive advantage, human resource planning will have a larger strategic role in the future. Along with increasing strategic importance, there also has been a trend toward decentralization of the responsibilities for human resource planning to line mangers.

Aside from the benefits of such planning, the problems that organizations incur when they fail to plan also were discussed. Such problems include having shortages or surpluses of employees with various skills and experiences, as well as higher operating costs, which result from failures to include staffing projections in strategic plans. A number of managerial issues related to planning also were discussed. These issues included the importance of human resource planning to individual managers, the changing receptivity toward human resource planning, and the paradox of the value of planning. Additionally, implications of European experiences with human resource planning were discussed.

Forecasting techniques also were discussed in some detail, beginning with the factors that determine the utilization of different techniques. These factors include the purpose of planning; organizational characteristics such as size and complexity; industry characteristics; the level of environmental turbulence; and other considerations such as data availability, forecasting horizon, the user's mathematical sophistication, and accuracy requirements. The discussion of supply forecasting techniques included replacement charts, succession planning, Markov analysis, renewal models, and computer simulation. Trends in the utilization of the various supply forecasting techniques also were reviewed. Techniques for forecasting the demand for human resources also were discussed, including the general category of heuristics, rules of thumb, the Delphi technique, operations research and management science techniques, and regression analysis. Differences in the utilization of these techniques also were discussed.

Endnotes

1. Eichinger, Robert W. Comments to the Metroplex Human Resource Planning Society, Plano, Texas, April 7, 1994.

2. Meehan, Robert H., and S. Basheer Ahmed. "Forecasting Human Resource Requirements: A Demand Model," *Human Resource Planning* 13, no. 4 (1990): 297–307.
3. Huselid, Mark A. "The Impact of Environmental Volatility on Human Resource Planning and Strategic Human Resource Management," *Human Resource Planning* 16, no. 3 (1993): 35–51.
4. Wood, D. Robley Jr., and R. Lawrence LaForge. "The Impact of Comprehensive Planning on Financial Performance," *Academy of Management Journal* 22, no. 3 (1979): 516–26; Pearce, John A. II, Elizabeth B. Freeman, and Richard B. Robinson Jr. "The Tenuous Link Between Formal Strategic Planning and Financial Performance," *Academy of Management Review* 12, no. 4 (1987): 658–75.
5. Zajac, Edward J. "CEO Selection, Succession, Compensation and Firm Performance: A Theoretical Integration and Empirical Analysis," *Strategic Management Journal* 11, no. 3 (1990): 217–30.
6. Nkomo, Stella M. "Human Resource Planning and Organizational Performance: An Exploratory Analysis," *Strategic Management Journal* 8, no. 4 (1987): 387–92.
7. Greer, Charles R., Dana L. Jackson, and Jack Fiorito. "Adapting Human Resource Planning in a Changing Business Environment," *Human Resource Management* 28, no. 1 (1989): 105–23.
8. Nkomo, Stella M. "The Theory and Practice of HR Planning: The Gap Still Remains," *Personnel Administrator* 31, no. 8 (1986): 71–84.
9. Risher, Howard W. "Strategic Salary Planning," *Compensation and Benefits Review* 25, no. 1 (1993): 46–50.
10. Henn, William R. "What the Strategist Asks from Human Resources," *Human Resource Planning* 8, no. 4 (1985): 193–200.
11. Risher. "Strategic Salary Planning," p. 47.
12. Walker, James W. *Human Resource Planning*. New York: McGraw-Hill, 1980; Milkovich, George L., and Thomas A. Mahoney. "Human Resources Planning and PAIR Policy," in Dale Yoder and Herbert G. Heneman Jr. (Eds.), *Planning and Auditing PAIR*. Washington, DC: Bureau of National Affairs, 1976, pp. 2-1–2-29; Middlemist, R. Dennis, Michael A. Hitt, and Charles R. Greer. *Personnel Management: Jobs, People, and Logic*. Upper Saddle River, NJ: Prentice-Hall, 1983; Niehaus, Richard J. "Models for Human Resource Decisions," *Human Resource Planning* 11, no. 2 (1988) 95–107.
13. Pitta, Julie. "The Cisco Kid," *Forbes* (January 10, 2000): 108–10; Gore, Gerald M., William Pyle, and Jay J. Jamrog. "Information Technology and HR," *Human Resource Planning* 19, no. 1 (1996): 56–61; Thurm, Scott. "Joining the Fold: Under Cisco's System, Mergers Usually Work; That Defies the Odds," *Wall Street Journal* (March 1, 2000): A1.
14. Baytos, Lawrence M. "A 'No Frills' Approach to Human Resource Planning," *Human Resource Planning* 7 (1984): 39–46.
15. Greer, Jackson, and Fiorito. "Adapting Human Resource Planning in a Changing Business Environment"; Mills, D. Quinn. "Planning with People in Mind," *Harvard Business Review* 63, no. 4 (1985): 97–105.
16. Greller, Martin M., and David M. Nee. *From Baby Boom to Baby Bust: How Business Can Meet the Demographic Challenge*. Reading, MA: Addison-Wesley Publishing, 1989, p. 124.
17. Mills. "Planning with People in Mind."
18. Goldstein, Michael. "Management Succession—Plan Now or Pay Later," *The CPA Journal* 62, no. 8 (1992): 14–20.
19. Mahlburg, Bob. "New Jail to Entail High Costs," *Fort Worth Star-Telegram* (September 7, 1989): 19, 21.
20. Greer, Jackson, and Fiorito. "Adapting Human Resource Planning in a Changing Business Environment."
21. Baytos, Lawrence M. "A 'No Frills' Approach to Human Resource Planning," *Human Resource Planning* 7 (1984): 39.
22. Mills. "Planning with People in Mind," p. 99.
23. Burack, Elmer H., and Thomas G. Gutteridge. "Institutional Manpower Planning: Rhetoric Versus Reality," *California Management Review* 20, no. 3 (1978): 13–22.
24. Niehaus. "Models for Human Resource Decisions."
25. Mills. "Planning with People in Mind."

26. Carter, Norman. Development Systems International, personal communication with the author, 1990.
27. Greer, Jackson, and Fiorito. "Adapting Human Resource Planning in a Changing Business Environment"; Tichy, Noel M. "Editor's Note," *Human Resource Management* 27, no. 4 (1988): 365–67; Mills. "Planning with People in Mind."
28. Ainsworth, Chris. "Strategic Human Resource Planning at Zeneca Pharmaceuticals," *Human Resource Planning* 8, no. 2 (1995): 11–15.
29. Verhoeven, C. J. *Techniques in Corporate Manpower Planning*. Boston: Kluwer-Nijhoff Publishing, 1982, pp. 3–4.
30. Alpander, Guvenc G. *Human Resources Management Planning*. New York: AMACOM, 1982.
31. Verhoeven. *Techniques in Corporate Manpower Planning*.
32. Bechet, Thomas P., and William R. Maki. "Modeling and Forecasting Focusing on People as a Strategic Resource," *Human Resource Planning* 10, no. 4 (1987): 209–17; Niehaus. "Models for Human Resource Decisions."
33. Niehaus. "Models for Human Resource Decisions"; Walker, James W. "Human Resource Planning, 1990s Style," *Human Resource Planning* 13, no. 4 (1990): 229–40; Fiorito, Jack, Thomas H. Stone, and Charles R. Greer. "Factors Affecting Choice of Human Resource Forecasting Techniques," *Human Resource Planning* 8, no. 1 (1985): 1–17; Walker, James W. *Human Resource Strategy*. New York: McGraw-Hill, 1992; Wikstrom, Walter S. *Manpower Planning: Evolving Systems*. New York: The Conference Board, Inc., 1971.
34. Niehaus. "Models for Human Resource Decisions"; Walker. "Human Resource Planning, 1990s Style"; Fiorito, Stone, and Greer. "Factors Affecting Choice of Human Resource Forecasting Techniques"; Walker. *Human Resource Strategy*; Wikstrom. *Manpower Planning: Evolving Systems*.
35. Mills. "Planning with People in Mind."
36. Stone, Thomas H., and Jack Fiorito. "A Perceived Uncertainty Model of Human Resource Forecasting Technique Use," *Academy of Management Review* 11, no. 3 (1986): 635–42.
37. Linden Dana W. "Dreary Days in the Dismal Science," *Forbes* (January 21, 1991): 68–71.
38. Ibid., p. 68.
39. Linden. "Dreary Days in the Dismal Science."
40. Georgoff, David M., and Robert G. Murdick. "Manager's Guide to Forecasting," *Harvard Business Review* 64, no. 1 (1986): 110–20.
41. Ibid., p. 119.
42. Georgoff and Murdick. "Manager's Guide to Forecasting."
43. Niehaus. "Models for Human Resource Decisions"; Greer, Jackson, and Fiorito. "Adapting Human Resource Planning in a Changing Business Environment"; Greer, Charles R., and Daniel Armstrong. "Human Resource Forecasting and Planning: A State-of-the-Art Investigation," *Human Resource Planning* 3, no. 2 (1980): 67–78.
44. Milkovich and Mahoney. "Human Resources Planning and PAIR Policy."
45. Hoffman, William H., Larry Wyatt, and George G. Gordon. "Human Resource Planning: Shifting from Concept to Contemporary Practice," *Human Resource Planning* 9, no. 3 (1986): 97–105.
46. Gatewood, Robert D., and B. Wayne Rockmore. "Combining Organizational Manpower and Career Development Needs: An Operational Human Resource Planning Model," *Human Resource Planning* 9, no. 3 (1986): 81–96.
47. Quintanilla, Carl. "For Its Profit Streak, Emerson's Reward Is a Laggard Share Price," *Wall Street Journal* (May 11, 1996): A1–A8; Emerson Electric Web Site, www.emersonelectric.com.
48. Quintanilla. "For Its Profit Streak, Emerson's Reward Is a Laggard Share Price," p. A8.
49. Walker. *Human Resource Planning*.
50. Wagel, William H. "Planning for Tomorrow's Human Resource Needs," *Personnel* 63, no. 11 (1986): 4–9.
51. Stahl, Robert J. "Succession Planning Drives Plant Turnaround," *Personnel Journal* 71, no. 9 (1992): 67–70.
52. Dyer, Lee. "Human Resource Planning at IBM," *Human Resource Planning* 7, no. 3 (1984): 111–25; Hall, Douglas T. "Dilemmas in Linking Succession Planning to Individual Executive

Learning," *Human Resource Management* 25, no. 2 (1986): 235–65; Petrock, Frank. "Planning the Leadership Transition," *Journal of Business Strategy* 11, no. 6 (1990): 14–16.

53. Hall. "Dilemmas in Linking Succession Planning to Individual Executive Learning," p. 239.
54. Greller and Nee. *From Baby Boom to Baby Bust: How Business Can Meet the Demographic Challenge.*
55. Walsh, James P. "Top Management Turnover Following Mergers and Acquisitions," *Strategic Management Journal* 9, no. 2 (1988): 173–83; Walker, James W. "Perspectives: Do We Need Succession Planning?" *Human Resource Planning* 21, no. 3 (1998): 9–11.
56. Walsh. "Top Management Turnover Following Mergers and Acquisitions," p. 180.
57. Wiersema, Margarethe F. "Strategic Consequences of Executive Succession Within Diversified Firms," *Journal of Management Studies* 29, no. 1 (1992): 73–94.
58. Ward, Dan. "Workforce Demand Forecasting Techniques," *Human Resource Planning* 19, no. 1 (1996): 54–55; Nardoni Associates, Inc. Web site, www.nardoni.com/html.
59. Rowland, Kendrith M., and Michael G. Sovereign. "Markov-Chain Analysis of Internal Manpower Supply," *Industrial Relations* 9, no. 1 (1969): 88–99; Heneman, Herbert G. III, and Marcus G. Sandver. "Markov Analysis in Human Resources Administration: Applications and Limitations," *Academy of Management Review* 2, no. 4 (1977): 535–42.
60. Ibid.
61. Heneman and Sandver. "Markov Analysis in Human Resource Administration: Applications and Limitations"; Bechet and Maki. "Modeling and Forecasting Focusing on People as a Strategic Resource"; Middlemist, Hitt, and Greer. *Personnel Management: Jobs, People, and Logic.*
62. Heneman and Sandver. "Markov Analysis in Human Resource Administration: Applications and Limitations."
63. Ibid.
64. Hopkins, David S. P. "Models for Affirmative Action Planning and Evaluation," *Management Science* 26, no. 10 (1980): 994–1005; Ledvinka, James. "Technical Implications of Equal Employment Law for Manpower Planning," *Personnel Psychology* 28, no. 3 (1975): 299–323; Heneman and Sandver. "Markov Analysis in Human Resource Administration: Applications and Limitations"; Flamholtz, Eric G., George T. Geis, Richard J. Perle. "A Markovian Model for the Valuation of Human Assets Acquired by an Organizational Purchase," *Interfaces* 14, no. 6 (1984): 11–15.
65. Dyer. "Human Resource Planning at IBM."
66. Bechet and Maki. "Modeling and Forecasting Focusing on People as a Strategic Resource"; Buller, Paul, and W. R. Maki. "A Case History of a Manpower Planning Model," *Human Resource Planning* 4, no. 3 (1981): 129–37.
67. Buller and Maki. "A Case History of a Manpower Planning Model."
68. Walker. *Human Resource Planning*; Burack, Elmer H., and Nicholas J. Mathys. *Human Resource Planning: A Pragmatic Approach to Manpower Staffing and Development.* Lake Forest, IL: Brace-Park Press, 1980.
69. Burack and Mathys. *Human Resource Planning: A Pragmatic Approach to Manpower Staffing and Development.*
70. Ibid.
71. Sheridan, James A. "Forecasts and Projections: Drawing Implications From Changes in Employee Characteristics," in Manuel London, Emily S. Bassman, and John P. Fernandez (Eds.), *Human Resource Forecasting and Strategy Development: Guidelines for Analyzing and Fulfilling Organizational Needs.* New York: Quorum Books, 1990, pp. 91–98.
72. Pinfield, Lawrence T., and Steven L. McShane. "Applications of Manpower Planning in Two School Districts," *Human Resource Planning* 10, no. 2 (1987): 103–13.
73. Ibid., p. 113.
74. Greer, Jackson, and Fiorito. "Adapting Human Resource Planning in a Changing Business Environment."
75. Frantzreb, Richard R. "Confessions of a Manpower Modeler," in Larry F. Moore and Larry Charach (Eds.), *Manpower Planning for Canadians*, 2nd ed. Vancouver, BC, Canada: Institute of Industrial Relations, University of British Columbia, 1979, pp. 480–89; Barrier, Michael. "Small Firms Put

Quality First," *Nation's Business* 80, no. 5 (1992): 22–32; Wikstrom. *Manpower Planning: Evolving Systems*; Atwater, Donald M. "Workforce Forecasting," *Human Resource Planning* 18, no. 4 (1995): 50–53; Ward, Dan. "Workforce Demand Forecasting Techniques," *Human Resource Planning* 19, no. 1 (1996): 54–55.

76. Wikstrom, *Manpower Planning: Evolving Systems.*
77. Dyer. "Human Resource Planning at IBM."
78. Malmborg, Charles J., and Gene R. Simons. "Planning Maintenance Human Resource Requirements Over the Life Cycle of a Repairable Equipment Population," *Human Resource Planning* 9, no. 1 (1986): 25–39.
79. Wikstrom. *Manpower Planning: Evolving Systems.*
80. Bryant, Don R., Michael J. Maggard, and Robert P. Taylor. "Manpower Planning Models and Techniques," *Business Horizons* 16, no. 2 (1973): 69–78; Milkovich, George L., and Thomas A. Mahoney. "Human Resource Planning Models: A Perspective," *Human Resource Planning* 1, no. 1 (1978): 19–30; Niehaus. "Models for Human Resource Decisions."
81. Milkovich, George L., Anthony J. Annoni, and Thomas A. Mahoney. "The Use of Delphi Procedures in Manpower Forecasting," *Management Science* 19, no. 4 (1972): 381–88; Greer, Charles R., and Daniel Armstrong. "Human Resource Forecasting and Planning: A State-of-the-Art Investigation"; Greer, Jackson, and Fiorito. "Adapting Human Resource Planning in a Changing Business Environment."
82. Niehaus. "Models for Human Resource Decisions"; Thornton, Billy M., and Preston, Paul. *Introduction to Management Science: Quantitative Approaches to Managerial Decisions.* Columbus, OH: Charles E. Merrill, 1977; Middlemist, Hitt, and Greer. *Personnel Management: Jobs, People, and Logic.*
83. Holloran, Thomas J., and Judson E. Byrn. "United Airlines Station Manpower Planning System," *Interfaces* 16, no. 1 (1986): 39–50.
84. Ibid.
85. Ibid.
86. Ibid.
87. Ibid., p. 49.
88. Meehan and Ahmed. "Forecasting Human Resources Requirements: A Demand Model."
89. Greer, Jackson, and Fiorito. "Adapting Human Resource Planning in a Changing Business Environment."

CASE 5
Human Resource Planning Support Systems

The description of United Airlines' short-range Station Manpower Planning System, which was presented in Chapter 5, provides an indication of the importance of having appropriate computer systems to support such efforts. Although the United system's forecasting range is on the short-term end of the spectrum, its computerized system has an obviously important financial impact in cost savings. While some human resource forecasting approaches are qualitative rather than quantitative and therefore require minimal computer support, many others require sophisticated software. As indicated in Chapter 5, because organizations' human resources are utilized more frequently today as sources of competitive advantage, human resource planning inputs will become more critical in the strategy formulation process. As a result, both human resource executives and other senior managers will need timely information on the future availability of critical human resources. Similarly, they will need timely information on the staffing requirements of a particular strategic alternative. Interestingly, even in the most traditional area of human resources—labor relations—computerized systems are already being used in union contract negotiations to provide on-the-spot cost evaluations of proposals and counterproposals.

Fortunately, a number of computer software packages are available for strategic human resource applications. For example, specialized software can be obtained for succession planning, human resource forecasting, and modeling human resource flows. In managing the software acquisition and implementation process, there are several factors to be considered. One suggestion is that the software evaluation team should include representatives from end-user groups, information technology (IT), and any other support groups. Because of the greater decentralization of human resource planning in many organizations, users' perceptions of the user friendliness and usefulness of software should be even more critical. As line managers take on more responsibilities for succession planning, human resource planning, and forecasting, there will be increased need for systems they can use without great difficulty. Along this line, efforts to educate line managers on use of these software packages should enhance the ultimate success of the company's human resource planning and forecasting efforts. While adequate representation from these groups is critical, the evaluation team should be small enough to perform its task in a timely manner. A second suggestion is that the evaluation team should develop a set of initial screening procedures for use in narrowing down the list of packages to a smaller set for in-depth evaluation. Potential screening procedures include checking the software's functionality against a requirements list, checking with human resource contacts in other companies using the software, viewing vendor presentations, and obtaining recommendations from industry associations.[1]

A third suggestion pertains to the in-depth examination phase. The assessment in this phase should assign highest priority to the mandatory requirements. Beyond whether the software performs the required functions, other components of this phase include an assessment of the technical compatibility of the software with the organization's other software systems; the software's functionality or types of operations it performs; the adequacy of documentation; ease of enhancing the software as future requirements and business conditions change; ease of maintenance; the level of training that will be needed for users; and an assessment of the vendor's staying power and the likelihood of satisfactory service in the future. More detailed checklists of factors for software evaluation are available in the practitioner literature.[2]

Although there is growing availability of human resource planning software, managers should remember that user dissatisfaction is still a problem with various software packages. Such dissatisfaction often results because the complexity of software has been underestimated and insufficient resources have been allocated to its implementation.[3]

Questions

1. What would be some critical parameters or assumptions in software used to forecast an organization's internal supply of human resources?
2. Which of a company's computerized databases should be integrated with a computerized succession planning system? Which ones should not?
3. What are the factors that could prevent a company from realizing the benefits of an investment in human resource planning software? Explain how each one affects the return on investment.
4. What organizational groups should be represented on a committee that will develop the requirements list against which human resource planning should be evaluated?

References

1. TenEyck, Gretchen. "Software Purchase: A to Z," *Personnel Journal* 69, no. 10 (1990): 72–79; Walker, Alfred J. "New Technologies in Human Resource Planning," *Human Resource Planning* 9, no. 4 (1986): 149–59.
2. TenEyck. "Software Purchase: A to Z"; Frantzreb, Richard B. (Ed.), *Microcomputers in Human Resource Management: A Directory of Software*. Roseville, CA: Advanced Personnel Systems, 1985.
3. Mandell, Mel. "Managing the Human Assets," *Computerworld* (April 6, 1992): 128.

CHAPTER 6

Strategy Implementation: Workforce Utilization and Employment Practices

The sixth component in the conceptual framework is strategy implementation. In order to accomplish their missions, organizations formulate requirements for returns on investment, scan the environment for opportunities and threats, formulate strategies, plan human resource requirements, and then implement their strategies. Unfortunately, implementation is usually the most difficult part of management and has often been overshadowed by the emphasis on strategy formulation. Fortunately, there is growing awareness of the actions needed for strategy implementation and an expanding literature on the topic. This chapter will cover several areas of implementation beginning with the efficient utilization of human resources through workforce flexibility and the widespread use of teams. Such efficiencies have become increasingly important because of pressure to control labor costs. Next, approaches for dealing with employee shortages will be discussed along with the related topic of human resource outsourcing. This discussion is followed by an extensive examination of selection practices. Approaches for dealing with employee surpluses are discussed after this examination. The chapter concludes with approaches for dealing with some special implementation challenges. Because of the breadth of this topic, the reward and developmental aspects of strategy implementation will be discussed in Chapter 7.

EFFICIENT UTILIZATION OF HUMAN RESOURCES

Several managerial practices have the potential to provide for more flexibility in workforce utilization. More recently, such flexibility has been obtained by cross-training and other innovative practices. A more traditional approach involves operating on a nonunion basis.

Cross-Training and Flexibility in Assigning Work

Flexibility in work assignment is a key to efficient utilization of human resources. Chaparral Steel in Midlothian, Texas, provides one of the most extreme examples of the efficiencies that can be obtained. Chaparral, which was established in 1973 as a start-up operation, has great workforce flexibility because it has only two job classifications in its production operations: one dealing with production activities and the other with maintenance. It has obtained flexibility in workforce utilization through extensive cross-training and by operating on a nonunion basis. By paying skill-based or knowledge-based pay, Chaparral has motivated its employees to master a broad range of skills, which enable them to perform wide-ranging activities. Even non-production employees are fully utilized. For example, security guards perform computer data-entry functions, serve as paramedics, and perform safety functions such as checking fire extinguishers. In addition to efficient utilization of human resources, Chaparral has achieved its position as one of the world's most efficient producers of steel through heavy emphasis on technological innovation and computerization.

Interestingly, most of Chaparral's research and development efforts come from its production employees, as it views product development as a responsibility of production personnel. Because of heavy emphasis on profit sharing and the avoidance of individualized suggestion systems, which discourage teamwork and information sharing, the company's employees are motivated to work together in developing technological advancements in production. Although Chaparral's research and developmental efforts come from its production employees, these are well-trained employees. Chaparral's production employees who have only high school educations go through two years of training in such areas as electronics, hydraulics, and statistical process control. Further, there is very high representation of college-trained engineers at Chaparral, such as those running the furnaces.[1] Admittedly, Chaparral has a production advantage in producing steel from scrap. However, its efficiencies are remarkable considering that with less than 1,000 employees, Chaparral's annual production of approximately 1.5 million tons of steel comprises about 1.5 percent of the steel produced in the United States.[2]

Interestingly, although Chaparral has achieved much of its productivity through technology, its managerial approach has also made substantial contributions. This is because the company's industry leadership in technological innovation is, in part, a result of its unique work environment. Major characteristics of this environment include encouragement of risk taking; challenge in the form of specific, reachable goals; the freedom to question; trust; and an absence of policies.[3] In fact, Chaparral has a "no fault" absence policy in which "an employee can be absent for a good reason, no reason, or a bad reason." [4] Interestingly, with this policy, "the daily absence rate is less than one percent." [5] Chaparral's former CEO, Gordon Forward, has explained the company's rationale for the absence of policies as follows:

> We don't have policies . . . We felt that a lot of the procedures in many organizations were designed to catch the 3 percent who were trying to cheat in one way or another. We decided to design our rules for the 97 percent we can trust. The others would stand out like sore thumbs, we figured, and they'd eventually leave. That's exactly what happened.[6]

The efficiencies made possible by technological innovation and human resource flexibility also are evident in the experiences of Frost, Inc., a small manufacturer in Grand Rapids, Michigan. Frost wanted to diversify its product line and decided that it needed greater flexibility in both its production facilities and its employees and managers. At the time it had machinery and employees who could perform only very limited numbers of functions. Frost replaced outdated machining equipment with robots and numerically controlled machine tools, introduced an automated inventory control system, and automated its office functions. Specific managerial and human resource changes included broadening employees' skills and job responsibilities, making each employee a stockholder of the company with options to purchase additional stock through its 401(k) plan, moving all hourly employees to salaried status, educating its employees on the new technology, eliminating perks such as reserved parking places, and eliminating several layers in the management hierarchy. Other changes included wide dissemination of company information, adding quarterly bonuses driven by the company's productivity, and increasing the level of employee participation in decision making. The productivity increases made possible by these changes, and a reduction in the number of employees to approximately 120, enabled the company to increase the level of sales per employee from $80,000 to $200,000.[7]

Commonalities in the approaches of Frost, Inc. and Chaparral include broadened employee job scope and responsibility, lean staffing, small size, informality, information availability, financial incentives based on company performance, and a flat organizational structure. It is important to note that the efficiencies obtained at Chaparral and Frost, Inc., through flexible work assignment and broadened jobs, were accompanied by corresponding changes in involvement in decision making, compensation, informality, and education.[8]

Using Work Teams

Requirements for Effective Teams

Several conditions must be present before teams are likely to be effective. One of the most important is that there must be a compelling purpose that is served by real teamwork. Team members have to buy in to the objective and feel responsible and accountable for performance, and their managers need to provide frequent reinforcement of the team's pursuit of this compelling purpose. Effective teams also have members whose skills are complementary; therefore, careful selection of team members is critical. Some companies select team members on the basis of their personality characteristics as well as their technical skills. Personality assessment instruments, such as the Myers-Briggs Type Indicator (MBTI), are being used for this purpose. Some companies also have begun to help ensure a better fit by collecting information about the work preferences of potential team members through the use of questionnaires.[9]

In addition, effective teams share feedback with each other. Teams require substantial training, and their members often benefit from being trained to present honest feedback in a skillful manner. Another ingredient of effective teams is that their members trust each other. As teams mature, they also can become self-governing as leadership responsibilities become shared within the team. Such self-governance reduces the amount of hierarchy needed in the larger organization's structure. The leadership that develops from teams also increases the stock of leadership talent within the whole organization.[10]

In addition to the conditions that must be present within the teams, compatible organizational systems also are required for team effectiveness. Compensation, other rewards, and performance appraisal systems must be adapted to teams with the move from individual to team contributions. For example, some companies have emphasized team contributions in the announcements of promotions.[11] TRW provides the following team-based compensation:

> "We have something going on called Project ELITE [Earnings Leadership in Tomorrow's Environment]," says director of compensation Harvey Minkoff, "where a number of people there are temporarily assigned to the effort, and it's expected they'll return to their units or to a fill-time permanent position sometime in the future. We have established specific goals for that project, and each individual, in turn, has established specific goals. A significant portion of their pay is tied to the accomplishment of their goals and the accomplishment of their organization's goals." This could range from 10 percent for lower-paid workers to 25 percent for those at higher levels. (Why do lower-paid workers get less?) The thinking is that they should be exposed to less risk in their total compensation packages than should higher-paid workers.[12]

Interestingly, the larger organization should have high performance standards before teams can be expected to produce at a high level. Managers also need to be aware that a substantial amount of time is often required for the development of effective teamwork. Teams go through phases before they reach peak performance, and certain behaviors occur at different phases. For example, teams go through the *forming phase* as they attend to organizational issues such as who will perform various tasks. Next, they typically encounter conflict with each other as they work through procedures for dealing with various issues. This phase is often referred to as the *storming stage*. The next phase, called *norming*, involves the establishment of understanding of how things should operate and what conduct is acceptable behavior. Finally, when the team has worked through these growing pains and has developed team skills, it reaches the *performing phase*.[13]

Managers also need to provide frequent feedback to teams about their performance. When teams are working on projects, they need to be tracked on their performance of the various milestones required for completion. In the case of project teams, it is important to celebrate the accomplishment of these milestones. For example, a product development team may have milestones for detailed development of the product specifications, development of a prototype, consumer testing, and so on. When teams complete these milestones, the team's members need to celebrate their accomplishment, and managers should provide rewards and contribute to such celebratory events. Managers also need to be aware that, because of the emphasis and focus on teamwork, that teams sometimes become inner-directed. As a result, they often fail to interact effectively with units outside of the team. When teams have been formed to work as a temporary task force pursuing a one-time project, instead of an ongoing permanent team, it is especially important to have the team report regularly to higher mangers and executives as well as outside units to keep others apprised of their progress.[14]

Executives and managers also need to be aware that teams require a substantial amount of their attention and are sometimes referred to as "high-maintenance" entities. One observer has likened teams to a Ferrari in that they can produce high performance but they also require high maintenance. Teams are not a silver bullet solution for all organizational problems, and they are often ineffective because the conditions necessary for teamwork are not present.[15]

An Example of an Effective Team

The Murder Squad of the Kansas City, Missouri, Police Department provides an excellent example of how effective teams operate. As a result of the squad's teamwork, the city has the highest percentage of murders solved of any city in the United States. Most of the team members are detectives who have many years of experience. All started as patrol officers and worked their way up to be detectives. Team members share a strong desire to solve murders.[16] This is consistent with research on teams, noted earlier, which shows that in order for teams to be effective, they must have a compelling purpose.

Many of the murders occur in an inner-city area in which there is a trend toward the killing of strangers. When a murder case is assigned to the squad, a team of approximately 8 to 10 detectives works 28 consecutive days on the case, going home only to sleep. While normal working hours are 8:00 A.M. to 4:00 P.M., teams are called back to work any time a murder occurs, and they may work for 24 consecutive hours. The teams are racially mixed and consist mostly of men, although there are some female members. Like most teams, there are members who make unique contributions. For example, a team may have a member who is a master interrogator. Because the teams stay on the job, there is continuity of effort and a continuous flow of information within the team. As a result, leads do not fall through the cracks as easily as they do when detectives work independently. Finally, as with many teams, the work of the teams is stressful, and the detectives often use humor and play practical jokes on one another to break the tension.[17]

Operating on a Nonunion Basis

In order to gain greater flexibility, companies commonly pursue strategies of operating on a nonunion basis. Such strategies are sometimes a major determinant of the organization's structure, affecting divisional composition, plant size, and plant location.[18] Anil Verma has studied some large multiplant firms, having both union and nonunion operations. One strategy he found among firms desiring to reduce their exposure to labor relations problems was the approach of building small new plants that operate on a nonunion basis rather than investing in increased capacity in existing unionized plants.[19] Emerson Electric provides an example of such strategies. The company, which has both unionized and nonunion plants, has an effective organizational structure for economical manufacturing. This structure also has reduced the likelihood of unionization in some of its plants. Emerson has some divisions that carry well-known product line names, such as Skil tools, In-Sink-Erator kitchen appliances, Dremel hobby tools, and Ridgid tools, as well as industrial product manufacturing such as Fisher controls. As a result of locating its plants in small rural communities and organizing by divisions having strong name identifications, stronger employee commitment and lower costs may be obtained, as well as an increased likelihood of remaining nonunion.[20] In addition to these organizational characteristics, there are numerous other variables that affect the likelihood of unionism such as the individual characteristics of the workforce, job content, compensation, industry, job satisfaction, perceptions of union instrumentality, characteristics of unions, governmental regulation, and macroeconomic influences. Because of space limitations, a detailed discussion of these influences cannot be provided here.[21]

DEALING WITH EMPLOYEE SHORTAGES

The combination of demographic influences and a robust economy can produce severe labor shortages in many occupations. Upturns and downturns are normal features of the economy, and individual employers may experience skill shortages of qualified managerial and professional personnel at a particular point in time. Nonetheless, technology workers have been in particularly short supply. Companies have gone to great lengths to meet the demand for technical specialists. For example, Burlington Northern Santa Fe has implemented an employee referral program for technical employees in which current employees can receive a $3,000 reward for referring a technical employee who is hired.[22] Vmware Inc., a software company in Palo Alto, California, obtained most of its 62 new hires in one recent year mostly through word of mouth.[23] *Employee referrals* are often an excellent source of employees because employees often tend to refer people like themselves. If a company has a good workforce, then there should be good referrals. When minorities and women are underrepresented in a company's workforce, however, sole reliance on employee referrals will tend to perpetuate the problem of underrepresentation.

Strategic Recruiting

Interestingly, the use of the Internet has added another venue to recruiting and is serving a tremendous need for matching employees with employment opportunities. Company Websites often inform viewers of the company's mission and how it is being pursued. They typically provide a graphical presentation of how the company is organized and include a recruiting section. There are usually explanations of career fields, job opportunities, and provisions for e-mailing résumés directly to the company. The Internet provides another component that must be aligned with the company's recruitment strategy and can help provide the appropriate human resources for pursuing specific strategies.

There is empirical evidence of the importance of such a strategic alignment. An analysis of human resource practices of well- and poor-performing companies found that the well-performing companies in the retailing industry were much more strategic in their orientation to selection and recruiting. One of these well-performing companies, as a part of a major strategic change, broke with its traditional human resource practices by using a front-end strategy of combining higher selectivity with higher salaries. It had previously placed less emphasis on hiring quality and had used an attrition approach for eliminating marginal employees.[24]

One way in which recruiting can be more strongly linked with strategy is to focus on those sources providing the greatest number of desirable employees. Along this line, a number of studies have evaluated different recruiting sources in order to identify differences in important work-related outcomes such as performance, turnover, attitudes, and absenteeism. For example, one study focused on a company's research personnel who had bachelors, masters, or doctoral degrees in chemistry or biology. For these types of employees, those making recruiting contact with the company through newspaper ads and college placement offices had lower performance than those responding to professional journal/convention ads or contacting the company on their own volition. Employees who responded to newspaper ads also had higher absenteeism rates. Further, those recruited through college placement offices had the lowest levels of job satisfaction. These results indicate that for research employees, newspaper ads and college placement offices are less desirable recruiting sources.[25] Unfortunately, as with most of the research in this area, it is difficult to generalize from such results. In this case, the subjects were highly educated research personnel. Employees having doctorates are often active in professional associations that have well-developed job placement services at their conventions. Such employees might likely have a training deficiency if they do not understand how placement works in the professional discipline.

The study pointed out an interesting possible explanation for differentials in recruiting source success. The potential explanation was that the various recruiting sources provide differing amounts of information about companies and jobs. Those sources associated with greater applicant information produced better results because self-selection led to better job and applicant matching.[26] However, a more recent study was unable to lend support to the differential knowledge and self-selection explanation. Because of the equivocal nature of the literature and a failure to find any relationships between recruiting sources and performance, this same study concluded that it is probably counterproductive to attempt to identify differentials in success rates across various sources of recruits. Instead, the study recommended that companies focus on those characteristics of individual applicants that are stronger predictors of job performance.[27]

Another strategy-related recruiting issue is the extent to which the company should rely on internal or external recruiting, or a mixture of the two. Some well-managed companies hire externally only at the entry level and fill all higher-level positions from within the firm. Examples of such companies include Merck, 3M, and IBM. There are a number of advantages associated with internal recruiting. These include having more reliable information on internal applicants, the motivational impact of employees knowing that promotions will be filled from within the company, less recruiting and selection expense, quicker response time, and a shorter adjustment period in the new job because of the internal applicant's familiarity with the company. Unfortunately, internal recruiting may lead to managerial inbreeding, which may be particularly disadvantageous in rapidly changing environments in which old strategies may be ineffective. Further, external recruiting has the advantages of providing fresh ideas, requiring less internal employee development, and possibly facilitating affirmative action.[28]

Employee shortages may not even require recruiting. Aside from the obvious approach of assigning more overtime, another alternative to recruiting is provided by temporary help firms. As indicated in earlier chapters, in addition to reduced recruiting responsibilities, temporary workers provide greater flexibility in matching staffing with workload requirements. Because of heavy reliance on temporary workers, some companies have even created temporary worker programs within their own companies. For example, Fidelity Investments has temporary employees who cover about 90 percent of the company's needs for temporaries. Fidelity's program provides temporary employees with substantial stability in work, although it is not guaranteed. A benefit to Fidelity is that it obtains quality temporaries who are knowledgeable about its procedures.[29]

Special Recruiting for Minorities and Females

Organizations often have shortages in their numbers of minorities and females. Recruiting in this area is affected by a company's public image. Companies that have created positive public images, through their leadership in developing diverse workforces, have an advantage in attracting females and minorities.[30]

Companies such as "Merck, Xerox, Syntex, Hoffman-La Roche, and Hewlett-Packard have been aggressively using favorable publicity to recruit women and racioethnic minorities."[31] Typically, such companies have introduced greater flexibility in work assignment and have provided support services such as child care facilities, which also reduce turnover.[32] PepsiCo is another company that has placed heavy emphasis on diversity. As a result, it has excellent representation of minorities and females throughout its top-level positions. As a part of its efforts, the company has provided attractive scholarships and summer internships for talented minority MBA students. PepsiCo has been very successful in recruiting these talented individuals upon graduation. In addition to these actions, PepsiCo has also provided leadership as a corporate citizen. PepsiCo has also been active in sponsoring diversity management workshops for business professors.

Many companies have moved beyond the requirements of affirmative action and are now focusing on the management of diversity, which was discussed earlier in Chapter 2. Nonetheless, for this to be a meaningful emphasis, there must first be an adequate representation of minorities and females, at least at entry level. Thus, affirmative action is a prerequisite. For those companies that have been successful in obtaining good representations of minorities and females at entry level, their next concerns are how to retain and facilitate the advancement of minorities and females to top positions. Thus, companies seeking to get maximum production out of their workforces should identify and remove barriers that limit individual employees' contributions. Much of what is meant by the term *management of diversity* is directed toward increasing productivity.[33]

Flexible Retirement as a Source of Labor

With an aging population, it seems likely that labor shortages may be partially addressed by extending the number of years that employees work before retirement. In the future, a number of factors may motivate older workers to remain on the job. Some of these influences are limited retirement benefits or inadequacies in health care benefits for retirees.

As indicated in Chapter 2, the larger older-age cohorts and smaller younger-age cohorts may create a labor shortage.[34] Because of this shortage, older people may be called on to provide needed goods and services. This may be a fortuitous situation because the psychological well-being of older persons is enhanced if they are allowed options for *flexible retirement*. This could be implemented with *phased-in retirement* or a reduced number of working days, instead of total retirement. Because of the centrality of work to our lives, the opportunity to continue working could provide great benefit. Surveys of managers and executives indicate a desire to work more years through various flexible approaches, such as phased retirement, transfers, and job redesign. Nonetheless, even though mandatory retirement at a given age is prohibited for most types of employees, senior executives are sometimes opposed to flexible retirement approaches. Some of this resistance may be related to the difficulties involved in individually determining who should be allowed to continue working. Determinations of fitness for continued employment would presumably be based on performance and medical evaluations. It is easy to visualize the greater difficulty of telling a longtime, loyal employee that he or she must retire because of performance inadequacies instead of letting an impersonal policy serve as the standard. In addition to some executives' opposition to flexible approaches, a large number of older workers favor early retirement in the interests of the organization as well as the employee.[35]

> We were surprised to find that older respondents, compared to younger respondents, were more likely to agree that it is in the best interests of both the organization and the employee for senior exempt employees to retire at age 65 or even earlier.[36]

Managing Vendors of Outsourced Functions

As noted in earlier chapters, many human resource management functions have been outsourced. When such functions are outsourced, the human resource executive or manager's role changes from supervision of employees who perform these functions to managers of a vendor relationship. The skills required for managing such relationships are different than those of direct supervision and involve the negotiation of contracts, sensitivity to the more strategic issues such as the importance of avoiding dependency on one vendor, and the need to maintain service levels through a contractual relationship. A set of guidelines or suggestions for managing such relationships is presented in Table 6-1.

SELECTION OF EMPLOYEES

Excellent selection procedures are essential for obtaining a workforce that can become a source of competitive advantage. While training and employee development also are critical, it is very difficult to overcome the built-in headwind of poorly qualified or mismatched employees. Furthermore, while some skill deficiencies can be overcome by training, the additional financial outlays required to make up for poor selection can place a firm at a disadvantage to its customers. High-performing companies are very selective in their staffing decisions. (Chapter 8 presents evidence on the relationship of selective hiring and firm performance.)

Reliability and Validity

A number of requirements must be met before firms can make good selection decisions. First of all, selection procedures need to have the psychometric properties of reliability and validity. *Reliability* means that the procedure, be it a test or an interview, needs to produce approximately the same result when the procedure

TABLE 6-1 Guidelines for Human Resource Outsourcing

Making the Outsourcing Decision

- Don't allow sacred cows. Except for core competencies, all other human resource activities should be considered as candidates for outsourcing.
- Determine whether the desire to outsource an activity is driven by its low contribution to core competencies, influences from the external environment, or only a result of poor management of the activity.
- Recognize that performance is more important than low human resource department head counts or lower costs.
- Beware of vendors that supply off-the-shelf solutions that do not fit the company's needs.
- Avoid excessive reliance on vendors.
- Decide how much control is needed for various human resource activities and whether control can be retained with outsourcing.
- Identify critical personal benefits of outsourcing.

Selecting and Negotiating with Outsourcing Vendors

- Assign a high weighting to vendors' knowledge of the industry.
- Perform reference checks of potential vendors.
- Understand the costs involved in switching vendors for outsourced services.

Managing the Outsourcing Transition

- Expect the internal human resource team to resist outsourcing and develop ways of managing this resistance.
- Anticipate conflict and develop a plan for its resolution in a manner that supports the relationship with the vendor.
- Anticipate changes to human resource culture and careers.

Managing Vendor Relationships

- Develop long-term relationships with outsourcing vendors where such continuity is critical.
- Develop staff members to become effective managers of vendor relationships.
- Maintain stability of the in-house staff who oversee vendor relationships and understand the performance expectations originally negotiated.
- Require competitive bidding for each outsourced service at regular intervals.

Monitoring and Evaluating Vendor Performance

- Establish expectations, measures, and reporting relationships up front for both outsourcing parties.
- Insist on high-quality performance by human resource vendors.
- Insist on accurate and frequent status reporting by human resource vendors and immediate notification when problems arise.
- Establish performance targets for vendors with the assistance of outside consultants when necessary.
- Enhance vendor performance through the use of performance standards.
- Consider internal customer surveys to evaluate vendor performance.

Source: Charles R. Greer, Stuart A. Youngblood, and David A. Gray. "Human Resource Management Outsourcing: The Make or Buy Decision," *Academy of Management Executive* 13, no. 3 (1999): 85–96. Reprinted with permission of *Academy of Management Executive*.

is repeated. Thus, if a test is used, an applicant's score from one administration of the test should correlate well with his or her score on the next administration of the test. This form of reliability is called *test–retest reliability*. Similarly, when a manager interviews job applicants, his or her assessments of the applicants should correlate well if the interviews are repeated at a later date. In addition, better results are achieved when multiple interviewers are used. Interviews are reliable when there is agreement among the interviewers about an applicant, which means that their ratings are correlated. This form of reliability is called *interrater reliability*. Greater reliability is possible when interviewers can be trained to gather information from applicants on dimensions that can be assessed with some degree of accuracy, such as communication and interpersonal skills. Interviewers also gain useful information by using interviews to fill in gaps in information obtained from the résumé, application, and references.

Selection procedures also must be valid. Validity means that the procedure predicts what it is supposed to predict. With selection procedures, this means that the test or interview predicts job performance in the position for which applicants are being selected. In order for selection procedures to be valid, they must first be reliable. There are several forms of validity relevant to selection. The first is *predictive validity*. With predictive validation, potential selection procedures, such as batteries of tests, are given to job applicants. However, during the validation procedure, selection is based on procedures other than the tests. After sufficient time for those hired to have learned their jobs, their job performance is then correlated with test scores. Tests having a significant and substantial statistical relationship with job performance are said to have predictive validity.

Another form of validity is *concurrent validity*, which has the practical advantage of not requiring a time lag before tests can be used. With concurrent validity, tests are given to current employees and their test scores are compared with their job performance. Both predictive and concurrent validation are called criterion-related forms of validity because they are validated on the criterion of job performance. A third form of validity is *content validity*. There is no statistical basis for assessing the content validity of a selection procedure, such as a test. Instead, content validity is established by having a panel of subject matter experts review the test items in order to determine that the test covers the domain of the subject. All three forms of validity can be used to defend the use of tests when selection decisions are appealed. There are other forms of validity and reliability that are relevant for test developers and testing specialists; however, the details of these are beyond the purposes of this discussion.

Job Analysis

Job analysis provides the foundation for good selection by identifying the knowledge, skills, abilities, and other requirements (KSAs) necessary to perform the job. Knowledge of the KSAs is necessary before selection can begin. Traditional job analysis identifies the tasks that make up a job, and these tasks form the basis for job descriptions. There are two approaches for collecting information for job analysis: interviews of job incumbents and their supervisors and the use of task inventory questionnaires. A system is available for job analysis in the form of the Position Analysis Questionnaire (PAQ). The PAQ is a highly sophisticated job analysis questionnaire consisting of 195 items that can be used to collect information about jobs in a highly organized and quantitative form. The PAQ has been used to develop compensation structures that reflect greater contribution for jobs that are more demanding. Nontraditional forms of job analysis are evolving to deal with situations in which there is extensive teamwork or flexible work assignments.[37]

Interviews

Interviews are a universal feature of selection systems. Recent research has shown that interviews can have substantial validity, particularly when they have more structure and are conducted appropriately. One very large-scale research study found a validity coefficient of .47 for interviews and .62 when more structured interviewed were used. (Validity coefficients range from 0 for no predictive ability to 1.0 for perfect predictive ability.) Thus, the predictive ability of interviews can be increased with more structure, which means that the interviewers ask the same questions of applicants so that they can be compared on the same dimensions. Other suggestions for improved interviewing include restricting the range of dimensions to be assessed to a small number of skills and abilities and knowledge that is most important for the job. Another suggestion is to limit the amount of information about the applicant that is reviewed by the interviewer before the interview. By limiting this information, the interview remains an independent predictor and the interviewer is less biased by information obtained from other means. In addition, the use of multiple interviewers helps improve predictive validity, although the use of panel interviews with simultaneous participation of multiple interviewers may not add predictive power.[38]

Behavioral Interviews

Another way to improve selection interviews is to use behavioral interviews. Essentially, in a behavioral interview, a candidate might be asked to describe how he or she dealt with a particular situation in the past. For example, an applicant might be asked to describe how he or she dealt with an employer who made a serious mistake. When interviewers ask applicants about past experiences, more predictive information can be obtained than through questions couched in hypothetical situations. Greater predictive power results from questions about past experiences because past behavior is generally a good predictor of future behavior.

Because of the greater predictive ability of behavioral interviews, more companies are using the approach. Bank One's use of the procedure provides a good example. At Bank One, applicants are informed about how they will be interviewed. For example, Bank One provides a preparation sheet that tells applicants that they will be asked about a specific situation such as, " 'How did you help pull your team together to meet goals?' "[39] The same questions are asked of applicants, which helps improve interrater reliability and the validity of the selection procedure.

Testing

The use of selection tests provides another means for improving the selection process. There are several types of tests that are relevant to selection. Some of the more common types of tests used for selection include cognitive or mental ability tests, personality tests, work sample or performance tests, and integrity tests.

Cognitive ability tests are commonly used to assess an applicant's capability to perform a job. Furthermore, they often have fairly high predictive ability. For example, studies have found the following validity coefficients between jobs and cognitive test scores: arithmetic reasoning for computer programmers = .57, general mental ability for first-line supervisors = .64, and mechanical comprehension for operators in the petroleum industry = .33. *Personality tests* also are commonly used for selection purposes. Researchers have established that the "big five" personality dimensions, as measured by the NEO–Personality Inventory and Personality Characteristics Inventory (PCI), can be very useful for selection. The big five personality dimensions are extroversion, agreeableness, conscientiousness, emotional stability, and openness to experience. Conscientiousness has been found to be a good predictor of job performance for almost all types of jobs and, not surprisingly, extroversion has been found to be related to performance in sales jobs. Finally, paper-and-pencil integrity tests have been found to be useful in predicting theft and other undesirable behavior, even though applicants may attempt to fake their responses.[40]

Performance or *work sample tests* require job applicants to perform some of the actual tasks required for the job. For example, applicants for machinist jobs could be given a set of blueprints and be asked to produce a part, while applicants for a computer technician job might be asked to diagnose a problem with a network server. Work samples or performance tests have the advantage of legitimacy because it is easy to see the connection with the job. Because applicants are frequently potential customers of the company, they may be more likely to feel that they have been treated fairly if they have been given work sample tests. Work samples or performance tests also tend to be free from racial or gender biases as well. Work samples also can be obtained from applicants for positions such as graphic designer, commercial artist, or business writer by asking applicants to supply portfolios of their work for review.

Assessment Centers

Assessment centers are another selection procedure that offers relatively high predictive validity for managerial and supervisory jobs. Assessment centers are intensive selection procedures that may last one to two days, in which multiple assessors observe the abilities of applicants in a wide range of settings. These procedures can be used for selection and are particularly useful for promotions to supervisory-level positions where there is no prior experience to assess; they are also well suited for development. Assessment centers combine several traditional selection procedures, such as interviews and tests, with procedures that simulate managerial work in a job setting. For example, in-basket exercises are an almost universal feature of assessment centers. In-basket exercises ask applicants to prioritize and describe the actions they would take to deal with the items that would be typically encountered in a manager's in-basket. Such items might include memos, phone messages, requests from employees, and short internal reports.[41]

Other examples of simulation components in assessment centers include business games and the leaderless group, in which applicants may be asked to make a presentation to a group of other applicants in an attempt to support a hypothetical employee for a promotion. Because none of the applicants have any authority, only their personal abilities to influence others can apply. Research indicates that the simulations account for much of the predictive ability of assessments centers. In addition, when done properly, assessments centers involve training for assessors in interviewing and observational skills. One reason for the high predictive validity of assessment centers is that they involve high ratios of assessors. Another reason is that the assessors normally are higher-level managers, from at least two levels higher in the organization, who have performed the job themselves.[42] An example of a very elaborate assessment simulation is the Looking Glass, Inc.® exercise developed by the Center for Creative Leadership in Greensboro, North Carolina. In this assessment simulation, which is used for developmental purposes, assessees play the roles of managers and executives in a hypothetical company.

Because only limited space can be devoted to selection issues here, readers who wish to learn more about this subject are encouraged to refer to *Human Resource Selection* by Robert Gatewood and Hubert Feild.

DEALING WITH EMPLOYEE SURPLUSES

As discussed in Chapter 1, there are several methods by which companies may reduce the likelihood that they will have to lay off employees. These include both short-range and long-range approaches. Several of these approaches need further explanation. Two of these are redeployment and retraining, with the latter often being required before employees can be redeployed without being laid off.

Redeployment and Retraining

The prevention of skill obsolescence and career plateauing were covered in Chapter 1. Unfortunately, obsolescence is not always prevented and retraining may be required. With the increased rate of technological change and potential for skill obsolescence, *retraining* may become more important. As a result, many companies provide retraining for managers whose skills have become obsolete. A critical determinant in the success of such programs is managers' self-efficacy beliefs, or expectations that they will be successful in mastering the new skills. Interestingly, some companies send the wrong message.[43]

> Executives often adopted a "slash and burn" strategy when retraining efforts failed to realize objectives, laying off managers who did not acquire new competencies, behaviors, and attitudes. Layoffs following retraining programs may send a message to the workforce that retraining is a futile endeavor.[44]

IBM is an example of a company that provided extensive retraining for employees to be *redeployed* within the company. However, most companies do not provide retraining for the employees they lay off. A study by Leana and Feldman found less than 10 percent of laid-off workers receive such assistance from their former employers. Because governmental agencies provide various retraining programs, the response of most companies is to leave such training to these agencies. However, there are exceptions, for example, the Ford Motor Company, which funds and operates the National Development and Training Center. Laid-off workers going through the Center receive individualized retraining, specific to their needs.[45]

Early Retirement

In dealing with an excess of employees, companies frequently offer *early retirement* incentives in which employees currently ineligible for retirement receive additional years' credit and a bonus payment that enhances pension benefits. Major concerns with this practice are the effects on the company's pool of talent and the impact on early retirees. Ann Howard conducted a longitudinal study of AT&T and Bell System managerial employees that addressed these concerns. One of the study's major conclusions was that there were no significant differences at the 20-year mark in the performance ratings of managers who took early retirement versus those who did not.[46] The study concluded the following:

> Thus, the companies suffered no loss in quality of management talent as a result of the early retirements . . . there are no indications that the most capable managers leave the company if a golden handshake for those nearing retirement age is offered. Nor, of course, are the least capable most likely to leave.[47]

The same study also investigated other characteristics between managers taking early retirement and those remaining. Although performance ratings at their 20th year were not significantly different, for those retiring early, work had a lower priority in their lives, they were less conscientious about quality work, perceived lower likelihood of future promotion, and were more dissatisfied with their present jobs. In addition, they were more dissatisfied with their supervisors and the company. Further, they were more dissatisfied with the company a number of years before they retired. In retrospect, some of this greater dissatisfaction may have been manageable because there were warning signs of its development. Nonetheless, the overall evaluation of the early retirement program was that the more highly motivated managers who had better work and company attitudes remained.[48]

On the other side, from the perspective of those taking early retirement, these managers seem to be motivated by an instrumentality rationale. They had fewer financial concerns and stronger life interests outside of work, such as hobbies and socializing. Nonetheless, there was some dissatisfaction with the manner in which the early retirements were handled. A particularly troublesome issue was a change in the performance appraisal approach, because it was perceived as a means of shoving them out of the company.[49] One manager describes this perception as follows:

> About the time they introduced the new benefit plan, they also introduced a new appraisal plan. I had always been rated above average, but the new appraisals were done by managers upstate. I became the bottom of the list. My boss and I both broke into tears. Rather than face another unsatisfactory rating, I decided to leave the company.[50]

A reaction such as this indicates that abrupt changes in performance appraisal approaches are likely to be viewed as deceptive and may create ill will. Thus, one guideline for downsizing through the use of early retirements is that abrupt changes in performance appraisal should be avoided. Further, a truly voluntary approach is preferred because coercive approaches will be seen for what they are.[51] To protect themselves from charges of age discrimination, employers downsizing through voluntary early retirement programs typically request that employees sign waivers against claims under the Age Discrimination in Employment Act (ADEA). As indicated in Chapter 3, several specific conditions must be met before such waivers will constitute valid defenses against such charges.[52]

Of course, it is sometimes more desirable to focus on eliminating the poorer performers, which necessitates another approach. From the standpoint of employee welfare, those opting for early retirement will probably be better prepared from a financial standpoint. Because some retirees indicate that they would like to work to maintain contact and earn extra money, the company should also consider providing part-time employment. Finally, the early retiree's contributions to the company should be recognized with a demonstration of the company's appreciation. Although performance may have declined at some point, an employee's many years of service to the company merit recognition, and the conclusion of a long career should not carry the stigma of a forced retirement.[53]

Retreat from Employment Security Policies

From the late 1980s to the mid-1990s, structural changes in the economy, increases in productivity resulting from technology, computerization, and intense global competition led scores of companies to abandon employment security policies and downsize their workforces.[54] Although a recession also accounted for some layoffs, many were the result of permanent structural changes as companies were able to accomplish the same or more work with fewer employees. Many companies that had maintained no-layoff policies in the past reverted to layoffs.[55] For example, IBM, which had long maintained a no-layoff policy, announced plans to reduce employment by 10,000, but planned to avoid layoffs through use of a financial incentive program.[56] Nonetheless, by 1992, the company found that it had to reduce its employment by 40,000 during that year alone. IBM tried to become more responsive by shifting to semiautonomous or free-standing units, a process called *deconstructing*. Essentially, IBM tried to obtain some of the quickness and accountability advantages of rapidly responding personal computer and workstation manufacturers such as Sun Microsystems and Dell.[57] By the middle of the 1990s, IBM had made massive cuts in its workforce. The business press reported that "The promise of 'employment security,' not long ago a bright hope for curing America's competitive problems, has faded." [58] Job security or income security, however, is still a goal of major importance to employees.

Downsizing and Layoffs

Before conducting *layoffs*, there should be a careful analysis of their effects in the long run, as well as in the short run. For example, if a company conducts layoffs in response to short-term losses, it may find that its long-term survivability is endangered. A short-term problem may only be symptomatic of a larger problem that is not addressed by layoffs, such as lack of adaptability. In reality, layoffs, such as in the research and development area, may place a company in the position of mortgaging its future. Such cuts may prevent a company from pursuing its intended strategies because it has focused on short-term tactical moves to the detriment of strategy. Thus, before conducting layoffs, companies should seek an appropriate balance between short-term and long-term demands, as well as between the goals of workforce stability and organizational adaptability. Downsizing strategies are also more effective when the most effective performers can be retained. In some instances, the performance evaluation system may need improvement for accurate identification of such individuals. Further, the reward system may require modification to obtain the flexibility needed to retain them. Such flexibility is necessary because of resource scarcities that often prompt downsizing strategies but may be obtained through future-oriented rewards such as stock ownership and profit sharing.[59]

Companies also must be aware that even their short-term problems may not be solved by downsizing because of the loss of skills resulting from the departure of experienced employees who are offered early retirement options or severance packages. There is empirical support for this caveat, as the study of declining industries, mentioned earlier, found that "The poor performers [companies] looked at their actions (e.g., layoffs or early retirements) as individual events without considering the long-term consequences." [60] As noted in Chapter 1, it has been hypothesized that organizations having previous experience with layoffs will reduce their workforces through methods that are less severe, because their managers are predicted to have more timely insight of surpluses. With this recognition, they should take remedial action more quickly and should be in a position to rely more on attrition or redeployment. It has also been hypothesized that companies having less slack in their resource base are more likely to reduce employment by resorting to more severe approaches, such as layoffs.[61]

The Carlson Travel Network, a large travel agency that had conducted layoffs, provides an example of short-term problems related to layoffs. One important client, who had planned to travel to Taiwan after completing business in Japan, found while in Japan that he could not travel to Taiwan without a visa. This necessitated his flying back to Minnesota before going on to Taiwan. An inexperienced agent had made a mistake. Eventually, Carlson's quality of service improved to desired levels and the company obtained desired efficiencies. However, this and other problems occurred during the learning period.[62] As noted earlier, in conducting layoffs, companies must be careful not to deplete their knowledge base such that their distinctive competencies are lost.[63]

Downsizing strategies, which often involve layoffs, along with other approaches such as attrition and hiring freezes, have been widespread throughout the U.S. economy. Nonetheless, companies sometimes find that downsizing and associated layoffs begin a vicious cycle. Typically, the cycle is initiated by more intensified competition that cuts into the company's revenues. Lower revenues then lead to efforts to quickly cut costs and some employees are laid off. Although the company is left with fewer employees, the workload remains constant. "Survivors" often experience overwork, stress, frustration, and declining morale as they operate in crisis mode, attending only to immediate problems. Additionally, remaining employees also tend to become more risk averse and narrow-minded. As a result, there are insufficient workers available to examine the underlying causes of problems and fewer resources available for research and developmental efforts. Because of these detrimental effects, customer satisfaction wanes, causing revenues to decline further, thus precipitating another round of layoffs to cut costs. Another problem with downsizing strategies is that companies frequently do not obtain the benefits of reduced expenses, profitability, and increased return on investment that they had hoped to achieve. Cost savings are also wasted when consultants have to be hired to supply the expertise lost from staff layoffs. Some observers have even estimated that replacements eventually have to be hired for 10 to 20 percent of the employees who were laid off.[64]

After all alternatives have been exhausted and there is no other alternative, layoffs sometimes become unavoidable. To enhance the likelihood of success, downsizing should be viewed more systematically. Typically, downsizing strategies must be accompanied by changes in other factors that have an impact on organizational efficiency, such as the design of the organization and elimination of redundancies.[65] Some key findings about the conduct of downsizing are presented in Table 6-2.

TABLE 6-2 Key Findings About Downsizing

Far too many companies are not well prepared for downsizing; they begin with no retraining or redeployment policies in place, and they fail to anticipate the kinds of human resource problems that develop subsequently.

Six months to a year after a downsizing, key indicators often do not improve: expense ratios, profits, return-on-investment to shareholders, and stock prices.

Survivors' syndrome is a common aftermath. Be prepared to manage it. Better yet, try to avoid it by actively involving employees in the planning phase of any downsizing effort.

Recognize that downsizing has exploded the myth of job security, and has accelerated employee mobility, especially among white-collar workers. It has fundamentally altered the terms of the psychological contract that binds workers to organizations.

To bring about sustained improvements in productivity, quality, and effectiveness, integrate reductions in head count with planned changes in the way that work is designed.

Downsizing is not a one-time, quick-fix solution to enhance competitiveness. Rather, it should be viewed as part of a process of continuous improvement.

Source: Extracted from Wayne F. Cascio. "Downsizing: What Do We Know? What Have We Learned?" *Academy of Management Executive* 7, no. 1 (1993): 103. Reprinted with permission of *Academy of Management Executive*.

Further, layoffs have too frequently been conducted without sufficient regard for employees. In order to minimize the adverse consequences to employees, managers should consider the guidelines that are presented in Table 6-3 and discussed in the following paragraphs.

Companies should give employees advance notice that they are going to be laid off. Reasons for not providing notice are based on fears that employees will sabotage equipment or quit, leaving the company without workers to complete production prior to the plant's closure. In a study of layoffs in the steel industry and work related to National Aeronautics and Space Administration (NASA)

TABLE 6-3 Guidelines for Conducting Layoffs

Give Early Warnings/Announcements of Layoffs
Soften the Impact with Compensation and Benefits
Utilize the Services of Outplacement Firms
Supply Retraining Services
Provide Equitable and Decent Treatment of Laid-Off Employees
Ensure Supportive Treatment of Survivors
Maintain a Cooperative Approach with Unions
Uphold Obligations to the Community

Source: Adapted from Daniel C. Feldman and Carrie R. Leana. "Managing Layoffs: Experience at the Challenger Disaster Site and the Pittsburgh Steel Mills," *Organizational Dynamics* 18, no. 1 (1989): 52–64.

programs, researchers found that less than less than 50 percent of employees had received advance notice.[66] There is evidence that employers' concerns about the dangers of providing advance notice are unfounded and that there are no associated declines in productivity or greater instances of sabotage. In contrast, companies actually benefit by providing advance notice because they are likely to be perceived more positively by the public.[67] As noted in Chapter 2, The Worker Adjustment and Retraining Notification Act (WARN) applies to companies having 100 or more employees. Under the act, employers must provide 60 days' advance notice of plant closings to employees, unions, and officials at state and local levels when 50 or more employees will lose their jobs.[68] Additionally, employees tend to receive other benefits from advance notice. One benefit is that early notification enables employees to prepare for their departure from the company.[69] Another is that their period of unemployment may be shorter. Empirical evidence indicates that the period of unemployment for those receiving advanced notice is shorter than for those who do not.[70]

Those being laid off should receive severance pay and benefits should be extended. Aside from humanitarian reasons, providing severance pay may preserve the company's relationship with the employee and enhance the company's chances of rehiring the employee after business improves. Additionally, severance pay may be perceived to reduce the likelihood of litigation.[71]

Employers also should make outplacement services available to employees. Outplacement services tend to stimulate laid-off workers to pursue retraining opportunities and to relocate. Likewise, they provide opportunities for building social support. Although the effectiveness of outplacement services varies by employee level and needs, their role in providing a base of operations for contacting employers appears to be uniformly valuable. Additionally, employees' perceptions of fair treatment are probably enhanced by outplacement services. Although research evidence has not definitively established that outplacement programs are effective in helping workers become reemployed, such programs may have an additional major benefit of facilitating employees' psychological adjustment to the loss of their jobs and in helping them regain their self-confidence.[72]

Other suggestions for carrying out layoffs include supplying additional training, particularly where declines in industries have made employees' skills obsolete; attending to the morale of remaining employees, such as by not making derogatory remarks about laid-off employees; pursuing cooperative efforts with unions to avoid layoffs; and displaying corporate social responsibility by helping to defray the costs incurred by the community in which layoffs or a plant closure are conducted. A final suggestion is to avoid preferential treatment of minorities and women even if the company has an affirmative action objective of increasing their representation. Such treatment has not been well received by the courts, particularly where seniority systems are circumvented.[73]

The impact on remaining employees or survivors should be taken into account when conducting layoffs. Whether layoffs are perceived to be conducted according to random criteria or on the basis of merit, they may have an impact on the work performance of survivors. A laboratory experiment, drawing on the tenets of equity theory, has demonstrated that subjects who survived layoffs conducted on a random basis were more productive in terms of quantity after the layoffs. The theoretical basis for this finding is that the survivors of a random layoff experience positive inequity. Positive inequity results because survivors believe their ratio of outcomes to inputs to be more favorable than those who were laid off. This is because their performance or inputs were no greater, but the outcomes of those laid off—losing their jobs—were less. In order to restore equilibrium and to reduce feelings of guilt, the survivors worked harder and produced more. Experimental conditions ruled out an alternative explanation: that the survivors' increased productivity may have resulted from feelings of anxiety regarding future layoffs.[74]

Regardless of the layoff strategy used, the impact in human terms will be considered by all but the most cold-blooded managers. The human cost of a layoff or termination may be assessed in terms of the anticipated length of the period of unemployment. Clearly, the morale of remaining employees will be adversely affected by prolonged periods of unemployment of those laid off or terminated, except in the most extreme cases of misbehavior. Unfortunately, it is difficult to predict the average length of time employees will remain unemployed because there are numerous explanatory factors. However, a New York outplacement firm has used a 60-variable formula to predict the period of unemployment for its clients.[75] A rule of thumb also exists. Although its predictive accuracy is unknown, the rule predicts that a terminated manager will remain unemployed for "one month for every $10,000 of income."[76]

Termination Strategies

Although terminations may be indicative of deficiencies in other human resource management systems, they are often required for organizational change and have even been categorized as an organizational development process. As such, terminations may be critical for the implementation of a shift in the strategic direction of an organization. Terminations of managers have been necessary in organizational evolutions in which managers, who can work effectively within an informal structure, cannot adapt to the more formal structure required with growth in size. Terminations also have been used where entrepreneurs, who were effective in founding companies, could not make the transition to the different managerial requirements of a bureaucratic environment.[77]

Companies should develop approaches toward termination that assure employees that termination will be for just cause and that the performance appraisal, coaching, and counseling systems will have warned them that their performance must improve or that certain behaviors are unacceptable. However, companies also must terminate employees in a manner that communicates that substandard performance and inappropriate behaviors will result in termination.

Companies need an approach that eliminates unsatisfactory performers while allowing competent employees to feel secure in their jobs, committed to the company, capable of taking reasonable risks, and deserving of their loyalty. In the absence of such an approach, the company will not have a performance culture, nor will it have employee commitment. Interestingly, experienced outplacement consultants have observed that managerial terminations are usually due to personality-related conflicts with the terminated employee's manager. In contrast, fewer than 5 percent of managerial terminations are based on the grounds of incompetence.[78]

In terminating unsatisfactory performers, U.S. employers have an advantage over many European competitors in that they have much greater latitude. For example, in Italy, governmental regulations require an employer to pay up to $130,000 in benefits to terminate an employee 45 years of age who has been employed for 20 years. Termination costs are not as expensive in all European countries as the cost in Ireland would be $13,000 under the same circumstances.[79]

Unfortunately, even with an appropriate balance between employment security and the maintenance of performance and behavioral standards, the implementation of such balanced termination strategies often leaves much to be desired. In recent years, terminations have been conducted too frequently with little regard for the dignity of the employee. Employees are frequently told of the termination and escorted by security personnel to their desks to pick up their personal property, and then taken to the door. Although often related to fears that the terminated employee will sabotage a computer system or other company assets, this rationale is not always applicable.[80] The following examples are more typical of termination actions than they should be.

> A supervisor at a tractor plant in Dubuque, Iowa, got the ax while he was on vacation. "He got a call at home. Company officials told him to meet them in the parking lot of a local fast-food restaurant. He got in his boss's car and [his boss] read him a brief notice," says Earl Payson, a lawyer who represented the client in an age-discrimination suit against the same company. "They wouldn't answer any questions. My client had been with the company for over 25 years." [81]
>
> My own son was terminated [recently] by an advertising company with a note on the door. It said, 'You're fired. Come and see me.' It was signed by his boss.[82]

Although the literature on terminations is largely prescriptive and anecdotal, there are some practical guidelines. One is that terminations should be conducted as business decisions. Employees should be told that the termination is an irrevocable business decision. In contrast to the advice offered by some attorneys, employees should be told the reasons for their termination.[83] The advice of some attorneys is that providing the reason for the termination simply gives the employee another rationale for initiating litigation. Nonetheless, such advice hardly meets the standard of fairness that managers themselves should apply, as well as the expectations of fairness held by other employees.

Outplacement services should be provided to help the employee make the adjustment from ending the employment relationship to beginning the search process. This adjustment process is sometimes equated to a grieving process in which the employee goes through predictable steps. It has been suggested by some observers that these steps are analogous to the Kübler-Ross five stages of dying: denial, anger, bargaining, depression, and acceptance.[84] Outplacement counselors may be of assistance in helping the terminated employee work more quickly through these stages to acceptance, at which point constructive steps can be taken toward obtaining a new job. Career counseling and realistic assessments of strengths and weaknesses may also be helpful in shortening the period of time before the employee can obtain a new job. Employees receiving outplacement assistance feel more fairly treated by the company.[85]

Another suggestion is to exercise care in the timing of terminations. Employees frequently want to take positive action to obtain another job as quickly possible. Therefore, terminating employees before a weekend or during a holiday may be unduly stressful because they cannot pursue job search activities at this time. Further, during these times, the employee may have too much time to brood over the termination. Managers also should consider the impact of a termination on other employees because how a coworker is terminated may have a lasting impact on employees' perceptions of the company. Terminations should be conducted only after prior warning, real attempts to improve the employee's performance or correct unacceptable behavior, and a thorough investigation surrounding the last-straw incident. Managers often delay too long before terminating employees. One reason for delay is that managers tend to feel guilty about terminating employees and may blame the employee's failures on themselves.[86]

In conducting the termination session, the manager should describe the conditions of the separation, benefits, and the nature of recommendations the company is willing to make. A practical suggestion is that the severance package and explanation of benefits should be in writing because the employee may not "hear" the information during such a traumatic time. In the termination session, the manager should cover the essential information, convey appropriate appreciation for the employee's contributions, and treat the employee with respect and as humanely as possible, but the session should not be a debate and should be fairly short, usually about 15 minutes.[87]

SPECIAL IMPLEMENTATION CHALLENGES

Several developments in the area of employment practices and policies provide special implementation challenges. Career paths for technical professionals pose one problem. Dual-career couples provide another important challenge to strategies requiring a mobile labor force.

Career Paths for Technical Professionals

Technical professionals, such as engineers or information technology specialists, often face limited opportunity for career advancement unless they leave their specialties for management positions. Professionals who make such choices and serve in management positions for some time find that it is difficult to return to their previous field because their technical knowledge has become obsolete. Companies have attempted to remedy this problem by establishing a dual-career path system that allows advancement on a separate technical ladder as the employee acquires more expertise and experience. Technical professionals need not move to the management path in order to move ahead in compensation, increasingly more challenging work assignments, and title. Dual-career paths are also used to help retain technical professionals. For example, Alcon Laboratories has implemented technical and management tracks for its professionals in information technology. Dual-career paths or ladders also have been implemented at Air Products and Chemicals for its research and development staff. Examples of corresponding levels on the ladders are the following: Level 9—Director (managerial), Consultant (technical ladder); Level 10—Assistant Vice President (managerial ladder), Senior Consultant (technical ladder); and Level 11—Vice President (managerial ladder), Executive Consultant (technical ladder). In addition to a progression in job titles, employees in the technical ladder receive the same compensation as those on the same level in the managerial ladder.[88]

Dual-Career Couples

Increasingly, companies are facing challenges in transferring employees because of the rising number of dual-career couples. Two-income families are now involved in a high proportion of transfers as the spouses of 65 percent of employees also work. Further, the woman is more frequently the employee who is being transferred. With women now comprising a large percentage of professional occupations, it is not surprising that they are increasingly the employees being transferred. An obvious problem companies face in transferring employees involved in dual-career situations is the spouse's ability to find a commensurate position. Such fears are well grounded: 51 percent of those spouses who were reemployed after the move received lower salaries and benefits than in their previous jobs.[89]

Another problem encountered with dual-career couples is their frequency of turnover when the spouse works for another large employer that transfers employees. For female employees, there is a perception, whether valid or not, that they may be more susceptible to turnover in such circumstances. This perception is as follows: "Because the female manager is seen as more often following her spouse in a relocation decision, her dual-career family status is considered more of a liability." [90] A related problem concerns travel requirements. Where both individuals have jobs that necessitate extensive travel, there are difficult problems with caring for children and in finding enough time for the couple to be together.[91]

Most employees in dual-career situations have a strong desire for assistance in obtaining employment for their spouses. Fortunately, companies' human resource personnel are in an advantageous position to provide such assistance, because they are the most attuned to job opportunities and are frequently networked with other area employers. One such example is an employer network in Columbus, Ohio, which is made up of over 40 organizations.[92] As specific examples, General Motors provides referrals and counseling assistance for spouses and IBM provides similar assistance.[93] More specific examples of employer assistance are the following:

> Atlantic Richfield Company, The Dow Chemical Company, Eastman Kodak, IBM, Merck & Co., Procter & Gamble, US Sprint, and Warner-Lambert will all help spouses find jobs. Many will give serious consideration to hiring them.[94]

Aside from obtaining another job for the spouse, another problem faced by dual career couples is the details of moving. In the past, the wife, who was less likely to be employed, typically handled these details. Further, family support systems now handle more duties such as childcare, housekeeping, and assistance with elderly parents. These support systems must be reestablished with a move to a different geographic location. With dual-career couples, the details involved with transfers have increased and cannot be handled by a spouse who is not employed. As a result, more time is required for the transfers, along with earlier notice.[95]

A related issue of greater importance in recent years is requests for transfer assistance when the other half of the dual-career couple is not a spouse. A survey revealed that almost 20 percent of companies furnish relocation assistance in such situations.[96]

> However, there are a number of problems companies face in these situations, such as, "How significant does the other have to be to be considered a partner? Is the length of time the relationship has existed a factor in defining partners? What about same-gender couples?" [97]

Another response to problems such as these is that more companies are adapting their policies to deal with the special issues involved with dual-career couples. A survey of nepotism policies (employment of relatives) indicates that, of the companies planning to change their nepotism rules, 58 percent intended to make them more liberal. Companies at the forefront in liberalizing policies to accommodate dual-career couples are in high-tech industries.[98] It is not surprising that high-tech industries offer more liberal nepotism rules because high-tech industries must attract high-quality talent, and will therefore bypass traditional approaches. As indicated in Chapter 2, women have benefited from the progressive policies of such companies and have made great strides into the managerial ranks of high-tech firms because these firms have strong needs for talent.[99]

Summary

This chapter has covered methods by which companies obtain the efficiencies needed for implementation of their strategies. Employers have become more efficient and flexible by broadening the duties and responsibilities of their employees. Cross-training has been used effectively in these efforts to gain flexible work assignments so that employees' time may be more efficiently utilized. In addition to producing benefits for the organization, cross-training has appeal for employees when combined with skill-based pay systems, which are discussed in Chapter 7. Organizational cultures emphasizing trust appear to promote flexibility through such practices as the elimination of rules. Approaches for operating on a nonunion basis were also discussed as means of obtaining flexibility.

Several methods for dealing with shortages of employees and skills were discussed. These included strategic recruitment from both internal and external sources and special recruiting for minorities and females. Suggestions were provided for the conduct of flexible retirement programs as a means of dealing with employee shortages. The requirements for effective selection were briefly reviewed and several methods for improved selections were discussed—including behavioral interviews, testing, and assessment centers. Methods for dealing with employee surpluses also were reviewed, including retraining and redeployment within the organization and early retirement. A brief description of the abandonment of employment security policies in the United States also was provided. Problems of downsizing and layoffs were then examined in some depth along with means for eliminating the dysfunctional effects of these actions. In addition, termination problems were discussed, along with suggestions for improving the effectiveness of these personnel actions.

Finally, the special challenges to strategies requiring a mobile workforce were discussed. Some of the most important of these challenges are encountered with technical employees and dual-career couples. Several suggestions for dealing with technical professionals and dual-career couples were provided.

Endnotes

1. Forward, Gordon E. "Wide-Open Management at Chaparral Steel," *Harvard Business Review* 64, no. 3 (1986): 96–102; Luthans, Fred. "Conversation with Gordon Forward," *Organizational Dynamics* 20, no. 1 (1991): 63–72; Personal conversations of the author with Gordon Forward, CEO, Dennis Beach, Vice President for Administration, and Larry Clark, Controller.
2. Forward. "Wide-Open Management at Chaparral Steel"; U.S. Bureau of the Census. *Statistical Abstract of the United States: 1990*, 110th ed., 1990; Greer, Charles R., and Robert T. Rhodes. "A Contrasting View of the Effect of Foreign Competition on Labor Unionism in the United States," *West Virginia Law Review* 93, no. 4 (1991): 945–55; Luthans. "Conversation with Gordon Forward."
3. Luthans. "Conversation with Gordon Forward."
4. Forward, Gordon E., Dennis E. Beach, David A. Gray, and James Campbell Quick. "Mentofacturing: A Vision for American Industrial Excellence," *Academy of Management Executive* 5, no. 3 (1991): 36.

5. Ibid.
6. Luthans. "Conversation with Gordon Forward," p. 69.
7. Galante, Steven P. "Frost Inc. Technological Renewal and Human Resource Management: A Case Study," *Human Resource Planning* 10, no. 1 (1987): 57–67.
8. Ibid.
9. Katzenbach, Jon R., and Douglas K. Smith. *The Wisdom of Teams*. New York: HarperCollins, 1993; McIntyre and Eduardo Salas. "Measuring and Managing for Team Performance: Emerging Principles from Complex Environments," in Richard A. Guzzo, Eduardo Salas, and Associates (Eds.), *Team Effectiveness and Decision-Making in Organizations*. San Francisco: Jossey-Bass, 1995; Ancona, Deborah G., Thomas A. Kochan, Maureen Scully, John Van Maanen, and E. Eleanor Westney. *Managing for the Future: Teams in Organizations*. Cincinnati, OH: South-Western College Publishing, 1996; Croft-Baker, Nancy. "Giving Teams a Winning Edge," *Corporate University Review* (February 1, 1999).
10. Ibid.
11. Croft-Baker. "Giving Teams a Winning Edge"; Pascarella, Perry. "Compensating Teams," *Across the Board* (February 1, 1997): 16.
12. Pascarella. "Compensating Teams."
13. Katzenbach and Smith. *The Wisdom of Teams*; McIntyre and Salas. "Measuring and Managing for Team Performance: Emerging Principles from Complex Environments"; Ancona, Kochan, Scully, Maanen, and Westney. *Managing for the Future: Teams in Organizations*; Croft-Baker. "Giving Teams a Winning Edge."
14. Ibid.
15. Ibid.
16. "Solving Murders: Kansas City Style." *Turning Point*, televised program on the Learning Channel narrated by Peter Jennings, December 1, 1999.
17. Ibid.
18. Mills, Daniel. *Labor–Management Relations*. New York: McGraw-Hill, 1978; "Emerson Electric's Rise as a Low-Cost Producer," *Business Week* (November 1, 1976): 47–48.
19. Verma, Anil. "Relative Flow of Capital to Union and Nonunion Plants Within a Firm," *Industrial Relations* 24, no. 3 (1985): 395–405.
20. Mills. *Labor–Management Relations*; "Emerson Electric's Rise as a Low-Cost Producer," *Business Week*.
21. Fiorito, Jack, Daniel G. Gallagher, and Charles R. Greer. "Determinants of Unionism: A Review of the Literature," in Kendrith M. Rowland and Gerald R. Ferris (Eds.), *Research in Personnel and Human Resources Management*. Greenwich, CT: JAI Press, 1986, pp. 269–306.
22. Cook, Barbara, Assistant Vice President, Burlington Northern Santa Fe. Comments to the Human Resource Roundtable, Texas Christian University, April 5, 2000.
23. "Innovative Companies Hire Family and Friends of Employees, and Even Clients," *Wall Street Journal* (February 22, 2000): A1.
24. Cook, Deborah S., and Gerald R. Ferris. "Strategic Human Resource Management and Firm Effectiveness in Industries Experiencing Decline," *Human Resource Management* 25, no. 3 (1986): 441–57.
25. Breaugh, James A. "Relationships Between Recruiting Sources and Employee Performance, Absenteeism, and Work Attitudes," *Academy of Management Journal* 24, no. 1 (1981): 142–47.
26. Ibid.
27. Williams, Charles R., Chalmer E. Labig, and Thomas H. Stone. "Recruitment Sources and Posthire Outcomes for Job Applicants and New Hires: A Test of Two Hypotheses," *Journal of Applied Psychology* 78, no. 2 (1993): 163–72.
28. Breaugh, James A. *Recruitment: Science and Practice*. Boston: PWS-Kent Publishing Company, 1992.
29. Bassett, Joan. "Recruitment: Fidelity Investments Brings Temporary Employment In-House," *Personnel Journal* 68, no. 12 (1989): 65–70.
30. Cox, Taylor H., and Stacy Blake. "Managing Cultural Diversity: Implications for Organizational Competitiveness," *Academy of Management Executive* 5, no. 3 (1991): 45–56.

31. Ibid., p. 49.
32. Cox and Blake. "Managing Cultural Diversity: Implications for Organizational Competitiveness"; Cox, Taylor Jr. "The Multicultural Organization," *Academy of Management Executive* 5, no. 2 (1991): 34–47.
33. Thomas, R. Roosevelt. "From Affirmative Action to Affirming Diversity," *Harvard Business Review* 90, no. 2 (1990): 107–17.
34. Fullerton, Howard W. "Evaluation of Labor Force Projections to 1990," *Monthly Labor Review* 115, no. 8 (1992): 3–14; Fullerton, Howard W. "New Labor Force Projections, Spanning 1988 to 2000," *Monthly Labor Review* 112, no. 11 (1989): 2–12.
35. Rosen, Benson, and Thomas H. Jerdee. "Retirement Policies: Evidence of the Need for Change," *Human Resource Management* 28, no. 2 (1989): 87–103.
36. Ibid., p. 99.
37. Gatewood, Robert D., and Hubert S. Feild. *Human Resource Selection*, 4th ed. Fort Worth, TX: Dryden Press, 1998; Heneman, Herbert G. III, and Robert L. Heneman. *Staffing Organizations*. Middleton, WI: Mendota House, 1994.
38. Gatewood and Feild. *Human Resource Selection*.
39. Kleiman, Carol. "True to Life: Behavioral Interviews Focus on Experience," *Fort Worth Star-Telegram* (February 20, 2000): Careers Section.
40. Gatewood and Feild. *Human Resource Selection*.
41. Cascio, Wayne F. *Applied Psychology in Personnel Management*, 4th ed. Upper Saddle River, NJ: Prentice Hall, 1991.
42. Ibid.
43. Hill, Linda, and Jaan Elias. "Retraining Midcareer Managers: Career History and Self-Efficacy Beliefs," *Human Resource Management* 29, no. 2 (1990): 197–217.
44. Ibid., p. 213.
45. Leana, Carrie R., and Daniel C. Feldman. "Job Loss and Employee Assistance: Joint Efforts to Help Displaced Workers," in Manual London, Emily S. Bassman, and John P. Fernandez (Eds.), *Human Resource Forecasting and Strategy Development*. New York: Quorum Books, 1990, pp. 127–40.
46. Howard, Ann. "Who Reaches for the Golden Handshake?" *Academy of Management Executive* 2, no. 2 (1988): 133–44.
47. Ibid., p. 134.
48. Howard. "Who Reaches for the Golden Handshake?"
49. Ibid.
50. Ibid., p. 140.
51. Howard. "Who Reaches for the Golden Handshake?"
52. Player, Mack A. *Federal Law of Employment Discrimination in a Nutshell*, 3rd ed. St. Paul: West Publishing Co., 1992; Mitchell, Charles E. "Waiver of Rights Under the Age Discrimination in Employment Act: Implications of the Older Workers Benefit Protection Act of 1990," *Labor Law Journal* 43, no. 11 (1992): 735–44.
53. Howard. "Who Reaches for the Golden Handshake?"
54. Hoerr, John, and Wendy Zellner. "A Japanese Import That's Not Selling," *Business Week* (February 26, 1990): 86–87.
55. Kochan, Thomas A., John Paul MacDuffie, and Paul Osterman. "Employment Security at DEC: Sustaining Values Amid Environmental Change," *Human Resource Management* 27, no. 2 (1988): 121–43.
56. Burke, Steven. "PC Operations Spared the Worst of IBM's Cost-Cutting Programs," *PC Week* 6 (December 11, 1989): 1, 6.
57. Verity, John W. "Deconstructing the Computer Industry," *Business Week* (November 23, 1992): 90–100.
58. Hoerr and Zellner. "A Japanese Import That's Not Selling," p. 86.
59. Greenhalgh, Leonard, Robert B. McKersie, and Roderick W. Gilkey. "Rebalancing the Workforce at IBM: A Case Study of Redeployment and Revitalization," *Organizational Dynamics* 14, no. 4

(1986): 30–47; Ferris, Gerald R., Deborah A. Schellenberg, and Raymond F. Zammuto. "Human Resource Management Strategies in Declining Industries," *Human Resource Management Strategies in Declining Industries* 23, no. 4 (1984): 381–94.

60. Cook and Ferris. "Strategic Human Resource Management and Firm Effectiveness in Industries Experiencing Decline," p. 448.
61. Greenhalgh, Leonard, Anne T. Lawrence, and Robert I. Sutton. "Determinants of Work Force Reduction Strategies in Declining Organizations," *Academy of Management Review* 13, no. 2 (1988): 241–54.
62. Harper, Lucinda. "Hazardous Cuts: Travel Agency Learns Service Firms' Perils In Slimming Down," *Wall Street Journal* (March 20, 1992): A1, A6.
63. Greer, Charles R., and Timothy C. Ireland. "Organizational and Financial Correlates of a 'Contrarian' Human Resource Investment Strategy," *Academy of Management Journal* 35, no. 5 (1992): 956–84.
64. Schneier, Craig E., Douglas Shaw, and Richard W. Beatty. "Companies' Attempts to Improve Performance While Containing Costs: Quick Fix Versus Lasting Change," *Human Resource Planning* 15, no. 3 (1992): 1–25; Cascio, Wayne F. "Downsizing: What Do We Know? What Have We Learned?" *Academy of Management Executive* 7, no. 1 (1993): 95–104.
65. Cascio. "Downsizing: What Do We Know? What Have We Learned?"
66. Feldman, Daniel C., and Carrie R. Leana. "Managing Layoffs: Experiences at the Challenger Disaster Site and the Pittsburgh Steel Mills," *Organizational Dynamics* 18, no. 1 (1989): 52–64.
67. Ibid.; Leana, Carrie R., and John M. Ivancevich. "Involuntary Job Loss: Institutional Interventions and a Research Agenda," *Academy of Management Review* 12, no. 2 (1987): 301–12.
68. Rothstein, Mark A., Andria S. Knapp, and Lance Liebman. *Cases and Materials on Employment Law*, 2nd ed. Westbury, NY: The Foundation Press, 1991.
69. Leana and Ivancevich. "Involuntary Job Loss: Institutional Interventions and a Research Agenda."
70. Feldman and Leana. "Managing Layoffs: Experiences at the Challenger Disaster Site and the Pittsburgh Steel Mills"; Love, Douglas O., and William Torrence. "The Value of Advance Notice of Worker Displacement," *Southern Economic Journal* 55, no. 3 (1989): 626–43.
71. Feldman and Leana. "Managing Layoffs: Experiences at the Challenger Disaster Site and the Pittsburgh Steel Mills."
72. Ibid.; Leana and Ivancevich. "Involuntary Job Loss: Institutional Interventions and a Research Agenda."
73. Feldman and Leana. "Managing Layoffs: Experiences at the Challenger Disaster Site and the Pittsburgh Steel Mills"; Kleiman, Lawrence S., and Robert H. Faley. "Voluntary Affirmative Action and Preferential Treatment: Legal and Research Implications," *Personnel Psychology* 41, no. 3 (1988): 481–96.
74. Brockner, Joel, Jeff Greenberg, Audrey Brockner, Jenny Bortz, Jeanette Davy, and Carolyn Carter. "Layoffs, Equity Theory, and Work Performance: Further Evidence of the Impact of Survivor Guild," *Academy of Management Journal* 29, no. 2 (1986): 373–84.
75. Hymowitz, Carol, and Timothy D. Schellhardt. "After the Ax: Formula Aims to Predict Length of a Fired Manager's Job Search," *Wall Street Journal* (October 20, 1986): 25.
76. Ibid.
77. Morin, William J., and Lyle Yorks. *Outplacement Techniques: A Positive Approach to Terminating Employees*. New York: AMACOM, 1982.
78. Ibid.
79. Conte, Christopher. "Labor Letter," *Wall Street Journal* (May 12, 1992): A1.
80. Alexander, Suzanne. "Firms Get Plenty of Practice at Layoffs, But They Often Bungle the Firing Process," *Wall Street Journal* (October 14, 1991): B1, B3.
81. Ibid., p. B1.
82. Ibid.
83. Coulson, Robert. *The Termination Handbook*. New York: The Free Press, 1981; Dessler, Gary. *Personnel Management*, 4th ed. Upper Saddle River, NJ: Prentice Hall, 1988.

84. Rice, F. Philip. *Human Development: A Life-Span Approach*. New York: Macmillan, 1992; Kübler-Ross, Elisabeth. *Questions and Answers on Death and Dying*. New York: Macmillan Publishing Company, 1974.
85. Morin, William J., and Lyle Yorks. *Outplacement Techniques: A Positive Approach to Terminating Employees*. New York: AMACOM, 1982.
86. Dessler. *Personnel Management*; Coulson. *The Termination Handbook*.
87. Alexander. "Firms Get Plenty of Practice at Layoffs, But They Often Bungle the Firing Process"; Coulson. *The Termination Handbook*; Dessler. *Personnel Management*; Morin and Yorks. *Outplacement Techniques: A Positive Approach to Terminating Employees*.
88. Tsumpis, Nick, Vice President of Information Technology Applications. Comments to the Human Resource Roundtable, Texas Christian University, April 5, 2000; Thayer, Ann M. "Dual Career Ladders," *Chemical and Engineering News* 76, no. 44 (1998): 51–57; Kinsman, Michael. "At Work These Days, Company Ladder Doesn't Always Lead to the Top," *San Diego Union-Tribune* (October 2, 1992): E-1; Gomez-Mejia, Luis R., David B. Balkin, and Robert L. Cardy. *Managing Human Resources*. Upper Saddle River, NJ: Prentice Hall, 1995.
89. Clark, Wayne. "Spouse's Career Should Figure in Employee Relocation," *Milwaukee Journal Sentinel* (August 2, 1999): 4; Collie, H. Cris. "Two Salaries, One Relocation: What's a Company to Do?" *Personnel Administrator* 34, no. 9 (1989): 54–57.
90. Guinn, Stephen L., and Lori G. Russell. "Personnel Decisions and the Dual-Career Couple," *Employment Relations Today* 14, no. 1 (1987): 84 (whole article on pp. 83–89).
91. Guinn and Russell. "Personnel Decisions and the Dual-Career Couple."
92. Collie. "Two Salaries, One Relocation: What's a Company to Do?"
93. Taylor, Alex III. "Why Women Managers Are Bailing Out," *Fortune* 114, no. 4 (1986): 16–23.
94. Morgan, Hal, and Kerry Tucker. *Companies That Care*. New York: Simon & Schuster, 1991, p. 333.
95. Collie. "Two Salaries, One Relocation: What's a Company to Do?"; Guinn and Russell. "Personnel Decisions and the Dual-Career Couple."
96. Collie. "Two Salaries, One Relocation: What's a Company to Do?"
97. Ibid., p. 55.
98. Newgren, Kenneth E., C. E. Kellogg, and William Gardner. "Corporate Responses to Dual-Career Couples: A Decade of Transformation," *Akron Business and Economic Review* 19, no. 2 (1988): 85–96.
99. Naisbitt, John, and Patricia Aburdene. *Megatrends 2000: Ten New Directions for the 1990's*. New York: William Morrow and Company, 1990.

CASE 6 The Health Care Industry

The health care industry has been going through major structural changes in order to become more efficient to help stem rising costs of health care. During the previous decade, health care organizations hired MBAs to help streamline their organizations, introduce new efficiencies, and market their services. In addition, many physicians are obtaining MBAs in order to help introduce better management into the health care industry. Health maintenance organizations (HMOs) continue to hold down costs by emphasizing prevention, by limiting access to specialists, by requiring copayments to make patients more sensitive to the costs of health care, and through increased bargaining power resulting from their size. There also have been mergers among health care organizations and hospitals. Unfortunately, many health care organizations have encountered financial difficulties and some have failed. The federal government also has tried to hold down costs by limiting Medicare and Medicaid reimbursements.[1]

At the same time that the health care industry is struggling to become more efficient, the demand for health care is increasing and is expected to increase in the future because of an aging population, increased affluence, and advances in technology. By 2008, 7.2 percent of the U.S. population will be 75 years or older. This compares with 5.2 percent in 1978.[2] Actual employment levels in selected health care occupations in 1998 and projections for 2008 are as follows:[3]

Occupation	1998	2008
Physicians	577,000	699,000
Dentists	160,000	165,000
Optometrists	38,000	42,000
Physician's assistants	66,000	98,000
Registered nurses	2,079,000	2,530,000
Physical therapists	120,000	161,000
Respiratory therapists	86,000	123,000
Dental hygienists	143,000	201,000
Clinical lab technologists and technicians	313,000	366,000
Licensed practical and licensed vocational nurses	692,000	828,000
Speech–Language pathologists and audiologists	105,000	145,000

Questions

1. Most people have some familiarity with hospitals and the health care industry. (If you lack such familiarity, you may want to interview someone who works in health care.) Based on your knowledge, in which quadrant of the staffing policies matrix (Figure 4-3) do you think hospitals are located? Are the staffing policies of hospitals more like baseball teams, academies, clubs, or fortresses? Explain your reasoning.
2. Examine the projections for the various health care occupational specialties. Are there substantial differences in the rates at which employment is expected to grow in the different occupations? How have the strategic actions by health care organizations, such as mergers, shifts to preventative approaches, and the focus on cost control, affected the expected growth of the different specialties? How is the market demand for medical care expected to affect employment in the different specialties?

3. Given the uncertainty of the demand for health care workers, how can health care organizations be prepared to meet their future needs for such employees? How can they help their employees prepare for their employment futures?
4. Do Porter's competitive strategies of cost leadership, differentiation, and niche or focus apply to hospitals or health care organizations? Explain.
5. Interview someone from the health care industry about the changes in utilization of human resources that have taken place. What are the major changes? What are their personal views about the value of these changes? How does this person view the effectiveness of the implementation of these changes?

References

1. Braddock, Douglas. "Occupational Employment Projections to 2008," *Monthly Labor Review* 122, no. 11 (1999): 51–80.
2. Ibid.; Fullerton, Howard N. "Labor Force Projections to 2008: Steady Growth and Changing Composition," *Monthly Labor Review* 122, no. 11 (1999): 19–32.
3. Braddock. "Occupational Employment Projections to 2008."

CHAPTER 7

Strategy Implementation: Reward and Development Systems

The seventh component of the conceptual framework presented in the Preface deals with strategy implementation through the use of reward and development systems. Reward systems provide the incentives and reinforcement for workforce behaviors that contribute to the implementation of strategies while development systems provide the workforce skills required for implementation. This chapter begins with a discussion of performance measurement systems, which provide the information required for allocation of rewards and developmental needs. Next, following a discussion of the limitations of traditional compensation systems, there is a discussion of strategically oriented compensation systems, including skill-based pay, team-based pay, broadbanding, variable compensation, and executive compensation. The chapter then discusses employee development approaches, including various training programs and methods, apprenticeships, management development approaches, management development for international assignments, and the strategic fit dilemma of whether to focus on selection or development of managers.

STRATEGICALLY ORIENTED PERFORMANCE MEASUREMENT SYSTEMS

The strategic importance of performance measurement systems is indicated in the following quotation by Clinton Longenecker and Dennis Gioia:

> A shipping firm executive captured his personal credo in the phrase: "You get what you measure." And we might add: "You measure what you value." If the organization values short-term results, that is what it will measure and get. If it values executive development, a different emphasis emerges.[1]

Various approaches to performance measurement are available to help assess the degree to which the behavior of employees at all organizational levels contributes to the implementation of strategies. Measures of performance are necessary for the functioning of reward systems, which are discussed in the next section. All methods of performance measurement and evaluation are potentially useful means of providing feedback on the degree to which behaviors are congruent with organizational strategies. Likewise, they are all potentially useful means, although to varying degrees, of informing reward systems of the extent to which employees are deserving of increased compensation, promotions, recognition, and the like. Further, they are all potentially valid sources of guidance for future developmental efforts, although they differ in their appropriateness in this regard.

Performance Measurement Approaches

A number of evaluation approaches have been traditionally used for performance measurement. Some of the most common are management by objectives, graphic rating scales, and narratives. The most advanced performance evaluation systems are those utilizing behaviorally anchored rating scales. These approaches will be discussed in the following section, beginning with management by objectives.

Management by Objectives

Management by objectives (MBO) is a widely used performance evaluation approach. In the case of MBO, the linkage with the implementation of strategies is easy to establish because the objectives can be specified as outcomes or milestones in the strategy implementation process. MBO typically begins with an initial phase in which the subordinate generates goals or objectives to be accomplished over the next time period. As a part of this process, the subordinate specifies the measures by which accomplishment of such objectives will be determined and outlines action plans he or she will use to achieve these objectives. The superior also generates objectives for the subordinate and then meets with the subordinate to work out a joint agreement. At the end of the next time period, the subordinate is evaluated on the extent to which the objectives were accomplished and the existence of factors beyond the subordinate's control that may have affected objective accomplishment. Unfortunately, as with all performance evaluation approaches, MBO has disadvantages as well. Objectives for some jobs are more difficult to write, such as for staff jobs, and problems occur when objectives are not well thought out. Further, the process may be viewed with cynicism if higher-level executives are not evaluated by MBO.[2]

Despite its disadvantages, a recent survey of *Fortune* 100 firms found that MBO was used by 80 percent of the respondents to evaluate executives and managers while 70 percent of the respondents used the approach for professionals. Furthermore, as with all evaluation approaches, organizations sometimes offset their disadvantages and take advantage of the strengths of various evaluation approaches by combining MBO, graphic rating scales, narratives, and other approaches.[3]

Graphic Rating Scales

The same survey also addressed the use of graphic rating scales and found that 31 percent of the *Fortune* 100 responding companies used such scales for nonexempt employees.[4] *Graphic rating scales* involve a format of multiple-interval response scales carrying numerical values with short descriptive anchors. For example, a seven-point scale might be used for an item tapping an employee's work quality. At the low end of the scale, the blank carrying a value of one might be anchored by characterization of "low quality of work" while the high-end blank carrying a value of seven would be anchored by a characterization of "high quality of work." Graphic rating scales differ in whether their anchors are absolute, such as in the example just provided, or relative. An example of a productivity scale constructed with relative anchors would be where the low end of the scale would be anchored with "one of the least productive" while the top end would be anchored with "one of the most productive." There is some evidence that anchors expressed in relative terms are superior to those expressed in absolute terms.[5]

Unfortunately, although graphic rating scales can be improved with the use of anchors expressed in relative terms, they are typically not anchored in terms of behaviors and often have items that measure only traits. However, an advantage of graphic rating scales is that their lack of behavioral specificity allows a standardized performance evaluation approach that can be used across large numbers of jobs. Organizations often find standardized approaches useful for comparison purposes, such as in developing a list of employees to be laid off on the basis of performance. However, because evaluators differ in the degree to which they are strict or lenient raters, some means of converting individual evaluators' ratings into a standardized score is required when evaluations are to be used for comparison purposes. Finally, the results of graphic rating scales are fairly easily translatable into numerical indices, which can then be used for determination of raises. However, they have somewhat limited value for use in developmental counseling.[6]

Narratives

Another traditional approach to performance evaluation is the *narrative* description of performance written by an employee's supervisor. Such approaches, which can be highly individualistic according to the unique aspects of the employee's job, are sometimes used with higher-level professionals and managerial personnel. Disadvantages to this approach are the writing skills required on the part of the evaluator and the time taken to write thoughtful narratives. Further, it is difficult to translate narratives into increases in compensation. Nonetheless, they are very useful in developmental counseling.

Behaviorally Anchored Rating Scales

The most advanced of the approaches to performance evaluation are *behaviorally anchored rating scales* (BARS). With BARS approaches, job incumbents are evaluated according to their performance on a relatively small set of job dimensions. A major advantage of the approach is that for each dimension, specific anchor points on the rating scale are provided in the form of observable behaviors. Thus, the evaluator is not forced to choose between the ambiguous meanings of adjective or numerical scale values. For example, in rating an employee's performance as a consumer credit representative in handling denials of credit, the rater does not have to decide whether the employee merits a rating of 6 or 7 on a 10-point scale. With the BARS approach, the evaluator typically chooses among an array of observable behaviors for the one that is most representative. In the case of the credit representative, such behaviors might range from "tactfully informs the customer that credit cannot be extended at this time and encourages the customer to reapply at a later date" to "tells customer that he or she is a bad credit risk and that it would be pointless to reapply." Because the evaluator is reporting observations, rather than making inferences about the mental processes of an employee, there may be increased validity and less likelihood of bias. Unfortunately, research to date on BARS has not yet demonstrated that they are superior to other rating approaches in interrater reliability or in reducing leniency or halo errors. (Halo errors occur when an outstanding rating on one dimension of performance carries over to affect ratings on other dimensions.)[7]

In spite of the failure of research to demonstrate the superiority of BARS, the greatest contribution of the BARS approach may be through its role as a feedback mechanism. Because of its focus on behaviors, the use of BARS may be less likely to lead to employee defensiveness and the feedback may be heard. Likewise, the BARS format produces ratings that are directly useful in developmental counseling because the employee knows the behaviors that should be adopted or discontinued. Further, its behavioral anchors carry numerical values, which can be summed across performance dimensions to provide an index translatable into merit increases in compensation. Unfortunately, BARS are applicable to only the specific jobs for which they are developed. As a result, it is practical to use them only for jobs having large numbers of incumbents because of their considerable developmental expense and the statistical expertise required. This is unfortunate, because further up the job hierarchy, there are ordinarily fewer job incumbents at the managerial and professional levels. However, large organizations may have sufficient numbers of managers at lower levels, such as sales managers, store managers, and the like to justify their development. Likewise, many organizations have lower-level professional jobs with many incumbents, such as staff accountants, insurance claims adjusters, and registered nurses, who could be evaluated with BARS.[8]

Behavioral Observation Scales

Behavioral observation scales (BOS) are a variation of the BARS approach in that they add graphic rating scales to the observable behaviors that are developed from critical incidents as in BARS. Each of these observable behaviors and their response scales constitute a rating item, and there are multiple items for each dimension of performance. Ratings on each item are summed to produce a quantitative evaluation of performance in each dimension. Thus, instead of choosing which observable behavior within a dimension is the most characteristic of the employee's performance, the evaluator rates several observable behaviors.[9]

360-Degree Feedback

Performance feedback from superiors, peers, and subordinates can provide good information for developmental purposes. One of the problems with performance evaluations in which only superiors rate their subordinates is that performance is evaluated from only one direction or perspective. While a manager may appear to be performing well when viewed from above, a very different evaluation may be obtained if evaluated from below from the subordinate's perspective. For example, a manager may be taking driving subordinates in order to achieve short-term results instead of leading, motivating, and developing them for the future. In addition, when viewed from a horizontal perspective, a manager's peers at the same level may have a very different evaluation as well, particularly if the manager does not cooperate with other departments and focuses only on the welfare of his or her own unit to the detriment of the organization as a whole. Because of these limitations of traditional top-down performance evaluation approaches, it is no surprise that *360-degree feedback* systems have been almost universally adopted among *Fortune* 500 firms and in many other companies. Companies using 360-degree feedback systems include Shell Oil, Exxon, IBM, Caterpillar, GE, AT&T and Levi Strauss.[10] Otis Elevator has even implemented a 360-degree feedback system on the Internet with encryption for security purposes. Evaluators can simply perform the evaluation by clicking on the Internet site where the forms are provided and e-mail it to the consulting firm that summarizes the evaluations.[11]

Evaluators in 360-degree feedback systems can include superiors, peers, subordinates, and even major customers. By using evaluations from each of these constituencies, a much more comprehensive picture of a manager's developmental needs can be obtained. In addition, because the ratings in 360-degree feedback systems can be anonymous, a much more honest evaluation may be possible. The 360-degree feedback system also is better suited to the interdependent nature of many of today's organizations, which are decreasing their reliance on centralized control and hierarchical decision making.[12]

As with any system, there can be problems with the implementation of 360-degree feedback systems. For example, the 360-degree feedback system is supposed to be more appropriate for developmental purposes than for appraisal purposes. Nonetheless, they are sometimes used for performance appraisal where anonymity and breaches of privacy can become major issues. Because so many people are involved in 360-degree feedback systems, there is substantial likelihood that evaluators will discuss the ratings with others and violate the manager's privacy. Thus, there are real challenges to the confidentiality and privacy of the system. When used for appraisal purposes, there is much room for mischief and self-serving behaviors because anonymous evaluators could intentionally evaluate a manager lower than he or she should be in order to increase their own chances for a promotion. In addition, there is greater likelihood that rating biases will influence evaluations because so many evaluators are involved and there is less assurance that all have been adequately trained to provide valid evaluations. In order to prevent this source of inaccuracy, organizations should train their raters before implementing 360-degree feedback systems.[13]

While there are problems with 360-degree feedback systems, just as with other evaluation systems, the approach has substantial potential to resolve many of the problems of more traditional approaches to developmental feedback and performance appraisal. In addition, some of its limitations as a performance appraisal approach also may be overcome.

Performance Evaluation of Executives

In spite of the value of performance evaluation systems, Longenecker and Gioia have found that such systems are not used very frequently for executives. More specifically, "the higher one rises in an organization the less likely one is to receive quality feedback about job performance."[14] Several questionable beliefs or myths are apparently responsible for the low regard for performance evaluation at the executive level. These myths are that performance evaluation is (1) not needed or desired by executives, (2) inconsistent with an executive's dignity, (3) too time consuming for the schedules of the superiors of executives, (4) detrimental to executive creativity and autonomy, (5) irrelevant since executives must meet "bottom line" criteria, and (6) executive performance is too intangible for description. Nonetheless, Longenecker and Gioia found that these myths lack a factual basis. In marked contrast, their research found that executives desire feedback and that even though bottom line results are critical for executives, they still need process-type feedback. Further, when executive performance is considered too intangible for description, the vacuum of explanation may be filled by political explanations. Some suggestions may be helpful in encouraging the use of performance evaluation at executive levels. For example, the process should utilize written narratives instead of standard rating forms because of the highly individualistic nature of executive work. It should also include clarification of organizational goals, discussions of how success will be defined, and assessment of the executive's management style. Also, the process should be a regularly occurring activity and should be based on both process considerations and outcomes.[15]

Effectiveness of Performance Measurement

Human resource managers are sometimes criticized for the attention they place on the format of evaluation instead of the management of the evaluation process. Even the most unsophisticated evaluation approach can be effective while the most sophisticated can be ineffective. When employees understand the dimensions of performance on which they will be evaluated, know that they are being evaluated on relevant aspects of their jobs, view the evaluation process as valid, feel that their evaluations are fair, and see reward contingencies, they will "buy in" to the evaluation system. At this point, the evaluation system can help strategy implementation. Further, performance evaluation will have a greater impact on strategy implementation when evaluators make meaningful distinctions among different levels of performance. Unfortunately, there have always been political aspects of performance evaluation that reduce its effectiveness, such as when evaluators rate subordinates lower than they deserve in order to establish managerial authority, encourage them to leave, or establish a convincing paper trail in the event that the employee is terminated.[16]

STRATEGICALLY ORIENTED COMPENSATION SYSTEMS

One of the critical means by which organizations implement their strategies is to reward employees for behaviors that are consistent with strategic goals. Reward systems provide the ability to reinforce desired behaviors and serve the traditional functions of attracting and maintaining a qualified workforce. Because of the centrality of compensation to strategy, the following discussion will focus only on rewards distributed through compensation systems. As indicated earlier in this chapter, a critical determinant of whether a strategy will be successfully implemented is the degree of flexibility of the workforce. In order to gain more flexibility from their workforces, many organizations have implemented new compensation approaches. Four of the more well-known compensation innovations are (1) skill-based pay, (2) broadbanding, (3) team-based pay, and (4) variable compensation. These approaches will be examined in this section along with executive compensation. However, before examining these approaches, a review of traditional compensation systems should be helpful.

Traditional Compensation Systems

Millions of employees are compensated through traditional job-based pay systems. Such systems typically incorporate the use of *job analysis* to determine the knowledge, skills, and abilities required to perform jobs. Job analysis information is then incorporated into the process of *job evaluation*, which determines the relative standing of each job in the salary or wage hierarchy of an organization. Essentially, the process of job evaluation involves a review of each job to determine the extent to which *compensable factors* are present. Typically, jobs are evaluated on only a small set of compensable factors such as knowledge, knowhow, accountability, effort, and problem solving. The *point system* is a common job evaluation approach, which uses a job evaluation manual to assign points to each job on the basis of compensable factors. Another job evaluation system is the *factor comparison system*, which involves a rather complicated approach of comparing jobs directly with each other in order to determine differences in the presence of compensable factors. *Hybrid systems*, which often involve a combination of the point system and factor comparison system, also are widely used. An example of a hybrid system is the *Hay Guide Profile Method.* Traditional approaches involving job evaluation are used to determine *internal equity* or fairness in compensation among jobs in an organization. Salary surveys are then used to determine *external equity* with market rates. Managers then set rates of compensation by balancing considerations of internal and external equity.[17]

Strategic Inadequacies of Traditional Compensation Approaches

Unfortunately, traditional compensation systems leave much to be desired from a strategic perspective. One of the strongest criticisms involves the evaluation of jobs on compensable factors such as problems solving or know-how. By assigning differential points to various jobs on the basis of these factors, the process tells job incumbents—whose jobs are evaluated low on problem solving or know-how—that they are not being paid to solve problems or think. A further criticism is that because of the job-based focus, each employee is compensated only for the performance of a specific job. Thus, the compensation system introduces constraints on managers' flexibility in utilizing the workforce. When a person is asked to perform work outside of his or her job classification, there are problems in assignment of a pay rate to such jobs. The presence of a union complicates this further as the pay rates for the various job classifications are the result of collective bargaining. Additionally, traditional compensation systems do not work well with managers and professionals. With such employees, the job-based focus of traditional systems conflicts with the individualized nature of their work. With increasing professionalization of the workforce, the importance of this problem will be magnified. To summarize, when compensation systems limit workforce flexibility and discourage workers from using their intelligence, they cannot facilitate the implementation of today's competitive strategies.[18]

Skill-Based Pay

Skill-based pay or *knowledge-based pay*, in contrast to traditional compensation approaches, focuses on the individual, not the job. In fact, with skill-based pay, employees perform a number of jobs and receive the same pay rate, irrespective of the job. As noted earlier, in Chaparral Steel's application of skill-based pay, there are only two general job classifications in its production environment. With skill-based pay, employees are able to increase their compensation as they acquire a broader range of skills. Thus, they have a strong incentive to learn. With the rapid rate of change in today's business environment and the need for flexible assignment of work, there is an obvious need for employees to develop or broaden their skill repertoires.[19] The flexibility of skill-based pay is revealed in the following description of its application in a container plant:

> For example, a plant technician at the top of the skill range may work on electrical assignments when such work needs to be done or may be assigned to quality assurance or to operate a specific machine if no electrical problems require attention.[20]

Because of such characteristics, companies dealing with stiff foreign competition have a higher propensity to implement skill-based pay approaches. Likewise, in companies in which promotional opportunities have been reduced because of the delayering of organizational structures, there also are higher propensities to implement skill-based pay.[21] The extent of skill-based pay usage is revealed by a survey, which found that 51 percent of responding companies had implemented the approach. However, companies generally apply this pay approach to fewer than 20 percent of their employees.[22]

Because of the advantages of skill-based pay, numerous companies have adopted this approach. For example, General Mills, Northern Telecom, and Honeywell have substantial experience with skill-based pay. Skill-based pay approaches have been frequently implemented in high-involvement manufacturing settings, and they also are being implemented in service environments. Although there are variations in how skill-based pay is implemented, employees typically start out at a base rate and increase their compensation as they master a sequence of skill blocks. Typically, employees take several years to master the content of all skill blocks because they are generally fairly broad. For example, at a General Mills plant, all of the production processes are contained in four skill blocks. One of the more difficult aspects involved in the administration of skill-based pay involves the determination of the amount of pay that should be assigned to skill blocks. Nonetheless, market survey data are often used to establish the range and average values for skill blocks.[23]

Skill-based pay is often implemented in conjunction with semiautonomous work teams. In such applications, employees master the skills required for a job and then rotate into another job in the team until its skills are mastered, and then into the next, and so on. Upon completion of the rotation, the employee can then move into another team and acquire more skills by rotating through its various jobs. Certification and recertification of skill block mastery is assessed through various approaches. Testing approaches, which constitute one means of certification, often involve sample observations of work, written tests, and oral examinations. Other certification approaches include assessment by multiple evaluators, including supervisors, peers, technical experts, management committees, and human resource personnel. Skill-based pay's focus on compensation for skills also is contained in approaches used with professional employees who are paid according to maturity curves. In maturity curve approaches, with increasing experience and development following the completion of formal education, professionals receive increased compensation.[24]

Aside from the flexibility advantages already noted, skill-based pay also has some other desirable effects although average wage rates tend to be higher. An important advantage is that the costs of higher wages are offset by higher productivity and increased quality. Other advantages include employees' heightened motivation for training, greater task variety, employee-induced pressures on companies to provide training, and increases in employees' self-esteem, which accompany the acquisition of skills. With skill-based pay, it also is easy to fill in for absences because of the availability of cross-trained employees. Skill-based pay also tends to give employees a broader understanding of production processes. Further, because employees gain compensation increases by expanding their skill sets, seniority is not the determinant of progression to higher-paying jobs. Another advantage of skill-based pay is that it provides greater job security for employees because they can perform a wider range of jobs.[25]

Often skill-based pay is implemented in conjunction with total quality management (TQM) programs because higher quality often requires more highly skilled employees. It also is implemented frequently in participative environments, and as noted earlier, in conjunction with semiautonomous work groups or self-managed teams. With teams, participative management, and high-involvement environments, employees can make meaningful contributions that result from their broader understanding of the production environment.[26]

Although there are numerous benefits of skill-based pay, there are also problems, as with any other compensation approach. One problem involves compensating employees who have topped out on the skill progression. For these employees, some observers have recommended incentives in the form of gain sharing, in which benefits from cost reductions or increased productivity are passed on to employees. Another problem is that training is frequently insufficient to support skill-based pay approaches. Some managers have even been reluctant to release sufficient funds from their training budgets to support skill-based pay.[27]

Broadbanding

In contrast to skill-based pay, *broadbanding* retains some of the components of the traditional approaches described earlier, such as a job focus and some utilization of job evaluation for *key jobs*—visible jobs having identifiable market wage rates. However, like skill-based pay, broadbanding can be helpful in strategy implementation because it is directed toward obtaining greater flexibility. Typically, broadbanding involves a reduction in the number of salary bands (pay grades). Interestingly, General Electric was able to reduce its number of bands to five for all employees. With broadbanding, the organization might reduce its salary bands for white-collar employees to three. For example, the first band for professionals might range from $55,000 to $91,000, the second for management might range from $58,000 to $121,000, and a third for leadership might range from $110,000 to $205,000. As these salary levels indicate, the salary ranges within each band cover a wide range of compensation. The advantage of maintaining fewer bands is that employees' salaries can be raised substantially even without a promotion. Likewise, employees' salaries could conceivably be reduced without resort to a demotion.[28]

Broadbanding is used frequently in conjunction with other changes that facilitate strategy implementation. For example, it may be used with reengineering, delayering of organizational hierarchies, employee empowerment efforts, and cross-functional initiatives. Although a very different compensation approach than skill-based pay, it also encourages skill acquisition and development. With broadbanding, an employee who is paid the market value for a job, such as $56,000 for the professional band, can earn more by acquiring more skills. A second-generation version of broadbanding abandons most of the traditional compensation system components, such as job evaluation, and shifts to an individual focus rather than a job focus. For example, the second-generation approach would develop a market value for an individual based on his or her individual skills.[29]

In moving toward a broadbanding approach, some of the same advice applies as with conventional compensation systems. There must be sufficient employee understanding of the salary determination process, trust, a culture that emphasizes performance, and sufficient communication. Employees also must be aware of the skills that must be mastered for increased compensation as well as the means for their acquisition.[30]

Team-Based Pay

With the growing importance of work teams noted in earlier chapters, compensation systems are needed to reward team members for behavior that facilitates strategy implementation. *Team-based pay* is being used more frequently in such settings. Typically, team-based pay is operationalized by specifying a goal or desired outcome and then allocating to all team members a reward for its accomplishment. Objective goals or outcomes are commonly specified, such as production levels, cost savings, or project completions, although goals also may be some form of subjective executive assessment. A wide variety of rewards may be used, cash as bonuses, stock ownership, trips, and time off from work.[31]

Team-based pay offers a number of advantages, one of which is that it overcomes the difficult problem of measuring individual contributions. Another advantage is that it is likely to facilitate cooperation. Further, bonuses to teams, such as for the completion of a major project, can be given very shortly after the event, thereby strongly linking desired behaviors with desired rewards. A further advantage of team approaches to compensation may occur where team rewards are linked to the development of skills. In situations in which the team reward is not given until all team members are cross-trained, the team members may help train or motivate those who have not yet acquired the necessary skills.[32]

One type of team setting that is likely to appear more frequently in the future is the research and development team. There is evidence that team-based pay systems have worked well in such settings. One study of research scientists and engineers specifically examined the effectiveness of team-based bonuses. The study examined the impact of such pay on several criteria of effectiveness, including performance on projects as well as individual performance, satisfaction with pay, and a measure of cognitive withdrawal or propensity to leave. The study found that team pay was superior to individual-based bonuses and merit pay when evaluated according to these criteria. In contrast, the individual-based forms of compensation were not significantly related with the criteria. Further, other aggregate compensation in the form of stock ownership plans and profit sharing tended to enhance the retention of employees. With any group- or team-based pay system, there is always a concern that some individuals may not do their share of work, preferring instead to be free riders on the efforts of more productive members. Interestingly, this study found that team members did not become free riders. Potential explanations for the absence of such behaviors include the combination of challenging work and the intrinsic motivation of professional employees.[33]

Team-based pay often involves some form of *gain sharing*. However, unlike gain-sharing approaches such as the Scanlon Plan or the Rucker Plan, the gains to be shared are sometimes linked to the accomplishment of strategic objectives. Some strategic objectives tend to be more ambiguous than tactical objectives and require commitment from employees because desirable performance on their part may also be difficult to specify. The Fibers Department at Du Pont provides an example of a very large-scale team-based approach that incorporated gain sharing. The department wished to increase the emphasis on participation and team work and decided to pursue a goal of increasing annual earnings by 4 percent.[34] The plan was operationalized as follows:

> The Achievement Sharing Program is being phased in over approximately five years. At the end of this period, Fibers Department employees will be earning 6 percent less in their base pay than their counterparts elsewhere in the company. If the department meets its annual profit, the employees will collect the 6 percent difference; if profits fall below 80 percent of the goal, they will receive a 3 percent bonus, and at 150 percent they will receive a 12 percent bonus.[35]

Unfortunately, the Du Pont plan, which also constituted a form of variable pay, was terminated two years after its implementation. The plan failed because of poor business conditions, which severely restricted or eliminated bonuses, and employees' failure to cope with the downside risk. The plan also conflicted with Du Pont's centralized culture and strategy by compensating employees for departmental results. The plan's failure highlights the importance of careful planning and preparation necessary for successful implementation of such compensation programs. In contrast to Du Pont's experience, Nucor Steel's gain-sharing plan has been in existence for over 25 years. Part of the success of Nucor's plan is probably due to its compatibility with the company's "no frills" culture.[36]

Because of the broader application of gain sharing, its impact on the productivity of white-collar workers has been the subject of recent research. An office of a large public accounting firm operationalized gain sharing as a percentage of labor savings, which were determined by subtracting actual labor costs from allowable labor costs. The study found that gain sharing increased productivity and that employees worked "smarter." [37]

Variable Compensation

Variable pay plans have been implemented by a number of companies, such as Xerox, Westinghouse, and Nucor Steel. A major purpose for such plans has been to create among employees a sense of shared destiny. Such plans seek to accomplish this purpose by linking a portion of employee compensation to various performance measures. A common element of such plans is the concept of having a portion of employees' compensation "at risk." [38] The rationale for variable compensation is appealing and, at first glance, seemingly uncomplicated. However, there is a level of complexity to these programs that must be understood.

An important consideration of variable pay plans is the form they will take. The first form is an increment to base pay, which is frequently called *add-on*. Bonuses based on company performance would constitute a form of add-on variable pay. The second is *at-risk* pay, which is normally operationalized by reducing employees' base pay by a certain percentage and then allowing them to receive various amounts of that percentage and more, depending on performance measures. The third form, "potential base pay at risk," is related to the second. This form of variable pay might be operationalized in situations in which the company has a tradition of steady raises, for example, averaging approximately 6 percent per year. This practice would be changed by allocating only 3 percent as a regular raise. The remaining 3 percent is set aside for allocation with greater increases if performance targets are met or exceeded. While there are no strict guidelines for identifying the circumstances in which these forms of variable pay are implemented, companies encountering heavy pressure to reduce labor costs are more likely to use at-risk variable pay. Companies dealing with less pressure might use add-on pay to pave the way for a later introduction of other forms of variable pay. They might also use add-on pay for very high performance standards.[39]

Another element of complexity with variable pay involves the measures of performance to which pay is to be linked. Unfortunately, the use of some seemingly rational performance measures can lead to very dysfunctional results. For example, if one links variable pay to the profitability of an insurance company, claims representatives may not pay customer accident claims as they should. If these same representatives are paid according to customer satisfaction, however, they may be too generous in the settlement of claims. In any event, the measures should reflect the organization's overall strategies. The range of measures may include profitability, improvements in quality, various financial ratios, and customer satisfaction. It is recommended that productivity not be defined in too narrow a fashion since some units could receive pay increases while the company becomes unprofitable.[40] Several recommendations regarding measures are presented in the following:

> Therefore, even though different goals are used, it is best that these measures not pay off unless the organization gains real bottom-line results. This is central to new variable pay. Productivity measures may be used at the team level as long as they do not result in awards when the organization's profit performance and quality have not improved . . . It is best for plans to generate awards only if both profit and productivity measures are satisfied.[41]

Aside from creating a feeling of shared destiny, another potential benefit of such plans is better labor cost control.[42] Variable pay plans may help provide employment security because with part of employees' compensation being derived from the company's profitability, with declines in business conditions and profits, total labor costs decline and employees may not need to be laid off.

Executive Compensation

The human resource function has been criticized for its failure to provide compensation systems that support companies' strategies. Probably the first and most important step needed to obtain alignment between strategy and compensation systems involves designing the system for compensating executives.[43] The impact of executive compensation systems has been described by Luis Gomez-Mejia and David Balkin as follows:

> Executive pay is perhaps the most crucial strategic factor at the organization's disposal. It can be used to direct managerial decisions and indirectly channel the behavior of subordinates. Because most organizations follow a pyramidal structure, whatever is rewarded at the top is likely to have a multiplier effect throughout all segments of the business . . . mechanisms used to reward executives are likely to have an enormous effect on the company's future.[44]

The approaches used for executives are obviously critical to the implementation of strategies. Unfortunately, the problems of executive compensation, particularly with chief executive officers, continue to be particularly troublesome in the United States and are a frequent subject of controversy to both employees and the public alike, particularly when executive compensation seems to run to excess. Regardless of the controversy, there is still need for sound executive compensation systems. For many years, executive compensation systems have involved a myriad of bonus systems, stock options, deferred compensation, and an elaborate set of perquisites. Nonetheless, there is increasing skepticism whether separate systems should exist for executives. Rosabeth Moss Kanter has described this problem as follows:

> Every year routine company surveys of employees find greater skepticism about the fairness of traditional pay practices. Every year the numbers seem to get worse, possibly because traditional practices are skewed toward rewarding the climb to high positions rather then [than] the contribution to organizational success.[45]

As a result of problems with compensation and the notion that compensation should be directed toward employees' contributions instead of their positions, Kanter has recommended the following: "Large executive bonuses or stock options should not be allowed at all unless comparable bonus systems exist for employees in general." [46] If Kanter's recommendations are an indicator of future reality, executive compensation systems will be largely indistinguishable from those of lower-level employees except for the magnitude of differentials based on contributions. However, in accordance with the compensation innovations presented in this chapter, lower-level employees also are likely to receive a larger component of their compensation in the form of variable pay and gain sharing.

EMPLOYEE DEVELOPMENT

Several approaches are available for the development of workforce skills that are needed for strategy implementation. The discussion of employee development will begin with training programs.

Training Programs

Companies having an investment perspective of human resource management view training as an opportunity to increase long-term productivity. Training also may be viewed as the solution to a number of problems, such as substandard quality resulting from skill deficiencies and voluntary turnover of employees seeking more rewarding jobs. It also may reduce involuntary turnover of employees who are terminated because of skill deficiencies and provide a means of preventing skill obsolescence. Aside from training's value in enhancing productivity and helping companies to avoid these problems, it also is a means for avoiding shortages of qualified workers.

At the lowest-level jobs in the skill hierarchy, there is a need for training in basic skills. Even the most basic skills of reading and writing cannot be taken for granted in today's environment. Because of these skill inadequacies, when there are labor shortages, companies may become more involved in remedial teaching. Further, with high levels of immigration, there will be a need to train immigrant workers in the United States cultural norms, language, values, and job expectations. Managers also may need training, such as in the immigrants' language and culture. Further, the disadvantaged and traditionally unemployed may need training in basic skills such as work norms.[47]

In addition to training at the lower end of the skill hierarchy, a common need for workers in today's information age is that they need more training in thinking skills or analytical skills. Workers need to have skills in drawing inferences, synthesizing, categorizing, and generalizing from data.[48] Professor Edward de Bono of Cambridge University has developed programs for teaching thinking skills and has trained thousands of individuals through these programs, including executives from major corporations. An interesting outcome of the information age has been that we now have vastly more information but will never have enough time to teach it. Therefore, we need to be better thinkers to benefit from this information.[49] Naisbitt and Aburdene have summarized this need as follows:

> The more information we have, the more we need to be competent thinkers. This is the quandary of the information society: We have an overabundance of data. But we lack the intelligence, the thinking ability, with which to sort it all out. That is why thinking is now as basic as reading.[50]

Unfortunately, training programs often focus on mid- to upper-level managers and do not place much emphasis on lower-level employees.[51] The survey results in Table 7-1 indicate that salespeople, professionals, and first-line supervisors receive the most training: 40.7, 35.5, and 35.4 hours per year, respectively. Further, middle managers, first-line supervisors, and executives are the most likely to receive training, with 75.9, 73.3, and 67.3 percent of companies providing such training, respectively. In contrast, production workers are the least likely to receive training as only 33.3 percent, respectively, of organizations provide such training.[52]

Aside from an uneven distribution of training across job categories, the extent to which companies provide training over time also is irregular. During good economic times, many corporations invest heavily in the training of their employees. Even though the cyclical nature of training is well known, some observers have became convinced of the commitment of U.S. companies to

TABLE 7-1 Distribution of Training by Job Category

Job Category	*Percent of Organizations Providing Training*	*Mean Number of Hours Delivered*
Middle Managers	75.9	35.1
Professionals	59.6	35.5
Executives	67.3	32.9
Salespeople	40.4	40.7
First-Line Supervisors	73.3	35.4
Senior Managers	58.5	31.2
Production Workers	33.3	30.7
Customer Service People	45.0	33.0
Office/Administrative Workers	66.7	19.0

Source: Extracted from Jack Gordon. "Where the Training Goes," *Training* 27, no. 10 (1990): 52. Reprinted with permission from the October issue of *Training* magazine.

training. For example, trend forecasters Naisbitt and Aburdene concluded the following:

> The recognition that people are a company's critical resource—and its greatest storehouse of knowledge—is creating a boom in corporate training and education. Corporations are finally willing to invest in people and their skills through training and education to the degree that they have always invested in equipment.[53]

Unfortunately, while it is hoped that this excerpt characterizes the current commitment of companies to training, past practices indicate that when economic activity wanes many companies slash their training outlays. Thus, the commitment that Naisbitt and Aburdene observed may be illusory, at least in some companies. An additional problem is that for training to be most effective, it needs to be systematic and continuous. Companies that conduct training on a "boom-and-bust" basis are unlikely to develop the kinds of human resources they need to gain a competitive advantage. Nonetheless, there are excellent companies that demonstrate a genuine commitment to their human resources, such as Motorola. A sense of this commitment is provided by a comment from a previous chief executive officer of Motorola, who stated that people are "the ultimate high technology." [54] Further, such comments are more than just rhetoric at Motorola. For example, the company is teaching automated production concepts to its production employees, even those who have previously performed only manual assembly work. In this training, employees learn concepts of computer-integrated manufacturing (CIM) and receive hands-on experience in programming robots.[55] "One of Motorola's goals is for manufacturing employees at all levels to achieve literacy in modern automated factory concepts." [56] Similarly, Corning, Inc. is investing heavily in training its employees, particularly as a part of its efforts to improve quality. All of Corning's employees have received two days of training in quality, and each year 5 percent of each employee's hours are devoted to training. Corning is convinced that these investments in employee training have paid off in improved quality.[57]

Training Methods

Training covers a broad area of human resource activities. Because of its breadth and importance, medium- and larger-sized companies typically have specialized training staffs. Although training is an area of specialization, general managers should be acquainted with several general training methods and instructional approaches. The methods discussed in this section include orientation training, socialization of new employees, on-the-job training (OJT), apprenticeships, coaching, mentoring, computer-based training, computer-assisted instruction, and experiential training. Job rotation also will be considered as a component in management development programs.[58] Apprenticeships and management development will be covered later in greater depth. Many specifics of both on-the-job training and management development were covered in Chapter 1 as part of a discussion of an investment perspective toward human resources.

Larger organizations generally have some type of *orientation program* for new employees. This training is important because it provides the first real work contact with the company and the first opportunity for new employees to develop an understanding of the company's culture. Because of its importance, some companies are very careful about the content and approach of their orientation programs so as to impart a particular impression. One useful suggestion for orientation and socialization is to assign an experienced employee to be the sponsor of each new employee. During this training, employees are actually introduced to the company's norms and values. In designing orientation programs, it is probably advisable to place greater emphasis on imparting the company's values to new employees, with less emphasis being placed on details, such as the technical issues of health care programs and retirement plans. With respect to the latter, employees should be given only "survival skills" or only enough information to get them through the first few weeks of employment. Details can be provided at a more leisurely pace when there is more time and less chance for information overload.[59]

Socialization of new employees is extremely critical because it can have a major impact on employees' understandings of such basic cultural norms as the company's performance expectations. Socialization also is important because turnover often occurs during the early months of employment.[60] Such turnover frequently occurs because there are delays before new employees become "permanent" members of work groups. In their permanent work groups, new employees form friendships, begin to make real contributions to the company, gain acceptance, and learn "how things really work." [61] Unfortunately, quick entry into a permanent work group is at odds with job rotational approaches for new managerial employees. In rotational program approaches, trainees may be rotated from one functional area to another after assignments of two or three months. Only after completion of the rotational phase are trainees given a permanent assignment. The logic of such approaches is that the trainees will have a broader understanding of the company and how the components fit together. One means of reducing the turnover associated with rotational programs is to move new trainees in pairs or small groups to each new temporary assignment. In this manner, they have some peer group support and can begin to develop permanent friendships and support systems within their group. They also should be assigned "real" work, which provides a challenge and receive frequent and timely feedback.[62]

Coaching consists of the day-to-day feedback, instruction, and advice provided by the employee's supervisor. Some observers have noted that the first supervisor is very critical to an employee's career. This is because basic values, performance standards, confidence in one's proficiency, and skills are developed by the first supervisor. Unfortunately, the importance of this assignment is often overlooked and opportunities are lost when new employees are assigned to mediocre supervisors.[63]

Mentoring is another important method for training managers and professionals. Many of the subtle skills needed to advance to the highest-level positions are learned through mentoring relationships. Aside from providing viable role models, candid feedback, instruction, insights into the company's politics, advice, and other support, mentors also serve in other valuable capacities. Mentors are frequently in the position of sponsors who help their proteges gain visibility and responsibility. One of the barriers to the advancement of women to the top positions of their companies has probably been the lack of female mentors in male-dominated career fields. Although men are sometimes the mentors of women and women the mentors of men, mixed genders introduce special complexities such as concerns about how others may perceive the relationship.[64] An example of problems of perceptions and their heavy toll on those involved is provided by the case of Mary Cunningham, a young Harvard MBA, and Bill Agee, the CEO at the former Bendix Corporation, now part of Honeywell.[65]

Aside from providing an invaluable service to the developing manager or professional and the organization, mentoring can provide a great deal of satisfaction to the mentor. Mentors are usually 8 to 15 years older than the junior employee. Given the age and experience requirements, mentoring would be expected to begin at the midpoint of managers' and professionals' careers. Nonetheless, contrary to intuition, both younger managers in their thirties and managers over 50 appear to have stronger interests in serving as mentors than those in the midstages of their careers. An interesting explanation is that midcareer individuals are not as available for mentoring roles because they themselves are often preoccupied with midlife crisis and the accompanying self-doubts and anxieties about the future. Mentoring can be a particularly valuable role for a manager who has reached a relatively high level in the company, but who will not be promoted further. Likewise, for those in the latter part of their career cycles, who may have stepped down from the highest positions, mentoring may be a very important role. Finally, in contrast to expectations, mentoring activity tends to increase during times of corporate stress, such as during downsizing. This is because for the mentor, the activity provides a source of esteem perhaps not otherwise available because of curtailed opportunities for advancement, and the like, and the junior employee may seek out mentors during such times for coaching and guidance.[66]

Computer-based training or *instruction* involves computer-generated presentation of material, through video and audio media, with interaction on the part of the student. For example, material may be presented in a format that requires the student to respond. The student's correct responses then receive positive reinforcement from the computer and incorrect responses are diagnosed, followed by additional instruction until the correct response is learned.[67] An example of such training is provided by the American Airlines Flight Academy, which uses such an approach for transition training, in which pilots and flight engineers learn to operate another type of aircraft. It also is used for upgrade training, such as in the case of flight engineers preparing for copilot duties.[68] An example of this training is provided in the following:

> American's Flight Academy, adjacent to Dallas/Ft. Worth International Airport, has 85 microcomputer high-resolution, color touch-screen monitors linked with audio tapes and slide projectors to present coursework and testing for pilots' transition training . . . A pilot beginning the day goes to the library and pulls the binder containing the program he or she is to work on that day . . . tapes, a slide tray, and a script . . . There are generally about 60–70 programs for a transition course, each lasting about 8–10 min., explaining the nature of a specific aircraft system or set of controls . . . After each presentation, with the pace controlled by the pilot, the crewmember is tested to determine whether he or she can do what is required, such as set up the hydraulic panel using the touch screen. A correct response lets the program proceed. If the pilot answers incorrectly, the system will set up the panel correctly, and the slide device and audio tape come on to explain why the answer was incorrect.[69]

This computer-based instruction is in addition to the very complex and expensive flight simulation training that American Airlines conducts on 20 flight simulators. These simulators are designed for specific aircraft, such as the Boeing models 767 and 727, McDonnell Douglas (now Boeing) models MD-80, DC-10, and the Airbus A300-600R. American's training operations are extensive. In a recent year, the company expected to conduct over 100,000 pilot man-days of training at the academy.[70]

Another example of computer-based instruction is one for training sales personnel, which builds in role-playing:

> Using a video camera mounted above the monitor, the student is filmed interacting with the customer segments, contained on a laser disk. The interface is an IBM Info-Window monitor with a touch screen. The final tape merges the student's and customer's responses for review.[71]

Interestingly, computer-based instruction or training has low delivery costs but is expensive to develop. In contrast, the lecture instructional approach involves low development costs but is very expensive to deliver. Nonetheless, the advantages of computer-based instruction are meaningful. It can be readily available and accessible on demand at the student's convenience, allows for self-pacing, and provides for active involvement through the interactive features of computerization. It also provides in-progress testing, reinforcement, and remedial training based on incorrect responses, and can be operated on a stand-alone basis. Such training also provides standardized training that can be widely disseminated within a company, and can provide realistic simulation of pragmatic work simulations.[72]

Another training approach is called *computer-assisted instruction.* In this approach, the computer may not be the primary instructional mode but may be used to augment more conventional training. The distinction between the terms is somewhat blurred because they are sometimes used interchangeably. Nonetheless, computer-assisted instruction seems to have a more general connotation. In recent years, there has been a substantial amount of research in the management information systems literature on how to design human–computer interfaces in computer-assisted training so as to obtain active involvement of the student. One important finding is that the design can have a significant impact on learning effectiveness.[73] Obviously, the Internet has tremendous ability to supply training. Companies and universities are rushing to increase their distance learning capabilities and taking advantage of the Internet's capabilities. For example, Duke University now offers an Executive MBA over the Internet. Several other universities also offer masters' degrees on the Internet.

Apprenticeships

Apprenticeship programs are not used extensively in the United States. Currently, they involve a very small proportion of the workforce, estimated to be only 0.16 percent. In contrast, apprenticeships involve 6.5 percent of the workforce in Germany.[74] Apprenticeship programs are most highly developed in Germany, where they lead to examination and certification in approximately 400 occupations.[75] As institutionalized in Germany, "About 65 percent of each class of middle school graduates enter apprenticeship training in fields ranging from skilled manufacturing to office work. Over 3 years, these would-be-apprentices spend 4 days per week in on-the-job training and at least 1 day per week at a state-supported vocational school."[76] The majority of students involved in the apprenticeship program, also called *dual training*, begin when they are 15 or 16 years old and finish in three years.[77]

German students not going on to college see the value of making good grades because scholastic performance is one of the factors employers consider in selecting apprentices. Further, students see that completing an apprenticeship and passing the examination for certification leads to a good job with attractive compensation. Following completion of their training programs, large German manufacturing companies retain approximately 80 to 90 percent of their apprentices as regular, long-term employees, and placement rates are high for all sizes of companies. At six months after successful completion of their certification examinations, 68 percent of German apprentices have jobs in the occupations in which they apprenticed. In contrast, in the United States, unless one is going on to college, the grades one makes in elementary school and high school are not an important determinant of employment because the jobs typically require only low skill and provide low pay. Therefore, there is little incentive to do well in school.[78]

German employers spend approximately two times as much on worker training than their counterparts in the United States. Further, their investments in apprenticeship training are partially funded by the German government. However, they usually do not pay apprentices the regular wage rate, typically lower than one-third of the regular rate. German firms also benefit from apprenticeships through the increased productivity of their workforce as well as stronger relationships among workers and supervisors. Supervisors and managers tend to understand the jobs of their subordinates because many of them were trained in apprenticeship programs.[79]

Unfortunately, there are a number of barriers or arguments in opposition to the adoption of German-type apprenticeship programs in the United States. One anticipated argument is that students will be forced to make the critical decision whether to pursue a vocational or university track while they are too young. Clearly, there will be a need for greater career awareness so that students can make informed decisions. Another argument is that because of the narrower focus of apprenticeship programs, students will not have sufficient breadth in their educations. A counter to this is that many students are already dissatisfied with school at a relatively early age and drop out anyway under the current system. Another argument is that because of the specificity of the training, the skills learned will become obsolete too quickly. This is not necessarily true because some skills can have broad applications. A final argument is that disadvantaged students, who are more likely to be minorities, will be disproportionately represented in the vocational track. As a result, they will have limited occupational mobility and truncated career paths. Unfortunately, the current reality is that the occupational outlook for disadvantaged youth is already abysmal and limited by the absence of networking relationships for good jobs. Apprenticeship programs provide employment relationships, networks, and mentorships that help build good work habits and self-esteem.[80]

Interestingly, as good jobs offering career prospects for young people in the United States have become increasingly bleak for those without extensive education, there is some attention on apprenticeship programs. U.S. employers facing competition from Germany, Japan, and China have great need for technically qualified workforces and may become the champions of apprenticeship programs. For example, Sears has been involved in a pilot apprenticeship program in appliance repair. In the program, students attend high school half of the day and then, during the other half, participate in an apprenticeship program designed by Sears. The program is paid for by their high school and a grant of federal money through the National Alliance of Business. Other apprenticeship programs are being conducted for surgical technicians, medical secretaries, metalworkers, accountants, and printing. Such programs should counter employer complaints that high school graduates do not have the knowledge required in today's more technological work environment. Unfortunately, in the United States, as contrasted with Germany and Britain, there is no comprehensive system for administering apprenticeship training. The German program is well integrated into the educational system. In Britain, students of ages 16 and 17 who have discontinued their schooling are guaranteed two years of such training.[81]

Management Development

Approaches to management development commonly emphasize *job rotation* through successively more responsible positions. Unfortunately, past organizational restructuring has eliminated many positions in the middle-management training ground. It may be challenging to groom managers for top-level positions in organizations in which middle-management positions have been eliminated.[82] As a result, there may be more management development efforts in the future that utilize rotating leaderships of task forces or product development teams.

However, one of the most commonly used approaches of management development is still the rotation of managers through successively more responsible positions or a combination of broadening assignments and vertical assignments. A departure from these traditional rotational programs involves *cross-functional assignments*. An important insight into these assignments is provided in the following description:

> While expertise-oriented managers are the bedrock of any organization, they succumb to Peter Principle traps when in leadership positions . . . But if one moves a manager who is thought to have leadership potential to another area of expertise, that person is obligated to develop leadership skills in delivering results through people who have more expertise. The duration of this cross-functional job should be at least 3–4 years (contrary to the practice of many firms)—otherwise people will only develop skills in starting things off, not in implementation and execution.[83]

A good description of management training practices is provided by a study that surveyed training practices for managerial personnel in 611 companies having at least 1,000 employees. Although systematic assessment of formal training would seem prudent, the study found that only 27 percent of the responding companies reported having needs assessment procedures. However, needs assessment and company size were significantly correlated as larger companies are more likely to have needs assessment procedures. A number of other important aspects of training also were found related to company size. Larger companies were more likely to involve their managerial employees in formal training programs, more likely to use job rotation as a training or development approach, and more likely to conduct career planning. There also were some significant industry differences as service industry companies were least likely to use job rotation as a management training approach and also were least likely to send their managers through university management development programs.[84]

One of the major results of the study was that the respondents expected to do more managerial training in the future in order to keep managers informed on current concepts and update their skills. The respondents also expected more managerial training in the future because of more corporate-level emphasis. Furthermore, managerial participation in such training was required by written policies in 22 percent of the companies.[85] Another study provides empirical evidence of performance-related differences in approaches toward training and development in the retailing industry. In this study, one of the good performers implemented a major change in strategy during a period of decline. As part of the change, the company increased its emphasis on training, particularly of a strategic nature, such as competitor analysis. In contrast, the poor performers either stopped or scaled back their programs.[86]

In addition to future changes in the amount and type of training, the speed of development has already changed. In the past, exceptionally talented individuals were developed for the highest positions through fast-track management development programs. For example, over a period of 32 years, Edgar S. Woolard Jr., moved through 20 jobs before he became the chief executive officer of Du Pont. While his tenure in these jobs ranged from only five months to three years, his experience was not unusual for fast trackers as promotions came after an average of 18 to 24 months on the job. Because of reductions in the numbers of middle-management jobs and the glut of the baby boomers, the rate of promotions has slowed dramatically.[87]

In spite of developmental slowdowns and a reduction in the middle-management training ground, there are still means for developing high-talent managers. One approach is to use lateral moves. By making *lateral assignments* of both average performers and stars, there is less chance that the assignment will be perceived as dead end. Increases in the span of supervision and magnitude of responsibility without vertical movement also can promote development. Specific examples are PepsiCo's use of lateral assignments for approximately 60 percent of its management-track assignments, and Hughes Aircraft's use of lateral moves in which electrical engineers are assigned to quality control. An obvious advantage of these lateral moves and the *slow-track* approach is that the manager develops a broader understanding of the company and is on the job long enough to see more of the fruits of his or her efforts. Another example of an alternative developmental approach is Du Pont's assignment of managers to overseas posts as a prerequisite to top management positions.[88]

Management Development for International Assignments

The use of overseas assignments for development is in sharp contrast to the past when managers having poorer prospects for higher positions were relegated to international assignments, as indicated by the following quotation: "At Du Pont, where nearly half the sales are foreign, overseas tours are becoming *de rigueur* for eventual moves up." [89] Unfortunately, U.S. companies have often failed to provide adequate training for expatriate assignments and have been dissatisfied with cross-cultural training. Nonetheless, such training can be more effective if it is supported by top management, based on adequate resources, and of sufficient duration. Where extensive cultural fluency is necessary, an immersion approach to training may be needed. Such approaches involve the use of field experiences, simulations, comprehensive training in languages, and sensitivity training.[90] There also may be greater support in the future from top management for such training. As early as the mid-1980s, Motorola was providing strategically oriented training on various countries in its senior-level executive development program.[91] A related issue is that in order to obtain world-class labor, human resource managers and executives must acquire the skills to recruit, hire, and develop managers and professionals from other countries for global operations.[92]

Product Life Cycles and Managerial Fit: Development vs. Selection

Earlier discussions have noted the importance of aligning human resource practices with the organization's overall strategy. A related issue concerns the importance of matching types of managers with the organization's strategies. Some strategists have proposed that different types of managerial skills or personalities are required for the different stages of product life cycles or different corporate strategies. Although there is no common agreement on the life-cycle stages, a common typology includes introduction, growth, maturity, and decline. Broader strategy categories might include steady-state and evolutionary stages. In the case of product life cycles, it is argued that in the introduction stage, a manager should be a risk taker or entrepreneur, while in the decline stage, the manager should be risk averse and focused on cost containment. There are problems with product life-cycle models stemming from ambiguities in stage identification, the validity of prescribed styles or personalities needed for each stage, and inaccuracies in style and personality measurement. However, they have value in focusing attention on alignment either through hiring, development, or the use of reward systems. With the limitations of these approaches in mind, a careful contingency approach to matching or fit may have some value.[93]

Along this line, some researchers have argued that for companies pursuing steady-state strategies, more effective matching will be obtained by placing greater emphasis on development rather than selection. With steady-state strategies, growth is achieved through internal expansion and managers must have a broad understanding of the business. Conversely, in organizations pursuing evolutionary strategies, selection should provide a more effective matching approach. Because evolutionary strategies rely on acquisitions and mergers for growth, the managerial talent needed to staff an unrelated acquisition can be obtained more easily through external selection.[94] These results indicate that for companies growing through internal expansion, management development will be an important means of aligning managerial talent with organizational strategies.

Summary

This chapter has discussed the role of reward and development systems in strategy implementation. Because performance measures are necessary for assessment of employees' contributions to the implementation of strategies, various measurement approaches were discussed as antecedents to reward and development systems. Management by objectives was discussed along with graphic rating scales, narrative descriptions of performance, behaviorally anchored rating scales, behavior observation scales, and 360-degree feedback systems. Additionally, the lack of performance evaluation at executive levels was discussed. The absence of such formal evaluation for executives was attributed to several unfounded beliefs or myths. Suggestions were offered for increased application of performance evaluation to executives.

Following the discussion of performance measurement, reward systems were considered from a compensation perspective. Traditional job-based pay systems were described, and their inability to provide the flexibility needed for today's competitive environment was discussed. Because of compensation's critical role in new work systems, organizational processes, and organizational structures, several innovative compensation approaches were discussed. These approaches included skill-based pay, which focuses on the individual as opposed to the job. Because workforces with high skill levels will be needed to obtain future competitive advantages, the alignment of rewards with skill acquisition can be critical to successful strategy implementation. The new compensation approach of broadbanding also was examined. Broadbanding, like skill-based pay, facilitates efficient workforce utilization. There also was a discussion of team-based pay, which rewards cooperative efforts, and a discussion of variable compensation. Variable compensation is becoming more widely adopted because it helps to create a sense of shared destiny among all employees. Such plans place a portion of employees' compensation at risk and then link that portion to the achievement of overall performance goals. Variable compensation also has the potential to contribute to employment security. The role and current status of executive compensation also were examined.

Following the discussion of compensation systems, employee and management development were discussed as means of strategy implementation. Several training methods were examined, including both traditional and evolving approaches. These included new employee orientation, socialization, coaching, mentoring, computer-based training, computer-assisted training, experiential training, and job rotation. The training approaches of apprenticeships, which may receive greater emphasis in the future, and management development were covered in detail. Management development was examined in terms of job rotation, cross-functional assignments, and lateral assignments.

Endnotes

1. Longenecker, Clinton O., and Dennis A. Gioia. "The Executive Appraisal Paradox," *Academy of Management Executive* 6, no. 2 (1992): 26 (whole article on pp. 18–28).
2. Richards, Max D. *Setting Strategic Goals and Objectives*, 2nd ed. St. Paul, MN: West Publishing Company, 1986.
3. Thomas, Steven L., and Robert D. Bretz Jr. "Research and Practice in Performance Appraisal: Evaluating Employee Performance in America's Largest Companies," *SAM Advanced Management Journal* 59, no. 2 (1994): 28–34.
4. Thomas and Bretz. "Research and Practice in Performance Appraisal: Evaluating Employee Performance in America's Largest Companies."
5. Cardy, Robert L., and Gregory H. Dobbins. *Performance Appraisal: Alternative Perspectives*. Cincinnati, OH: South-Western Publishing Co., 1994.
6. Ibid.
7. Ibid.

8. Ibid.
9. Gatewood, Robert D., and Hubert S. Feild. *Human Resource Selection*, 4th ed. Fort Worth: Dryden Press, 1998.
10. Ghorpade, Jai. "Managing Five Paradoxes of 360-Degree Feedback," *Academy of Management Executive* 14, no. 1 (2000): 140–50.
11. Huet-Cox, G. Douglas, Tjai M. Nielsen, and Eric Sundstrom. "Get the Most from 360-Degree Feedback: Put It on the Internet," *HRMagazine* 44, no. 5 (1999): 92–103.
12. Ghorpade. "Managing Five Paradoxes of 360-Degree Feedback."
13. Ibid.
14. Longenecker and Gioia. "The Executive Appraisal Paradox," p. 18.
15. Longenecker and Gioia. "The Executive Appraisal Paradox."
16. Longenecker, Clinton O., Henry P. Sims, and Dennis Gioia. "Behind the Mask: The Politics of Employee Appraisal," *Academy of Management Executive* 1, no. 3 (1987): 183–93.
17. Gomez-Mejia, Luis R., and David B. Balkin. *Compensation, Organizational Strategy, and Firm Performance*. Cincinnati, OH: South-Western Publishing Co., 1992; Milkovich, George T., and Jerry M. Newman. *Compensation*, 4th ed. Homewood, IL: Richard D. Irwin, 1993; Emerson, Sandra M. "Job Evaluation: A Barrier to Excellence?" *Compensation and Benefits Review* 23, no. 1 (1991): 39–51.
18. Emerson. "Job Evaluation: A Barrier to Excellence?"; Tosi, Henry, and Lisa Tosi. "What Managers Need to Know About Knowledge-Based Pay," *Organizational Dynamics* 14, no. 3 (1986): 52–64; Gomez-Mejia and Balkin. *Compensation, Organizational Strategy, and Firm Performance*.
19. Ledford, Gerald E. Jr. "Three Case Studies on Skill-Based Pay: An Overview," *Compensation and Benefits Review* 23, no. 2 (1991): 11–23; Lawler, Edward E. III, Ledford, Gerald E. Jr., and Lei Chang. "Who Uses Skill-Based Pay, and Why," *Compensation and Benefits Review* 25, no. 2 (1993): 22–26.
20. Tosi and Tosi. "What Managers Need to Know About Knowledge-Based Pay," p. 57.
21. Ledford. "Three Case Studies on Skill-Based Pay: An Overview"; Lawler, Ledford, and Chang. "Who Uses Skill-Based Pay, and Why."
22. Lawler, Ledford, and Chang. "Who Uses Skill-Based Pay, and Why."
23. Ledford. "Three Case Studies on Skill-Based Pay: An Overview."
24. Ibid.; Tosi and Tosi. "What Managers Need to Know About Knowledge-Based Pay"; Lawler, Ledford, and Chang. "Who Uses Skill-Based Pay, and Why."
25. Ibid.
26. Lawler, Ledford, and Chang. "Who Uses Skill-Based Pay, and Why"; Tosi and Tosi. "What Managers Need to Know About Knowledge-Based Pay."
27. Tosi and Tosi. "What Managers Need to Know About Knowledge-Based Pay"; Ledford. "Three Case Studies on Skill-Based Pay: An Overview."
28. Hofrichter, David. "Broadbanding: A 'Second Generation' Approach," *Compensation and Benefits Review* 25, no. 5 (1993): 53–58.
29. Ibid.
30. Ibid.
31. Gomez-Mejia, Luis R., and David B. Balkin. *Compensation, Organizational Strategy, and Firm Performance*. Cincinnati, OH: South-Western Publishing Co., 1992.
32. Gomez-Mejia, Luis R., and David B. Balkin. "Effectiveness of Individual and Aggregate Compensation Strategies," *Industrial Relations* 28, no. 3 (1989): 431–45; Gomez-Mejia and Balkin. *Compensation, Organizational Strategy, and Firm Performance*.
33. Gomez-Mejia and Balkin. "Effectiveness of Individual and Aggregate Compensation Strategies."
34. Ost, Edward J. "Team-Based Pay: New Wave Strategic Incentives," *Sloan Management Review* 31, no. 3 (1990): 19–27.
35. Ibid., p. 22.
36. Gross, Steven E., and Jeffrey P. Bacher. "The New Variable Pay Programs: How Some Succeed, Why Some Don't," *Compensation and Benefits Review* 25, no. 1 (1993): 51–56.

37. Bowie-McCoy, Susan W., Ann C. Wendt, and Roger Chope. "Gainsharing in Public Accounting: Working Smarter and Harder," *Industrial Relations* 32, no. 3 (1993): 432–45.
38. Gross and Bacher. "The New Variable Pay Programs: How Some Succeed, Why Some Don't"; Hogarty, Donna Brown. "New Ways to Pay," *Management Review* 83, no. 1 (1994): 34–36.
39. Schuster, Jay R., and Patricia K. Zingheim. "The New Variable Pay: Key Design Issues," *Compensation and Benefits Review* 25, no. 2 (1993): 27–34.
40. Ibid.; Kerr, Steven. "On the Folly of Rewarding A While Hoping for B," *Academy of Management Journal* 18, no. 4 (1975): 769–83.
41. Schuster and Zingheim. "The New Variable Pay: Key Design Issues," p. 31.
42. Gross and Bacher. "The New Variable Pay Programs: How Some Succeed, Why Some Don't."
43. Henn, William R. "What the Strategist Asks from Human Resources," *Human Resource Planning* 8, no. 4 (1985): 193–200; Gomez-Mejia, Luis R., and David B. Balkin. *Compensation, Organizational Strategy, and Firm Performance*. Cincinnati, OH: South-Western Publishing Co., 1992.
44. Gomez-Mejia and Balkin. *Compensation, Organizational Strategy, and Firm Performance*, p. 221.
45. Kanter, Rosabeth Moss. *When Giants Learn to Dance: Mastering the Challenge of Strategy, Management, and Careers in the 1990s*. New York: Simon and Schuster, 1989, p. 237.
46. Ibid., p. 368.
47. Magnus, Margaret. "Training Futures," *Personnel Journal* 65, no. 5 (1986): 61–71.
48. Ibid.; Naisbitt, John, and Patricia Aburdene. *Re-inventing the Corporation: Transforming Your Job and Your Company for the New Information Society*. New York: Warner Books, Inc., 1985.
49. Naisbitt and Aburdene. *Re-inventing the Corporation: Transforming Your Job and Your Company for the New Information Society*.
50. Ibid., p. 127.
51. Gordon, Jack. "Where the Training Goes," *Training* 27, no. 10 (1990): 51–69; Peters, Tom. *Thriving on Chaos: Handbook for a Management Revolution*. New York: Harper and Row, 1987.
52. Gordon. "Where the Training Goes."
53. Naisbitt and Aburdene. *Re-inventing the Corporation: Transforming Your Job and Your Company for the New Information Society*, p. 165.
54. Ibid.
55. Cheng, Alex F. "Hands-On Learning at Motorola," *Training and Development Journal* 44, no. 10 (1990): 34–35.
56. Ibid., p. 34.
57. Hammonds, Keith H. "Corning's Class Act," *Business Week* (May 13, 1991): 68–76.
58. Magnus. "Training Futures"; Wexley, Kenneth N., and Gary P. Latham. *Developing and Training Human Resources in Organization*, 2nd ed. New York: HarperCollins, 1991; Goldstein, Irwin L. *Training in Organizations: Needs Assessment, Development, and Evaluation*, 2nd ed. Monterey, CA: Brooks/Cole Publishing Company, 1986.
59. Ivancevich, John M., and William F. Glueck. *Foundations of Personnel: Human Resource Management*, 4th ed. Homewood, IL: Richard D. Irwin, 1989; Cherrington, David J. *Personnel Management: The Management of Human Resources*, 2nd ed. Dubuque, IA: William C. Brown Publishers, 1987; Dessler, Gary. *Personnel Management*, 4th ed., Upper Saddle River, NJ: Prentice Hall, 1988.
60. Ivancevich and Glueck. *Foundations of Personnel: Human Resource Management*.
61. Schein, Edgar H. *Career Dynamics: Matching Individual and Organizational Needs*. Reading, MA: Addison-Wesley, 1978, p. 117.
62. Wexley and Latham. *Developing and Training Human Resources in Organizations*; Schein. *Career Dynamics: Matching Individual and Organizational Needs*.
63. Schein. *Career Dynamics: Matching Individual and Organizational Needs*.
64. Ibid.; Hunt, David M., and Carol Michael. "Mentorship: A Career Training and Development Tool," *Academy of Management Review* 8, no. 3 (1983): 475–85.
65. Velasquez, Manuel, Dennis J. Moberg, and Gerald F. Cavanagh. "Organizational Statesmanship and Dirty Politics: Ethical Guidelines for the Organizational Politician," *Organizational Dynamics* 12, no. 2 (1983) 65–80.

66. Wexley and Latham. *Developing and Training Human Resources in Organizations*; Hunt and Michael. "Mentorship: A Career Training and Development Tool"; Kram, Kathy E., and Douglas T. Hall. "Mentoring as an Antidote to Stress During Corporate Trauma," *Human Resource Management* 28, no. 4 (1989): 493–510; Schein. *Career Dynamics: Matching Individual and Organizational Needs*.
67. Wexley and Latham. *Developing and Training Human Resources in Organizations*.
68. Shirfrin, Carole A. "American Meets Pilot, Fleet Increase With Computer-Intensive Instruction," *Aviation Week and Space Technology* (June 13, 1988): 139–41. Copyright © 1988 by McGraw-Hill. Reprinted by permission of McGraw-Hill.
69. Ibid., p. 139.
70. Shirfrin. "American Meets Pilot, Fleet Increase With Computer-Intensive Instruction."
71. Booker, Ellis. "Grading High-Tech Teaching," *Computerworld* (February 19, 1990): 114.
72. Ibid.; Granger, Ralph E. "Computer-Based Training Works," *Personnel Journal* 69, no. 9 (1990): 85–91.
73. Goldstein. *Training in Organizations: Needs Assessment, Development, and Evaluation*; Gal, Graham, and Paul John Steinbart. "Interface Style and Training Task Difficulty as Determinants of Effective Computer-Assisted Knowledge Transfer," *Decision Sciences* 23, no. 1 (1992): 128–43.
74. Hilton, Margaret. "Shared Training: Learning from Germany," *Monthly Labor Review* 114, no. 3 (1991): 33–37.
75. Lerman, Robert I., and Hillard Pouncy. "The Compelling Case for Youth Apprenticeships," *The Public Interest* no. 101 (Fall, 1990): 62–77.
76. Hilton. "Shared Training: Learning from Germany," p. 33.
77. Rachwalsky, Klaus. *Vocational Training—Investment for the Future: The Dual Training System in the Federal Republic of Germany*. Cologne: Carl Duisberg Gesellschaft, 1983.
78. Lerman and Pouncy. "The Compelling Case for Youth Apprenticeships."
79. Hilton. "Shared Training: Learning from Germany"; Phillips, Dennis. "How VW Builds Worker Loyalty Worldwide," *Management Review* 76, no. 6 (1987): 37–40; Lerman and Pouncy. "The Compelling Case for Youth Apprenticeships."
80. Lerman and Pouncy. "The Compelling Case for Youth Apprenticeships."
81. Wartzman, Rick. "Learning by Doing: Apprenticeship Plans Spring Up for Students Not Headed to College," *Wall Street Journal* (May 19, 1992): A1, A6.
82. Cascio, Wayne F. "Downsizing: What Do We Know? What Have We Learned?" *Academy of Management Executive* 7, no. 1 (1993): 95–104.
83. Evans, Paul A. L. "Management Development as Glue Technology," *Human Resource Planning* 15, no. 1 (1992): 93.
84. Saari, Lise M., Terry R. Johnson, Steven D. McLaughlin, and Denise M. Zimmerle. "A Survey of Management Training and Education Practices in U.S. Companies," *Personnel Psychology* 41, no. 4 (1988): 731–43.
85. Ibid.
86. Cook, Deborah, and Gerald R. Ferris. "Strategic Human Resource Management and Firm Effectiveness in Industries Experiencing Decline," *Human Resource Management* 25, no. 3 (1986): 441–57.
87. Weber, Joseph, Lisa Driscoll, and Richard Brandt. "Farewell, Fast Track," *Business Week* (December 10, 1990): 192–200.
88. Ibid.
89. Ibid., p. 196.
90. Mendenhall, Mark E., Edward Dunbar, and Gary R. Oddou. "Expatriate Selection, Training and Career-Pathing: A Review and Critique," *Human Resource Management* 26, no. 3 (1987): 331–45.
91. Bolt, James F. "Tailor Executive Development to Strategy," *Harvard Business Review* 63, no. 6 (1985): 168–76.
92. Hambrick, Donald C., James W. Fredrickson, Lester B. Korn, and Richard M. Ferry. "Preparing Today's Leaders for Tomorrow's Realities," *Personnel* 66, no. 8 (1989): 23–26.

93. Galbraith, Jay R., and Robert K. Kazanjian. *Strategy Implementation: Structure, Systems, and Process*, 2nd ed. St. Paul, MN: West Publishing Company, 1986; Kerr, Jeffrey. "Assigning Managers on the Basis of the Life Cycle," *Journal of Business Strategy* 2, no. 4 (1982): 58–65; Szilagyi, Andrew D. Jr., and David M. Schweiger. "Matching Managers to Strategies: A Review and Suggested Framework," *Academy of Management Review* 9, no. 4 (1984): 626–37.
94. Kerr, Jeffrey L., and Ellen F. Jackofsky. "Aligning Managers with Strategies: Management Development Versus Selection," *Strategic Management Journal* 10 (1989): 157–70.

CASE 7 CEO Compensation

Many readers have probably had a conversation in which a friend or coworker expressed amazement at the extremely high compensation of some chief executive officers (CEOs). Inevitably, there is a question of how such huge amounts of compensation can be justified. A notable example includes the Walt Disney Corporation's CEO who received $203 million in one year.[1] Another includes $58.5 million to the CEO of U.S. Surgical Corporation.[2] Still another includes a signing bonus of $10 million and $180 million in stock options for the incoming CEO of Global Crossings who resigned after one year.[3] Even severance packages for some CEOs are huge. The former CEO of Mattel resigned after substantial financial losses in the previous quarter and was given a $37 million package and over $708,989 per year for the remainder of her life.

Graef Crystal, a noted critic of CEO compensation, has spent a great amount of time studying the subject. For example, in his study of CEO compensation in health care organizations, in which there is great variance in compensation, he found no rationale according to organizational performance or size. Further, he discredited supply and demand explanations and attributed CEO high compensation to other sources of power.[4] Some of Crystal's conclusions are as follows:

> So is there any rhyme or reason to explain the huge variation of CEO pay levels? Short answer: Forget it . . . There's no justifiable theory on a shortage of CEO talent to drive up CEO pay. But there is a creditable theory at work, the theory of CEO power. Pack the board with your friends, hire consultants who are good at blowing smoke, float a lot of statistics about how other companies offer their CEOs a ton of money, and, voila, you, too, can make a lucrative sum no matter how you perform, and see your pay rise at a rate faster than people who fill other important jobs in the organization.[5]

On the other hand, there are defenders of current levels of CEO compensation. Consultants Ira Kay and Rodney Robinson have argued that the pay of CEOs is justified by the performance of their companies. Further, they have pointed out that academic research studies using time series methodologies provide the basis for such conclusions.[6] Even Crystal has found a small positive relationship between performance, in the form of shareholder returns, and CEO compensation. He has found that such performance explains only 19.8 percent of the variance in their compensation, however, which leaves approximately 80 percent to other factors.[7] Further, other critics have pointed out the vast differences between the United States and other countries in ratios of CEO compensation to the average worker's compensation. Reports indicate that CEO compensation in some U.S. companies is now 200 times higher than that of rank-and-file employees whereas others indicate that the ratio has risen as high as 475 to one. When compared to other industrialized countries, the ratios are much higher in the United States.[8]

Because of the problem of excessive compensation, several recommendations have been proposed. Some are very high-level policy recommendations, which would require legislation. One such recommendation is that the U.S. Glass-Steagall Act of 1933, which prohibits bankers from sitting on their customers' boards of directors, should be amended to permit such practices. Presumably, such bankers would be more cost conscious. A radical policy recommendation is that the United States should move to a German style of codetermination system in which worker representatives sit on boards of directors. In contrast, another recommendation is to avoid solutions that are based on legislation because they are likely to introduce even more problems. Still another is that tax deductions should be disallowed for companies in which the CEO's compensation is 25 times greater than the average for blue-collar workers.[9]

Several other recommendations are directed toward implementation at the organizational level. One is to link CEO pay to long-term profitability. A second is to put more stockholders and workers on boards of directors. A related recommendation is directed toward members of company boards of directors. That recommendation maintains that board members should ignore self-serving surveys that portray CEOs as underpaid in comparison to other CEOs. They also should be very skeptical of assessments concluding that CEOs are mobile. Still another recommendation is to use succession planning to develop an internal pool of qualified CEO candidates and thereby avoid seeking expensive replacements from the external labor market.[10] A final recommendation would attack the problem in a more indirect manner. In response to the problems of excessive CEO compensation, as well as other factors, the Financial Accounting Standards Board (FASB) has proposed that stock option grants be reflected on financial statements as a charge to earnings.[11] Without such a requirement, stock option grants to executives, which may eventually take on millions of dollars in value, are never reflected in financial statements.

Questions

1. Explain the potential adverse impacts on strategy implementation when the CEOs of companies receive extremely high compensation.

2. Discuss the merits of the various recommendations for solutions to the problem of extremely high CEO compensation.
3. What nonregulatory pressures are most likely to bring excessively high CEO salaries more in line with realistic levels?
4. Evaluate the argument that pay for performance justifies the level of compensation paid to the CEOs noted in the examples.
5. Evaluate the argument that the problem of excessive CEO compensation should not be addressed through legislation.

References

1. Hardy, Eric S. "Marathon Men," *Forbes* (May 23, 1994): 140–42.
2. Crystal, Graef. "Inefficient Market for CEOs in Health Care," *Compensation and Benefits Review* 25, no. 5 (1993): 74–75.
3. Strauss, Gary. "Homes, Cars, Jets Among Perks Piling Up for CEOs: Companies Generous With Compensation Packages," *USA Today* (May 22, 2000): 1B.
4. Crystal. "Inefficient Market for CEOs in Health Care."
5. Ibid., p. 75.
6. Kay, Ira T., and Rodney F. Robinson. "Misguided Attacks on Executive Pay Hurt Shareholders," *Compensation and Benefits Review* 26, no. 1 (1994): 25–33.
7. Crystal, Graef. "Speaking My Mind," *Compensation and Benefits Review* 26, no. 1 (1994): 34–37.
8. Bloom, Matt. "The Performance Effects of Pay Dispersion on Individuals and Organizations," *Academy of Management Journal* 42 (1999): 25–40; Schuler, Randall S., and Vandra L. Huber. *Personnel and Human Resource Management*, 5th ed. Minneapolis/St. Paul, MN: West Publishing Company, 1993, p. 437.
9. Collier, Gene. "Living Wage? Some Are Living Large," *Pittsburgh Post-Gazette* (May 3, 2000): E-1.
10. Wilhelm, Paul G. "Application of Distributive Justice Theory to the CEO Pay Problem: Recommendations for Reform," *Journal of Business Ethics* 12, no. 6 (1993): 469–82.
11. Kay and Robinson. "Misguided Attacks on Executive Pay Hurt Shareholders."

CHAPTER 8

The Performance Impact of Human Resource Practices

A major premise of the investment perspective of this book is that investments in human resources can provide a sustainable source of competitive advantage and can increase the likelihood of successful implementation of the firm's business strategies. Because of these effects, investments in human capital have the potential to produce attractive rates of return for the firm's shareholders. The process of investing in human resources goes beyond simply hiring and retaining good people, although these are fundamentals. Investments in human resources can take several forms. They may be relatively direct, such as in the case of training employees in order to increase their productivity. Human resource investments may take a more indirect approach as well. For example, such investments may be pursued through an attractive compensation plan that helps the firm boost employee productivity and facilitates retention of a highly talented workforce. Other examples might include investments in improved selection procedures, such as by acquiring more valid selection tests, or increasing the amount of advertising of job vacancies.

In recent years, human resource executives have been extremely interested in the empirical evidence on the relationship between various human resource management practices and sound measures of firm performance. This interest has been prompted in many cases by pressure from senior management for solid evidence that their human resource departments are making contributions to the firm's performance. This chapter will examine the impact of individual human resource practices and systems of such practices by reviewing some of the research on this subject. Most of the research studies drawn on in this chapter are empirical and use statistical techniques to control for other influences that may affect organizational performance. A few nonempirical works reporting findings from multiple observations also are incorporated into the discussion.

This discussion will begin by examining the impact of individual high-performance human resource practices, some of which have been asserted to be almost universally applicable best practices. It then addresses the limitations of individual best practices in terms of their effect on performance and of the evolution of individual practices to systems of practices. The discussion then focuses on the effects of systems of high-performance practices. The basis for expecting increased performance with systems of such practices is examined, followed by a consideration of the results of research studies attempting to determine whether systems provide superior performance to individual best practices. Finally, there is an examination of the contingency view of strategic human resource management, which maintains that the full benefit of individual best practices or systems of practices is realized only when these practices support the firm's business strategy and match well with the firm's organizational context.

INDIVIDUAL HIGH-PERFORMANCE PRACTICES

A number of researchers have identified several high-performance practices or best practices. One of the most prominent of these advocates of universal best practices is Professor Jeffrey Pfeffer of Stanford University. Pfeffer has addressed these best practices in two book-length treatments: *Competitive Advantage through People* and *The Human Equation: Building Profits by Putting People First.* The first book identified 16 best practices while the second combined several and winnowed the list down to seven. Pfeffer's research indicates that these seven management practices are nearly universal in their ability to enhance firm performance:

1. Employment security.
2. Selective hiring of new personnel.
3. Self-managed teams and decentralization of decision making as the basic principles of organizational design.
4. Comparatively high compensation contingent on organizational performance.
5. Extensive training.
6. Reduced status distinctions and barriers, including dress, language, office arrangements, and wage differences across levels.
7. Extensive sharing of financial and performance information throughout the organization.[1]

Empirical evidence on the performance effects of these and several other human resource practices will be presented in this chapter. Research results on whether such practices actually have a positive impact on various measures of firm performance will be presented by the major categories of individual practices.

Compensation

Despite the importance of compensation and financial incentives to employees and firms, there has been a surprising lack of good research on its performance effects. Furthermore, traditional compensation practices have come under criticism:

> Employees today are expected to work in teams rather than solely on their own. They are expected to keep learning new skills and to assume broader roles. They are expected to take more risks and responsibility for results. As a consequence we are slowly coming to the realization that we may be paying for the wrong things, sending inconsistent messages about the company to its employees, or creating artificial expectations of continued advancement and raises, no matter how well the company performs.[2]

Some researchers have asserted that there has only been one good study per year on the topic over the past 40 years.[3] Another barrier also has limited our understanding of compensation, as well as other areas of management. That barrier has been the difficulty of synthesizing the results of multiple studies in order to arrive at firm conclusions about their collective findings. Fortunately, meta-analysis techniques have been developed that allow researchers to draw rigorous conclusions from comprehensive empirical reviews of the literature. A recent meta-analysis was able to reach very definitive findings about the performance effects of financial incentives. In addition, it refuted assertions by some scholars that financial incentives act to kill intrinsic motivation:[4]

> Our meta-analysis explored whether the relationship between financial incentives and performance was stronger for *extrinsic* (i.e., dull and boring) tasks than for *intrinsic* (i.e., challenging and interesting) tasks. Presumably, if financial incentives erode intrinsic motivation, we would find them to be negatively related to performance for intrinsic tasks. The data show otherwise. It doesn't matter what kind of work people are doing—incentives improve performance . . . Taken together, then, the hard data are unambiguous—financial incentives improve performance quantity; they *do not* erode intrinsic motivation.[5]

Highly experienced executives who are compensation experts with the Hay Group have reached a similar conclusion:

> Deming is right in touting the merits of intrinsic motivation. Indeed many organizations have stifled that aspect of performance—and they have often done it through lousy pay and performance management strategies, as well as bad supervision and bureaucratic administrative practices. But to say that all extrinsic rewards are therefore bad is to miss the point. The fact is, a well-designed compensation program that is fully and properly aligned with an organization's values and culture does wonders for self-esteem and an eagerness to learn, not to mention performance.[6]

As this excerpt indicates, in addition to the ability of compensation practices to complement other sources of motivation, they tend to work best where organizational contingencies, such as culture, are taken into account. As the individual practices are discussed, a number of contingencies will be noted that are probably important to consider before implementing even the most robust of the potential "universal" best practices.

High Compensation Linked to Organizational Performance

As with many compensation issues, there are different perspectives on high compensation as well as on making it contingent on organizational performance. Professor Jeffrey Pfeffer has asserted that it is folly for some companies to claim that their employees are their source of competitive advantage while they pay their workforces only the market average. He points out that Home Depot has achieved success because of its superior workforce, maintained by paying relatively high wages in a low-wage industry.[7] Unfortunately, while there is anecdotal evidence that supports this assertion, there are few empirical studies on the impact of high wages other than those that focus on low wages as an indirect cause of turnover, which adversely affects firm performance.

However, there is substantially more evidence on the impact of contingent compensation. A contrary view is provided by the Vice President for People at Southwest Airlines who says that her company does not believe in fancy compensation programs. Noting that the company is 85 percent unionized, she explains that these employees are paid on the basis of time in grade and that they, like all Southwest employees, receive profit sharing.[8] Thus, the bulk of compensation is unrelated to performance. On the other hand, the remaining portion is linked to the collective performance of all employees at this high-performing company. The Southwest Airlines example does not provide strong evidence that contingent compensation is a universal best practice because its salaries are tied to seniority and its contingent compensation (profit sharing) is just one highly compatible component of the firm's extraordinary organizational culture.

Stock options and profit sharing, which are discussed later in a separate section, provide other means of making a portion of compensation contingent on the firm's performance. Many leading companies such as Microsoft, Bank of America, Intel, Owens Corning, and Starbucks have adopted stock option programs for all or very broad categories of employees, such as those having satisfactory performance. It has been asserted that such forms of compensation add value by (1) helping to attract and retain employees, (2) building organizational commitment, (3) reinforcing skill and knowledge acquisition, and (4) motivating behaviors in line with the company's strategic objectives. Thus, for broad-based stock options to have an effect on performance, they should make a positive contribution in at least one of these four ways.[9]

The literature indicates that broad-based stock options may not produce all of the benefits that their proponents have claimed. For example, there is little empirical evidence supporting the effectiveness of broad-based stock options in attracting potential employees. Likewise, stock options are probably not universally effective because there are several factors that influence their impact. As an example of their specific applicability, it has been observed that stock options work better for employees who are comfortable with risk. Employers such as Microsoft use stock options to attract risk-taking employees. Stock options can even help with retention because their impact can be enhanced by the use of vesting schedules that do not allow options to be exercised until employees have stayed with the company for a certain number of years.[10]

A review of the literature indicates several other factors that influence the performance effects of stock options. For example, organizational culture appears have an interaction effect with stock options. It has been found that a combination of participative organizational culture and stock options produces faster growth rates while neither produces such results alone. Productivity effects also appear to lag the implementation of stock options because three or four years are required before employees develop commitment and cooperative work practices. Stock options also appear to work better in smaller companies. In addition, employees must be well informed before stock options are likely to influence them to act like the owners of the company and to align their behaviors with the firm's goals. Information must be shared with employees and they must be trained so that they can understand financial measures and be knowledgeable about the financial drivers of the firm. Employees also need to be able to participate in decisions and understand the firm's goals. A healthy stock market is obviously important.[11]

Michael Beer has offered additional advice about the conditions that should be present before contingent compensation can be expected to have a positive impact on firm performance. His critical views also call into question whether contingent compensation is a universal best practice:

> Similarly, does it make sense for a company to ask its HR and line management executives to devote considerable valuable time and energy to administering tightly coupled contingent pay for performance compensation systems? Despite the rhetoric, these systems probably do not contribute much to the effectiveness of organizations. Systems that differentiate only at the extremes and payout on a variable ratio schedule for outstanding performances are effective—and far easier and less costly to administer . . . suffice it to say that some of the most successful companies in the world do not have executive bonus or commission systems, for example. They have thick team-based cultures . . . It appears that complex compensation schemes may not only take a lot of time, they also do not motivate and may actually be injurious to building the very team-based culture companies are aspiring to develop.[12]

Incentive-Based Compensation

The previous discussion on contingent compensation linked to firm performance overlaps with incentive-based compensation. Nonetheless, because incentives can be unrelated to organizational performance, this form of compensation will be discussed separately. For example, incentives can include commissions based on sales, individual sales goals, and the like.

John Delaney and Mark Huselid have addressed the question of the performance impact of incentive-based compensation with an analysis of data on 590 for-profit and nonprofit organizations from the National Organizations Survey. The study used perceptual measures of organizational performance framed in the context of how other organizations in the industry had performed during the past three years. The study found that incentive-based compensation was significantly related to organizational performance for the entire sample of companies.[13] As with other studies of firm or organizational performance, a number of control variables were employed in multiple regression analysis.

Profit Sharing

A study by Gary Florkowski and Kuldeep Shastri has examined the impact of profit sharing on shareholder wealth in unionized firms. This study examined shareholder returns after firms negotiated profit-sharing plans with their unions. The results of their study of 45 publicly traded firms indicated that shareholder returns increased following the announcements of such plans. Interestingly, the increases were the largest for firms having financial difficulties preceding the negotiated settlements. The results are meaningful because the researchers also concluded that the increased returns were not attributable to the conclusion of strikes or wage-reduction programs.[14]

The financial impact of profit sharing also has been studied in the banking industry. John Delery and Harold Doty's multiple regression analysis of data from 192 banks controlled for several potential influences on financial performance. Results of the analysis revealed that profit sharing had a positive impact on both return on assets (ROA) and return on equity (ROE).[15]

Another study provides further evidence on the impact of profit sharing. This study examined the five-year survival rates of 183 small nonfinancial firms that conducted initial public offerings (IPOs). The analysis of survival rates included several control variables expected to affect firm survival. The researchers utilized an organizational-based reward variable that captured the firms' practice of rewarding employees with profit sharing and stock options as well as gain sharing and other customized rewards. The variable took on greater values with more components and broader application to the whole workforce. Results indicated that the reward variable was a highly significant and positive predictor of the organization's survival.[16]

Team-Based Compensation

Team-based compensation also has been examined in recent research. One study examined the differential impact of bonuses based on the performance of teams. Looking at bonuses resulting from team performance, the study sought to determine the impact of bonuses distributed on the basis of equity (bonuses allocated on the basis of each team member's contributions) versus those distributed on the basis of equality (bonuses divided equally among team members). Data were obtained from 10 organizations for 57 teams with an average team size of 13 (team size ranged from 4 to 32). The study used perceptual measures of team effectiveness, productivity, and helping behaviors.[17]

Results indicated that teams were more effective and demonstrated more helping behaviors when bonuses were allocated within the team on the basis of equity. As the size of the bonuses increased, there was also a significant increase in team productivity and effectiveness. In addition, there was significantly greater satisfaction with the team bonuses when members perceived that team performance was linked to team bonuses and when they perceived clear goals for the team. While such compensation practices have a positive impact on team performance, these results are not reported in Table 8-1 because they do not address the direct impact on the performance of the firm.[18]

Financial rewards for results are only part of the compensation picture for teams. Teams are often asked to do things differently and to take risks that may not always produce desired results. If rewards are tied only to results, teams will not be motivated to take risks. Therefore, companies such as Motorola reward teams for desired activities and behaviors. Timely recognition for team members also is critical as with other employees.[19]

A comprehensive study by Matt Bloom of compensation and performance in baseball has provided good insights into the effects of pay compression and dispersion. The study found that great dispersion in compensation between the members of a team impairs team performance. The research, which studied team and individual player performance and compensation for 1,644 players over nine years, found the following results:

> Findings suggest more compressed pay dispersions are positively related to multiple measures of individual and organizational performance . . . The results of this study indicate that greater dispersion in pay within an organization is associated with lower individual and group performance, at least where work interdependencies are important.[20]

Diversity

As noted in Chapter 2, research on the creativity of groups has found that ethnic diversity is positively related with creativity.[21] Correspondingly, it has been asserted that the heightened creativity produced by a more diverse workforce can have a positive impact on the firm's performance if properly managed. While it is a desirable practice to hire people who will fit well with the organization, this practice can result in dysfunctional homogeneity if carried to an extreme. With extreme homogeneity, organizations may become less capable of adapting to changing circumstances and less flexible.[22]

Recent research has examined this assertion by analyzing the hiring for affirmative action purposes during economic downturns. This research has found that firms placing greater emphasis on such hiring have better financial performance than other firms, as measured by shareholder returns, two years after the economic recovery. Emphasis on hiring for affirmative action purposes was correlated with the lagged financial performance variable. As with the other studies of firm performance, an extensive set of control variables was employed. Not surprisingly, the effects of increased diversity do not result in immediate performance because time is needed for the benefits of diversity to be manifested in increased performance. Speculative interpretations are that such hiring for affirmative action purposes has the additional benefit of enhancing the firm's reputation among female and minority job applicants, as well as reducing the likelihood of litigation and its associated costs.[23]

Another study examined the performance impact of cultural diversity in international operations of 442 *Fortune* 500 firms. Culturally related international diversification was expected to have a positive impact on firm performance. One example, in which positive effects are expected, is the use of just-in-time inventory management techniques in cultures that are compatible with the technique, such as in Japan. In Japan, there is appreciation for efficient space utilization and group-oriented commitment to work duties. Another example in which positive effects are expected is by organizing marketing activities around commonalities such as exist between the United States and Canada, as opposed to the United States and Indonesia. Culturally unrelated global diversification was expected to have a negative result. For example, when companies diversify by establishing business units in countries with very different cultures, there is greater likelihood of misunderstandings and communication difficulties. With greater "cultural distances" between operations, there is need for more complex control systems and correspondingly higher transaction costs.[24]

The study, which employed a longitudinal design, measured performance by return on assets (ROA) and market-to-book value (MTB). Changes in these performance measures over various time periods were analyzed with regression equations including several control variables. Nonetheless, in contrast to expectations, the study found no impact on performance for either ROA or MTB resulting from several measures of cultural diversity. Stated optimistically, these results could mean that companies overcome factors that would produce declining returns as they deal with increasingly heterogeneous environments. One speculative interpretation is that increased cultural diversity produces increased innovation and creativity that enable companies to become better at marketing to more diverse customers.[25] This is a complex area that will need more research in the future before the effects are fully understood. However, for the companies that understand the relationships there are great opportunities for financial gain.

Employment

Countercyclical Hiring

Research also has examined the impact of the contrarian practice of hiring key employees during economic downturns. The practice is obviously a limited one because the firm is hiring while there is a downturn. Nonetheless, firms can obtain bargains in key personnel that may be needed to implement a strategy that will produce substantial returns after the recovery. For example, the firm may hire key research and development people on such a basis while the demand for their services from other companies is low. A recent study assessed the impact of this practice on shareholder returns. The study used a measure of executives' perceptions of the extent to which their firms engaged in such practices during the last economic downturn. Multiple regression employing a number of control variables found that shareholder returns two years after the downturn were positively related with the measure of countercyclical hiring.[26]

Downsizing

As noted in Chapter 6, downsizing has been the subject of a great deal of normative discussion in both the popular press and academic literature.[27] A void in this literature was its failure to address the financial impact of downsizing. However, a comprehensive study has examined the effects of downsizing. This study analyzed 5,479 instances of downsizing over a 15-year period. The study examined the impact of downsizing on firm profitability (ROA) as well as shareholder return. Interestingly, the study found that downsizing firms did not obtain significantly greater returns than the average for firms in their industries. However, firms that pursued a combined approach of coupling downsizing with a restructuring of their assets (plant and equipment) had substantially higher returns on assets two years later than those that only downsized. More impressively, after adjusting for industry, those firms combining employment and asset downsizing had substantially greater ROAs two years later than stable as well as employment-downsizing firms. These results indicate the importance of coordinated approaches in which downsizing is complementary with the firm's overall strategies, such as focus or retrenchment, in which plant and equipment are downsized as well.[28]

Another study found negative effects from the announcement of temporary staff reductions. Results of the study indicated that temporary staff reductions produced declines in shareholder returns. However, the researchers cautioned that these results are complicated by the fact that temporary layoffs, which convey a positive message about lower compensation costs, also communicate bad news about product demand.[29]

Early Retirement Programs

In the 1980s and 1990s, offers of early retirement became a regular news feature of the business press, although there was little evidence about the financial effects of such practices. Fortunately, an empirical study has examined the effects of early retirement practices on shareholder wealth. This study, which analyzed 51 announcements of early retirement programs, found that the effects were dependent on the firm's performance before the announcement. For those firms having declining shareholder returns during the year prior to the announcement, there was no relationship with announcements of early retirement programs. For those firms that had good returns, the announcement had a positive impact on shareholder returns.[30] One potential explanation for the significant results is that "Proactive downsizing made when a firm is doing well may signal an intended reorientation of personnel that goes well beyond a mere defensive reaction to decline through cost cutting."[31]

Employment Security

As noted in Chapter 1, employment security practices help to preserve the firm's investments in its human resources. They also provide the stability needed to unleash the innovativeness of employees for the benefit of the firm. It has been asserted that employees who are more secure in their jobs are more likely to use their knowledge to increase the firm's productivity.[32] However, there is also a downside to such practices, and an inverted "U"-shaped relationship between job security and work effort was noted in Chapter 1. A study cited earlier by Delery and Doty has addressed the issue of the performance impact of job security. Their study of banks found that employment security practices were positively related to ROA.[33] Unfortunately, as noted in Chapter 1, most of even the best-managed companies had to abandon their employment security practices in the 1980s and 1990s. Nonetheless, for those companies that provide the right amount of job security, there can be positive returns. Interestingly, Southwest Airlines, one of the best-performing companies for years, and which operates in a turbulent industry, has never had a layoff.[34]

Human Resource Outsourcing

Human resource departments have outsourced many of their activities over recent years. Indeed, recent surveys have found up to 91 percent of respondents reporting that their firms outsource some of their human resource activities.[35] There are a number of explanations for this trend and several are related to increased demands for greater performance. Cost reductions and greater efficiencies are often cited as benefits of outsourcing. However, practitioners are quick to point out that when outsourcing is adopted solely for cost reduction, the result is often disappointing. Sustainable competitive advantage appears to result from outsourcing when it allows human resource departments to focus on value-added activities and when outsourcing helps to support the strategic direction of the firm.[36] For example, by outsourcing employee relocation activities, the human resource department can reallocate its resources to higher-value activities such as performance management programs.

While there is little empirical evidence on the impact of human resource outsourcing, a recent study of small manufacturing firms has found that human resource outsourcing can contribute to several measures of firm performance. Although subjective measures of financial performance were used, the measures correlate well with objective financial data. The study found that outsourcing had an indirect but positive impact on subjective measures of financial performance and innovation. The fact that the firms' strategies moderated the relationships between outsourcing and firm performance provides support for the contingency view that human resource practices are more effective in some circumstances than others.[37]

Industrial Relations

Decertification of Union Bargaining Agents

While companies are legally prohibited from the instigation of employee attempts to decertify their unions, the nature of the labor relations environment can be expected to have some influence over such actions. Thus, the firm's practices that shape the labor relations climate have the potential to indirectly influence decertification actions. Accordingly, decertification elections are included in this discussion of the effects of human resource practices. A recent study has examined the effect on shareholder returns of 153 union decertification elections. Potential investors are assumed to anticipate that unionism will redistribute the firm's earnings toward wages at the expense of shareholder returns. Thus, the decertification of a union as the bargaining agent would be assumed to have a positive impact on shareholder returns.[38] In contrast to this expectation, the study found that elections retaining the union produced higher shareholder returns:

> This study finds that firms that retained union representation in decertification cases actually outperformed those that ousted the bargaining agent in a partitioned sample comparison.[39]

Positive Labor Relations

The manner in which firms handle relations with their unions and the workers they represent can have a number of effects. Such labor relations practices can affect the productivity of the workforce and financial performance. More specifically, it has been well established in the industrial relations or labor relations literature that unionism can have both positive and negative impacts on productivity. One explanation of the effects of unions is that through their representation of workers in grievance procedures and collective bargaining, unions provide workers with a means of expressing their concerns to management about workplace conditions. This means that unions provide a voice mechanism, which in some situations can have a positive impact on firm performance. For example, in situations in which management is unreceptive to the concerns of individual workers and there is no union to provide a voice, the only other alternative for dissatisfied workers is an exit response of leaving for better conditions elsewhere. Because of the voice mechanism, it is argued that unionized firms have lower quit rates and encourage firms to provide more rational and professional management. In turn, these secondary effects lead to greater productivity.[40]

Unions also can have a positive impact on productivity under certain labor market conditions. This can occur in situations in which the employer has monopoly power in the labor market (a condition of monopsony). When unions negotiate higher wages under such conditions, the economically rational response of employers is to add more capital per worker and to enhance the quality of labor. In turn, these secondary effects have the potential to increase productivity. However, unions may negotiate more restrictive work rules that lead to higher levels of employment than are necessary. Obviously, such secondary effects can lead to decreases in productivity.[41] A concise summary of the effects of labor relations on firm productivity is provided in the following:

> An important implication of the voice-response model is that productivity is likely to depend on the state of labor–management relations in shops. When those relations are poor, management is likely to have trouble getting high productivity. When they are good, workers and management may pull together for the benefit of the firm. Three studies have examined the link between productivity and the state of industrial relations at plants, and all three have found strong support for this proposition.[42]

In addition, it can be argued that under very specific conditions, the net effect of unionism and good labor relations may be positive. This argument is provided in the following:

> What unions do to productivity is one of the key factors in assessing the overall impact of unions. The new quantitative studies indicate that productivity is generally higher in unionized establishments than in otherwise comparable establishments that are nonunion, but that the relationship is far from immutable and has notable exceptions. Higher productivity appears to run hand in hand with good industrial relations and to be spurred by competition in the product market, while lower productivity under unionism appears to exist under the opposite circumstances.[43]

In spite of these findings, most employers probably do not feel that their firms obtain greater productivity as a result of unionism. Otherwise, they would encourage their workers to form unions, and this is obviously not the case with most employers. The effects of poor labor relations are more obvious. Strikes can provide an indication of the quality and impact of labor relations practices. While at first appearance strikes might not appear to be a human resource practice, they can reflect to some degree the quality of the firm's labor relations effort or the overall management of the firm. Obviously, unionization does not equate with strikes but it does bring their potential. Furthermore, there is probably more than a grain of truth to the old expression that firms that have unions usually deserve them. Indeed, there are abundant examples of firms that were unionized as a result of their poor treatment of employees. Thus, there is a question of causality here in that unionism and subsequent strikes or work stoppages are sometimes reflective of poor management.

Nonetheless, there are many factors, aside from the quality of a firm's labor relations function, that predispose a firm toward unionism.[44] For example, automobile manufacturing, railroads, and airlines are overwhelmingly unionized as are many public sector organizations such as fire departments and police departments. Even the best-managed firms or departments in such industries will most likely be unionized. As mentioned earlier, at Southwest Airlines, which is perennially in the top four on *Fortune*'s list of the 100 Best Companies to Work For, 84 to 85 percent of its employees are represented by unions.[45]

Strikes

The relationship between strikes and the financial performance of struck firms has been empirically examined using shareholder returns. One study found that after relatively long strikes (11 to 29 days), shareholder returns tended to increase. Conversely, after short strikes (1 to 10 days), the firms' financial performance tended to decline, and after extremely long strikes (30 days or more), shareholder returns tended to decline dramatically. These results provide evidence of the conventional wisdom that companies win longer strikes (11 to 29 days) and that unions win short strikes (1 to 10 days). For the extremely long strikes, financial returns decreased dramatically up to 24 months after the strike, perhaps because the parties' relationship may have taken on aspects of a death marriage.[46]

The recent strikes at American Airlines and Boeing, which involved highly educated pilots, engineers, and technicians, were unique because college-educated, unionized professionals were striking. In the Boeing strike, there were several issues of an economic nature but also some were related to perceptions that engineers were not treated well by the company's management.[47] In addition, one strike and one "sick out" by the pilots at American Airlines also were related to their perceptions of an unsatisfactory labor relations environment, a confrontational management style by the previous CEO, and perceptions that management was attempting to outsource routes that should be flown by American Airlines pilots.[48] Although the first strike lasted only a matter of minutes before it was stopped by U.S. presidential action, the second "sick out" was very costly for the company and for passengers whose travel arrangements were disrupted by the strike. (Airlines are covered by the Railway Labor Act of 1926, which has a number of provisions that limit efficient conflict resolution.) It is instructive to consider the following: "In contrast to American and its long history of strikes, Southwest has never lost an hour of flying time to a labor dispute even though its work force is the industry's most unionized." [49] It seems reasonable to conclude that failure to invest in good labor relations practices has negative financial consequences for firms.

While poor labor relations practices set the stage for poor financial performance, some conflict with unions may be unavoidable. In many instances, labor difficulties such as strikes are not representative of the quality of a firm's labor relations practices. In some cases, a firm may be struck irrespective of the quality of its labor relations. For example, if a firm bargains as part of a multiemployer bargaining association, such as in the trucking industry, all firms in the association may be struck if negotiations reach an impasse. In addition, in some instances, the decision to take a strike instead of settling on unfavorable terms with the union may be an investment in the future credibility of management negotiators and may be consistent with high-quality labor relations. Thus, a company that has "taken a strike" may gain some advantage in the future because when it says no to a union demand, the union may be convinced that the firm's response is credible and may not pursue the issue. Furthermore, although unionization levels are at historically low levels in the private sector in the United States, several recent strikes, such as those at United Parcel Service (UPS), American Airlines, General Motors, Boeing, and Lockheed-Martin, have captured the attention of management observers.

Internal Labor Market

Researchers also have examined the performance effects of internal labor markets that provide for promotion from within. The Delaney and Huselid study, cited previously, found through analysis of data from the National Organizations Survey that promotion from within is significantly related to perceptual measures of organizational performance. Such promotion practices were correlated with performance for the for-profit organizations in their sample. Interestingly, these results were not found when nonprofit organizations were included in the analysis. However, an alternate measure of internal labor markets assessed the degree of vertical hierarchy as an indicator of promotion ladders. While greater vertical hierarchy is inconsistent with tendencies toward flatter structure and decentralized decision making, this measure became significantly related with performance when nonprofit organizations were included in the analysis.[50]

Motivation

Decentralized Decision Making

A study by Varma and colleagues provides evidence on the performance effects of decentralized decision making. Their study examined the impact of a number of high-performance work practices and systems, including delegation of decision making. The research was based on a survey of 39 large firms (average of 18,000 employees) from several industries. The researchers referred to delegation as a system, as opposed to an individual practice, although they measured it with only one item. (Delegation was one of several items used to measure organizational culture.) Thus, while delegated decision making or decentralization is probably more complex than simple human resource practices such as structured interviews, it will be considered as an individual practice in this discussion. In addition, the study employed perceptual measures of financial and operational performance.[51] (In a later discussion and in Table 8-2, decentralized decision making appears as one of several practices making up a commitment-oriented system.)

The study's findings on the effects of delegated or decentralized decision making may be summarized as follows:

Not surprisingly, increased delegation has a significant positive relationship with operational outcomes. Once again, this confirms the notion that employees feel empowered by increased delegation, and this empowerment can lead to significant improvements in the operational outcomes of the organization. This is an important finding worthy of attention. The data suggest that organizations that make a conscious effort to increase delegation of work are likely to benefit by improving their operational outcomes.[52]

Self-Managed Teams or Autonomous Work Groups

Teams and teamwork have become critical to the success of many organizations, and self-managed teams fit with greater decentralization.[53] Self-managed teams are different than traditional work teams in that the team itself governs the sequence of work needed for the performance of a series of interdependent tasks. Such teams may order materials, perform maintenance, and perform inspections of the quality of the output. A recent study examined the impact of teams on quality and labor productivity in four different manufacturing areas of a unionized *Fortune* 500 company. The teams in this study did not have all of the autonomy of self-managed teams, but they had substantial latitude in problem solving and were provided with budgetary information about their plant and with information about the products of their competitors. In addition, team membership, which ranged from 4 to 18, was involuntary as members were assigned to their teams. The researchers termed these teams "High-Performance Work Teams."[54]

In order to determine the impact of teams, the researchers used a longitudinal research design with data series beginning before the implementation of teams. Their analysis examined 84 weeks of quality data (manufacturing defect rates) and 21 months of labor productivity data. Because there are many potential influences on quality and productivity, the analysis included several control variables. The researchers found that the implementation of the high-performance work teams produced significant improvements in quality (reductions in defect rates) and labor productivity.[55]

Open-Book Management or Sharing Financial and Performance Information

As explained in Chapter 2, the sharing of financial or performance information is often referred to as open-book management. Essentially, the practice encourages empowered employees to act in the best interests of the firm by making informed decisions and taking informed actions. The practice has the potential to enhance motivation by instilling a sense that employees are trusted and valued and by combining employee empowerment with various incentives such as profit sharing or cost savings. Although there is little empirical evidence on the performance impact of open-book management, there is a great deal of anecdotal evidence derived from the experiences of companies that have implemented the practice.

John Case has described numerous successful implementations in his book, *The Open-Book Experience: Lessons from Over 100 Companies Who Successfully Transformed Themselves*.[56] Firms have obtained positive impacts in achieving a number of specific firm goals such as reduced error rates, increased average sales per customer, improved quality, improved order accuracy, and reduced expenses for shop supplies.[57] Although anecdotal reports do not control for other factors that may have contributed to such performance improvements, the large number of positive reports argue for an optimistic view of the potential impact of this practice.

Reduced Status Differentials or Symbolic Egalitarianism

There is little empirical evidence that reduced status differentials have a positive performance effect. Nonetheless, there are several examples of top-performing companies that have devoted substantial effort to the elimination of status differentials. Executives in these companies believe that such differentials create dysfunctional divisions in the workforce and detract from the company's performance. Many high-performing companies, such as Whole Foods Markets, Lincoln Electric, Kingston Technology, Wal-Mart, and Southwest Airlines, have gone to great lengths to minimize status differentials in their organizations.[58]

For example, at Southwest Airlines, there is low tolerance for elitism. As the Vice President for People has explained: "Arrogant people will not fit in. Nor will someone who is really proud of his or her title." [59] The company's executives do not have big offices, and they provide their home telephone numbers for employees. Indeed, many of the firm's executives have worked their way up from the ranks. In addition, Southwest's reputation for casual attire is legendary.[60] At Chaparral Steel, another company known for managerial excellence and firm performance, there is no reserved parking for anyone, and casual attire is the norm except when there is a meeting with customers. At Intel Corporation, the CEO has a 9 × 12-foot cubicle for an office described as follows:

> WHAT YOU SEE: In true Silicon Valley tradition, a cubicle only slightly larger than Dilbert's. Steel-framed partitions are covered in gray fabric, desk and tabletops are gray Formica, bookcases and cabinets are gray plastic with mauve upholstery. At the doorless entryway, a gray plastic name plate reads "C. Barrett." [61]
>
> WHAT HE SEES: A very egalitarian company. There are no perks. Everybody has the same office, with a chair, a computer, a couple of bookshelves and some storage space. We spend most of our time in meetings anyway.[62]

Compensation also has important status implications in many organizations. The compensation of top executives can become a major status differential and thus a potential cause of decreased organizational performance.[63] Graef Crystal has analyzed the relationship between the compensation for 20 CEOs and the performance of their companies. As a measure of company performance, he used an index of total shareholder return weighted over a three-year period. For compensation, he included base salary, annual bonus, and the following forms of long-term incentives: stock options, restricted stock, and performance plans that generally involve cash payments for attaining goals. In order to determine the value of stock options, he used a version of the Black-Scholes Option Pricing Model. He also derived a market value for the CEOs reflecting differences in firm size, industry, and company performance. In another study of 279 CEOs from throughout the United States, he determined that the average total compensation was $8.7 million.[64]

On the basis of these data, Crystal provided a colorful categorization of the extent to which the CEOs were worth the compensation they received. In his top performance category, which he termed "worth it big time," he included some of the following: Gordon Bethune, the CEO of Continental Airlines whose shareholders received a 483 percent return over the three-year period while Bethune received annual compensation of $3,007,000; Herb Kelleher, the CEO of Southwest Airlines, whose shareholders received 68.2 percent return in 1997, while Kelleher received $651,000 in total compensation per year; John Mackey, the CEO of Whole Foods Market, whose total annual compensation was $332,000, while his shareholders received returns for the three years from 58 to 91 percent; Thomas Engibous, CEO of Texas Instruments, whose shareholders received 62.8 percent over the period, while he received $5,365,000 in total compensation. (Michael Dell was an exception as his total compensation far exceeded the other CEOs in this best category.)

In the worst category, "not worth it big time," he included the CEO of Enron, whose compensation totaled $13,701,000, while shareholders in 1997 received a −1.4 percent return when the Standard & Poor's 500 generated a return of 33.4 percent. He also included the CEO of Electronic Data Services (EDS) in the worst category and provided the following commentary on his compensation and the firm's performance:

> Although his performance was just plain terrible most of the time, EDS's board lavished upon him vast sums of money: a total compensation package worth more than $13.8 million in 1997. Yet you'd have to search long and hard during Alberthal's nearly twelve years as CEO to find an instance when EDS outperformed the Standard & Poor's 500 Index, a listing of five hundred stocks that is the premier gauge of the stock market. Actually, there is one instance that springs to mind, and that was August 7, 1998, the day after EDS announced his retirement. That day the company's stock price jumped 14 percent, adding $2.5 billion to the total market value of the stock. It's not often that a CEO can determine just how much impact he personally is having on his company's stock price, but for Alberthal, August 7 was one for the books.[65]

Performance Management

There is empirical evidence that results-oriented appraisals have a positive impact on firm performance. The study by Delery and Doty cited earlier, which drew on a sample of banks, also found that results-oriented appraisals have a positive impact on ROA.[66] In addition, companies that do not have good appraisal systems run the risk of not being able to justify terminations or the denial of promotions. Having no documentation of inadequate or substandard performance places the firm in danger of being on the losing side in litigation or arbitration and creates financial liability.

Nonetheless, performance appraisals do not always accurately reflect the performance of the employee nor do their ratings always have an impact on results such as compensation. Because of these and other problems, the practice of performance appraisal is being revised in some organizations because of fundamental questions about its contributions and the changing role of human resource management.[67] Indeed, 360-degree feedback approaches are being adopted by many organizations because of problems with traditional appraisal systems. Michael Beer has made the following critical observations about performance appraisal:

> Evidence has been accumulating for years that performance appraisal systems, no matter how well designed, do not differentiate employees sufficiently to make valid and reliable compensation, promotion and layoff decisions. They do not necessarily even lead to better coaching. Instead these systems have become bureaucratic nightmares and have put human resource professionals in the role of "cop." . . . effective individual performance evaluation and development are fostered not by a performance appraisal system, but by a high involvement organization, performance-oriented managers, and a culture that tolerates mistakes, encourages letting consistently poor performers go, and recognizes outstanding performers.[68]

Staffing

Several individual staffing practices have been found to be positively associated with various measures of firm performance. For example, a study by David Terpstra and Elizabeth Rozell examined the performance impact of five staffing practices that are commonly viewed as well-grounded selection techniques:

1. Yield analysis or follow-up studies of recruiting sources to identify those sources producing the highest percentages of high-performing employees
2. Validation studies of tests and other selection procedures
3. Use of structured selection interviews (asking the same questions of all applicants)
4. Use of ability and cognitive aptitude tests
5. Use of weighted application blanks (WABs) or biographical information blanks (BIBs)

A composite selection index was developed for all of these techniques.[69]

Terpstra and Rozell surveyed over 200 firms in order to determine the relationship between these selection techniques and the following measures of firm performance: annual profit, growth in profit over a five-year period, growth in annual average sales over a five-year period, and a composite or overall performance measure. The study did not use actual accounting data but instead asked respondents to report profit, profit growth, and sales growth in terms of percentage ranges. Nonetheless, these measures correlated highly with accounting data obtained for a subsample of over 60 of the firms in the survey.[70]

The results of the study provide strong evidence that these selection tools can have a positive impact on firm performance, particularly in certain industries. The study's failure to find uniform positive effects across all industries, even for such well-grounded selection practices such as these, indicates that the effectiveness of a particular selection practice depends, to a certain extent, on the firm's industry. The influence of industry also emphasizes the importance of the contingency perspective that will be addressed later. Not surprisingly, the study found that larger firms are more likely to use better selection practices. (It is possible that more positive relationships may have been found with more precise controls for different industries. Because profitability is affected by many influences, a more extensive set of control variables also may have produced even stronger evidence of the impact of these practices.)[71]

Cognitive Tests

Cognitive tests, or tests of mental ability, have been used for various selection purposes since the early 1900s. The use of such tests came under attack in the 1970s because firms sometimes used them without establishing their validity or the relationship between applicant scores and job performance. Nonetheless, while the process of validating such tests requires some statistical sophistication, validation procedures are well established. Furthermore, recent research indicates that the predictive ability of cognitive ability tests may have been underestimated in the past. These tests can be enormously helpful in improving selection accuracy when validated and administered properly.[72] The Terpstra and Rozell study found that cognitive tests were significantly associated with profit, sales growth, and overall performance in service industries. The study also found that the use of cognitive testing tended to be associated with greater firm size in terms of number of employees.[73]

Staffing Selectivity

The impact of selective staffing also has been subjected to empirical analysis. The Delaney and Huselid study cited also examined selective staffing through analysis of perceptual measures of the organizational performance. For organizations in the for-profit sector of the survey, staffing selectivity was significantly related in a positive direction to organizational performance. When the nonprofit organizations were included in the analysis no relationship was found with performance.[74]

Anecdotal evidence also supports the positive relationship found in empirical studies. Southwest Airlines, provides an example of a high-performance company that is highly selective in staffing.[75] Southwest's Vice President for People reported in a recent year that the company received 135,000 applications. Of these applicants, it interviewed 35,000 (with three different people interviewing each applicant), and hired approximately 5,000 people. Interestingly, Southwest includes some of its frequent flyers in the interviewing process for flight attendants to help ensure a good match with the company's culture.[76]

Strategy-Linked CEO Succession: Insiders vs. Outsiders

While the traditional selection literature typically provides guidance on how to select individuals for particular jobs, some firms have moved toward processes that may be more accurately described as strategic selection. In essence, such staffing attempts to find executives who have the best abilities to implement a desired strategy in a given industrial context. Interestingly, it has been proposed that with greater diversification at the corporate level, the firm-specific experience and knowledge of CEOs becomes less important than portfolio management skills. (Portfolio management skills refer to the ability to manage diverse businesses on the basis of general principles instead of in-depth knowledge of the specific business.)[77]

Conversely, with less diversified firms, knowledge of the core business is much more valuable. Such knowledge of less diversified firms typically develops with increasing organizational tenure. It has been argued that as executives acquire longer tenure within their firms, however, they apply fewer innovative or novel ideas to new situations. Accordingly, there appears to be a downside to the value of firm-specific knowledge as an inverse relationship has been found between firm performance and CEO tenure in nondiversified firms.[78]

These conflicting observations have led to a recent attempt to find answers to three related questions:

1. When firms differ in the extent to which their strategies emphasize diversification, are there differences in the tenure of the CEOs they select?
2. Does the tenure of an executive who is selected as CEO have an impact on the subsequent performance of the firm?
3. Does the firm's degree of diversification moderate the CEO tenure and firm performance relationship?

These questions were addressed by examining the succession of CEOs in 221 different firms. After the CEO successions, the performances of the firms were measured by return on assets over a three-year period. The study employed controls for the circumstances of the CEO succession, the firm's performance prior to the CEO's succession, firm size, and age of the firm. CEOs were considered as outsiders if they had five or fewer years of tenure with the firm at the time of succession.[79]

Interestingly, the results indicate that firms selecting CEOs from the ranks of executives inside the organization or CEOs with longer tenure experienced declines in their ROA during the period after their selection. Furthermore, for firms having low levels of diversification, the selection of outsiders or executives with low levels of tenure was associated with increased ROAs in the period after the CEO's selection.[80] Thus, the study provides strong evidence that better firm performance can be obtained when the selection practices are coordinated or matched with the firm's strategy. Some of the other implications of this study may be summarized as follows:

> These findings linking tenure with inferior performance contradict conventional wisdom and conventional practice. Traditionally, both conventional wisdom and practice have been that internal development and promotion, up to and including the CEO position, were the hallmark of the successful, effective, organization . . . The rapidity of environmental flux in recent years may dictate a heightened need for a constant reexamination of the status quo, and continuous innovation and change. A corollary of this proposition is that the relative value of firm-specific tenure may be diminishing. Knowledge of past practices, procedures, and strategies—perhaps more valuable in earlier, more stable competitive environments—may now sometimes impede progress and change.[81]

While these results favor the selection of outsiders, insiders also can acquire some of the abilities associated with outsiders. The NCR Corporation has found that the intraorganizational experience of executives can be enriched to develop adaptive abilities more characteristic of outsiders. In addition, these findings emphasize that while firms tend to select CEOs from outside when firm performance has declined, the performance of outsiders is better than that of insiders only when the firms are nondiversified. The researchers have speculated that with greater diversification, there may be some dilution of the CEO's impact, while with less diversification, the CEO can achieve results more quickly as a result of more focus.[82]

Structured Interviews

Terpstra and Rozell also examined the performance impact of structured interviews. Their multiple regression analyses found that structured interviews were associated with profit and profit growth in service industries. In contrast to the regression results, correlations of structured interviews with profit and profit growth across all industries were quite small.[83] The small bivariate correlations indicate the importance of the context in which the practices are implemented and thus provide some evidence for the contribution of the contingency perspective.

Validation Studies

Terpstra and Rozell's analyses found that validation studies were associated with profit, profit growth, and overall firm performance in service industries. As with cognitive tests, the results also indicated that the use of validation studies was associated with increased firm size in terms of number of employees. Cognitive testing and the use of validation studies were highly correlated.[84] This relationship was to be expected since the threat of potential litigation over the adverse impact of testing requires evidence of test validity, and test validation is a bedrock principle of good selection.

Weighted Application Blanks and Biographical Information Blanks

Terpstra and Rozell also examined the performance impacts of WABs and BIBs. Their analysis, which controlled for the number of employees, revealed that the use of WABs/BIBs was associated with overall firm performance in service industries. Relatively high correlations for WABs/BIBs were found with annual profit, profit growth, and overall performance.[85]

Yield Analysis of Recruiting Sources

Yield analysis involves the evaluation of the quality of various sources of employees such as the universities from which an organization obtains its better employees or the advertising media that produce the best job applicants. The Terpstra and Rozell study also examined the impact of yield analysis. They found that yield analysis was associated with sales growth and the overall measure of performance in service industries. They also found it to be associated with profit and firm overall performance in wholesale/retail industries. As noted earlier, their analysis also controlled for number of employees in the firms. Yield analysis had correlations across all industries with profit and overall firm performance.

Training

It has been estimated that U.S. companies spend $55.3 billion on training each year.[86] Although the U.S. lags behind several other industrialized countries in training, such an expenditure provides some indication that many firms view training as a high-performance practice. Nonetheless, until recently, there has been little evidence on its effect on firm performance. As will be discussed in Chapter 9, in the past, companies were slow to evaluate the effectiveness of their training programs. However, there is ample evidence that the value of training has come under increased scrutiny. For example, a recent survey of training professionals revealed that 93 percent of the respondents reported greater pressure to show a return for their employers' investments in training.[87]

A recent empirical study focused on the performance impact of training in an open-pit mining operation of the Cyprus Sierrita Corporation. Approximately 200 of the company's 770 employees at this site work in mining operations. A time series of normalized productivity data for total cycle time (truck tons per hour) was examined to determine the impact of training for mine crews. While no control group was employed, the data were exponentially smoothed to lessen the impact of temporal and weather influences. Examination of these productivity data before and after the training revealed that the there was a substantial impact on productivity. The costs of the training were determined in considerable detail to include the wages of employees while they were being trained, the costs for the trainer, idle time for equipment, and overtime premiums. As a result of the training, the company realized an annual savings of $1.9 million.[88]

Another recent study provides additional evidence on the financial impact of training. The study surveyed 40 companies from a number of industries.

Table 8-1 Individual Human Resource Practices Affecting Firm Performance

Human Resource Practices	*Positive Firm Performance Effects*
Compensation	
Broad-based stock options	Productivity (lagged), growth
Incentive-based compensation	Performance relative to industry (P), sales and customer satisfaction (in upscale markets)
Profit sharing	ROA, ROE, shareholder returns, survival
Diversity	
Minority hiring during downturns	Shareholder returns
Employment	
Countercyclical hiring	Shareholder returns
Downsizing (employment and assets)	ROA
Early retirement programs	Shareholder returns (with good returns prior to announcement)
Employment security	ROA
Human resource outsourcing	Financial performance (P), innovation (P)
Industrial Relations	
Decertification elections (union retained)	Shareholder returns
Positive labor relations (unionism)	Productivity
Strikes (11–29 days)	Shareholder returns
Internal Labor Market	
Internal career opportunities	ROA (prospectors), ROE (prospectors)
Motivation	
Decentralized decision making	Operational outcomes (P)
Open-book management	Numerous reports of goals obtained (A)
Participative decision making	ROA (defenders), ROE (defenders)
High-performance work teams	Quality, labor productivity
Reduced status differentials	High-performance firm adoptions (A)
Performance Management	
Results-oriented appraisals	ROA
Staffing	
Cognitive tests	Profit, sales growth, overall performance
Selectivity	Performance relative to industry (P)
Succession of "outsider" CEOs	ROA (with low firm diversification)
Structured interviews	Profit, profit growth
Validation studies	Profit, profit growth, overall performance
WABs and BIBs	Profit, overall performance
Yield analysis of recruiting sources	Sales growth
Training	
Training	Performance relative to industry (P), productivity

Note: P = perceptual measures of performance; A = numerous anecdotal reports of performance impacts; ROA = return on assets; ROE = return on equity. Many performance effects are industry specific. Industry differences in performance effects are not indicated in this table. Some performance effects are strategy specific.

Sources: Studies reported in this chapter provide the basis for these results.

When the respondents were categorized by their average training expenditures per employee, there was a substantial difference in their annual gross profit. Those companies in the top half had an average gross profit of $168,000 per employee, while those in the bottom half had an average of $121,000. The companies were also compared on the level of their training expenditures and their MTB ratios, which provide a rough indication of the company's intellectual capital as well as other intangibles. Those companies in the upper half of training expenditures had an average MTB ratio of 2.40 as compared with 2.00 for the companies in the lower half. When the companies were compared on the proportion of their workforces receiving training, the difference in MTB ratios was even larger. While these results should be regarded as being somewhat preliminary because of the study's lack of controls, the results provide an indication that the performance effects may be substantial.[89]

Training also has been found to have a positive impact on perceptual measures of organizational performance. The Delaney and Huselid study cited earlier using data from the National Organizations Survey also found training to be significantly related to such measures of performance for both for-profit and nonprofit organizations. Training was correlated with performance for the entire sample and for for-profit organizations.[90]

It also can be concluded that the type of training and its quality can have an impact on the financial and productivity effects to be realized by firms. In addition, there is probably a great deal of truth in the assertion that there is greater likelihood of positive performance effects when training is integrated into the culture of the firm.[91]

A summary of the performance impact of individual human resource practices is presented in Table 8-1.

LIMITATIONS OF INDIVIDUAL PRACTICES

As noted earlier, individual human resource practices tend to be highly intercorrelated. As a result, it is easy to overestimate their actual impact on performance. For example, if it is found that merit-based compensation practices have a significant correlation coefficient of $r = .40$ with firm profitability, then the statistical interpretation is that such compensation systems account for 16 percent (r^2) of the variance in firm profitability. Unfortunately, this would be a misleading interpretation because the compensation practice is probably only one of several other highly correlated human resource practices that are simultaneously influencing profitability. A more accurate interpretation would be that several high-performance practices are responsible for 16 percent of the variance in profitability.[92] Indeed, the Delaney and Huselid study cited earlier, based on the National Organizations Survey, found that simple relationships between individual human resource practices and measures of firm performance overstate their contributions because when additional practices are added to multiple regression equations, the size of their coefficients (magnitude of contribution) decreases and may even become statistically insignificant.[93]

EVOLUTION OF PRACTICES

While the individual practice perspective has limitations, it seems reasonable to infer that decisions about the adoption of human resource practices may occur, at least on occasion, on an individual practice basis. Indeed, until recently, much of the human resource literature focused on the impact of individual practices.[94] Furthermore, systems of human resource practices are not developed and implemented over night but appear to evolve. Brian Becker and Barry Gerhart have concluded that "HR systems are path dependent. They consist of policies that are developed over time and cannot be simply purchased in the market by competitors."[95] Firms have often adopted human resource practices to address specific competitiveness concerns, such as lagging product development. To counter such a weakness, the firm may have adopted an individual practice of compensation leadership in order to attract highly talented research and development personnel. Unfortunately, not all individual practices are effective by themselves. For example, a firm may make the decision to adopt another individual practice, such as work teams, without changes in supporting systems such as team-based compensation systems. Isolated decisions on individual practices, such as in the latter example, have sometimes resulted in a potpourri of disjointed practices that may even be incompatible with each other. For example, a firm would not be expected to maximize the benefits from the implementation of work teams while it retains a compensation system that reinforces individual performance.

SYSTEMS OF HIGH-PERFORMANCE HUMAN RESOURCE PRACTICES

A practical implication of the limitations of individual practices and their high intercorrelation is that it is unusual to find a firm that employs only one or two such practices. The more common situation is one in which the firm employs several such practices or systems of these practices. For example, practices such as highly selective recruiting practices, heavy investment in training, team-based compensation, and dual technical and managerial career tracks are compatible with each other and constitute systems that are critical for implementation of a business strategy that emphasizes innovation through research and development. Thus, the literature has asserted that such strategic human resource systems should produce superior performance because of such compatibilities or synergies.[96]

Because of the potential synergies that are possible when firms employ systems of complementary human resource practices, the question has arisen as to whether systems of such practices have a greater impact on firm performance than individual practices. Thus, we shall examine the effects of systems of practices.

Recently, sophisticated empirical studies have provided definitive answers to persistent questions about the bottom-line performance effects of systems of human resource practices. While the literature has long asserted that certain practices will produce higher performance, until recently there was only scattered evidence for individual practices and virtually no evidence on systems of practices. While there is now evidence on the performance effects of such systems, the particular practices to be included in the various systems are often a function of the research methodology. Many of the studies examining systems of human resource practices have employed statically derived groupings of practices. By using statistical procedures such as factor analysis, they usually identify groups or clusters of individual practices and then label each cluster as a system. Although the systems consist of empirically related practices, there may be less logical consistency than would occur if a human resource executive were asked to develop such systems. A summary of the performance impact of systems of human resource practices is presented in Table 8-2.

Mark Huselid has performed one of the most comprehensive studies of the financial effects of such systems. His study, which has been received with great interest by both academicians and practitioners, examined data from over 825 firms. The results of this study warrant substantial confidence as the study employed a comprehensive set of variables that controlled for various influences on firm performance. The study examined two separate systems of highly intercorrelated practices, the first being employee skills and organizational structures and the second being employee motivation and hiring selectivity. This skills system included the following practices:

- Information sharing
- Use of formal job analysis
- Promotion from within
- Use of attitude surveys of the workforce
- Use of quality of work life programs
- Profit sharing or gain sharing
- Employee training
- Employee access to grievance procedures
- Use of selection tests

The second system of motivation practices was made up of the following:

- Compensation based on performance appraisals
- Use of formal performance appraisals
- Merit-based promotions
- Hiring selectivity[97]

This comprehensive study found very strong evidence that systems of human resource practices have a positive impact on firm performance. In gen-

Table 8-2 Systems of Human Resource Practices Impacting Firm Performance

Systems of HR Practices as Defined in Individual Studies	*Positive Performance Effects for Each System*
Commitment-Oriented Systems	
Decentralized decision making	Labor productivity and scrap rates (lower)
General training	
Greater proportion of highly skilled employees	
Higher wages	
Greater emphasis on bonuses	
Human–Capital Enhancement	
Comprehensive training Developmental and behavior-based appraisal Selection for technical and problem-solving skills Selective staffing Training for technical and problem-solving skills	Labor productivity (P), equipment efficiency (P), and customer alignment (e.g., on-time delivery, quality) (all produced by combination of a quality strategy with a human–capital-enhancement system)
Human Resource Administrative System	
Hourly pay Individual equity Individual incentives Results-based performance appraisal Selection for manual and physical skills Training on policies and procedures	Equipment efficiency (P) (produced by a combination of low-cost strategy with a human resource administrative system)
Motivation and Commitment System	
Hiring on receptiveness to new learning Compensation contingent on firm performance Extent of status differentials (management vs. workers) Training for new employees Ongoing training for experienced employees	Labor productivity and quality (produced by combination of flexible production systems with motivation and commitment systems)
Motivation and Hiring Selectivity	
Formal performance appraisals Hiring selectivity Merit-based promotions Performance-based compensation	Sales per employee, Tobin's q
Skills and Organizational Structures	
Attitude surveys of the workforce Employee access to grievance procedures Formal job analysis Information sharing Profit sharing or gain sharing	Gross rate of return on assets

(continued)

Table 8-2 *(continued)*

Systems of HR Practices as Defined in Individual Studies	*Positive Performance Effects for Each System*
Skills and Organizational Structures *(continued)*	
Promotion from within	
Quality of work life programs	
Selection tests	
Training	

Note: P = perceptual measures of performance. Many performance effects are industry specific. Industry differences in performance effects are not indicated in this table. Systems of practices were often statistically defined by the studies from which this table was compiled. For example, individual practices were often categorized by factor analysis and assigned descriptive system labels.

Sources: Studies reported in this chapter provide the basis for these results.

eral, the system of employee skills was significantly related to increased gross rate of returns on assets. Thus, firms that use systems of high-performance skill enhancement practices generally have higher rates of return. Furthermore, firms that use systems of high-performance motivation practices generally have higher productivity (sales per employee) and values of Tobin's q, a crude measure of accumulated intellectual capital.[98] Obviously, a myriad of organizational, technical, economic, environmental, and temporal variables have influences on different measures of firm performance. Nonetheless, when the influence of these variables is controlled, analyses of the impact of systems of human resource practices clearly indicate increased likelihood of increased performance for firms that implement them under the appropriate circumstances.

Finally, the overall impact of the whole set of high-performance human resource practices in Huselid's study was captured in dollar terms as follows:

> The magnitude of the returns for investments in High Performance Work Practices is substantial. A one-standard-deviation increase in such practices is associated with a relative 7.05 percent decrease in turnover and, on a per employee basis, $27,044 more in sales and $18,641 and $3,814 more in market value and profits, respectively. These internally consistent and economically and statistically significant values suggest that firms can indeed obtain substantial financial benefits from investing in the practices studied here.[99]

INDIVIDUAL BEST PRACTICES VS. SYSTEMS OF PRACTICES

As noted earlier in the discussion of individual best practices, the Delaney and Huselid study, based on 590 for-profit and nonprofit organizations from the

National Organizations Survey, used perceptual measures of organizational performance. These measures were relative in the sense that survey respondents reported on how the performance of their organizations compared with others in the same industry. As noted in the discussions of individual practices, the results indicated that several such practices were significantly related to performance. Nonetheless, tests of whether systems of complementary practices provided greater performance found the following result: "Our results do not support the assertion that complementarities among HRM practices enhance firm performance."[100]

The evidence on the superiority of the approaches is mixed, with neither perspective clearly dominant in its performance effects. For the individual best practices perspective, there are some practices, such as selective staffing, that have very strong effects. Such practices can be expected to produce performance effects even in the absence of a complementary system of supporting practices, such as practices that help motivate and maintain a workforce. Nonetheless, the adoption of single practices or a single "silver bullet" practice is seldom a good means for increasing and sustaining firm performance. The fact that high-performance human resource practices tend to have high intercorrelations provides good evidence that firms tend to maintain systems of high-performance human resource practices. While they may adopt such practices incrementally and begin with only one such practice, over time the better-performing firms are likely to develop supporting systems of high-performance practices.

Before the impact of systems can be determined, the manner in which their components fit together within the context of the firm must be better understood. Effective systems are not likely to be collections of uncomplementary practices. This point has been made as follows:

> [I]t is difficult to grasp the precise mechanisms by which the interplay of human resource practices and policies generates value. To imitate a complex system, it is necessary to understand how the elements interact. Are the effects additive or multiplicative, or do they involve complex nonlinearities . . . researchers are a long way from understanding the precise nature of these interactions.[101]

UNIVERSAL PRACTICES VS. CONTINGENCY PERSPECTIVES

The universal approach maintains that there are several best practices that can have positive performance effects in nearly any organizational context. Furthermore, the approach applies to both individual best practices as well as systems of best practices. This approach maintains that the performance effects of such practices or systems are direct and that their effects are so general or robust that they increase performance regardless of other organizational conditions or circumstances. While human resource scholars have pointed out the lack of common agreement on which practices constitute best practices, some recurring themes among various studies tend to include the practices already discussed in this chapter. One group of researchers has offered this tentative description of best practices: (1) employee skill enhancement by selective staffing, training, and development; and (2) enhanced teamwork, empowerment, and worker involvement in problem solving through the mechanisms of job redesign, use of group-based incentives, and the progression to all-salaried work forces.[102]

The contingency or fit perspective maintains that firms should adopt systems of human practices that fit their human resource strategies. This perspective maintains that the performance effects of such practices are realized through their application in appropriate organizational circumstances. Thus, a company could obtain the greatest increase in performance from selective staffing practices when it simultaneously pursues a business strategy of differentiating itself from its competitors by producing the highest-quality products. Selective staffing practices would enable the firm to hire employees having enough talent to manufacture such high-quality products.

The contingency approach is consistent with the principles of strategic human resource management presented in Chapter 4. These principles maintain that the practices or systems of practices used to implement the firm's human resource strategies should fit with or conform to the firm's competitive business strategies. Examples of business strategies are provided by Porter's framework (Chapter 4) that specifies three strategies for competition: (1) cost leadership as the low-cost product or service provider; (2) differentiation, such as by superior quality or service; and (3) focus or niche strategies that concentrate on a narrow area of differentiation.[103]

Thus, the contingency view would maintain that if a firm has adopted a cost leadership strategy, then it should have human resource practices consistent with this strategy. With cost leadership, a firm would probably not have a compensation system that offers extensive perks for executives nor would it pursue a practice of wage leadership. Furthermore, the compensation system also should fit the firm's organizational culture, and additional matching will be required when the firm has several cultures.[104]

EMPIRICAL EVIDENCE: THE CASE FOR UNIVERSAL BEST PRACTICES

One approach for determining the superiority of the universal practices or contingency approach involves a comparison of the performance effects of external and internal fit. Such fit should be absent with a universal approach but present with a contingency approach. External fit (vertical fit) is defined as the degree to which a firm's system of human resource practices are complementary with its competitive strategies, such as cost leadership, differentiation, and focus. In contrast, internal fit (horizontal fit) is defined as the degree to which individual human resource practices are complementary with each other.[105] Huselid's comprehensive study, cited earlier, examined whether external fit or internal fit would result in improved firm performance. However, the study found little support for superiority of either type of fit over the effects of individual best practices:

> But despite the strong theoretical expectation that better internal and external fit would be reflected in better financial performance, on the whole the results did not support the contention that either type of fit has any incremental value over the main effects associated with High Performance Practices.[106]

The Delery and Doty study of human resource practices in the banking industry, noted earlier, also examined the performance impact of the universalistic and contingency approaches. Banks provide a good data source for such research because they are legally required to report a great deal of information to regulators and the data are relatively easy to obtain. The researchers tested the universalistic approach by examining the direct firm performance effects of several individual human resource practices on the key position of loan officers. These practices included (1) internal career opportunities, (2) extensive training, (3) results-oriented performance appraisals, (4) employment security, (5) participative decision making, (6) clear job descriptions, and (7) profit sharing. Firm performance was measured with two accounting ratios: return on assets (ROA) and return on equity (ROE). For tests of the contingency approach, the researchers used a product/market innovation instrument to categorize the banking firms into the Miles and Snow strategic types discussed in Chapter 4: prospectors (emphasis on innovation), analyzers (imitators of innovators and focused operations), and defenders (low-cost producers).[107]

As noted earlier in the discussion of individual practices, results of the tests of the universalistic approach revealed that results-oriented appraisals, profit sharing, and employment security all had a positive impact on ROA while profit sharing also had a positive impact on ROE. In order to test the contingency approach, the researchers examined the incremental impact on performance of the strategy interactions with each of the human resource practices. Results for the contingency approach indicated that for banks in the prospector strategic category, the use of results-oriented appraisals produced higher ROA and ROE. In contrast, when appraisals were less results oriented, the banks in the defender category had higher ROA and ROE. Interestingly, defender banks that allowed loan officers to participate in decision making had better ROA and ROE. Conversely, prospector banks performed better with less participative decision making. In addition, more internal career opportunities produced positive impacts on ROA and ROE in prospector banks while the reverse held for defender banks. As noted in the following excerpt, the study found strong support for the universalistic approach and some support for the contingency approach.[108]

> The results of this study provided relatively strong support for a universalistic perspective and some support for . . . the contingency . . . perspectives. Three individual HR practices, profit sharing, results-oriented appraisals, and employment security, had relatively strong universalistic relationships with important accounting measures of performance. Contingency relationships between strategy and three HR practices—participation, results-oriented appraisals, and internal career opportunities—explained a significant portion of the variation in the same performance measures.[109]

EMPIRICAL EVIDENCE: THE CASE FOR THE CONTINGENCY VIEW

Similar to the support for the universal best practices view, a study of human resource practices in manufacturing plants by Youndt and colleagues found strong support for the contingency approach. This study of 97 manufacturing plants found positive operational performance effects when systems of human–capital-enhancement practices were linked to complementary quality manufacturing strategies. Human resource practices were measured with multiple scales for the areas of staffing, training, performance appraisal, and compensation. Items for human resource practices were combined into indexes representing a human resource administrative system as well as a human–capital-enhancing system.[110]

The researchers' definition of the administrative system included measures of "selection for manual and physical skills, policies and procedures training, results-based performance appraisal, individual equity, individual incentives, and hourly pay." [111] Their definition of the human–capital-enhancing system included the following practices: "selective staffing, selection for technical and problem-solving skills, comprehensive training, training for technical and problem-solving skills, developmental and behavior-based performance appraisal, external equity [linking compensation to external market indicators], group incentives, skill-based pay, and salaried compensation." [112]

Operational performance measures were based on responses to questionnaires that asked general managers and functional managers to compare their firm's performance with other firms in their industry. Three indices of performance were developed from these responses: employee productivity, machine efficiency, and customer alignment in terms of quality products and on-time delivery. Manufacturing strategy was measured on four dimensions: cost, delivery flexibility (e.g., on-time delivery, ramping production up quickly), scope flexibility (e.g., handling nonstandard orders, adjusting product mix), and quality.[113] The results of this study found the following support for the contingency approach:

> Overall, however, the moderation results provide strong evidence that manufacturing strategy influences the HR-performance relationship with a quality strategy

interacting with human–capital-enhancing HR to predict performance and delivery flexibility and cost strategies interacting with administrative HR to predict performance. In short, maximizing performance appears to depend on properly aligning HR systems with manufacturing strategy.[114]

A recent study of steel mini-mills by Jeffrey Arthur also found support for the contingency view. This study examined whether systems of human resource practices designed to enhance employee commitment to the organization would produce greater performance than systems of human resource practices designed for controlling the workforce. In this study, mini-mills were categorized as either commitment or control oriented on the basis of several human resource variables. The commitment-oriented mini-mills differed significantly from the control-oriented mills in a number of respects. More specifically, the commitment-oriented mini-mills were (1) more decentralized (nonsupervisory personnel made more production decisions), (2) provided more general training, (3) had a higher proportion of more highly skilled employees (maintenance and craft), (4) paid higher wages, and (5) paid a greater proportion of compensation in the form of bonuses. As predicted, the study found correspondence between the systems of human resource practices and the firms' competitive strategies. Firms pursuing a cost leadership strategy tended to have control-oriented systems of human resource practices, while mini-mills pursuing differentiation strategies tended to have commitment-oriented systems. As predicted, commitment-oriented systems of human resource practices were found to be associated with higher labor productivity and lower scrap rates.[115]

Another manufacturing study by John McDuffie addressed the issue by examining the impact of systems of human resource practices in automobile manufacturing in several countries. The study proposed that positive performance effects would occur only if innovative human resource practices are integrated with or are compatible with the firm's production strategy. More specifically, the premise was that performance gains would occur only if the discretionary effort and motivation produced by such innovative practices were channeled by the production strategy into greater performance. The study analyzed the performance effects of an index for human resource systems based on the following measures:

1. Hiring criteria emphasizing receptiveness to new learning and interpersonal skills
2. The degree to which individual compensation was contingent on performance of the firm
3. The extent of status differentials between management and workers
4. The extent of training provided to new employees
5. The extent of ongoing training provided for experienced employees[116]

The statistical models, which employed a comprehensive set of control variables, analyzed labor productivity as measured by the number of hours involved in manufacturing a vehicle. They also analyzed quality as measured by the number of defects reported by consumers. Manufacturing also provides a good source of data because it is possible to obtain objective measures of productivity. The study found that the system of high-performance human resource practices was associated with greater productivity and quality. Furthermore, the index for the system of human resource practices had greater explanatory power for productivity and quality than the individual practices by themselves.[117]

> Overall, the evidence strongly supports the hypothesis that assembly plants using flexible production systems, which bundle human resource practices into a system that is integrated with production/business strategy, outperform plants using more traditional mass production systems in both productivity and quality. These results provide the strongest statistical evidence to date of a positive relationship between innovative human resource practices and economic performance . . .[118]

Another recent study that examined effects of bonus plans also supports the contingency view. This study examined 34 stores in a retail chain and tracked sales for a period of 77 months. Sales personnel received bonuses only if they reached sales goals (outcome-based compensation). Regression analysis results indicated that such outcome-based compensation practices had a significant positive impact on sales only when the store served an upscale market. In addition, the plans had a significant positive impact on customer satisfaction only in upscale markets.[119] These results also are supportive of a contingency perspective.

SORTING THROUGH THE EVIDENCE

Studies testing the contingency view and the value of strategic fit are challenged by a number of difficult methodological problems. For example, the various studies do not use the same measures of human resource practices. Thus, differences in measurement may contribute to inconsistent results across studies.[120] Also, it is often necessary to use crude proxy measures of firms' strategies, such as subjective respondent estimates of the proportion of their firm's sales from cost leadership, differentiation, or focus strategies.[121] In other instances, the classification of strategies may rely on only one common dimension that varies across the different strategic classifications. Thus, the empirical description of strategies poses a limitation on the amount of performance that contingency models are capable of explaining. In addition, it is often difficult to obtain sufficient numbers of companies in highly specialized industrial categories to make valid intraindustry comparisons. On the other hand, broader industrial classifications, such as manufacturing, that provide more companies in each category, often produce groupings of companies that have very little in common.

Furthermore, while strategic frameworks such as Porter's and others presented in Chapter 4 are useful conceptual and planning tools they are probably not sufficiently complex to capture complete business strategies. Consequently, their incomplete representation of strategies reduces the explanatory power of statistical tests used to test the superiority of contingency and fit versus universal best practices. These examples of methodological difficulties point out that it is probably unreasonable to draw conclusions that we should expect equivalent performance for universally applied best practices and internally and externally compatible systems of human resource practices. The methodological difficulties are sufficiently challenging that failures to find differences should not cause us to conclude that the approaches have the same effect. Such failures to find differences may simply indicate that we are not measuring the contingency or fit approach with sufficient accuracy to conduct valid tests. Thus, it may be too much to expect consistency across studies given the methodological challenges.

One of the paradoxes of research on the impact of human resource practices is whether the adoption of such practices produces superior performance or whether superior performance and accompanying financial returns allow companies to adopt better practices.[122] Unfortunately, much of the research is cross-sectional and does not allow inferences of causality. However, there have been a few recent studies that employ longitudinal methodologies or at least lags between adoptions of practices and outcome measures of firm performance.[123] Lagged examinations of the performance effects of human resource practices provide better evidence of causality in that researchers can mark the implementation or adoption of a practice at one point in time and then measure at a later time whether the firm's performance increased or decreased. Nonetheless, such longitudinal studies still do not allow researchers to rule out arguments of reverse causality.[124]

Fortunately, there are a couple of reasons to question the validity of the reverse causality argument. One is that there is little motivation for high-performing firms to invest in these human resource practices if they have reached such levels of performance without the aid of such practices.[125] The second is that some high-performance human resource practices have negligible costs. Examples of practices that can have very low costs include flextime and telecommuting or allowing employees to occasionally work at home. Because of the low costs of these example practices, companies without the resources of high-performing companies could just as easily have adopted the practices. Thus, the existence of financial resources does not always have an impact on whether the practices are adopted.[126]

Summary

This chapter has examined the recent research on the performance effects of human resource practices. In the past, there were anecdotal reports of individual company experiences with various practices and virtually no empirical evidence from methodologically sound studies. Current research based on sound methodology provides strong empirical support that many human resource practices and systems have a substantial impact on several objective measures of firm performance. Objective measures of firm performance have included market measures in the form of shareholder returns; accounting measures such as ROA, ROE,

Tobin's q, and profitability; productivity; scrap rates; and quality. In addition, while objective measures are generally preferable to perceptual measures, some aspects of firm performance, such as innovation and operational outcomes, can be measured reasonably well with perceptual measures or are not well-suited to objective measurement. Studies using perceptual measures also have found similar positive effects for several practices and systems of practices.

Results of this impressive collection of research studies indicates that several human resource practices—such as the use of cognitive tests in selection, staffing selectivity, and training—appear to be very robust in their ability to enhance firm performance in widely varying settings. Thus, there are some practices that are almost universal best practices. Nonetheless, it is easy to overestimate the impact of individual practices because other practices also make simultaneous contributions to firm performance. Because of these combined effects, it has been argued that systems of complementary human resource practices should have substantial impact on firm performance because of synergies. The research shows that such systems do indeed have a substantial impact on firm performance. Nonetheless, the evidence on whether systems of practices produce greater impacts on firm performance than individual practices has been mixed, although methodological limitations may have prevented more consistent results for the superiority of systems of practices.

Finally, the current research has examined the impact of contingent implementations of human resource practices and systems of practices. While there are some mixed results, there is substantial support for the proposition that human resource practices and systems of practices provide even greater impact when they are matched to the firm's strategies, organizational culture, context, and other human resource practices. Again, some of the mixed evidence may be a result of methodological challenges. There is substantial support for the contingency perspective that correspondence or fit between human resource practices and the firm's strategies and culture produce greater firm performance. However, as noted earlier, there are a few individual human resource practices that appear to be very robust in their ability to produce increased performance in almost any setting.

Endnotes

1. Pfeffer, Jeffrey. *The Human Equation: Building Profits by Putting People First*. Boston: Harvard Business School Press, 1998, pp. 64–65.
2. Flannery, Thomas P., David A. Hofrichter, and Paul Platten. *People Performance and Pay: Dynamic Compensation for Changing Organizations*. New York: The Free Press, 1996, p. 6.
3. Gupta, Nina, and Jason D. Shaw. "Let the Evidence Speak: Financial Incentives Are Effective!" *Compensation and Benefits Review* 30, no. 2 (1998): 26–54.
4. Kohn, Alfie. *Punished by Rewards: The Trouble with Gold Stars, Incentive Plans, A's, Praise, and Other Bribes*. New York: Houghton-Mifflin, 1993; Kohn, Alfie. "Why Incentive Plans Cannot Work," *Harvard Business Review* 71, no. 5 (1993): 54–63.
5. Gupta and Shaw. "Let the Evidence Speak: Financial Incentives Are Effective!", pp. 28, 30.

6. Flannery, Hofrichter, and Platten. *People Performance and Pay: Dynamic Compensation for Changing Organizations*, p. 3.
7. Pfeffer. *The Human Equation: Building Profits by Putting People First.*
8. Sartain, Libby, Vice President for People, Southwest Airlines. "Comments to the Human Resource Roundtable," Neeley School of Business, Texas Christian University, February 6, 1996.
9. Newman, Jerry M., and Melissa Waite. "Do Broad-Based Stock Options Create Value?" *Compensation and Benefits Review*, 30, no. 4 (1998): 78–86.
10. Ibid.
11. Ibid.
12. Beer, Michael. "The Transformation of the Human Resource Function: Resolving the Tension Between a Traditional Administrative and a New Strategic Role," in Dave Ulrich, Michael R. Losey, and Gerry Lake (Eds.). *Tomorrow's HR Management: 48 Leaders Call for Change*. New York: John Wiley and Sons, 1997, p. 89.
13. Delaney, John T., and Mark A. Huselid. "The Impact of Human Resource Management Practices on Perceptions of Organizational Performance," *Academy of Management Journal* 39 (1996): 949–69.
14. Florkowski, Gary W., and Kuldeep Shastri. "Stock-Price Response to Profit Sharing in Unionized Settings," *Journal of Labor Research* 13 (1992): 407–20.
15. Delery, John E., and D. Harold Doty. "Modes of Theorizing in Strategic Human Resource Management: Tests of Universalistic, Contingency, and Configurational Performance Predictions," *Academy of Management Journal* 39 (1996): 802–35.
16. Welbourne, Theresa M., and Alice O. Andrews. "Predicting the Performance of Initial Public Offerings: Should Human Resource Management Be in the Equation?" *Academy of Management Journal* 39 (1996): 891–919.
17. DeMatteo, Jacquelyn S., Michael C. Rush, Eric Sundstrom, and Lillian T. Eby. "Factors Related to the Successful Implementation of Team-Based Rewards," *ACA Journal* 6 (1997).
18. Ibid.
19. "Compensating Teams," *Research Technology Management* 40 (July/August 1997): 58, summary of an article by Perry Pascarella, "Compensating Teams," *Across the Board* (February 1997): 16–22.
20. Bloom, Matt. "The Performance Effects of Pay Dispersion on Individuals and Organizations," *Academy of Management Journal* 42 (1999): 25, 40.
21. McLeod, Poppy L., Sharon A. Lobel, and Taylor H. Cox Jr. "Ethnic Diversity and Creativity in Small Groups," *Small Group Research* 27 (1996): 248–64; McLeod, Poppy L., and Sharon A. Lobel. "The Effects of Ethnic Diversity on Idea Generation in Small Groups," *Best Papers Proceedings: Academy of Management* (1992): 227–31.
22. Becker, Brian, and Barry Gerhart. "The Impact of Human Resource Management on Organizational Performance: Progress and Prospects," *Academy of Management Journal* 39 (1996): 779–801.
23. Greer Charles R., Timothy C. Ireland, and John R. Wingender. "Contrarian Human Resource Investments and Financial Performance After Economic Downturns," *Journal of Business Research* (in press).
24. Gomez-Mejia, Luis R., and Leslie E. Palich. "Cultural Diversity and the Performance of Multinational Firms," *Journal of International Business Studies* 28 (1997): 309–35.
25. Ibid.
26. Greer, Ireland, and Wingender. "Contrarian Human Resource Investments and Financial Performance After Economic Downturns."
27. Cascio, Wayne F. "Downsizing: What Do We Know? What Have We Learned," *Academy of Management Executive* 7, no. 1 (1993): 95–104.
28. Cascio, Wayne F., Clifford E. Young, and James R. Morris. "Financial Consequences of Employment-Change Decisions in Major U.S. Corporations," *Academy of Management Journal* 40 (1997): 1175–89.
29. Abowd, John M., George T. Milkovich, and John M. Hannon. "The Effects of Human Resource Management Decisions on Shareholder Value," *Industrial and Labor Relations Review* 43 (1990): 203-S–236-S.

30. Davidson, Wallace N., Dan L. Worrell, and Jeremy B. Fox. "Early Retirement and Firm Performance," *Academy of Management Journal* 39 (1996): 970–84.
31. Ibid., p. 981.
32. Pfeffer. *The Human Equation: Building Profits by Putting People First.*
33. Delery and Doty. "Modes of Theorizing in Strategic Human Resource Management: Tests of Universalistic, Contingency, and Configurational Performance Predictions."
34. Pedersen, Daniel. "Wal-Mart of the Sky," *Newsweek* (March 1, 1999): 47.
35. Harkins, Philip J., Stephen. M. Brown, and Russell Sullivan. "Shining New Light on a Growing Trend," *HRMagazine* 40, no. 12 (1995): 75–79.
36. Greer, Charles. R., Youngblood, Stuart A., and Gray, David A. "Human Resource Management Outsourcing: The Make or Buy Decision," *Academy of Management Executive* 13 (1999): 85–96; Guthrie, James P., and Deepak K. Datta. "Corporate Strategy, Executive Selection, and Firm Performance," *Human Resource Management* 37 (1998): 101–15.
37. Gilley, K. M., and Abdul, Rasheed. "Outsourcing and Firm Performance: The Moderating Effects of Firm Strategy and Environmental Dynamism," *Journal of Management* (in press).
38. Pearce, Thomas G., James E. Groff, and John R. Wingender. "Union Decertification's Impact on Shareholder Wealth," *Industrial Relations* 34 (1995): 58–72.
39. Ibid., p. 58.
40. Freeman, Richard B., and James L. Medoff. *What Do Unions Do*? New York: Basic Books, 1984.
41. Ibid.
42. Ibid., p. 176.
43. Ibid., p. 180.
44. Fiorito, Jack, Daniel G. Gallagher, and Charles R. Greer. "Determinants of Unionism: A Review of the Literature," in Kendrith M. Rowland and Gerald R. Ferris (Eds.), *Research in Personnel and Human Resources Management,* 4th ed. Greenwich, CT: JAI Press, 1986, pp. 269–306; Fiorito, Jack, and Charles R. Greer. "Determinants of U.S. Unionism: Past Research and Future Needs," *Industrial Relations* 21 (1982): 1–32.
45. Menaker, Marvin, Gary Kearns, James Parker, and Ruth Landau. "Presentation on Labor Relations at Southwest Airlines," Southwest Region, National Academy of Arbitrators, Dallas, Texas, March 1996; Levering, Robert, and Milton Moskowitz. "The 100 Best Companies to Work For," *Fortune* (January 10, 2000): 82–110; Sartain. "Comments to the Human Resource Roundtable."
46. Greer, Charles R., Stanley A. Martin, and Ted A. Reusser. "The Effect of Strikes on Shareholder Returns," *Journal of Labor Research* 1 (1980): 217–29.
47. "The Slow Death of Boeing Man," *The Economist* 354 (March 18, 2000): 29.
48. Allied Pilots Association. *Special Report to the Membership*, March 15, 1999.
49. Pedersen. "Wal-Mart of the Sky," p. 47.
50. Delaney and Huselid. "The Impact of Human Resource Management Practices on Perceptions of Organizational Performance."
51. Varma, Arup, Richard W. Beatty, Craig E. Schneier, and David O. Ulrich. "High Performance Work Systems: Exciting Discovery or Passing Fad?" *Human Resource Planning* 22, no. 1 (1999): 26–37.
52. Ibid., p. 31.
53. Adsit, Dennis J. "Surveys and Survey Feedback: Essential Ingredients in Organizational Change," in Edward M. Malone and Manuel London (Eds.), *HR to the Rescue: Case Studies of HR Solutions to Business Challenges*. Houston: Gulf Publishing Company, 1998, pp. 68–88.
54. Banker, Rajiv D., Joy M. Field, Roger G. Schroeder, and Kingshuk K. Sinha. "Impact of Work Teams on Manufacturing Performance: A Longitudinal Field Study," *Academy of Management Journal* 39 (1996): 867–90.
55. Ibid.
56. Case, John. *The Open-Book Experience: Lessons from Over 100 Companies Who Successfully Transformed Themselves*. Reading, MA: Perseus Books, 1998.
57. Hall, Cheryl. "An Open-Book Policy," *Dallas Morning News* (June 28, 1998): 1H–2H.

58. Pfeffer. *The Human Equation: Building Profits by Putting People First.*
59. Sartain. "Comments to the Human Resource Roundtable."
60. Ibid.
61. Hold, Nancy D. "Workspaces: A Look at the Places Where Businesspeople Work," *Wall Street Journal* (April 7, 1999): B10.
62. Ibid.
63. Pfeffer. *The Human Equation: Building Profits by Putting People First.*
64. Crystal, Graef. "Pay Check," *Texas Monthly* (October 1998): 116–19.
65. Ibid., p. 116.
66. Delery and Doty. "Modes of Theorizing in Strategic Human Resource Management: Tests of Universalistic, Contingency, and Configurational Performance Predictions."
67. Beer. "The Transformation of the Human Resource Function: Resolving the Tension Between a Traditional Administrative and a New Strategic Role."
68. Ibid.
69. Terpstra, David E., and Elizabeth J. Rozell. "The Relationship of Staffing Practices to Organizational Level Measures of Performance," *Personnel Psychology* 46, no. 1 (1993): 27–48.
70. Ibid.
71. Ibid.
72. Gatewood, Robert D., and Hubert S. Feild. *Human Resource Selection*, 4th ed. Fort Worth: Dryden Press, 1998.
73. Ibid.
74. Delaney and Huselid. "The Impact of Human Resource Management Practices on Perceptions of Organizational Performance."
75. Pfeffer. *The Human Equation: Building Profits by Putting People First.*
76. Sartain. "Comments to the Human Resource Roundtable."
77. Guthrie, James P., and Deepak K. Datta. "Corporate Strategy, Executive Selection, and Firm Performance," *Human Resource Management* 37 (1998): 101–15.
78. Ibid.
79. Ibid.
80. Ibid.
81. Ibid., p. 110.
82. Guthrie and Datta. "Corporate Strategy, Executive Selection, and Firm Performance."
83. Terpstra and Rozell. "The Relationship of Staffing Practices to Organizational Level Measures of Performance."
84. Ibid.
85. Ibid.
86. Bassi, Lauri, and Mark E. Van Buren. "The 1998 ASTD State of the Industry Report," *Training and Development* 52, no. 1 (1998): 20–43.
87. Bassi, Lauri J., and Daniel P. McMurrer. "Training Investment Can Mean Financial Performance," *Training and Development*, 52, no. 5 (1998): 40–42.
88. Jones, C. M. "Financial Benefits of Training at Cyprus Sierrita," *Mining Engineering* 50, no. 11 (1998): 42–45.
89. Bassi and McMurrer. "Training Investment Can Mean Financial Performance."
90. Delaney and Huselid. "The Impact of Human Resource Management Practices on Perceptions of Organizational Performance."
91. "Ineffective Training Kills the Bottom Line," *USA Today* (December 1998): 14–15.
92. MacDuffie, John P. "Human Resource Bundles and Manufacturing Performance: Organizational Logic and Flexible Production Systems in the World Auto Industry," *Industrial and Labor Relations Review* 48 (1995): 197–221; Ichniowski, Casey, Kathryn Shaw, and Giovanni Prennushi. "The Effect of Human Resource Management Practices on Productivity," unpublished paper, Columbia University (1993).

93. Delaney and Huselid. "The Impact of Human Resource Management Practices on Perceptions of Organizational Performance."
94. Ibid.
95. Becker and Gerhart. "The Impact of Human Resource Management on Organizational Performance: Progress and Prospects," p. 782.
96. Huselid, Mark A. "The Impact of Human Resource Management Practices on Turnover, Productivity, and Corporate Financial Performance," *Academy of Management Journal* 38 (1995): 635–72.
97. Ibid.
98. Ibid.
99. Ibid., p. 667.
100. Delaney and Huselid. "The Impact of Human Resource Management Practices on Perceptions of Organizational Performance," p. 965.
101. Becker and Gerhart. "The Impact of Human Resource Management on Organizational Performance: Progress and Prospects," p. 782.
102. Youndt, Mark A., Scott A. Snell, James W. Dean Jr., and David P. Lepak. "Human Resource Management, Manufacturing Strategy, and Firm Performance," *Academy of Management Journal* 39 (1996): 836–66.
103. Porter, Michael E. *Competitive Advantage: Creating and Sustaining Superior Performance*. New York: Free Press, 1985.
104. Flannery, Hofrichter, and Platten. *People, Performance, and Pay: Dynamic Compensation for Changing Organizations*.
105. Huselid. "The Impact of Human Resource Management Practices on Turnover, Productivity, and Corporate Financial Performance."
106. Ibid., pp. 665–66.
107. Delery and Doty. "Modes of Theorizing in Strategic Human Resource Management: Tests of Universalistic, Contingency, and Configurational Performance Predictions."
108. Ibid.
109. Ibid., p. 825.
110. Youndt, Snell, Dean, and Lepak. "Human Resources Management, Manufacturing Strategy, and Firm Performance."
111. Ibid., p. 850.
112. Ibid.
113. Youndt, Snell, Dean, and Lepak. "Human Resources Management, Manufacturing Strategy, and Firm Performance."
114. Ibid., p. 853.
115. Arthur, Jeffrey B. "Effects of Human Resource Systems on Manufacturing Performance and Turnover," *Academy of Management Journal* 37 (1994): 670–87.
116. MacDuffie. "Human Resource Bundles and Manufacturing Performance: Organizational Logic and Flexible Production Systems in the World Auto Industry."
117. Ibid.
118. Ibid., p. 218.
119. Banker, Fajiv D., Seok-Young Lee, Gordon Potter, and Dhinu Srinivasan. "Contextual Analysis of Performance Impacts of Outcome-Based Compensation," *Academy of Management Journal* 39 (1996): 920–48.
120. Delaney and Huselid. "The Impact of Human Resource Management Practices on Perceptions of Organizational Performance."
121. Huselid. "The Impact of Human Resource Management Practices on Turnover, Productivity, and Corporate Financial Performance."
122. Ibid.
123. Ibid.; Huselid, Mark A., Susan E. Jackson, and Randall S. Schuler. "Technical and Strategic Human Resource Management Effectiveness as Determinants of Firm Performance," *Academy of*

Management Journal 40 (1997): 171–88; Greer, Ireland, and Wingender. "Contrarian Human Resource Investments and Financial Performance After Economic Downturns."

124. Huselid. "The Impact of Human Resource Management Practices on Turnover, Productivity, and Corporate Financial Performance."
125. Kravetz, Dennis J. *The Human Resources Revolution: Implementing Progressive Management Practices for Bottom-Line Success*. San Francisco: Jossey-Bass, 1988.
126. Greer, Ireland, and Wingender. "Contrarian Human Resource Investments and Financial Performance After Economic Downturns."

CASE 8

360-Degree Feedback on the Internet

Performance appraisal systems serve many purposes, such as providing formal feedback to employees on how they stack up with respect to the organization's performance standards, serving as input for compensation decisions, identifying areas in which future development is needed, reinforcing good performance, providing input for promotional decisions, and establishing the documentation needed to justify termination of employment. Nonetheless, while performance appraisal is one of the fundamental activities in human resources, it has always been a lightning rod for criticism and has recently come under renewed attack as indicated in this chapter.

Some criticisms of traditional performance appraisal systems, in which supervisors appraise subordinates, are that they frequently do not provide good assessments of managers. More specifically, traditional performance appraisal systems often do not provide accurate evaluations of opportunistic managers who take advantage of their own subordinates in order to enhance their superiors' perceptions of their own performance. For example, such managers may not give credit where credit is due, such as to employees who may have created an innovative process that helped improve the unit's productivity. Instead, they may attribute improved performance to their managerial skills and take the credit for themselves.

With this background in mind, there is much to be learned from the experiences of the Otis Elevator Company. The company had concerns that its old paper-based performance appraisal system was too slow and cumbersome. There were also concerns about whether the raters could be assured of the confidentiality of their ratings. Because of these problems, the company wanted a better system for appraising and developing the performance of its engineering managers. Specifically, the company was interested in enhancing these managers' project management and project team leadership skills. The engineering managers needed substantial improvement in their skills, and the company wanted a performance appraisal system that would provide feedback from the managers' subordinates, peers, and customers as well as their direct superiors.[1]

Given these concerns, it is not surprising that Otis Elevator decided to develop a 360-degree feedback system. With 360-degree feedback systems, superiors, peers, and subordinates evaluate managers. The innovative aspect of the company's approach to the 360-degree system is that the company decided to base the system on the Internet and its own intranet. An independent contractor, E-Group, developed the system and handles the collation and analysis of the feedback information.[2]

E-Group chose a 75-item survey called LEAPS, which measures seven dimensions of leadership, for the 360-degree instrument. The instrument was loaded on a Web site so that all raters can pull up the information and complete the appraisal in approximately 20 minutes. After completing the appraisal, they simply submit the results via e-mail to E-Group to process. Because the system is encrypted, the company is able to provide greater confidentiality and anonymity for the raters than with the previous paper-and-pencil system. In addition to the LEAPS items, the company included a fairly large set of other items to assess managers' technical competency and their contributions to the business. E-Group was able to provide appraisal profiles for the managers within three days after the last of the evaluators e-mailed their input for the manager. In addition, the profile of actual ratings for each manager from E-Group also includes an ideal leadership profile developed by Otis executives. By comparison on his or her actual ratings with the ideal profile, managers can identify areas for future development. Otis Elevator chose to use the system only for developmental purposes, although recently it began to consider other purposes for the system.[3]

Questions

1. Aside from the advantage of instantaneous transmission of information, what other advantages do you see with this type of performance appraisal system on the Internet?
2. What problems do you think Otis Elevator experienced once the 360-degree system was successfully implemented on the Internet?
3. In the past, many human resource professionals have been almost obsessed with the forms or format used in performance appraisal systems. How is the Internet application of 360-degree performance appraisal systems different from the old obsession with form or format?
4. What else is necessary to help ensure that a performance appraisal system will be successful? How would you determine if the system affects the firm's performance?

References

1. Huet-Cox, G. Douglas, Tjai M. Nielson, and Eric Sundstrom. "Get the Most from 360-Degree Feedback: Put It on the Internet," *HRMagazine* 44, no. 5 (1999): 92–103.
2. Ibid.
3. Ibid.

CHAPTER 9

Human Resource Evaluation

The ninth and final component of the conceptual framework is human resource evaluation. With the increasing emphasis placed on strategic contribution, competitiveness, and cost control, there has been a greater need to justify the existence of human resource practices, activities, and programs. As will be noted in this chapter, the evaluation of human resource programs has not been a high priority in most organizations. Nonetheless, as noted in Chapter 8, evaluation will be more important in the future because of the increased need to demonstrate efficient utilization of resources. Chapter 8 presented evidence from the literature on the impact of human resource practices and systems of such practices on overall firm performance. This chapter will explain how to conduct such evaluations of practices and systems. It will deal with several aspects of evaluation, beginning with an overview and a description of different analytical approaches. The chapter will discuss approaches for evaluating the strategic contributions of traditional human resource areas as well as emerging areas. Explanations of the different analytical approaches to evaluation will be provided along with specific guidance for evaluation in the various human resource functional areas. Finally, there will be a discussion of macro-level evaluations of human resource effectiveness.

Several human resource theorists and practitioners have presented compelling arguments for the evaluation of human resource management and the human resource function. Such evaluations have been advocated for a number of reasons including:

- Promotion of the human resource function, for example, through demonstration of bottom-line contributions through reduced turnover

Author's Note: Although this chapter draws on many sources, the numerous works of Anne Tsui and Luis Gomez-Mejia were particularly helpful in its development and are cited several times. Similarly, Wayne Cascio's and Irwin Goldstein's works on the evaluation of training were also particularly helpful and are cited several times. Those readers desiring to learn more about evaluation are referred to the extensive works by these authors.

- The demonstration of accountability in utilization of resources
- Promotion of change by identifying strengths and weaknesses
- Introduction of financial assessment as a decision tool in human resource program selection
- Highlighting key human resource practices
- Gauging the performance of the human resource function
- Demonstrating the function's role in the accomplishment of company goals[1]

The intensive emphasis on cost control, justifying efficient allocation of resources, contributing to the bottom line, and capability of human resources to provide a competitive advantage, appear likely to result in more emphasis on evaluation.[2]

OVERVIEW OF EVALUATION

Before evaluating human resource management, a suitably comprehensive definition of evaluation must be accepted, as well as the criteria and measurement approach. From an organizational perspective, *organizational effectiveness* is generally viewed as a multidimensional construct and typically involves multiple criteria, such as productivity and flexibility. *Productivity measures* sometimes tap efficiency, quantity, and quality, while *flexibility measures* may also tap the effectiveness with which the organization deals with schedule changes, crash programs, or emergencies. In some instances, adaptability is operationalized separately and includes measures of problem anticipation, knowledge of new technology, and adaptation to change. Because of the multidimensionality of the effectiveness concept, policies capturing statistical procedures have been developed for constructing multiple measures of subunit effectiveness.[3]

Scope of Evaluation

Within the narrower confines of human resource management, there has been substantial progress in the evaluation literature. Although dozens of effectiveness measures have been proposed for evaluation of the function, including composite indexes, the literature has suffered from a lack of an organizing, theoretical framework. This void has since been filled by Anne Tsui and Luis Gomez-Mejia's comprehensive conceptual framework. Their framework differentiates between outcomes or processes affected by line management and those under control of the human resource management function. In order to evaluate broader human resource performance, a company might examine turnover, grievance rates, or workers' compensation claims, which are largely affected by the actions of the company's line managers.[4] Tsui and Gomez-Mejia's conceptual model of human resource effectiveness is presented in Figure 9-1.

In contrast, a narrower evaluation of the human resource management function would focus on its efficiency in administering a benefit program or

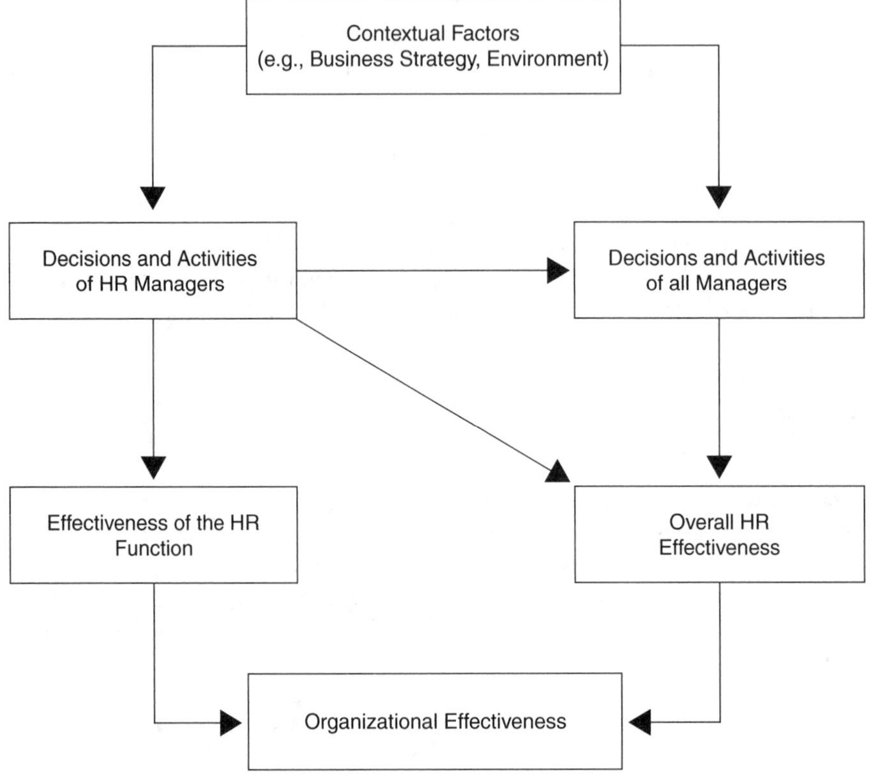

FIGURE 9-1 Model of Human Resource Effectiveness

Source: Anne S. Tsui and Luis R. Gomez-Mejia. "Evaluating Human Resource Effectiveness." Reprinted with permission, p. 1-211 from *Human Resource Management Evolving Roles and Responsibilities*, edited by Lee Dyer. Copyright © 1988 by the Bureau of National Affairs, Inc., Washington, DC 20037.

recruiting and screening applicants. Thus, with broader evaluations, measures of the company's use of human resources would be affected by the performance of the company's line managers. With narrower evaluations, the measures are affected only by the performance of the human resource staff. Human resource departments are unique in that their activities and responsibilities apply to all managers and employees in all departments. Thus, the evaluation of human resource departments is a complicated but important matter.[5] While it may be tempting to simplify matters with a narrower evaluation, there are shortcomings with this approach. Donald Jarrell has cautioned that isolated evaluations of human resource departments run the risk of communicating that others have no responsibilities in the area. Because all managers and departments affect the quality of human resource management and have related responsibilities, this would be an undesirable side effect of evaluation. In addition, another aspect of the scope of evaluation involves a time dimension.[6]

The length of time between implementation of a program and its impact on performance can vary depending on the nature of the program. Likewise, its effects may be stable or may diminish or increase over time. In addition, different stakeholders, such as shareholders, executives, and production workers may have a very different perspective on the time frame that should be used for evaluation. Clearly, there are problems when evaluation is performed on only a one-shot basis instead of a continual and systematic basis. There are obvious advantages with longitudinal approaches as opposed to cross-sectional approaches because of the latter's inability to provide insights into causality.[7]

Strategic Impact

Another aspect of human resource evaluation is that the nature of the process is changing from a reactive focus on how well a problem is solved or how successful a program has been to an emphasis on the organizational and employee impact of human resource policies, programs, and activities. For example, in contrast to past evaluation practice in which a company might have examined narrow criteria such as turnover rates, a more strategic approach would examine whether it is losing high performers. Essentially, more strategic approaches to evaluation recognize the organizational interdependencies and relationships of human resource policies, systems, and activities. As a result, they have moved from narrow determinations of whether human resource activities are working to broader analyses of their contributions.[8]

Level of Analysis

Another dimension of evaluation involves the *level of analysis*, which is the level of aggregation or level within the organizational structure. Tsui and Gomez-Mejia have identified three levels of analysis in human resource management evaluation: strategic, management, and operational. The objective of evaluation at the strategic level is to determine whether human resource policies and programs are consistent with the company's strategy. At the management level, the focus is on control, such as the cost effectiveness of a benefit program. At the operational level, the focus is on the quality of human resource services and programs. Since there are multiple constituencies at this level, the service provided and level of satisfaction with the human resource department may vary across these constituencies.[9]

Criteria

In another comprehensive study, Anne Tsui identified criteria by which the effectiveness of human resource departments can be assessed. Her results emphasize that the various constituencies of human resource departments have differing views of the importance of the various services provided. Results of factor analytic statistical procedures indicate that there are five clear categories of effectiveness criteria for human resource departments: (1) responsiveness, (2) managing cost and negative performance, (3) proactivity and innovativeness, (4) training and development, and (5) affirmative action accomplishments.[10]

Level of Constituents

Another of Tsui's findings is that the *level of constituents* has a major impact on the effectiveness criteria they apply. Managers and nonsupervisory employees tend to place importance on the department's ability to provide services on matters of immediate or short-term importance. Operating line executives, who have production responsibilities, also hold similar views. In contrast, when corporate-level human resource executives evaluate human resource departments, they tend to place greater importance on such activities as organizational development and human resource planning, which have strategic implications. Thus, human resource departments are subject to incompatible expectations that need to be taken into account in an evaluation strategy.[11]

Ethical Dimensions

In addition to determining the impact of human resource practices on financial or operational measures, all activities, practices, and programs should be evaluated from an ethics perspective. While human resource management operates within a highly regulated environment, as described in Chapter 3, compliance with the law or regulations does not always ensure ethical behavior. Fortunately, the investment perspective of human resources is consistent with high ethical standards. Employers who invest in their employees are more likely to treat them ethically because they have an investment to protect. Nonetheless, the investment perspective is not sufficient to ensure ethical behavior. In addition, the technological advances that have done so much to enhance productivity, make jobs less monotonous, and allow greater flexibility in where work is performed also have brought new ethical challenges. Information technology and the rapidly evolving Internet and software industries pose special challenges, as described in the following account of ethical problems in the Silicon Valley:

> Among the common infractions: companies stealing one another's intellectual property, cheating employees out of promised stock options . . . or intercepting private e-mail, as when Interloc, the corporate predecessor of rare-book company Alibris, started collecting messages sent from Amazon.com to its customers.[12]

Nonetheless, the guidelines for evaluation of the ethics of various practices and programs are available, and it is often the role for those in human resources to take the lead when it comes to ethical treatment of employees. Michael Losey has provided the following guidance on the matter of ethics:

> Advocacy and ethics are important for any profession, but they are especially significant roles for human resource managers . . . It is customary that the HR exec-

utive makes his or her contribution by first and always being a member of management. At the same time, HR executives are paid to understand their communities, workplace, employee attitudes, and government regulations and requirements. It is up to the HR professional to balance and advance the interests of all parties within the business and strategic thrust of the organization. On occasion, the HR executive may even find it necessary to put him- or herself at risk in order to balance these interests. This is especially the case when situations are not clearcut or where a double standard may appear to exist.[13]

APPROACHES TO EVALUATION

There are a number of general approaches to human resource evaluation, as well as various measures and criteria of effectiveness. Some of the classifications of these components of evaluation are not mutually exclusive—they may fit several categories.

Audit Approaches

In addition to different evaluative foci, criteria, and levels of analysis, there are also two general approaches that have been traditionally used in human resource evaluation. The first is the *audit* approach, which relies on (1) personnel indices, such as per-capita recruiting costs, absenteeism rates, or workers' compensation experience rates, or (2) service/user reactions, such as the perceived equity of the job evaluation system. Typically, data pertaining to the latter would be obtained through the use of surveys or interviews.[14] Usually, items for such surveys can be obtained from published sources. Audit approaches also may be referred to as stakeholder approaches. Stakeholder approaches determine the satisfaction of key users or consumers of human resource services. Such stakeholders may be individuals or units within the organization. There also may be external stakeholders, such as unions, community organizations, or suppliers. An example of a stakeholder approach to evaluation is provided by Honeywell's Aerospace and Defense Division, which has used the process to clarify the human resource department's role in the company.[15]

Analytical Approaches

The second approach is *analytical* and involves either (1) experimental designs, such as the pretest–posttest control group design, which will be described later in the discussion of evaluation of training; or (2) cost–benefit analysis, such as utility theory, which was discussed in Chapter 1 and will be considered in more detail in this chapter. Although the cost–benefit analytical approach has been used with success, the valuation of benefits poses a major problem for human resource applications. *Utility analysis* is a specific type of cost–benefit analysis, which has applicability to human resource evaluation. It has the advantage of expressing evaluations in economic terms, which are probably more understandable by decision makers from other functional areas. Several human resource activities have been evaluated with utility analysis, including appraisal systems, equal employment policies, recruiting, selection, training, and turnover. Although utility analysis has broad applicability and represents a quantitatively superior means of evaluating human resource activities, the process is quite difficult for some applications. As a result of these difficulties and the amount of resources and effort required for analysis, its use has been limited to only selected applications. (An example of an application of utility analysis to a selection problem is provided later in this chapter.) Human resource practices such as succession planning and career development, which may have greater strategic impact, often defy quantitative measurement.[16]

Quantitative and Qualitative Measures

Other evaluation issues are whether to use *quantitative* or *qualitative* measures. A number of quantitative and qualitative measures can be constructed to measure the effectiveness of a company's human resources or the human resource function. Quantitative measures can sometimes be combined in the form of composite indices, and, as indicated earlier, weighting schemes necessary for such indices can be developed through policy capturing approaches. Further, the human resource function can also be evaluated as a cost center. Additionally, the benefits resulting from human resource management programs, such as reduced turnover or improved percentages of good hires, can sometimes be determined in dollar values. In such cases, the effectiveness of the function can be measured as a profit center. It is worth noting that an inordinate emphasis on quantitative evaluation measures can become dysfunctional. This occurs when the focus on goals or objectives, as operationalized in terms of such measures, does not contribute to accomplishment of strategic goals. Changes in the attitudes of an organization's workforce also can provide a partial indication of the effectiveness of the human resource function. These indicators, although inherently more qualitative than many other organizational characteristics, can be captured in measures that allow them to be subjected to statistical analysis.[17]

Outcome and Process Criteria

A final evaluation issue is whether the criteria will involve *outcomes* or *processes*. The distinction between the two types of criteria is that outcomes are results or end products of work while processes concern behaviors or how activities are performed. An example of an outcome criterion might be productivity ratios for a company's workforce. In spite of the appeal of their link to production activity, ease of measurement, and objective nature, outcome or output criteria are often contaminated by external factors unrelated to the activity being evaluated.[18] For example, high turnover rates could be more indicative of low unemployment rates in the local labor market than weaknesses in a company's selection or compensation systems.

Conversely, an example of a process criterion could be whether a unit meets affirmative action milestones according to a schedule, such as completing a utilization analysis by the end of the first quarter, conducting an availability analysis by the end of the next quarter, and so on. Many managers experience difficulties in defining objectives in terms of processes. When they have difficulty in articulating a desired process by which an activity should be performed, it is sometimes useful to reverse the question and ask them if they can describe how the activity should not be performed. Almost without exception, they can describe how the activity should not be performed, which then helps to stimulate and organize their thinking on desired or efficient processes.

A matrix of these two categories of evaluative criteria are presented in Figure 9-2, with separate breakdowns for evaluations of the effectiveness of the company's human resources and the human resource management function itself.

Balanced Scorecard Perspective

Another perspective on measures is presented in the balanced scorecard approach developed by Robert Kaplan and David P. Norton. Kaplan and Norton's work on evaluation concluded that companies commonly use three measures in human resource evaluation: employee satisfaction, retention, and productivity. Kaplan and Norton explain that satisfaction is a prerequisite for improvements in productivity, quality, responsiveness, and customer service. They note that the relationship with customer service is straightforward, as satisfied employees tend to have more satisfied customers. They also endorse annual surveys of employee satisfaction or monthly rolling surveys of samples of the workforce. Similarly, they endorse the measurement of employee retention for its importance in preserving the organization's investments in intellectual capital.[19]

Their most pointed advice is reserved for measurements of employee productivity. While ratios such as revenue per employee are commonly used, there are problems with such measures. More specifically, the preferable approaches to improving productivity ratios involve actions directed at increasing the numerator (output or revenues). However, the same improvement in productivity ratios can be obtained by less preferred actions. Actions directed at reducing the denominator (downsizing or outsourcing) are often dysfunctional because of the long-term loss in organizational capabilities.[20] The following provides more specific advice on the use of measures of revenue per employee:

> One way to avoid the incentive to outsource to achieve a higher revenue-per-employee statistic is to measure value-added per employee, subtracting externally purchased materials, supplies, and services from revenues in the numerator of this ratio. Another modification, to control for the substitution of more productive but

	Overall HR Effectiveness		HR Function Effectiveness	
	Quantitative	**Qualitative**	**Quantitative**	**Qualitative**
Process	**Cell 1**	**Cell 2**	**Cell 5**	**Cell 6**
	• Absenteeism rate • Minority turnover • Grievances • Job acceptance rate	• Lack of conflict • Innovativeness • Union relations • Flexibility	• Average time to fill jobs • Cost per employee • Number of minority applicants • Training hours per employee	• Time to answer inquiries • Quality of HR services • Cooperativeness of HR staff • Quality of HR programs
Outcome	**Cell 3**	**Cell 4**	**Cell 7**	**Cell 8**
	• Revenue per employee • New inventions • Productivity • Loss of key employees	• Employee morale • Stakeholder approval • Company reputation for HR	• Value added on HR investment • HR budget per employee • Number of new HR programs • Personnel ratio	• Executive satisfaction • Line manager satisfaction • Employees' opinion of HR

FIGURE 9-2 Effectiveness Criteria Matrix

Source: Anne S. Tsui and Luis R. Gomez-Mejia. "Evaluating Human Resource Effectiveness." Reprinted with permission, p. 1-213 from *Human Resource Management Evolving Roles and Responsibilities*, edited by Lee Dyer. Copyright © 1988 by the Bureau of National Affairs, Inc., Washington, DC 20037.

> higher paid employees, is to measure the denominator by employee compensation rather than number of employees . . . If a revenue-per-employee measure is used to motivate higher productivity of individual employees, it must be balanced with other measures of economic success so that the targets for the measure are not achieved in dysfunctional ways.[21]

Benchmarking

In addition to these approaches, criteria, and measurements, another general evaluation approach has been applied to human resource practices in recent years. This approach is called *benchmarking*.[22] The origination of benchmarking in the United States is generally credited to Xerox, which used the approach to reduce its manufacturing costs. In essence, benchmarking involves studying how competitors, and sometimes even companies in unrelated industries, are better at certain activities. For example, Ford studied 400 different features of the automobiles of competing manufacturers, with the goal of designing and producing a car that would be better than, or at least as good as, the best competitor in each feature.[23]

Similarly, benchmarking in human resource applications involves the collection of information about specific human resource practices, from large numbers of respondents across many companies. At a macro-analysis level, Ulrich, Brockbank, and Yeung at the University of Michigan collected information on 21 human resource practices in the general areas of staffing, development, performance appraisal, rewards, communication, and organizational design. Questionnaires composed of five-interval response scale items (where 1 = low and 5 = high) were used to measure these practices. The questionnaires were completed by 11,300 respondents in 91 companies. Of the respondents, 1,315 were human resource professionals while 9,985 were from associates of these professionals from various functional areas throughout their companies. The data provided by this large number of respondents provide benchmarks for various human resource practices in 10 different industries. Much of the data concern practices and perceptions of the human resource function's competencies in such areas as recruitment, training, and designing benefit programs. The data also provide benchmarks of perceived competencies across the various other functional areas (e.g., finance, marketing, research and development) and allow a comparison with the human resource function on competencies in such areas as business knowledge, change management, and the like.[24]

Through benchmarking, a company can compare its human resource practices and competencies with other companies. In addition to some of the benefits of evaluation noted earlier, benchmarking can also enable a company to see how its competencies in human resource practices stack up against those of world-class competitors and whether it has improved over time when longitudinal data are collected. An implication of benchmarking of particular relevance to human resource management's strategic role is that it enables a company to better concentrate its resources so that it can obtain a competitive advantage.[25]

> Benchmarking HR practices provides the means of focusing attention on highest value-added HR activities—those practices which are more likely to be practiced by successful companies. Rather than fall into the trap of trying to do everything well and please everyone with insufficient resources—which results in no one being satisfied—HR professionals could use benchmarking to focus limited resources on critical activities.[26]

Industry Influences

One important consideration in evaluating human resources is industry differences. What may constitute effective human resource practice in one setting may be ineffective in another. A study of high-technology entrepreneurial start-up firms provides some good examples of industry differences in effective human resource practices. This study points out that the entrepreneurial and high-technology literatures provide contradictory guidance in the areas of human resource planning, compensation, and the work environment. For example, in high-technology industries, higher company performance is associated with the use of internal sources for managerial recruitment. Extrapolating from this relationship, the researchers reasoned that human resource planning would be needed to ensure the availability and development of internal sources of talent. Thus, they hypothesized that in high-technology companies, human resource planning is associated with company performance. In contrast, the entrepreneurial literature suggests that there is insufficient time for such planning, relative to other demands, and that planning is inconsistent with the rapid rate of change and flexibility required in entrepreneurial companies.[27]

The researchers also examined compensation issues. The high-technology literature argues that high-technology firms should exercise salary leadership in order to attract talent. Although the entrepreneurship literature recognizes these benefits, it maintains that cash flow problems in entrepreneurial firms typically preclude salary leadership practices. The high-technology literature also argues that since its key employees, scientists and engineers, adhere to norms of autonomy, an autonomy-oriented work environment will be associated with company performance. However, the entrepreneurial literature argues that a control-oriented work environment is necessary to focus employees' efforts on short-term goals.[28]

The study, which tested the hypotheses in high-technology entrepreneurial start-up companies, found no relationship between human resource planning and performance. In contrast, compensation leadership was found to be related to sales growth and measures of innovation, as predicted by the high-technology literature. Also, as predicted by the high-technology literature, work environments emphasizing professional autonomy were found to be associated with company performance.[29] An important conclusion from this study is the following:

> Researchers interested in the effects of HR policies and practices on organizational effectiveness are advised to take into account such contingencies as industrial setting, stage in the lifecycle, and business strategy. Failure to do so may result in prescriptions which are inapplicable or inappropriate in particular settings.[30]

PREVALENCE OF EVALUATION

In spite of advocacy for evaluation, a relatively small proportion of companies conduct human resource management evaluations. Likewise, few companies express the results of their evaluations in economic terms. Even with billions of dollars being spent on training every year, many companies do not even evaluate training.[31] Tsui and Gomez-Mejia's survey results found the following: "Systematic, periodic evaluation of HR effectiveness does not occur frequently in American business organizations." [32] There are several potential explanations for this difference between the normative views of the human resource literature and industry practice. These explanations include human resource executives' fears of the outcomes of evaluation, difficulties in obtaining meaningful and valid measures of human resource activity, and lack of a meaningful evaluative framework. Nonetheless, important variables are positively correlated with the conduct of such evaluation, including: financial performance, aggressiveness in marketing strategy, economically oriented goals, and top-level involvement of human resource executives in setting the strategic direction of their companies.[33] Because of these positive contributions of evaluation and the cost consciousness resulting from the pressures of the global economy, evaluations should become more prevalent in the future.

EVALUATING STRATEGIC CONTRIBUTIONS OF TRADITIONAL AREAS

As indicated in Figure 9-2, there are many areas within the traditional functions of human resource management that probably should be evaluated. Major human resource functions of obvious strategic importance are human resource planning, staffing, performance evaluation, compensation and reward systems, training and development, and labor relations.[34] The first to be considered is human resource planning. The potential strategic contributions of human resource planning were discussed in earlier chapters, and the evaluation of this area should be of importance to general managers.

Human Resource Planning

The effectiveness of human resource planning can be viewed from a behavioral perspective. This includes the degree to which managers accept human resource planning as an activity that helps them perform their jobs. Line management's willingness to supply information to be used in the development of forecasts and actually use human resource forecasts in their own planning provide other indicators of human resource planning effectiveness. Even when forecasts are inaccurate, the human resource planning process has value. This is because, as in any planning effort, the process of forecasting is often more valuable than the forecast itself because managers are forced to reexamine fundamental operating assumptions.[35] Such reexamination and resultant communications are often valuable side effects.

From a quantitative perspective, for companies that have strong preferences to fill vacancies from internal sources, the extent to which the organization must hire in the open labor market, instead of from its internal labor market, may be an indicator of the effectiveness of the human resource planning process. To the extent that shortages in certain skill areas are forecasted and prepared for with the development of employees, the organization has less need to hire externally. Companies that hire from the external market only at entry levels must have effective human resource planning programs. The failure to plan is probably no more obvious than in professional sports when a team finds itself with a roster of aging athletes and then must endure years of rebuilding because it did not have an effective planning process for bringing in younger players.

Another standard or criterion of human resource planning and development effectiveness is provided by the concept of *just-in-time talent*, which means that vacancies can be filled quickly from within the company by a person qualified for promotion. The promoted individual should have been developed by previous assignments and training but should not have to wait in a holding pattern in which his or her skills are underutilized.[36] The concept of just-in-time talent has a great deal of appeal because, from the company's standpoint, during the period in which the individual is underutilized, the company is not obtaining a return on its investment in development. From the individual's perspective, there is the obvious advantage of not having to spend time in positions that underutilize one's talents. Such situations lead to turnover, which has costly implications for the company as well.

It is interesting to speculate about a potential cause for inaccuracies of human resource forecasts. This explanation points to the rationales for planning. Although paling in comparison to the effects of global expansion or recession, demographic influences, immigration, and intensified international competition, at the micro-level individual companies probably plan for the forecasted shortages. For example, when expecting labor shortages, companies may invest heavily in labor-saving equipment. This may be evident in industries in which productivity is growing rapidly. Such investments helped U.S. companies meet international competitive pressures by increasing the productivity of their employees. Awareness of forecasted shortages in labor supply may contribute to companies' decisions to make investments in labor-saving equipment. Thus, increased investment in labor-saving equipment may be influenced, to some extent, by companies' awareness of forecasted labor shortages through their environmental scanning activities. At least in some small portion, forecasted labor shortages may not materialize because companies do human resource planning and take appropriate actions.

This speculative explanation is also consistent with a general description of an effective human resource management function. James Walker has explained this as follows:

> One company suggested that the most effective function is the one that ensures that there are no pressing human resource issues to concern management. The most proactive, strategic approach to managing resources anticipates and addresses emerging issues before the "pain" is felt. Because conditions continually change, however, there are always issues to be addressed. Through human resource planning, the function may bring these issues to management's attention and create a sense of urgency for action.[37]

Staffing

Obviously, a company's recruiting and selection procedures are critical to its ability to acquire the human resources needed to obtain competitive advantage. Further, as indicated in the Tsui and Gomez-Mejia model in Figure 9-1, human resource effectiveness is influenced by factors outside the human resource function. Accordingly, evaluation approaches for staffing functions must control these other influences before valid assessments can be obtained. In addition to the traditional approaches to selection, which attempt to match applicants with job requirements, some new views of selection may pose different evaluation challenges. For example, David Bowen has pointed out that some companies are now placing primary emphasis in matching applicants with the characteristics or culture of the organization, instead of the job.[38] Thus, future evaluations may need to focus on developing measures of staff compatibility with organizational characteristics.

There are a several measures that can be used in the evaluation of recruiting effectiveness (e.g., cost per hire, number of résumés received, recruiter activities).[39] In turn, the effectiveness of recruiting has an impact on the effectiveness of a company's staffing. To the extent that a company performs staffing functions poorly, the impact may be potentially manifested in problems such as excessive turnover, line management dissatisfaction, poor quality, litigation, underrepresentation of minorities and women, and so on, which detract from human resource effectiveness. Utility analysis may be used as an evaluation approach for assessing the effectiveness of selection processes. An interesting feature of the utility analysis approach to cost–benefit analysis is that it can be linked with capital budgeting processes. In turn, this link with capital budgeting may make such evaluation of much greater interest to general managers. Like capital budgeting, utility analysis of selection procedures deals with projected cash flows, such as in the form of savings from increased productivity. The results of the utility analysis of such cash flows can be expressed as net present values.[40]

Application of Utility Analysis to Selection

Neal Schmitt and Richard Klimoski have used the approach of Frank Schmidt, M. J. Mack, and John Hunter, to provide a relatively straightforward explanation of the application of utility analysis. Schmitt and Klimoski's explanation of the determination of the utility for a new selection test has been modified in this presentation for application to sales personnel. In this example, a company has decided to pursue a strategy of increasing its market share. To implement this strategy, it needs to 15 additional sales persons this year. The company's current selection procedures are based solely on interviews that have a validity coefficient of .15, while the new test will produce a validity coefficient of .30. Validity coefficients indicating the accuracy of selection procedures range in value from .0 to 1.0, with values of 1.0 indicating perfect prediction.[41]

Because the new test holds out the prospect of making better selection decisions (i.e., selecting a higher percentage of applicants who turn out to be better salespersons), an estimate of the dollar value of better performance is needed to determine the benefit of the new procedure. The company knows the contribution margin for each salesperson, which is sales minus all variable costs including costs of goods sold and his or her compensation. Based on these data, the company determined that the value of better performance is $20,000.

Given the $20,000 value of better performance, utility analysis then involves comparison of the associated costs with the benefits. In order to make comparisons, the company has determined that its current interviewing costs are $100 per applicant and that the new test, which requires special scoring, will cost $250 per applicant. It also knows that salespersons stay with the company for an average of three years. If the company chooses the top 10 percent of all applicants, the formula provided by Schmitt and Klimoski indicates that the utility of the new test would be approximately $215,000. The cash flows from such utility gains can then be projected out into the future and then discounted to arrive at a net present value of investing in the new test. However, the period of time over which such gains will be accrued will be reduced by changes in the jobs that reduce the validity coefficient. (For readers who desire to probe further into the details of methods for determining the value of better performance or the standard deviation of dollar contributions, selection ratios, standardized scores, validity, and the formula used in this example, books by Schmitt and Klimoski and Wayne Cascio provide excellent reference sources.)[42]

Training

As noted earlier, one of the most neglected areas in human resource management is the evaluation of training effectiveness. Such failures to evaluate training have been identified by Steven Kerr, as a classic example of misdirected reward structures, or "rewarding A while hoping for B." In a typical scenario, the proponent of the training, who championed the financial outlay, will collect anecdotes and testimonials that provide "evidence" of the success of the program.[43]

> The last thing many desire is a formal, systematic, and revealing evaluation. Although members of top management may actually *hope* for such systematic evaluation, their reward systems continue to *reward* ignorance in this area.[44]

There is probably a great deal of truth in Kerr's comments even today. Scott Tannenbaum and Steven Woods suggest that with expensive training programs, strong forms of evaluation are sometimes unlikely because of personal risk to the proponent of the program, in the event of failure. The alternative in such cases is a trade-off of risk for a weaker form of evaluation, such as participants' reactions or satisfaction with the program.[45]

However, as noted earlier, because of international competition and increased focus on costs, human resource programs have been subjected to greater scrutiny. Consequently, human resource managers have had to become more sophisticated in justifying their programs because the costs of investments in training can be substantial. For example, during one year training costs for

IBM and were more than $2 billion.[46] Thus, conducting credible evaluations of training effectiveness should be more important in the future.

Although training should normally be expected to contribute to increased productivity, reduced expenses, reduced turnover, improved morale, and so on, training is also conducted for other reasons that may be difficult to quantify. For example, training is sometimes conducted in attractive off-site locations to reward performance and to communicate to those being trained that they are important to the organization. It may also be conducted to allow employees to build informal relationships and to develop personal networks that facilitate communication and coordination. Training also may be conducted for the purpose of allowing a managerial coalition to propagate its views at the expense of another or for other political purposes that cannot be acknowledged in assessment measures.[47] Further, some companies' cultures may require objective data before an evaluation will have any credibility, while in others, elaborate evaluations of training employing objective measures may be rejected because they are incompatible with the company's culture.[48]

Nonetheless, in spite of such difficulties, training can normally be evaluated with relevant, acknowledgeable criteria. Traditional levels of evaluative criteria are (1) reaction, (2) learning, (3) behavior, and (4) results. In addition, some researchers consider attitude change as another category of evaluative criteria.[49]

Measures of *reaction criteria* typically tap participants' satisfaction with training or their perceptions of its quality or relevance.[50] Student evaluations of professors are examples of such measures. Whether reaction criteria actually provide valid standards of effectiveness is arguable because they may indicate only satisfaction. In most industrial settings, some level of satisfaction with training probably is a necessary, although insufficient, condition for effectiveness. The essence of this intuitive interpretation has been supported by a recent empirical study that found no linear relationship between reactions and learning. Instead, the study found that reactions moderate the training motivation and learning relationship. It also found that reactions have a complex relationship with other facets of training and effectiveness criteria. In fact, the best training results occur under conditions in which trainees are highly motivated to learn and have a positive reaction to the training.[51]

Learning criteria are concerned with whether participants have absorbed the concepts or content of training. As such, they are concerned with whether the trainees have learned facts, information, techniques, strategies, and the like.[52] An application of this criterion would be a test to determine whether stockbroker trainees have learned the content of training on Securities and Exchange Commission regulations.

Behavior criteria go a step beyond whether the trainee has learned the relevant concepts. These criteria are concerned with whether the lessons of the training program are translated into changes in the behavior of the trainee on the job. For example, there should be changes in the managerial behavior of employees who have completed a management-training program. Unlike the other criteria, a period of time is usually needed for the training to become manifested in behaviors. Therefore, a minimum of three months between the completion of training and measurement of behavior is recommended.[53]

Finally, *results criteria* are bottom-line criteria. Measures of such criteria might be breakage and scrap rates that are affected by the skill levels of production workers. Similarly, measures of turnover and morale could be relevant applications of results criteria for managerial training programs.[54] With results criteria, it is easy to visualize potential contaminants of broader or more global outcomes, such as morale, because a multitude of factors other than training may impact morale.

Criteria can also be classified as internal and external. *Internal criteria* are reactions, attitude change, and learning, while *external criteria* are behavior and results. External criteria have an advantage of going beyond the measurement of satisfaction with training or learning of material as they provide information on whether the training has an impact on job performance.[55] A final point on evaluation criteria is that when measuring the effectiveness of training methods, such as lectures, behavioral modeling, role-plays, and so on, the choice of evaluative criterion makes a difference. In other words, the effectiveness of different training methods depends on the type of criterion to be measured in the evaluative process. For example, a comprehensive meta-analysis of 70 studies by Michael Burke and Russell Day found that when objective performance standards are applied, evaluations of general management training indicate that it is usually quite effective. These findings differ from the conclusions of evaluations applying learning and subjective behavioral criteria.[56]

In addition to the criteria used, it is critical to have an appropriate and practical research design that guides the collection of data and the choice of measures of the evaluative criteria. The potential contaminants to valid measurement of training effectiveness must be eliminated or controlled through use of an appropriate research design. Both experimental and quasi-experimental designs can be used in a wide range of evaluative applications. Two experimental designs have particular relevance to the assessment of training effectiveness in many organizational settings. Experimental designs are presented in Table 9-1.

The first is the *pretest–posttest control group design*, which includes both experimental and control groups. Assignment of participants to these groups is based on random selection in order to control for such contaminants as differences in ability, experience, and the like. Prior to the commencement of training, both groups are pretested on the effectiveness criteria (e.g., knowledge of concepts, skill levels). The experimental group then receives the training while the control group does not. After completion of the training, and any appropriate time lags for behaviors to be manifested, both groups are posttested. The statistical approach for assessing the significance of results involves the computation of gain scores, in which each individual participant's pretest score is subtracted from the posttest score. Mean values of gain scores are computed within the experimental group and the control group. The significance of the difference in

TABLE 9-1 Experimental Designs

Pretest–Posttest Control Group Design

Assignment	Group	Pretest	Training	Posttest
Random	Experimental	Yes	Yes	Yes
Random	Control	Yes	No	Yes

Posttest-Only Control Group Design

Assignment	Group	Pretest	Training	Posttest
Random	Experimental	No	Yes	Yes
Random	Control	No	No	Yes

Source: Adapted from Donald T. Campbell and Julian C. Stanley. *Experimental and Quasi-Experimental Designs for Research*. Boston: Houghton Mifflin Company, 1966; and Wayne F. Cascio. *Applied Psychology in Personnel Management*, 4th ed. Upper Saddle River, NJ: Prentice Hall, 1991.

means of the gain scores between the two groups can then be tested with a t-test. In realistic company settings, a control group should not be too difficult to obtain. Members of the control group can be employees, who may even participate in the same training at some point in the future, after its effectiveness has been determined. When assigning employees to control groups, evaluators must be able to provide justifications as to why control group members are not being trained when they know that another group is receiving training. Another aspect of control groups, of which evaluators should be aware, is the group's knowledge of the training. In work settings, it is often likely that members of the control group may be receive substantial information about the training through discussions with other employees.[57]

The second experimental design is the *posttest-only control group design*. This design also utilizes an experimental and control group with random assignment of participants. Unlike the pretest–posttest control group design, there is no pretest. With randomization and sufficient sample size, the two groups may be assumed to have equivalent characteristics, such as ability and experience. This design is useful where a pretest cannot be used because it may sensitize employees to a subtle objective of the training and therefore defeat its purpose.[58] An example might be where "asking questions of the members of the control group regarding their management style might cause them to become sensitized to this aspect of their behavior and, inadvertently, cause them to change their style in some systematic way." [59] Further, the statistical testing with this design is straightforward, as the significance of the difference in the means between the experimental and control groups is determined with a t-test. Unfortunately, the researcher may have nagging doubts as to whether the experimental and control groups are truly equivalent.[60] This is an important point because decision makers, who must be convinced of the value of the training, may not truly understand randomization and research design.

Although these two experimental designs should be adequate for most evaluation needs, the *Solomon four-group design* can eliminate other threats to the validity of evaluation.[61] However, the exceptions that require this level of analysis are probably beyond the scope of interest for most general managers.

A final research design appropriate to the assessment of training programs is the *quasi-experimental design* based on a time series. This design may be appropriate in situations in which no control group can be obtained. The essence of the approach is to obtain measures of the evaluation criterion at repeated intervals, such as every month for six months, prior to the conduct of training. After the training, the measures would be collected again at repeated intervals. Unfortunately, analysis of the significance of the results is not as straightforward as with the two experimental designs because of the nonindependence of observations.[62] In some cases, the interpretation of the results may rest on a simple visual examination of observation trend lines.

The CIGNA Corporation has used the quasi-experimental design to assess the effectiveness of its basic management skills training program. In one unit, repeated measures of productivity were collected for several months prior to and after the training in order to assess the program's effectiveness. In another unit, measures of outstanding collectibles were collected in the same manner. Additionally, projections of collectibles were also developed in this unit to indicate the performance that would have occurred in the absence of the training. These projections allowed the calculation of financial returns on the training investment. Other aspects of its program provide an indication of the comprehensiveness of CIGNA's evaluation approach. In addition to these evaluations based on the time series quasi-experimental design, the company also used reaction, learning, and behavioral criteria to assess training effectiveness. In the case of assessments of behaviors, the company had the participants' supervisors assess their managerial behaviors prior to and after the training on such dimensions as leadership, setting standards, and planning.[63]

Performance Evaluation Systems

Unfortunately, in response to complaints and unfavorable comments, many organizations may respond in a technical manner by changing their performance evaluation format instead of addressing more basic problems, such as inadequate training for evaluators, absence of linkage between ratings and rewards, or failures to consider strategic contributions. Maintaining an effective performance measurement system requires training for evaluators, adequate time to perform evaluations, adequate time to conduct performance counseling, and rewards to distribute according to performance. Periodic surveys of managers' views on these aspects of the performance evaluation system can provide indicators of its effectiveness. Another effectiveness indicator can be obtained by correlating employees' ratings with their percentage merit increases in compensation. Although structural adjustments for external equity or other adjustments can sometimes legitimately alter the relationship, on average there should be a positive correlation. While it is hoped that an effective performance evaluation system will reduce the frequency of litigation, another indicator of effectiveness may be its track record in litigation.

Compensation Systems

As indicated in Chapter 7, the human resource function has been faulted for the existence of compensation systems that are not congruent with organizational strategies. Several aspects of compensation systems must be evaluated in order to determine their value in strategy implementation. The *compensation mix* is a critical issue that needs monitoring. Unfortunately, while there is movement toward more variable compensation in the United States, the compensation mix does not yet promote workforce stability, as it does in Japan. In the United States, the bulk of employees' compensation comes in the form of fixed levels of salaries or wages over time, regardless of the performance of their companies or the state of the economy. When demand for their company's product diminishes or performance factors cause profits to decline, employees are laid off. As discussed in Chapter 7, one means of providing more employment stability is to change the compensation mix by building in a larger proportion of variable compensation, such as profit sharing or bonuses, which is the approach used in Japan. When profitability and demand decline, compensation costs also decline, making it less necessary to lay off employees.[64]

Another critical issue in evaluating the effectiveness of compensation systems is their flexibility. Unfortunately, as indicated in Chapter 7, traditional compensation systems based on job evaluation and determination of internal equity among jobs tend to be inflexible. As noted, the process of job evaluation, commonly performed according to the point system, assigns different numbers of points for various levels of characteristics, such as "know-how," which refers to operational knowledge of different jobs. Unfortunately, for some nonmanagerial jobs, there are no "know-how" points in the evaluation system. Thus, the job evaluation system places some employees in "nonthinking" categories. One consequence of placing employees in such pigeonholes is that some tend to stop thinking and maintain a level of ignorance in order to conform to the job requirements. Another consequence is that some employees who are dissatisfied with the "nonthinking" requirements, proceed on their own to develop other knowledge. As a result of these employees' initiatives, managers attempt to have their positions upgraded, which introduces another source of distortion to the wage structure.[65]

In addition to these major issues, there are several other aspects of compensation that should be evaluated for their contribution to the strategic goals of the company. These may include subjective measures of the extent to which the compensation system provides for internal equity; conforms to legal requirements for race, gender, and age; and provides pay satisfaction. Objective measures of compensation system effectiveness may include overtime utilization, payroll complaints, and comparisons of the company's wages for various jobs with those in relevant labor markets.[66]

Labor and Employee Relations

It is important for unionized companies to evaluate the effectiveness of their labor relations functions and line managers' conduct of labor relations. For unionized companies, there are numerous indicators of labor relations effectiveness, such as the frequency or length of work stoppages, degree to which collective bargaining agreements are restrictive, degree of cooperation between the union and management, managerial flexibility in work assignment, ability to impose reasonable work rules, other management prerogatives, discretion to promote or lay off on the basis of ability or merit, ease of administering the labor agreement, and the company's grievance experience. In the case of grievances, caution must be used in drawing inferences of effectiveness, because there is a multitude of potential influences on the incidence of grievances. Such influences include managerial behavior, the technology of the workplace, the personality and motivation of union representatives, the company's relationship with the union, and individual employee characteristics.[67]

It is also important for nonunion companies to evaluate the effectiveness of their employee relations functions. For such companies, the prospects of unionization should not be discounted even though overall union membership is only 16.5 million or approximately 13.9 percent of wage and salary workers. (Union members account for 9.4 percent of wage and salary workers in the private sector.[68]) One reason is that downsizing and layoffs are now commonplace in the U.S. economy, and job security has become a major concern for many U.S. workers. As noted in Chapter 1, in the past, several industry leaders such as Hewlett-Packard and IBM maintained no-layoff approaches or employment security policies.[69] Such approaches and policies were probably a major reason why these companies were able to remain nonunion. However, because of competitive pressures, many such companies have abandoned these policies.[70] In addition, the casual approach of many companies to downsizing and the emergence of unbundled or network organizations have probably reduced employee loyalty to the extent that more employees may be willing to unionize in order gain job security. The question remains as to whether employees will see unionization as instrumental to their job security or as a futile effort.

In the past, unions were often able to confine layoffs to the most junior employees, as the vast numbers of layoffs were conducted according to inverse seniority.[71] They were successful to the extent that they could organize extensively in an industry and make all competitors pay the same wages and offer similar working conditions. Their strategy was to "take wages out of competition."[72] The cost of wage increases and favorable terms of employment were then largely passed on to consumers in the form of price increases. However, with today's international marketplace, the power of unions has declined. Unions cannot organize all international manufacturers in a given industry, as demonstrated by abortive attempts at multinational union cooperation.[73] As a result, there will be adverse employment effects to the extent that employment security agreements put domestic manufacturers at a disadvantage to international competitors. Further, unions seem to be unable to prevent domestic manufacturing companies from shifting production facilities to other countries. It will be interesting to see whether unions will be able to devise strategies to help employees obtain greater job security.

Regardless of the eventual direction of unionization in the future, unionization is very much a reality in many industries. For example, unionized workers constitute the following percentages of workers in the following industries: 25.5 percent in transportation and public utilities, 19.1 percent in construction, and 15.6 percent in manufacturing. Furthermore, 37.3 percent of governmental employees are unionized.[74] Nonunion companies should not become complacent to the prospects of unionization and should periodically evaluate their organizational climate and human resource policies in order to determine whether they may encourage unionization.

EVALUATING STRATEGIC CONTRIBUTIONS IN EMERGING AREAS

There are a number of challenges from emerging areas related to human resource management that have major consequences for most companies. Two of the most important of these are (1) equal employment opportunity and the management of diversity, and (2) quality readiness. The following sections will cover these areas in some detail.

Equal Employment Opportunity and Management of Diversity

The relevance of the *management of diversity* to the topic of evaluating human resource effectiveness is that effective management in this area enables organizations to tap the potential of their workforces. Thus, management of diversity can be related to the effectiveness with which companies avoid labor shortages. For example, African-American employees tend to have higher turnover.[75] By correcting those factors leading to the turnover of African-Americans, companies should be able to reduce their shortages of labor. Evaluations of effectiveness in this area should measure turnover of minority and female employees.

Corning, Inc. provides an example of a company that has had considerable success in this area. The company has made remarkable progress in increasing the number of African-American and female managers, both in total numbers and in their representation in executive positions. This accomplishment is all the more impressive when it is noted that the company is located in a small town in upstate New York. One specific example of Corning's approach was to take a leadership position in making the local area more attractive to African-American managers and professionals. Attrition of African-Americans declined from 15.3 to 11.3 percent over a three-year period. Additionally, over the same time period, the attrition of females declined from 16.2 to 7.6 percent.[76]

Some suggestions from the literature appear to have value in enabling organizations to be more effective in the management of diversity. One suggestion deals with the advancement of minorities and females. Advancement to upper-level positions requires information that is obtained through informal networks from which minorities and females are often excluded. Because the pathway to promotion for companies' highest-level jobs becomes more subtle and ill defined with moves up the organizational hierarchy, it is desirable for organizations to devote more attention to these subtleties. Being networked and acquiring upward pull from a mentor are critical before minorities and females can rise to the top.[77] Roosevelt Thomas has explained this process as follows:

> Another widespread assumption, probably absorbed from American culture in general, is that "cream will rise to the top." In most companies, what passes for cream rising to the top is actually cream being pulled or pushed to the top by an informal system of mentoring and sponsorship.[78]

Unfortunately, performance evaluation processes frequently do not provide managers with the feedback that they need to advance to the highest-level positions. This weakness of performance evaluation systems is often offset by informal feedback through personal mentoring or networks. When lack of access to networks deprives an individual of honest feedback, performance appraisal systems must be improved for increased effectiveness.[79]

A second suggestion for improved effectiveness is that, where the problems of minorities and females are unrelated to prejudice, remedial efforts should facilitate the advancement of all groups of people. In contrast, when remedial programs give special consideration only to particular groups, they become enormously time consuming and are inconsistent with the spirit of diversity. A third suggestion is that, since the management of diversity is not an exact science, mistakes will be made and setbacks will occur. Accordingly, in the interests of fairness, managers should not be penalized for their efforts. A fourth suggestion is that the focus of the management of diversity should be a broad one, extending even to education, personality, background, and age. Such a broad orientation should facilitate the development of a heterogeneous culture, instead of attempting to assimilate those who differ into a dominant culture of white males.[80] A fifth suggestion is to conduct training courses on diversity, which may deal with communication style differences, increase self-awareness, and reduce biases through skill-building exercises. Leading companies in this type of training include Hewlett-Packard and Ortho Pharmaceuticals. Such training can be evaluated with the approaches discussed earlier. A sixth suggestion is to incorporate management of diversity into the company's performance evaluation and reward system so that those managers doing a good job in this regard are rewarded. Companies providing leadership in this area include Coca-Cola and Exxon-Mobil.[81]

Quality Readiness

Although *total quality management* (TQM) has received a great deal of attention, the importance of the role of human resource management is not well known. Christopher Hart and Leonard Schlesinger have pointed out that TQM is relevant to the evaluation of human resources in at least three respects:

1. The quality that can be achieved by a company's workforce is in part determined by its motivation and training.
2. The quality of the activities and services of the human resource function are evaluated in TQM approaches.
3. The Malcolm Baldrige National Quality Award framework provides a TQM guide for evaluation of human resources.

Interestingly, human resource management and development make up one of the seven major components on which companies are evaluated for the Baldrige Award, comprising 150 of the total of 1,000 points. The importance of the Baldrige framework, however, is not attributable to its role in the granting of awards for quality. Instead, its importance lies with its usefulness in providing a guide to obtaining quality and its value in evaluation or assessment.[82]

Under TQM, the ultimate objective is to provide customer satisfaction. By satisfying customers, a company increases its market share and enhances the likelihood of increased profitability. The traditional objectives of the human resource function, which seek to improve performance, productivity, employee satisfaction, and motivation, are indirectly related to customer satisfaction. This is because employee retention and a well-trained workforce are required for the production of quality goods and services. Since TQM emphasizes the importance of a systematic, comprehensive approach toward quality, the interrelated role of the human resource function and its indirect impact on the workforce make it critical to this objective. One outcome of TQM is that a stronger case is made for the importance of funding training.[83]

As a model for evaluation, the Baldrige guidelines make several important points. Among those most relevant to human resource management are its emphasis on (1) the use of objective performance data and (2) benchmarking based on external comparisons or based on the company's own performance in earlier time periods. Hart and Schlesinger have noted that the guidelines also deal with the specifics of assessment, such as described in the following:

> What Baldrige examiners look for, though, is objective evidence, like job definitions that include clearly delineated quality responsibilities. The criteria ask, among other things, for "indicators, benchmarks, or other bases for evaluating and improving organizational structure" (1.2.b), and "key methods and key indicators

the company uses to evaluate and improve awareness and integration of quality values at all levels of management and supervision" (1.2.d).[84]

By using the Baldrige framework as a questionnaire, a company can use the guidelines like the award examiners do to evaluate its strengths and weaknesses in quality. This assessment would be a first step toward adoption of TQM and improvement of quality. Following this evaluation or assessment, a triage process would be undertaken in which priorities would be established for actions to be taken. One practical suggestion is to fix first those problems that have easy solutions or pick the "low-hanging fruit" first. Another TQM-related suggestion is that the human resource function should adopt a perspective that is similar to an independent contractor providing services to a customer. When viewed from this perspective, those in the human resource function would begin to ask themselves whether the customer, the company, would renew their contract. When viewed in this manner, the importance of customer satisfaction is more evident.[85]

Finally, the use of the Baldrige framework as a guide for evaluation and its emphasis on objective data deserve comment. Many important organizational phenomena may not meet all parties' definitions of objective. Dysfunctional results occur when important phenomena are ignored because they cannot be expressed in an objective format.

MACRO-LEVEL EVALUATION OF HUMAN RESOURCE EFFECTIVENESS

Although the focus of this chapter has been to describe approaches, methods, and criteria of evaluation, two end results of macro-level human resource effectiveness evaluations deserve mention. The first concerns differences in effectiveness across industries. The Ulrich, Brockbank, and Yeung benchmarking study, discussed earlier, reached the following conclusions: One is that "HR professionals demonstrate higher competencies in service, aircraft, and electronics industries, and lower competencies in manufacturing, utilities, and petroleum industries." [86] One explanation for such results may be that human resource management plays a more strategic role in the service, aircraft, and electronics industries because competitive advantages in these industries are based more on human resources. Interestingly, their findings also suggest that top-level general managers perceive greater competencies in human resource professionals than do executives and managers in other functional areas.[87]

The second macro-level finding is from Anne Tsui's examination of human resource departmental effectiveness. Her investigation found greater satisfaction among line executives than among operating managers, probably because of the human resource department's "tendency to 'cater' to the needs of the more powerful constituencies." [88] One implication of this result is that human resource managers need to devote more attention to the remainder of the company's managers and employees. For example, they need to obtain these managers' and employees' input on the content of human resource programs.[89] This finding is somewhat ironic, given the history of human resource management. In the past, human resource professionals decried their inability to gain the confidence of their top executive and to participate in the strategic management process. Human resource managers must not forget the importance of generating user satisfaction throughout the middle and lower levels of the organizational hierarchy as well.

Summary

This chapter has reviewed concepts related to the evaluation of effectiveness from a strategic management perspective. As a part of this discussion, the Tsui and Gomez-Mejia framework was utilized to illustrate the interrelated nature of human resource management with other functional areas and the necessity of considering (1) the impact of line management on human resource measures and (2) the level of analysis at which evaluation is directed. Methodological aspects of evaluation were reviewed, including audits, analytical approaches, quantitative and qualitative measures, outcome and process criteria, benchmarking, and industry considerations. In spite of the logical appeal of evaluation, human resource evaluation has not been a widespread practice. Nonetheless, the cost and competitive pressures of today's global economy and the focus on quality will probably serve as a stimulus for more evaluation in the future.

Greater attention was devoted to the evaluation of strategic human resource management contributions in the traditional areas. Specific approaches were described for evaluating human resource planning, which is likely to take on greater importance with growing human resource strategic contributions. Measures for assessing the effectiveness of staffing were discussed, along with an example of utility analysis applied to staffing issues. Effectiveness measures and research designs were also presented for evaluating the effectiveness of training. Although training has not received the evaluation attention warranted, the financial resources that will be required for training in the future also will serve as a strong incentive for more evaluation. Evaluation needs and approaches for assessment of performance measurement systems and compensation systems also were discussed, along with evaluation of labor and employee relations.

Beyond the traditional areas of human resource management, evaluation approaches in two newer areas of strategic importance were discussed: (1) equal employment opportunity and the management of diversity and (2) quality readiness. Although the management of diversity literature is still evolving, some important insights have been developed for evaluating effectiveness in this area. Finally, the contributions of human resource management to quality were discussed, along with approaches for evaluating such contributions.

Endnotes

1. Tsui, Anne S., and Luis R. Gomez-Mejia. "Evaluating Human Resource Effectiveness," in Lee Dyer (Ed.), *Human Resource Management: Evolving Roles and Responsibilities*. Washington, DC: Bureau of National Affairs, Inc., 1988, pp. 187–227; Ulrich, Dave. "Assessing Human Resource Effectiveness: Stakeholder, Utility, and Relationship Approaches," *Human Resource Planning* 12, no. 4 (1989): 301–15; Gomez-Mejia, Luis R. "Dimensions and Correlates of the Personnel Audit as an Organizational Assessment Tool," *Personnel Psychology* 38, no. 2 (1985): 293–308.
2. Ulrich. "Assessing Human Resource Effectiveness: Stakeholder, Utility, and Relationship Approaches."
3. Steers, Richard M. "Problems in the Measurement of Organizational Effectiveness," *Administrative Science Quarterly* 20, no. 4 (1975): 546–58; Mott, Paul E. *The Characteristics of Effective Organizations*. New York: Harper and Row, 1972; Hitt, Michael A., and R. Dennis Middlemist. "A Methodology to Develop the Criteria and Criteria Weightings for Assessing Subunit Effectiveness in Organizations," *Academy of Management Journal* 22, no. 2 (1979): 356–74; Hitt, Michael A., R. Dennis Middlemist, and Charles R. Greer. "Sunset Legislation and the Measurement of Effectiveness," *Public Personnel Management* 6, no. 3 (1977): 188–93.
4. Tsui and Gomez-Mejia. "Evaluating Human Resource Effectiveness"; Tsui, Anne S. "Personnel Department Effectiveness: A Tripartite Approach," *Industrial Relations* 23, no. 2 (1984): 184–97.
5. Tsui and Gomez-Mejia. "Evaluating Human Resource Effectiveness"; Tsui. "Personnel Department Effectiveness: A Tripartite Approach."
6. Jarrell, Donald W. *Human Resource Planning: A Business Planning Approach*. Upper Saddle River, NJ: Prentice Hall, 1993; Peterson, Donald J., and Robert L. Malone. "The Personnel Effectiveness Grid (PEG): A New Tool for Estimating Personnel Department Effectiveness," *Human Resource Management* 14, no. 4 (1975): 10–21.
7. Rogers, Edward W., and Patrick M. Wright. "Measuring Organizational Performance in Strategic Human Resource Management: Looking Beyond the Lamppost," Working Paper #98-24, Center for Advances Human Resource Studies, Cornell University, 1998.
8. Portwood, James D. "Process Management vs. Problem Solving: Choosing an Appropriate Perspective for Evaluating Human Resource Systems," in Richard J. Niehaus and Karl F. Price (Eds.), *Creating the Competitive Edge through Human Resource Allocations*. New York: Plenum Press, 1988, pp. 181–91.
9. Tsui and Gomez-Mejia. "Evaluating Human Resource Effectiveness"; Tsui. "Personnel Department Effectiveness: A Tripartite Approach."
10. Tsui, Anne S. "Defining the Activities and Effectiveness of the Human Resource Department: A Multiple Constituency Approach," *Human Resource Management* 26, no. 1 (1987): 35–69.
11. Ibid.
12. "New Ethics—or No Ethics?", *Fortune* (March 20, 2000): 82.
13. Losey, Michael R. "The Future Human Resource Professional: Competency Buttressed by Advocacy and Ethics," in Dave Ulrich, Michael R. Losey, and Gerry Lake (Eds.), *Tomorrow's HR Management: 48 Thought Leaders Call for Change*. New York: John Wiley and Sons, 1997, pp. 297–98.
14. Tsui and Gomez-Mejia. "Evaluating Human Resource Effectiveness"; Peterson and Malone. "The Personnel Effectiveness Grid (PEG): A New Tool for Estimating Personnel Department Effectiveness"; Phillips, Jack J., and Anson Seers. "Twelve Ways to Evaluate HR Management," *Personnel Administrator* 34, no. 4 (April 1989): 54–58.
15. Ulrich. "Assessing Human Resource Effectiveness: Stakeholder, Utility, and Relationship Approaches."
16. Tsui and Gomez-Mejia. "Evaluating Human Resource Effectiveness"; Phillips and Seers. "Twelve Ways to Evaluate HR Management: The Best Methods to Measure HR's Effectiveness"; Steffy, Brian D., and Steven D. Maurer. "Conceptualizing and Measuring the Economic Effectiveness of Human Resource Activities," *Academy of Management Review* 13, no. 2 (1988): 271–86; Ulrich. "Assessing Human Resource Effectiveness: Stakeholder, Utility, and Relationship Approaches."
17. Hitt and Middlemist. "A Methodology to Develop the Criteria and Criteria Weightings for Assessing Subunit Effectiveness in Organizations"; Phillips and Seers. "Twelve Ways to Evaluate HR Management: The Best Methods to Measure HR's Effectiveness."

18. Tsui and Gomez-Mejia. "Evaluating Human Resource Effectiveness"; Schmitt, Neal W., and Richard J. Klimoski. *Research Methods in Human Resources Management*. Cincinnati: South-Western Publishing Co., 1991.
19. Kaplan, Robert S., and David P. Norton. *The Balanced Scorecard: Translating Strategy into Action*. Boston: Harvard Business School Press, 1996.
20. Ibid.
21. Ibid., p. 132.
22. Ulrich, Dave, Wayne Brockbank, and Arthur Yeung. "Beyond Belief: A Benchmark for Human Resources," *Human Resources Management* 28, no. 3 (1989): 311–35.
23. Jorgensen, Les. "How to Steal the Best Ideas Around," *Fortune* (October 19, 1992): 102–06.
24. Ulrich, Brockbank, and Yeung. "Beyond Belief: A Benchmark for Human Resources."
25. Ibid.
26. Ibid., p. 312.
27. Bamberger, Peter, Samuel Bacharach, and Lee Dyer. "Human Resources Management and Organizational Effectiveness: High Technology Entrepreneurial Startup Firms in Israel," *Human Resource Management* 28, no. 3 (1989): 349–66.
28. Ibid.
29. Ibid.
30. Ibid., pp. 362–63.
31. Tsui and Gomez-Mejia. "Evaluating Human Resource Effectiveness"; Phillips and Seers. "Twelve Ways to Evaluate HR Management"; Petersen and Malone. "The Personnel Effectiveness Grid (PEG): A New Tool for Estimating Personnel Department Effectiveness"; Cascio, Wayne F. "Responding to the Demand for Accountability: A Critical Analysis of Three Utility Models," *Organizational Behavior and Human Performance* 25, no. 1 (1980): 32–45; Tannenbaum, Scott I., and Woods, Steven B. "Determining a Strategy for Evaluating Training: Operating Within Organizational Constraints," *Human Resource Planning* 15, no. 2 (1992): 63–81.
32. Tsui and Gomez-Mejia. "Evaluating Human Resource Effectiveness," p. 200.
33. Tsui and Gomez-Mejia. "Evaluating Human Resource Effectiveness"; Peterson and Malone. "The Personnel Effectiveness Grid (PEG): A New Tool for Estimating Personnel Department Effectiveness."
34. Butler, John E., Gerald R. Ferris, and Nancy K. Napier. *Strategy and Human Resources Management*. Cincinnati: South-Western Publishing Co., 1991.
35. Mills, D. Quinn. "Planning with People in Mind," *Harvard Business Review* 63, no. 4 (1985): 97–105; Robbins, Stephen P. *Management*, 3rd ed. Upper Saddle River, NJ: Prentice Hall, 1991.
36. Walker, James W. *Human Resource Strategy*. New York: McGraw-Hill, 1992.
37. Ibid.
38. Bowen, David E., Gerald E. Ledford Jr., and Barry R. Nathan. "Hiring for the Organization, Not the Job," *Academy of Management Executive* 5, no. 4 (1991): 35–51.
39. Cascio, Wayne F. *Applied Psychology in Personnel Management*, 4th ed. Upper Saddle River, NJ: Prentice Hall, 1991.
40. Ibid.; Cronshaw, Steven F., and Ralph A. Alexander. "One Answer to the Demand for Accountability: Selection Utility as an Investment Decision," *Organizational Behavior and Human Decision Processes* 35, no. 1 (1985): 102–18; Schmitt and Klimoski. *Research Methods in Human Resources Management*; Boudreau, John W. "Economic Considerations in Estimating the Utility of Human Resource Productivity Improvement Programs," *Personnel Psychology* 36, no. 3 (1983): 551–76.
41. Schmitt and Klimoski. *Research Methods in Human Resources Management*; Schmidt, Frank L., Murray J. Mack, and John E. Hunter. "Selection Utility in the Occupation of U.S. Park Ranger for Three Modes of Test Use," *Journal of Applied Psychology* 69, no. 3 (1984): 490–97.
42. Schmitt and Klimoski. *Research Methods in Human Resources Management*; Schmidt, Mack, and Hunter. "Selection Utility in the Occupation of U.S. Park Ranger for Three Modes of Test Use"; Cascio, Wayne F. *Costing Human Resources: The Financial Impact of Behavior in Organizations*, 3rd ed. Boston: PWS-Kent Publishing Company, 1991.

43. Kerr, Steven. "On the Folly of Rewarding A While Hoping for B," *Academy of Management Journal* 18, no. 4 (1975): 769–83.
44. Kerr. "On the Folly of Rewarding A While Hoping for B," p. 774.
45. Tannenbaum and Woods. "Determining a Strategy for Evaluating Training: Operating Within Organizational Constraints."
46. Ibid.
47. Boettger, Richard D., and Charles R. Greer. "The Wisdom of Rewarding A While Hoping for B," *Organization Science* 5 (1994): 569–82.
48. Tannenbaum and Woods. "Determining a Strategy for Evaluating Training: Operating Within Organizational Constraints."
49. Cascio. *Applied Psychology in Personnel Management*; Goldstein, Irwin L. *Training in Organizations: Needs Assessment, Development, and Evaluation*, 2nd ed. Monterey, CA: Brooks/Cole Publishing Company, 1986; Tannenbaum and Woods. "Determining a Strategy for Evaluating Training: Operating Within Organizational Constraints."
50. Cascio. *Applied Psychology in Personnel Management*; Goldstein. *Training in Organizations: Needs Assessment, Development, and Evaluation.*
51. Mathieu, John E., Scott I. Tannenbaum, and Eduardo Salas. "Influences of Individual and Situational Characteristics on Measures of Training Effectiveness," *Academy of Management Journal* 35, no. 4 (1992): 828–47.
52. Cascio. *Applied Psychology in Personnel Management*; Goldstein. *Training in Organizations: Needs Assessment, Development, and Evaluation*; Tannenbaum and Woods. "Determining a Strategy for Evaluating Training: Operating Within Organizational Constraints."
53. Cascio. *Applied Psychology in Personnel Management*; Goldstein. *Training in Organizations: Needs Assessment, Development, and Evaluation.*
54. Ibid.
55. Cascio. *Applied Psychology in Personnel Management.*
56. Burke, Michael J., and Russell R. Day. "A Cumulative Study of the Effectiveness of Managerial Training," *Journal of Applied Psychology* 71, no. 2 (1986): 232–45.
57. Campbell, Donald R., and Julian C. Stanley. *Experimental and Quasi-Experimental Designs for Research.* Boston: Houghton Mifflin Company, 1966; Tannenbaum and Woods. "Determining a Strategy for Evaluating Training: Operating Within Organizational Constraints."
58. Campbell and Stanley. *Experimental and Quasi-Experimental Designs for Research*; Cascio. *Applied Psychology in Personnel Management.*
59. Schmitt and Klimoski. *Research Methods in Human Resources Management*, p. 385.
60. Campbell and Stanley. *Experimental and Quasi-Experimental Designs for Research*; Cascio. *Applied Psychology in Personnel Management.*
61. Ibid.; Goldstein. *Training in Organizations: Needs Assessment, Development, and Evaluation.*
62. Campbell and Stanley. *Experimental and Quasi-Experimental Designs for Research.*
63. Paquet, Basil, Elizabeth Kasi, Laurence Weinstein, and William Waite. "The Bottom Line," *Training and Development Journal* 41, no. 5 (1987): 27–33.
64. Gomez-Mejia, Luis R., and David B. Balkin. *Compensation, Organizational Strategy, and Firm Performance.* Cincinnati: South-Western Publishing Co., 1992; Henn, William R. "What the Strategist Asks from Human Resources," *Human Resource Planning* 8, no. 4 (1985): 193–200.
65. Emerson, Sandra M. "Job Evaluation: A Barrier to Excellence?" *Compensation and Benefits Review* 23, no. 1 (1991): 39–51.
66. Gomez-Mejia. "Dimensions and Correlates of the Personnel Audit as an Organizational Assessment Tool."
67. Labig, Chalmer E., and Charles R. Greer. "Grievance Initiation: A Literature Survey and Suggestions for Future Research," *Journal of Labor Research* 9, no. 1 (1988): 1–27; Allen, Robert E., and Timothy J. Keaveny. "Factors Differentiating Grievants and Nongrievants," *Human Relations* 38, no. 6 (1985): 519–34.
68. U.S. Bureau of Labor Statistics. "Union Members Summary," *Labor Force Statistics from the Current Population Survey*. Internet address: **stats.bls.gov/newsrels.htm** (January 19, 2000).

69. Hewlett-Packard Corporation. *Annual Report*, 1985; Peters, Tom. *Thriving on Chaos: Handbook for a Management Revolution*. New York: Harper and Row, 1987; Hoerr, John, and Wendy Zellner. "A Japanese Import That's Not Selling," *Business Week* (February 26, 1990): 86; Burke, Steven. "PC Operations Spared the Worst of IBM's Cost-Cutting Programs," *PC Week* (December 11, 1989): 1, 6.
70. Hoerr and Zellner. "A Japanese Import That's Not Selling"; Wilke, John R. "Digital Equipment, in Its First Layoffs, To Dismiss About 3,500 Workers by July," *Wall Street Journal* (January 10, 1991): A3; Burke. "PC Operations Spared the Worst of IBM's Cost-Cutting Programs."
71. Freeman, Richard B., and James L. Medoff. *What Do Unions Do?*. New York: Basic Books, 1984.
72. Mitchell, Daniel J. B. *Human Resource Management: An Economic Approach*. Boston: PWS-Kent Publishing Company, 1989.
73. Northrup, Herbert R., and Richard L. Rowan. "Multinational Union Activity in the 1976 U.S. Rubber Tire Strike," *Sloan Management Review* 18, no. 3 (1977): 17–28.
74. U.S. Bureau of Labor Statistics. "Union Members Summary."
75. Cox, Taylor H., and Stacy Blake. "Managing Cultural Diversity: Implications for Organizational Competitiveness," *Academy of Management Executive* 5, no. 3 (1991): 45–56.
76. Hammonds, Keith H. "Corning's Class Act," *Business Week* (May 13, 1991): 68–76.
77. Thomas, R. Roosevelt. "From Affirmative Action to Affirming Diversity," *Harvard Business Review* 90, no. 2 (1990): 107–17.
78. Ibid., p. 114.
79. Thomas. "From Affirmative Action to Affirming Diversity."
80. Ibid.
81. Cox, Taylor Jr. "The Multicultural Organization," *Academy of Management Executive* 5, no. 2 (1991): 34–47.
82. Hart, Christopher, and Leonard Schlesinger. "Total Quality Management and the Human Resource Professional: Applying the Baldrige Framework to Human Resources," *Human Resource Management* 30, no. 4 (1991): 433–54.
83. Hart and Schlesinger. "Total Quality Management and the Human Resource Professional: Applying the Baldrige Framework to Human Resources."
84. Ibid., pp. 442–43.
85. Hart and Schlesinger. "Total Quality Management and the Human Resource Professional: Applying the Baldrige Framework to Human Resources."
86. Ulrich, Brockbank, and Yeung. "Beyond Belief: A Benchmark for Human Resources," p. 329.
87. Ulrich, Brockbank, and Yeung. "Beyond Belief: A Benchmark for Human Resources."
88. Tsui. "Defining the Activities and Effectiveness of the Human Resource Department: A Multiple Constituency Approach," p. 65.
89. Ulrich, Brockbank, and Yeung. "Beyond Belief: A Benchmark for Human Resources."

CASE 9 Assessment of Human Resource Utilization

A bank has foreclosed on Core-Line Software, a software development company. Although Core-Line has a strong level of sales, its costs are far too high and it cannot repay its loans. The bank had hoped to line up a buyer before foreclosing; however, none was willing to pay the bank's price. As a result, the bank has been forced to foreclose and operate the company until a buyer can be found. In order to recoup as much of its loans as possible, the bank has decided to seek advice on how to improve the operating efficiency of the company. With increased efficiency, the bank hopes to obtain a higher price. Because the bank's staff has no experience in the software business, it has retained a consulting firm to advise it on how to improve the efficiency of the company's operations. Because labor costs constitute the bulk of software firms' expenses, Core-Line's utilization of human resources is an obvious area in which to look for potential improvement. Like most software companies, Core-Line has a full array of specialists, including programmers, graphic artists, systems analysts, project managers, systems architects, and the like. The consulting firm has decided to begin by assessing Core-Line's efficiency in the utilization of programmers by comparing its utilization level with other software developers.

In order to obtain data for its recommendations to the bank, the consulting company has conducted a survey of other software developers. The survey was designed to obtain information on several business practices, including questions about staffing levels and human resource utilization. (The consulting firm has already determined that Core-Line's salaries are average for the industry.) Unfortunately, although the consulting firm has done some work with software developers and has a good reputation, many firms refused to supply data. Consequently, only 40 percent of the questionnaires were returned, for a total of 65 responses. Nonetheless, the consulting firm has decided to proceed with an analysis of the data.

The analysis of the data will employ a comparative approach in which each responding company's staffing level of programmers (dependent variable) will be compared with potential explanatory variables (independent variables). In order to control the influence of each independent variable, the consulting firm has decided to use the statistical technique of multiple regression analysis. Each of the 65 responses will constitute a separate observation in the analysis. Thus, in the regression analysis, the dependent variable (Y) is the number of programmers. The independent variables are the dollar volume of annual software sales

(X_1), average number of hours worked each year by programmers including overtime (X_2), average years of experience of programmers (X_3), a rating of the quality of programming supervision (X_4), and a rating of the complexity of the software produced by each company (X_5). The rating of the quality of supervision is a five-interval scale ranging from 1 (poor) to 5 (good). Similarly, the software complexity rating scheme is a five-interval scale ranging from 1 (simple) to 5 (complex). The regression model is $Y = \alpha + \beta_1X_1 + \beta_2X_2 + \beta_3X_3 + \beta_4X_4 + \beta_5X_5 + \varepsilon$, where α is the intercept or constant; β_1, β_2, β_3, β_4, and β_5 are the respective regression coefficients derived in the model; and ε is the error term.

In order to derive the values for α, β_1, β_2, β_3, β_4, and β_5, the consulting firm will run the regression analysis, with each observation being composed of matched data from one of the 65 different software companies. (Under most conditions, the value for ε is assumed to be 0.) If the model is adequately specified, statistically significant, and a substantial amount of variance in the dependent variable is accounted for, the consulting firm will have confidence in the statistical justification for using its parameters. The adequacy of explanatory power is indicated by the R^2 and the overall model's F values. (For the purposes of this case, assume that the model is statistically adequate on all of these indicators.)

To predict the number of programmers that Core-Line should be using, which is the value for $\hat{Y}$, the consulting firm will plug into the regression model Core-Line's X values for annual sales, average annual hours worked by programmers, average experience of programmers, rating of the quality of programmer supervision, and rating of software complexity. Using this model or equation, the consulting firm will then compute the number of programmers ($\hat{Y}$ value). This predicted value or industry standard will then be compared with Core-Line's actual utilization of programmers in order to determine if it is overstaffed. Further, for each independent variable having a statistically significant relationship with the dependent variable, the positive or negative sign of the regression coefficient will provide direction for potential solutions to utilization problems.

Questions

1. What are the implications of using data from a survey of other companies in which only 40 percent of the sample chose to respond? How could one determine whether there is any potential bias in the returned questionnaires?
2. What potential variables has the consulting firm left out of its model? How would any omitted variables affect the results?
3. Because the consulting firm has employed a cross-sectional approach, it cannot pick up any productivity trends. How might this be a problem?
4. What other methods should be used to determine whether Core-Line is utilizing its programmers efficiently?
5. How is the process of benchmarking similar to the process employed by the consulting firm?

Index